RETIREMENT ISSUES, PLANS AND LIFESTYLES

SOCIAL SECURITY REFORM: DISABILITY, INDEXING AND FINANCING

RETIREMENT ISSUES, PLANS AND LIFESTYLES

Additional books in this series can be found on Nova's website at:

https://www.novapublishers.com/catalog/index.php?cPath=23_29&seriesp=Retirement+Issues%2C+Plans+and+Lifestyles

Additional e-books in this series can be found on Nova's website at:

https://www.novapublishers.com/catalog/index.php?cPath=23_29&seriespe=Retirement+Issues%2C+Plans+and+Lifestyles

RETIREMENT ISSUES, PLANS AND LIFESTYLES

SOCIAL SECURITY REFORM: DISABILITY, INDEXING AND FINANCING

JANET U. BURLINGTON
EDITOR

Nova Science Publishers, Inc.

New York

For permission to use material from this book please contact us:
Telephone 631-231-7269; Fax 631-231-8175
Web Site: http://www.novapublishers.com

LIBRARY OF CONGRESS CATALOGING-IN-PUBLICATION DATA

Social security reform : disability, indexing, and financing / editor, Janet U. Burlington.
p. cm.
Includes index.
ISBN 978-1-61668-354-2 (hardcover)
1. Social security--United States. 2. Social security--United States--Finance. 3. Social security--Law and legislation--United States.
I. Burlington, Janet U.
HD7125.S59936 2010
368.4'300973--dc22

2010012282

Published by Nova Science Publishers, Inc. ✝ New York

CONTENTS

PREFACE

The programs administered by the Social Security Administration (SSA) form the foundation for the nation's social insurance network that has greatly reduce poverty among the elderly through the retirement and survivors program and provides income support to people with disabilities, widows and widowers, and young children. This book addresses the current challenges facing the Social Security Administration including issues for disability and dependent benefits, the implications of different indexing choices, the need for greater transparency with regard to general revenue financing, possible effects on the elderly poor and mitigation options, legal analysis and the costs of reform.

Chapter 1 features a letter to the Social Security Administration.

Chapter 2 features a letter to the U. S. House of Representatives.

Chapter 3 - Social Security has significantly reduced elderly poverty. The elderly poverty rate has fallen from 35% in 1959 to an all-time low of 9% in 2006, in large part because of Social Security. If Social Security benefits did not exist, an estimated 44% of the elderly would be poor today assuming no changes in behavior. The Supplemental Security Income (SSI) program, also provides benefits to the poorest elderly, many of whom do not qualify for Social Security benefits. However, despite these programs, about 3.4 million elderly individuals remained in poverty in 2006.

The Social Security system faces a long-term financing problem. The Social Security Trustees project cash-flow deficits beginning in 2017 and trust fund insolvency in 2041. Many recent proposals to improve system solvency would reduce Social Security benefits in the future. Benefit reductions could affect the low- income elderly, many of whom rely on Social Security benefits for almost all of their income. Such potential benefit reductions could lead to higher rates of poverty among the elderly compared to those projected under the current benefit formula. Because the low-income elderly are especially vulnerable to benefit reductions, many recent Social Security reform proposals have included minimum benefits or other provisions that would mitigate the effect of benefit cuts on the elderly poor.

This report analyzes the projected effects of four possible approaches to mitigating the effects of Social Security benefit reductions on elderly poverty in 2042, the first full year of projected trust fund insolvency. The options are compared to a *payable baseline*, which assumes current-law benefits would need to be cut across the board to balance Social Security's annual income and spending at the point of insolvency. The four options examined are (1) a poverty-line Social Security minimum benefit; (2) a sliding-scale Social Security minimum benefit; (3) a poverty- line SSI benefit; and (4) a poverty-line SSI benefit with liberalized eligibility.

Chapter 4 - In recent years, an initiative by former President Bush to restructure Social Security through the creation of individual accounts moved Social Security reform to the forefront of the political debate. While much attention has been focused on the issue, there has been no legislative action. In the *Fiscal Year 2010 President's Budget*, President Obama stated that he does not support the creation of individual accounts within the Social Security system.

The spectrum of ideas for reform range from relatively minor changes to the pay-as-you-go social insurance system enacted in the 1930s to a redesigned, "modernized" program based on personal savings and investments modeled after IRAs and 401(k)s. Proponents of the fundamentally different approaches to reform cite varying policy objectives that go beyond simply restoring long-term financial stability to the Social Security system. They cite objectives that focus on improving the adequacy and equity of benefits, as well as those that reflect different philosophical views about the role of the Social Security program and the federal government in providing retirement income. However, the system's projected long-range financial outlook provides a backdrop for much of the Social Security reform debate in terms of the timing and degree of recommended program changes.

Currently, the Social Security system is generating surplus tax revenues. However, its board of trustees projects that the trust funds will be depleted in 2037, at which point an estimated 76% of scheduled annual benefits will be payable with incoming receipts (under the intermediate projections). The primary reason is demographics. Between 2010 and 2030, the number of people aged 65 and older is projected to increase by 75%, while the number of workers supporting the system is projected to increase by 8%. In addition, the trustees project that the system will begin running cash flow deficits in 2016, at which point other federal receipts will be needed to meet benefit costs. If there are no other surplus governmental receipts, policymakers would have three options: raise taxes or other income, reduce spending, or borrow.

Public opinion polls show that fewer than 50% of respondents are confident that Social Security can meet its long-term commitments. There is also a public perception that Social Security may not be as good a value for future retirees. These concerns, and a belief that the nation must increase national savings, have led to proposals to redesign the system. At the same time, others suggest that the system's financial outlook is not a "crisis" in need of immediate action. Supporters of the current program structure point out that the system is now running surpluses, continues to have public support and could be affected adversely by the risk associated with some of the reform ideas. They contend that only modest changes are needed to restore long-range solvency to the Social Security system.

During the 110th Congress, six Social Security reform measures were introduced, five of which would have established individual accounts. None of the measures received congressional action. During the 111th Congress, two Social Security reform measures have been introduced. This report will be updated as legislative activity warrants.

Chapter 5 - Calculations indicating that in the long run the Social Security program will not be financially sustainable under the present statutory scheme have fueled the current debate regarding Social Security reform. This report addresses selected legal issues which may be raised regarding entitlement to Social Security benefits as Congress considers possible changes to the Social Security program, and in view of projected long-range shortfalls in the Social Security Trust Funds.

Social Security is a statutory entitlement program. Beneficiaries have a legal entitlement to receive Social Security benefits as set forth under the Social Security Act. However, the fact that Social Security benefits are financed by taxes on an employee's wages does not limit Congress's power to fix the levels of benefits under the Social Security Act, or the conditions upon which they may be paid. Congress's authority to modify provisions of the Social Security program was affirmed in the 1960 Supreme Court decision in *Flemming v. Nestor,* wherein the Court held that an individual does not have an accrued "property right" in his or her Social Security benefits. The Court has made clear in subsequent court decisions that the payment of Social Security taxes conveys no contractual rights to Social Security benefits.

Congress has the power to legislatively promise to pay individuals a certain level of Social Security benefits, and to provide legal evidence of Congress's "guarantee" of the obligation of the federal government to provide for the payment of such benefits in the future. While Congress may decide to take whatever measures necessary to fulfill such a obligation, courts would be unlikely to find that Congress's unilateral promise constitutes a contract which could not be modified in the future. In addition, a congressional promise not to reduce a specific level of Social Security benefits payable to certain eligible individuals would likely not overcome the constitutional principle, subject to due process considerations, that one Congress may not bind a subsequent Congress to legislative action or inaction.

The calculations concerning the possible future insolvency of the Social Security Trust Funds raise a question whether that result would affect the legal right of beneficiaries to receive full Social Security benefits. While an entitlement by definition legally obligates the United States to make payments to any person who meets the eligibility requirements established in the statute that creates the entitlement, a provision of the Antideficiency Act prevents an agency from paying more in benefits than the amount available in the source of funds available to pay the benefits. The Social Security Act states that Social Security benefits shall be paid only from the Social Security Trust Funds and the act appropriates all payroll taxes to pay benefits. Although the legal right of beneficiaries to receive full benefits would not be extinguished by an insufficient amount of funds in the Social Security Trust funds, it appears that beneficiaries would have to wait until the Trust Funds receive an amount sufficient to pay full benefits in the case of a shortfall, unless Congress amends applicable laws.

Calculations indicating that in the long run the current Social Security program will not be financially sustainable under the present statutory scheme have fueled the current debate regarding Social Security reform.[1] This report addresses selected legal issues which may be raised regarding entitlement to Social Security benefits as Congress considers possible changes to the Social Security program and in view of projected long-range shortfalls in the Social Security Trust Funds.[2]

Social Security benefits are administered pursuant to Title II of the Social Security Act, known as the *Old Age, Survivors and Disability Insurance (OASDI)* program.[3] Title II is part of a larger social insurance program in which Congress uses its power to tax and spend for the general welfare to promote the social goals of aiding the aged, survivors of workers, disabled persons and persons of limited means. Beneficiaries under title II have a legal entitlement to receive Social Security benefits as set forth by the Social Security Act and as administered by the Social Security Administration (SSA), an independent agency in the executive branch.

An individual's right to Social Security benefits is in a sense "earned," since there is a general relationship between OASDI benefits and wages earned and the tax paid thereon. However, benefits are not directly measured by the amount of payments made through the years into the system. Thus, the fact that Social Security benefits are financed by taxes on an employee's wages does not provide a limit on Congress's power to fix the levels of benefits under the Social Security Act, or the conditions upon which they may be paid.[4]

Chapter 6 - Many recent Social Security reform proposals to improve program solvency include elements that would reduce benefits currently scheduled for future recipients. To date, debate has focused primarily on the potential impact on retirees, with less attention to the effects on other Social Security recipients, such as disabled workers and dependents. As these beneficiaries may have fewer alternative sources of income than traditional retirees, there has been interest in considering various options to protect the benefits of disabled workers and certain dependents.

This report examines (1) how certain elements of Social Security reform proposals could affect disability and dependent benefits, (2) options for protecting these benefits and how they might affect disabled workers and dependents, and (3) how protecting benefits could affect the Social Security program. To conduct this study, GAO used a microsimulation model to simulate benefits under various reform scenarios. GAO also interviewed experts and reviewed various reform plans, current literature, and GAO's past work.

Chapter 7 - The financing shortfall currently facing the Social Security program is significant. Without remedial action, program trust funds will be exhausted in 2040. Many recent reform proposals have included modifications of the indexing currently used in the Social Security program. Indexing is a way to link the growth of benefits and/or revenues to changes in an economic or demographic variable.

Given the recent attention focused on indexing, this report examines (1) the current use of indexing in the Social Security program and how reform proposals might modify that use, (2) the experiences of other developed nations that have modified indexing, (3) the effects of modifying the indexing on the distribution of benefits, and (4) the key considerations associated with modifying the indexing. To illustrate the effects of different forms of indexing on the distribution of benefits, author calculated benefit levels for a sample of workers born in 1985, using a microsimulation model. The author have prepared this report under the Comptroller General's statutory authority to conduct evaluations on his own initiative as part of a continued effort to assist Congress in addressing the challenges facing Social Security. The author provided a draft of this report to SSA and the Department of the Treasury. SSA provided technical comments, which author have incorporated as appropriate.

Chapter 8 - Absent reform, Social Security's financing gap will grow until currently scheduled benefits can no longer be paid in full. Recent reform proposals often include general revenue (GR)—a major change that can have significant implications for the budget as a whole. This report addresses these issues: (1) What information is available about GR in recent proposal scorings by Social Security's Office of the Chief Actuary (OCACT)? (2) What common mechanisms, especially GR mechanisms, are used to increase program revenue? (3) What are the implications of GR for the trust fund and the federal budget? We have prepared this report under the Comptroller General's statutory authority to conduct evaluations on his own initiative as part of a continued effort to assist Congress in addressing the challenges facing Social Security.

Chapter 1

CHALLENGES FACING THE SOCIAL SECURITY ADMINISTRATION: PRESENT AND FUTURE

Social Security Advisory Board

Susan M. Daniels
James Roosevelt
Transition Team for the President-Elect
Social Security Administration
400 Virginia Ave, SW Suite 700
Washington, D.C. 20024

Dear Ms. Daniels and Mr. Roosevelt:

When the Social Security Advisory Board was established in 1994, it was directed to provide advice to the President, the Congress, and the Commissioner of Social Security on matters pertaining to the Retirement, Survivors, and Disability programs, as well as the Supplemental Security Income program. During the past 14 years, the Board has issued over 40 reports and issue briefs that have recommended improvements in program administration, development and application of policies, and service delivery. The report that we are submitting to the President-Elect's Transition Team is a reflection of our past study as well as an analysis of the current state of the Social Security Administration.

The Social Security Administration has a strong commitment to the programs it administers and to the public that it serves; and it has carried out these responsibilities admirably over the past 70 years. However, the Social Security Advisory Board believes that the agency has reached a tipping point wherein continuing to do business with outdated 20th century tools hinders its ability to meet the needs and expectations of the American public. SSA needs to develop a vision and focus on the integration of processes, investment in a modern technology platform, and development of a highly skilled and creative workforce. This will not be an easy task, but we believe that with proper planning and implementation of new business processes, it will, once again, be regarded as a premier federal agency.

In addition, the Board is charged with making recommendations with respect to policies that will ensure the solvency of the Old-Age, Survivors, and Disability Insurance programs, both in the short term and the long term. In that capacity, we would be remiss if we did not voice our concern over the vacancies in the Public Trustees positions, which have not been filled since late 2007. It is important for the credibility of the Trustees Reports that these positions be filled quickly by diligent, fair and knowledgeable people who act with integrity in a bipartisan manner, and that the positions be filled by early summer, so that the 2010 Trustees Report can reflect their influence and views.

We greatly appreciate the opportunity that we had last week to share our perspectives with you. The attached report expands on a number of those ideas and highlights the challenges that confront the Social Security Administration in the near term and into the future.

Sincerely,
/s/
Sylvester J. Schieber
Attachment

INTRODUCTION

The programs administered by the Social Security Administration (SSA) form the foundation for the nation's social insurance network that has greatly reduced poverty among the elderly through the retirement and survivors program and provides income support to people with disabilities, widows and widowers, and young children. As such, the agency has performed admirably since 1936 when it came into being. On an annual basis, SSA issues payments to 60 million people who have established eligibility to Social Security or Supplemental Security Income benefits, a total of $650 billion—an amount equal to 20 percent of all federal spending and 5 percent of the national gross domestic product.

Despite this impressive accomplishment, the world is changing and the agency has reached a critical juncture. Due to the demographic changes that will result from nearly 80 million baby boomers, SSA's workloads will increase dramatically over the next 10 years. Retirement claims will jump by over 40 percent and disability claims will rise by at least 10 percent. Given the impact of Social Security on the national economy, the current state of the agency is disquieting—even as nearly overwhelming challenges loom on the horizon.

Current State and Future Burdens

- The agency is severely stressed now:
    - 750,000 hearings cases are backlogged; the average wait for a decision by an administrative law judge is over 500 days.
    - There is a 50 percent busy rate at the 800 number, in addition to the growing number of unanswered phone calls in the field office.

    - The waiting times in field offices are climbing—each month over 300,000 individuals who walk into a field office wait over an hour to be served.
    - Computer systems capacity and slow response time continue to be issues. The agency cannot offer 24/7 service because the antiquated systems must be backed up each night, necessitating taking the electronic services off line.
- SSA has estimated that over the next five years they will experience tremendous growth in their workloads. But these numbers do not reflect the likely increase in benefit applications that may occur due to the recent downturn in the economy:
    - RSI and Medicare by 28 percent.
    - SSI applications by 23 percent.
    - Disability applications by 5 percent.
    - New and replacement Social Security cards issued will increase by 9 percent to 18.8 million.
- In addition to core workloads, the agency has been tasked with unfunded additional responsibilities:
    - Medicare Prescription Drug program.
    - Verification of employment eligibility.
    - Medicaid and Food Stamp programs.
- SSA must maintain a system of records that is used as a key identifier for nearly all financial and health records in the country. The maintenance of this information embodies security risks never imagined by the creators of the Social Security Act:
    - 270 million earnings items are posted yearly to workers' records.
    - The records of over 60 million Social Security and Supplemental Security Income beneficiaries are currently maintained.
    - 250 million medical records are currently stored, increasing at the rate of 2 million per week.

To continue to serve the public in the myriad of ways necessary to fulfill its mission, the Social Security Administration must make fundamental changes in the processes used to deliver services. The current SSA structure is comprised of a number of functional units that handle a variety of tasks. The processes used by each unit to accomplish its assigned tasks have usually been developed within the narrow context of the particular needs and duties of the separate entities. The systems and procedures have been created over time to fulfill a specific purpose or program requirement, often without integrating the needs of other parts of the organization or capitalizing on tools already in place. The silo-nature of developing administrative procedures has had, after all these years, the impact of locking the agency into inefficient processes harnessed to outmoded technology. In turn, these outdated procedures and processing tools have limited creativity, innovation and have stymied continuous improvement efforts, leading to a workforce that it is doing its best, but is unable to meet the ever-increasing challenges the agency faces.

The Social Security Advisory Board believes that the agency has reached a tipping point wherein continuing to do business with outdated 20th century tools hinders its ability to meet the needs and expectations of the American public. SSA needs to develop a vision and focus on the integration of processes, investment in a modern technology platform, and development of a highly skilled and creative workforce. This is not merely tinkering around the edges—by addressing fundamental organizational change in these three areas—process, platform, and people, the agency has the potential to make the administration of the Social Security programs more effective in meeting the public's demand for service.

SSA must have a *process* capable of delivering services in an efficient and cost-effective manner; a process that transcends organizational boundaries. The agency has struggled to redesign its processes—but the approaches to date have been implemented against a backdrop of artificial rules in a stove-piped organization. These constraints have not allowed them to address the root cause of bottlenecks, inefficiencies, and redundant operations. They need to take a fresh look at *what and how and why* they do what they do.

SSA must have a technology *platform* that enables and supports an integrated process and does not compromise the integrity of the data. The underlying databases are based on obsolete computer languages. By the 1980s experts had concluded that these structures were inferior to the newer relational data models because they severely limited the ability to use more modern and flexible software tools; yet SSA is only just now confronting the need to convert key parts of its infrastructure.

SSA must have a workforce comprised of *people* in the proper organizational alignment and with the skills necessary to manage innovation and deliver quality service. The agency faces the challenges of an aging workforce as well as staffing losses. While SSA states that it is "managing" the retirement wave, it has continued practices such as early-out retirement that raises questions about their approach to sound human capital planning and oversight.

To make the fundamental changes required in the processes used to deliver services, SSA must have the resources to provide for a modern technological infrastructure and the people required for creative design and implementation. In past reports addressing SSA resources, the Board has urged that the agency's administrative funding should not be subject to discretionary caps in the budget process. SSA must act, and act quickly, to replace outmoded technology—this can only be accomplished with a temporary multi-year capital fund to modernize the systems at all levels. The Board urges SSA to continue to educate Congress and the Administration on the long-term goals and strategic plans of the agency, and provide additional transparency in the budgeting process. This will enable Congress to better understand the needs of the agency, in the midst of so many competing national priorities.

Process

High-performing organizations can be identified by their forward-looking and creative vision of a business process that is efficient, fosters consistent application of program policy, and is agency-wide. These organizations are goal-oriented, emphasizing the overall process in order to achieve the intended outcome. Effective processes cross organizational boundaries and are cross-functional. That is, the focus is on the activity, not on a narrow band of people who are "responsible" for a particular set of tasks.

SSA's service delivery methodology consists of a series of tasks performed by separate components. Each person performs a specific task and hands the case off to the next person in the production line. There is little concern, or even awareness, of what the others are doing and, perhaps more importantly, little sense of the overall framework that ties the pieces together. New procedures and the accompanying tasks—and even the supporting electronic tools—are developed in a stove-pipe fashion; thus they are not able to take advantage of information from downstream components leading to redundancy and rework. The agency is inwardly-focused and seems to place more value on minimizing internal burden and less emphasis on the effect on customers.

In order for SSA to deliver high quality service in an efficient and effective fashion and meet changing customer expectations, they must seriously analyze the current adjudication system, identify non-value added steps and reorganize the essential parts into a sequence of activities that eliminates hand-offs, and establish measures of success that transcend discrete components. This will require a significant culture shift away from "it is not my issue" to one of taking responsibility for results.

Current Service Delivery Process

The current methodology is built around a variety of discrete tasks, which are implemented by several different components:

- The network of **Field Offices** and **Teleservice Centers** provide the basic points of contact through which the public can access service and transact business.
- **Disability Determination Service (DDS)** units in each state make the initial disability determination for claims filed in SSA field offices and handle the first level of appeal (reconsideration).
- **Hearing Offices** in the **Office of Disability Adjudication Review** (ODAR) conduct hearings for applicants who choose to appeal claims that were denied at the DDS level.
- The **Appeals Council** handles appeals for applicants who were denied at the hearing level.
- **Program Service Centers** complete much of the post-entitlement work and maintain beneficiary records.
- In addition to processing post-entitlement workloads, the **Office of Central Operations** is responsible for issuing Social Security numbers and maintaining earnings records.

The ability to deliver quality service through a wide network of component sites and electronic services requires processes that are integrated; otherwise, the result is fragmented service and wasted resources. Therefore, SSA should:

- Fully **integrate services** across programs: Processes should be designed to cover the full cycle of service, regardless of which component initiates the action - beginning at the point a claim is filed, continuing through all appeals to payment or denial, and extending to post-entitlement actions for beneficiaries.

- Initiate effective **policy research and development**: Processes should be developed in conjunction with policy to avoid unneeded complexity. SSA needs to take the initiative to research and develop policy in a strategic, visionary manner, identifying policy improvements that will make the program easier to administer.
- Eliminate **redundancy** in the collection of information: Processes should pull information from internal SSA systems and from data stores maintained by other agencies and organizations in order to eliminate the need to ask the public to provide duplicate information or to seek services from other sources.
- Collaborate with **outside agencies and organizations:** SSA does not take full advantage of integration with outside agencies and organizations who furnish information to verify eligibility for benefits, or from whom the public must also seek service—the Veterans Administration, Immigration, and state assistance agencies. SSA should find areas of common methodologies in order to share information and utilize shared physical locations to provide overarching service to the customer.

Disability Process

There is a long history of concern regarding the effectiveness of the disability process. In 1998, the SSAB concluded that *from the standpoint of applicants for benefits, the current disability decision process is difficult to understand, as well as slow and fragmented into multiple levels of processing and decision making*. SSA has, however, made repeated attempts to improve the overall process, but in each case they did not take advantage of the opportunities to re-think the work flow.

- **Disability Redesign**—a long-term strategy to redesign the entire disability claims process from initial application up to the appeals process was initiated in 1994. The original plan and three subsequent revisions in 1997, 1999, and 2001 yielded only limited success.

- **Prototype**—eliminated the reconsideration level of appeal and implemented the single decision maker process. Even though this was implemented in 10 states in 1999 and remains in place in those states, the elements of the Prototype process have never been fully implemented nationwide. Thus, the appeals process has been inconsistent for nearly 10 years.

- **Disability Service Improvement (DSI)**—a process improvement plan that focused on improving the accuracy, timeliness, and consistency in decision making was initiated in August 2006 and suspended in early 2007. Most of the DSI initiatives were never implemented beyond the Boston Region due to ongoing systems problems and the unanticipated administrative costs.

After all these years of redesign efforts, the agency is left with a disability process that does not meet service expectations. The process still is not integrated, and the national disability program continues to be applied inconsistently throughout the DDSs, the quality review components, and the hearing offices. The disconnect between DDS and ODAR adjudication procedures and application of agency policy is cited as one reason for the wide variation in DDS and ODAR allowance rates.

Incremental improvements to the current processes: The agency's recently released strategic plan addresses several important improvements to current processes; however, they do not address the process as an integrated whole.

- The **Quick Disability Determinations (QDD)** system identifies applicants who have a disability that will in all likelihood result in an allowance without extensive case development—such as cancer, end-stage renal disease, and low birth-weight babies.
- The **Compassionate Allowance** initiative identifies individuals who are likely to be disabled by the nature of their disease or condition. This initiative, like QDD, speeds up the decision making process by fast tracking claims through the current process.

Elimination of the hearings backlog: Another series of initiatives outlined in the strategic plan address the need to eliminate the hearings backlog and prevent its recurrence. The tactical steps outlined below should stop the growth in the backlog and provide the agency some breathing room while they develop and implement new electronic tools, simplify and unify program policies, and expand adjudicatory capacity.

- Increase the capacity to hear and decide cases through increasing the size of the ALJ cadre and support staff;
- Increase the use of video hearings;
- Open National Hearing Centers to provide operational flexibility;
- Remand certain cases back to DDS for possible allowance;
- Increase adjudicative actions by senior attorneys; and
- Automate scheduling, file preparation and centralized notice functions.

Even though the focus is almost solely targeted to the elimination of the hearings backlog, it is also directed toward *preventing its recurrence*. This is an excellent opportunity for the agency to pause and reassess the tasks and eliminate or restructure the steps that are inefficient or redundant. Moreover, *preventing the recurrence* is not just an ODAR issue—some of the backlog is attributable to procedures and rules in the field offices and disability determination services that result in rework in the hearings offices. For example, last year ODAR returned over 52,000 cases to the DDSs under the informal remand procedures; nearly 33 percent of these were allowed—many without additional evidence. This raises a very basic question of whether these cases should have been allowed at an earlier step in the process. If a fundamental redesign of the adjudication phases is undertaken, then many of the complexities and rework in the hearings process may be eliminated.

It is not clear whether the initiatives the agency has implemented will eliminate the backlog or just keep up with the level of receipts. The agency's strategic plan has established as an objective *to reduce the time it takes an individual to receive a hearing decision to an average of 270 days.* SSA has stated that this is the optimum time the current process is capable of delivering. Even if the process improvements under development do materialize and deliver some processing time efficiencies, it is not at all clear that they will achieve this goal without some fundamental process changes.

Retirement Process

SSA anticipates *nearly 80 million boomers will file for retirement benefits over the next 20 years—an average of 10,000 per day.* SSA is planning to introduce *Ready Retirement*, a new internet application for filing retirement claims, to address the anticipated growth in the retirement workload. It is designed to *simplify the filing process and shorten the time it takes to file online from 45 to 15 minutes while also eliminating the need for most individuals to visit their local field office*. There are three supporting actions associated with this initiative.

- Expand the use of automated data exchanges—to eliminate the need to submit paper copies of birth certificates, death certificates, and earning information.
- Simplify policies and procedures—to eliminate the need to ask for information already contained in SSA systems or databases.
- Provide online tools to plan for retirement—to eliminate the staff resources needed to respond to requests for retirement benefit estimates.

Despite the improvements in process, this initiative raises the question—is *Ready Retirement* a fresh approach for the retirement process, or simply an overlay of technology onto the paper process? *Ready Retirement* provides the agency an opportunity to push beyond current paradigms about how the process works for establishing and confirming eligibility. Given the amount of information stored in the SSA system and available through interfaces with IRS and other systems, it is possible to eliminate the necessity of filing a claim altogether. Entitlement at full retirement age could be established automatically, with payment made contingent upon some type of claimant response to authenticate identity and verify circumstances. This process would require little, if any, human intervention and merge policy and technology into a singular end-to-end process that would help the agency manage those 80 million benefit claims.

SSA's current estimates for growth in the retirement application workload are most likely understated. The country has been in a recession for over a year and the economic down turn shows no signs of abating in the near term. Due to job loss some workers who are in their early 60s may find themselves contemplating claiming retirement benefits sooner than they had expected. When to claim Social Security retirement benefits is a very important decision in the lives of most workers and should be made within the context of an individual's unique circumstances.

The Social Security Administration has developed a variety of public information tools designed to present the salient issues relevant to that decision, but many of them unintentionally send unclear messages about the relationship between the claiming of benefits and withdrawing from the workforce—between taking "retirement benefits" and actually "retiring" from work. The agency inadvertently frames the benefit election choice in a manner that treats these very different and separate decisions as if they were inextricably linked, and as a result may send mixed signals to potential retirees about how continuing to work affects their benefits. The *Social Security Statement* is mailed to over 149 million individuals each year and is the agency's primary communication tool with the American public. Given the important role that Social Security benefits play in providing income security in retirement and in disability, the *Social Security Statement* should function as a state-of-the-art communications vehicle that presents this critical information clearly, accurately, and succinctly.

Supplemental Security Income process

The SSI program, as part of our national economic security structure, provides a monthly income to help meet the basic needs of people who have little or no income or resources and are age 65 or over, have a severe disability, or are blind. The issues raised in the disability discussion above also affect the SSI disability process. However, the program is further complicated by the non-disability rules, many of which have roots in the federal-state welfare programs of the 1960s.

- The SSI program is over 35 years old, but there has not been a fundamental review of the policies and processes used in the program. The income and resource limits have not been changed for almost 20 years and SSI policies are some of the most complex administered by SSA. Documentation and verification procedures are labor intensive and remain mired in a paper process. For example, wage reporting is the leading cause of SSI overpayments. SSI payments are computed using a process known as retrospective monthly accounting. That is, correct payment amounts for prior months are calculated and applied retroactively, resulting in overpayments for many working SSI beneficiaries. Retrospective accounting is easier for SSA to administer, but does not serve the best interests of the beneficiaries who live at or near poverty level.
- Integration and collaboration with outside parties, particularly financial institutions and state assistance agencies, is even more important to the SSI process given the need to verify income and resources and the number of places claimants must contact to request assistance or establish eligibility.

Management Information and Policy Development

High-performing organizations recognize that there cannot be a commitment to process change without an equal commitment to performance measurement. Identifying and targeting the root cause of bottlenecks and vulnerable processes is the first step; implementing performance measures that track outcomes across the organization must follow. SSA collects a wealth of data on case characteristics, decisional outcomes, timeliness, productivity, quality, and cost. The data are collected by each functional operating component, tallied and put into charts, and then used as "management information." The data, like the process, are not integrated—it is virtually impossible to track the end-to-end adjudicative processing of a cohort of cases in the normal course of the business process, making trend analysis difficult at best. The cadre of economists, statisticians and other technical analysts in Social Security's research operations could help in devising appropriate analyses if they were simply brought into the process and given a free hand to do so. Without complete information, the agency's ability to lay out sound arguments for legislative changes, for shaping public policy, and for supporting its budget requests are compromised.

PLATFORM

It is imperative that the agency commit to implementing a modern technology platform that will support the agency's mission *and* is sufficiently flexible to grow and support future program changes. The infrastructure must enable change; new tools should stimulate alternative approaches to process implementation, but it cannot be the sole driver. Process change has been stymied in the past because the outmoded IT system has placed constraints on the extent to which SSA could redesign its work and has limited data sharing across components. The SSA system must be able to support internal processes, deliver services online to the public in a method that is secure and private, and maintain all the records accurately.

Replacement of Basic Computer Infrastructures

SSA's basic system is outdated, and could prove unreliable and subject to security risk if not replaced. At the request of SSA, in 2007 the National Research Council (NRC) of the National Academies conducted a strategic assessment of SSA's proposed e-government strategy and the underlying infrastructure. Many of the recommendations from the NRC have been included in the agency's strategic plan.

SSA's **National Computer Center** is 30 years old and the NRC recommended that it be replaced. Prior to this recommendation, SSA initiated a project to complete a second data center in Durham, NC; however, it will not be fully operational for three years. It is our understanding that when the concept for a second site was conceived, it was to provide full redundant processing for the National Computer Center (NCC) as a disaster recovery operation. However, SSA recently estimated that the NCC in Baltimore will be unable to handle the expected computer processing workload and will be near collapse by the end of 2012, when the Durham site is projected to be fully operational. The mission of the second site has evolved in view of this, but it appears that it will fall short of being able to fully protect the agency's data. It is estimated that the Durham site will provide no more than 50 percent redundant coverage and will have to provide front-line operating capacity to support the workload. More important, as the agency moves forward on modernizing its infrastructure, it must make comprehensive disaster recovery a priority.

The agency is at risk—both in the near term and in the future—to protect all of its data in a secure and responsible fashion. It therefore needs to:

- Convert the **COBOL-based information technology infrastructure**. SSA's database platform, Master Data Access Method, was developed in-house by SSA staff in the early 1980s. The NRC concluded that *it is technologically obsolete and functionally primitive compared with readily available commercial technologies and products.* SSA has begun the conversion process but on a lengthy schedule that extends beyond 2014.

- Replace the **telephone system** with one capable of integrated e-mail and web-based communication. The agency has awarded a contract to replace current telephone systems over the next five years with Voice-Over-Internet-Protocol (VOIP) systems which will provide greater flexibilities for telephone and internet services.

All of this is long overdue, and will be extremely costly to accomplish. SSA must work with Congress to obtain a no-year capital budget and determine how all of these major changes can be achieved in a relatively short time given the risk of involved for loss of vital information, and the resources that continue to be wasted in working with an ineffective system. In his April 2008 testimony before the Committee on Ways and Means, Chairman Schieber noted that *"this capital budget would be for limited duration and come with a stipulation that the net results be a modern integrated system that delivers efficiencies in the operation, increases output of workloads, and shortens the processing time for applicants."*

Strategies for Technology Transformation

Effective IT strategies support organizational goals in a holistic manner and enable the continuous improvement and transformation of business processes from the first point of contact through post-entitlement actions. Technology has been used to automate current processes; however, this has been mostly a project to convert current paper-based claims processes into an electronic reflection of that process. Moreover, because the IT planning process is driven more by internal politics than a true strategic plan, technology has not been used as a catalyst for process change.

There is a plan underway to build a **common processing system** for the DDSs that will replace the 54 state DDS systems with a single system. However, focusing *first* on the middle segment of the disability adjudication process, without consideration of how changes in the front-end of the adjudication process will affect the DDS, and then how the accumulated data will impact the hearings process, fails to consider the disability process as an integrated whole. This fragmented approach has been used in the past and has not been successful because it does not follow the flow of data. SSA needs to develop a comprehensive IT system that supports a full service process from end-to-end—from initial claim through appeals to final decision and on into post entitlement actions for beneficiaries.

To address inconsistency and improve documentation of the initial claim determination, a software program, **Electronic Case Analysis Tool (eCAT)** is under development for the DDSs. At nearly the same time a similar program, the **Findings Integrated Template (FIT)** was developed with the same purpose for the ALJs to use for hearing decisions. An opportunity to unify the application of policy and process could have been capitalized upon if SSA had chosen to develop one integrated tool that could have been used across adjudicative levels.

Electronic services are a part of the agency's long-term service delivery strategy; however they are viewed as an "add-on" and not as *the* way to conduct business. As a result, they are not well-integrated into the business lines. Some of this is most likely attributable to the antiquated systems platform which constrains how data elements are accessed and shared. SSA has developed several online software applications, but many are not user friendly, causing the public to abandon them after attempted use. The agency has acknowledged this and recently announced plans for a new online initiative—*Disability Direct*—that will simplify the application process, eliminate redundant questions and provide links, prompts, and other tools to assist the user. The National Research Council recommended that SSA consider the experiences of private sector organizations such as large-scale financial institutions—to examine the approaches they used to change the public's preference for face-to-face contact to a preference for access through ATMs and the internet.

Plans are under development to work with the medical community to adapt SSA systems to **Health Information Technology** standards, thereby creating a uniform electronic format for the storage and transmission of medical records. An electronic exchange of information with medical sources, and with the federal courts, is also being developed. They are also looking beyond the current state of "receiving and storing" electronic images which places a significant strain on storage capacity and can cause slow response times for the end-users. In addition, they are exploring how intelligent systems could be used to analyze medical evidence.

Imbed **management information** in the technology platform. The technology platform should include a structure to deliver management information and data timely, in a format that enables leaders to draw conclusions and make effective decisions. In order to measure success, critical data elements must be identified and built into the system. SSA does not have a comprehensive data measurement structure that monitors the success of outcomes and service delivery levels across the enterprise or that provides the kind of organizational analyses needed for process improvement.

Develop needed technology to ensure the **security of records.** SSA recognizes the importance of protecting the information entrusted to it by the public, and has taken steps to obtain the technology to ensure that protection. However, this is becoming more difficult as systems hackers become more sophisticated. SSA faces a formidable challenge in assuring that users are properly authenticated as they move forward with making information stored in the agency's systems available via the internet. This is an area where SSA should seek to capitalize on lessons learned from the other organizations and the technology industry.

PEOPLE

Processes and platforms are only the vehicles through which the ingenuity of the people flows to ultimately provide the services. It is the people that make the ultimate difference. To operate as a high-performing agency, the organizational structure of SSA must be properly aligned, and have a sufficiently staffed workforce that possesses the skills and knowledge that are critical for success.

The SSA workforce is not appropriately staffed with the right skill sets and knowledge levels to meet the challenges of today, let alone in the future.

- Over 53 percent of the total workforces, including 70 percent of the supervisors, are eligible to retire by FY 2017.
- Since 1999, nearly 32,000 employees have left the agency with just under 28,000 people hired to replace staffing losses (through FY 2007).
- Staffing levels are at an historic low exacerbated by the retirement of the agency's own baby boomers and by their continued use of the "early out" retirement incentive. In the last three years, 28 percent of all retirees took advantage of the early out provisions.

Organizational Structure

Although the agency has undergone many re-organizations, usually when a new Commissioner is appointed, it is not clear which structure is the most effective from a functional point of view However, it is clear that none have resulted in the ability to foster innovation and change as a cultural expectation.

SSA's current organization is stove-piped—even though many of the programs administered by the agency cut across these organizational lines. To a significant degree, this current structure has, while dispersing responsibility, narrowed accountability.

The disability process remains one of the areas most affected by fractured organizational structure. The two primary processing components for disability—the DDSs and the hearing offices—are the responsibility of two different deputy commissioners. Disability policy and disability systems are the responsibility of two additional deputy commissioners. While the agency maintains that these executives work across program lines, the very existence of the disparate structures has created obstacles.

The governance of the IT planning process is a similarly fractured process. The primary responsibility for planning, developing and implementing systems initiatives is divided between the agency's CIO and the Deputy Commissioner for Systems. However, there are several other agency executives who have major responsibilities for parts of the process. In addition, the oversight of IT planning is managed by an (internal) information technology advisory board where all components compete for resources to implement their specific projects.

Workforce Composition

Over 60 percent of SSA employees deliver direct services, mainly in field offices and teleservice centers; the remaining personnel provide indirect and support services through processing centers, regional offices, and headquarters. There are literally hundreds of different positions within these components and, while many duties are unique to a given position, many of the duties are overlapping. SSA needs to:

- Assess the **type of position** and **skill sets** needed. As SSA works to achieve more effective integrated processes, it must also assess the impact of those changes on the types of positions and skill sets needed at every level of the process. The types of positions that are filled, and the locations in which they will work, must correlate to the processes developed for use in direct services as well as in the various components that provide support behind the scenes.

- Update **employee skill mix** to maximize the use of technology. Since technology is now and will continue to be an integral part of every process, more emphasis must be placed on recruiting staff with the skills to effectively utilize the ever-increasing scope of technology in all involved components. SSA must continue to deliver services through its network of community-based offices; however, the public expects to be able to access alternative service delivery options such as online services, videoconferencing, and interactive web-based "chat rooms." This will require the development of more flexible job classifications and position descriptions that will enable employees to perform diverse tasks and deliver comprehensive service at the earliest point in the process.
- **Develop data** needed to effectively staff and train the agency. In order to determine how many people are needed, the types of training they require, the proper locations to provide services and the appropriate staffing mix for each location, management information and data are essential. Currently, the agency does not have a good mechanism to capture descriptive data on training activities offered, and more significantly, data that facilitates planning for and acquiring the types of training that are *not* offered, but are essential for job performance. Without that data, it is impossible to measure the resources required to process workloads or provide administrative support. SSA's limited ability to gather and analyze workload measures reflects the stove-piped organizational structure and restricts their capability to anticipate fluctuations in workload and make pro-active adjustments. They need to develop comprehensive management information across the entire organization using standard measures and uniform definitions of productivity.

CONCLUSION

The Social Security Administration is at a critical juncture in its ability to continue to fulfill the mission that was set out for it in 1935. Granted, the mission has grown and the scope of the agency's responsibilities undoubtedly far exceeds what the original framers had in mind. Historically, SSA has been the "can-do" agency that has always stepped up to meet new challenges. But today change is rapidly overwhelming the agency's capacity to adjust. Challenges such as shifting demographics, growing workloads, changing customer expectations combined with an aging workforce, deteriorating systems infrastructure, and chronic under funding have pushed SSA's ability to deliver high quality service to the brink.

Despite these challenges, the agency can step up once more—with proper planning and attention to improving their processes, designing and implementing modern technology, and investing in its staff. Short term initiatives that will restore the balance within the agency are essential and SSA is, once again, relying on such activities. But they are not enough and they have diverted the agency's attention away from critical long-term planning. The foundation for such initiatives must be a longer range vision for the future that lays out a compelling roadmap for the future that transcends changes in Administration and agency leadership. And that makes a persuasive case for sufficient and stable funding. SSA has massive administrative challenges ahead and time is running short.

APPENDIX A: SELECTED EXCERPTS FROM SOCIAL SECURITY ADVISORY BOARD REPORTS, TESTIMONIES, AND PRESENTATIONS

Budget

The SSA has always stepped up to meet every new challenge and it can do it again. But it takes adequate resources and investment in its staff. Chronic under-funding has contributed to the current crisis and has diverted the agency's attention away from long-term planning. *Statement to the Subcommittee on Social Security of the Committee on Ways and Means, U.S. House of Representatives—September 2008*

Rather than commit to long-term increased support of what is an unsatisfactory process for stakeholders at all levels, maybe it is time to restore a temporary multi-year capital fund to modernize the functions at all levels of this operation and develop systems to implement the solutions. *Statement to the Full Committee on Ways and Means, U.S. House of Representatives—April 2008*

One of the bad choices that managers have to make when administrative funding is inadequate is whether or not they should divert funds from activities which have a long-run payoff in lower costs in order to meet the immediate pressures of rising claims backlogs. In that sort of competition, the needs of the disabled claimant obviously and correctly win out. But funding at a level that forces that choice is the ultimate in penny-wise and pound-foolish behavior. *Statement to the Subcommittee on Social Security of the Committee on Ways and Means, U.S. House of Representatives—February 2007*

Although the administrative costs of the Social Security program are treated as "discretionary" from a budget perspective, these programs are a very basic and direct Federal responsibility, and the failure to provide adequate funds to administer them has results that are anything but discretionary. If the agency does not have adequate funding, it will have to continue to postpone program integrity actions, which means losing programmatic savings well beyond the administrative resources involved. *Letter to the Chairs and Ranking Members of the House and Senate Appropriations Committees and Subcommittees—April 2004*

Disability Program

There are several workgroups in place looking at the content and format for collecting initial disability claim information…it must be tied to an overarching unified business process. There needs to be a purposeful analysis of why we do what we do and how can it be done in a better way that will be useful to any adjudicator anywhere in the system. *Speech to the National Association of Disability Examiner—September 2008*

The DDS "one system"…will require compromises. But the creative aspects of hammering out what the system will look like and how it will work should generate new thinking about the process and its interconnectedness with the field offices and the hearings offices, about the platform on which it is built, and how people will use it. *Speech to the National Association of Disability Examiners—September 2008*

But we were dismayed when we recently learned that ODAR has had limited involvement with the development of the DDS eCat initiative. ODAR has not been able to explore fully how eCat can lead to efficiencies in the hearings development process. *Address to the National Educational Conference, Association of Administrative Law Judges—August 2008*

The focus of this hearing—clearing the backlogs and providing adequate resources—needs to be about more than just the state of the workload at the hearings level. It must take into consideration the critical steps all along the determination process. It must recognize the problems with the systems infrastructure that supports the work being done by staff at all levels. *Statement to the Full Committee on Ways and Means, U.S. House of Representatives—April 2008*

Our Nation's policymakers need to acknowledge that the current disability programs, though well intentioned, are badly fractured and disjointed. A unifying point of vision, oversight and management is desperately needed. *A Disability System for the 21st Century—September 2006*

The Social Security disability programs had their origins in the 1950s—a world vastly different from today's world in several important respects including the nature of available work, the educational levels of the workforce, medical capacity to treat disability conditions and the nature and availability of rehabilitative technology...but the core design of the programs, rooted in a definition of disability as inability to do substantial work, has remained unchanged. *The Social Security Definition of Disability—October 2003*

With regard to the disability program, dispersion of functions throughout many different entities within the agency poses a difficult problem; the disability program lacks the tightly defined policy and administrative parameters of the RSI programs. *Charting the Future of Social Security's Disability Programs: The Need for Fundamental Change—January 2001*

Information Technology

I am concerned that all the separate initiatives to build electronic pathways to solve Social Security's disability problem may fail because no one is making sure they link up to create a path to a real solution. *Address to the National Educational Conference, Association of Administrative Law Judges—August 2008*

SSA has made tremendous strides in the development of the electronic folder. For all of its strengths, it has some striking weaknesses; primarily that it is not a "single system." Case production processes are not coordinated from beginning to end. *Testimony to the Full Committee on Ways and Means, U.S. House of Representatives—April 2008*

This is about moving away from COBOL-based operating systems, a 1950s' technology, to modern software languages and tools. This is about moving away from manual work sampling to integrated data collection that permits inline measurement and quality review systems that can assess what works, what does not, and the difference between the two. We are talking about the potential for redesigning work in an organization that is stifled by institutional barriers between components and work rules that are crippling productivity advances. *Statement to the Full Committee on Ways and Means, U.S. House of Representatives—April 2008*

A strategy is needed to address the growing demand for telephone service; field offices are "virtually impenetrable" by phone. Better information is needed regarding how the public views the nature and quality of the agency's telephone service. *Challenges Facing the New Commissioner of Social Security—December 2001*

Efforts to improve SSA's systems must be strengthened. With expected growth in workloads, systems improvements must be accelerated to meet the demand, particularly with regard to the disability processing systems. *How the Social Security Administration Can Improve Its Service to the Public—September 1999*

SSA must develop new ways of delivering service beyond the traditional office or telephone service. Internet has significant potential for helping alleviate resource problems while improving service; other technologies should also be explored such as kiosks and videoconferencing. *How the Social Security Administration Can Improve Its Service to the Public—September 1999*

Management Information

The only way to truly prevent the backlog from recurring is by identifying and targeting the root cause of bottlenecks and vulnerable processes and then implementing performance measures that track outcomes. *Address to the 2008 National Educational Conference, Association of Administrative Law Judges—August 2008*

Part of the problem here may be that data itself is often of little value if not refined into information and knowledge that managers on the ground can use to improve the efficiency of the units they run. (For example) data on individual ALJ productivity can only be properly assessed in an analysis that controls for other environmental variables—number of support staff, workload characteristics, percentage of remanded decisions and other variables. *Address to the 2008 National Educational Conference, Association of Administrative Law Judges—August 2008*

The agency urgently needs a quality management system to produce program information needed by policy makers; the system must incorporate all parts of the disability determination process. *Charting the Future of Social Security's Disability Programs: The Need for Fundamental Change—January 2001*

The agency does not have the ability to accurately measure workloads and therefore cannot assess its workforce needs accurately. Automation expected to improve productivity and efficiency often is not delivered on schedule or does not produce expected savings; however no adjustments are made to resource levels. *How the Social Security Administration Can Improve Its Service to the Public—September 1999*

Policy/Process Development

A third suggestion I would make is for a thorough evaluation of the Social Security programs with a view of finding policy improvements that might suggest ways to make the program easier to adminster. As we move into a future with larger workloads and continuing budgetary limits, it would be useful to evaluate existing procedures and rules to see if they can be made more objective. *Statement to the Subcommittee on Social Security of the Committee on Ways and Means, U.S. House of Representatives—February 2007*

SSA's Demonstration Projects: While there have been some positive outcomes, projects have not always been focused to enhance policy decision-making. For example, projects that focus all of the RTW efforts inside the structure of the disability program missed assessment of early intervention. *A Disability System for the 21st Century—September 2006*

A single presentation of policy is critical to ensuring consistent/fair decisions. Policy makers need far better information than is now available in order to develop and implement the kinds of changes in policies and procedures that are needed to improve accuracy and consistency in decision making. *Challenges Facing the New Commissioner of Social Security—December 2001*

Workforce

Unlike other newly hired federal employees, administrative law judges do not serve a probationary period. Adding a probationary period as a condition of employment would provide the agency with a more formal mechanism wherein struggling employees could receive additional policy training and guidance on workload management. *Letter to The Honorable Sam Johnson, Ranking Member, Subcommittee on Social Security of the Committee on Ways and Means, U.S. House of Representatives—October 2008*

In view of the fact that SSA employs more than four out of five ALJs and pays a proportional share of the costs of the selection process, it should have a process that identifies candidates that meet its unique needs. *Address to the Subcommittee on Social Security of the Committee on Ways and Means, U.S. House of Representatives—September 2008*

We talk about our commitment to public service and our willingness to address the needs of those individuals who turn to Social Security on a daily basis. But the reality is that thousands of disability cases languish for years as the claims representatives, the disability adjudicators, and the administrative law judges struggle with crushing backlogs and steadily declining numbers of workers. *Statement to the Full Committee on Ways and Means, U.S. House of Representatives—April 2008*

The offer of early out retirement is part of the agency's overall staffing strategy to manage the retirement wave. Our concern with the agency's use of early out is twofold: first is the obvious loss to SSA of experienced staff, and secondly, the example it sets with regard to the employment of older workers. *Letter to Commissioner Michael J. Astrue—March 2008*

The fact that most administrative law judges are admirable employees does not mean that the agency should ignore it stewardship responsibilities here. It seems to me that ALJs who are carrying out their duties in a responsible manner should want to work with the management of the agency to develop reasonable standards and procedures that will fully protect decisional independence while identifying and seeking appropriate correction of situations where there is failure to meet those standards. *Address to the 2007 National Educational Conference, Association of Administrative Law Judges—July 2007*

There are long-standing institutional problems that must be addressed. The agency's culture discourages open discussions and timely resolution of issues; there are weaknesses in communication between headquarters and field, and ongoing issues have resulted in inadequate teamwork among various components (especially with regard to the disability program). *Challenges Facing the New Commissioner of Social Security—December 2001.*

APPENDIX B: LISTING OF UPCOMING REPORTS

The following reports will be published over the next several months. All documents will be posted to the SSAB website at http://www.ssab.gov/index.html. Printed copies can also be ordered through the website or by calling 202-475-7700.

Working for Retirement Security—this report summarizes the policy issues involved in extending the working lives of older Americans. The report discusses the barriers to working at older ages and highlights the work of experts who participated in a forum on policies pertaining to older workers sponsored by the Social Security Advisory Board and the University of Illinois Center for Business and Public Policy.

Social Security Administration: 21^s Century Service Delivery (working title)—Focusing on the development of information technology (IT), this report outlines the agency's current problems with service delivery and discusses how and why its systems infrastructure must change if the agency is to meet 21st Century challenges.

The Social Security Statement: Is It Achieving Its Intended Purposes? (working title)—in developing this report, the Board has taken an in-depth look at the *Social Security Statement*, its purpose, its content, and its impact on public understanding. This report outlines a number of recommendations for improving and clarifying the information provided.

Unexpected Consequences of SSA Policies: Substantial Gainful Activity—this paper is the second in a series of issue briefs that looks at the unexpected consequences of certain SSA policies and offers some recommendations for policy change both in terms of more immediate actions and long term restructuring.

Unexpected Consequences of SSA Policies: Representative Payees—the third in this series of issue briefs focuses on issues involving the appointment of representative payees who receive and manage Social Security payments for incapable beneficiaries. Some of the issues discussed include accounting practices, misuse, payees for difficult populations, and systems improvements.

In: Social Security Reform: Disability, Indexing and Financing ISBN: 978-1-61668-354-2
Editor: Janet U. Burlington

Chapter 2

COSTS ASSOCIATED WITH THE ADMINISTRATION'S EFFORTS TO PROMOTE PROGRAM REFORMS*

United States Government Accountability Office

August 10, 2007

The Honorable Henry A. Waxman
Chairman
Committee on Oversight and Government Reform
House of Representatives

Subject: *Social Security: Costs Associated with the Administration's Efforts to Promote Program Reforms*

Dear Mr. Chairman:

You requested that we identify the official Social Security reform public speaking events and other promotion initiatives involving administration officials, and their costs to the federal government, since January 2005. As you know, the Social Security[1] Board of Trustees is projecting in its 2007 report that as early as 2017 Social Security benefit payments will exceed tax revenues. After that time, the gap between costs and tax revenues grows continuously, and unless action is taken to close this gap, it is currently estimated that the Social Security trust funds will be depleted by 2041. In his 2005 State of the Union Address, the President emphasized the need to reform Social Security, and he announced his intention to work with the Congress to achieve reforms. On March 2, 2005, the Secretary of the Treasury announced the "60 Stops in 60 Days" tour[2] in which the President and other administration officials would speak to the public about the need for reform in a series of town hall meetings across the country in an attempt to gain popular support for program

* This is an edited, reformatted and augmented version of a U. S. Government Accountability Office publication dated August 2007.

reforms. Your request asked us to include events such as those associated with the "60 Stops in 60 Days" tour and initiatives such as the Social Security Information Center (SSIC) established at the Department of the Treasury (Treasury) to provide a focal point for the administration's Social Security reform activities.

To answer your question about the list of public speaking events and other promotion initiatives, we relied upon information supplied by the Social Security Administration (SSA), Treasury, and the Executive Office of the President (EOP), including information posted to Treasury's and the White House's Web sites.[3] To answer your question about the cost of the public speaking events and other promotion initiatives, we focused our work on the activities of SSA, Treasury, and EOP, which accounted for approximately 75 percent of the public speaking events. In addition to data obtained from SSA, Treasury, and EOP, we received information pertaining to EOP activities from the United States Air Force (Air Force), and the Departments of Labor (Labor) and Health and Human Services (HHS). We specifically asked the Air Force to provide cost data related to the President's and Vice President's use of Air Force One and Air Force Two in traveling to promote Social Security reform. We asked Labor and HHS to confirm the costs reported by EOP as being reimbursed by Labor and HHS through interagency agreements supporting the President's and Vice President's public speaking events. As agreed with your office, we did not ask the agencies that participated in a minimal number of public speaking events to verify their events or to provide us with costs related to those agencies' speaking events. Also, we did not determine Secret Service and other security costs or the salaries of the government officials, such as the President and Vice President, who participated in the Social Security reform events within the context of performing their larger duties, which we view as fixed costs.[4] We obtained and reviewed interagency agreement data from EOP, Treasury, Labor, and HHS supporting presidential and vice presidential public speaking events; travel data related to public speaking events from SSA, Treasury, EOP, and the Air Force; and activity and cost data related to other promotion initiatives from Treasury.

Except for the records access limitation discussed below, we performed our work in accordance with generally accepted government auditing standards from June 2005 through June 2007 in Washington, D.C., and are reporting the information obtained from Treasury, SSA, EOP, the Air Force, Labor, and HHS. Although we cannot provide reasonable assurance that the costs are complete and fully supported, we found that the data provided by these agencies were sufficiently reliable to substantially meet our objectives.

While EOP provided certain cost information, it withheld from us the detailed source records showing how the funds transferred pursuant to the interagency agreements with Treasury, HHS, and Labor were spent as well as the travel documentation we requested. EOP provided some summary and other cost data on April 25, 2007, which was after the scheduled end of field work and about 3 weeks into the 30-day agency comment period in which the agencies involved in this review had the opportunity to comment on a draft of this report. The information EOP provided was in response to our written request for the information first made in August 2006. EOP stated that much of the requested information contained personal information for EOP personnel (such as Social Security Numbers, personal contact information, and credit card numbers). EOP also stated that some of the information could pose security concerns (such as travel patterns, identities of vendors used, and names used for arranging White House–related travel and supplies). We disagree with EOP's decision to withhold this information from GAO, but decided to report this limitation on our work without initiating the process to enforce our right of access to EOP financial and related information under 31 U.S.C. § 716(a) because of the disproportionate amount of time and resources needed to pursue this matter and the limited amount of funds involved. Under the circumstances, we decided that it was appropriate to report EOP's decision to withhold basic financial and related information and have the Congress decide whether to pursue this matter further as part of its own oversight and investigative agenda. A full description of our scope and methodology, including the limitation on our work, can be found in enclosure I.

RESULTS IN BRIEF

We identified 228 public speaking events to promote the Social Security reform initiative, of which there were 40 presidential events, 7 vice presidential events, and 122 events with officials from EOP, SSA, or Treasury. As agreed with your office, we primarily focused on these 169 events (almost 75 percent of the 228 public speaking events) and are reporting cost information we obtained for these events. We also identified many other promotion initiatives, including radio addresses and interviews and the establishment of a Treasury Web site.

The direct and incremental costs for the 169 events and other initiatives were a reported $2,588,367 for staging, travel, and other direct costs. The largest portion was for reported reimbursements to EOP from Treasury, HHS, and Labor for staging costs totaling $1,651,460, while reported travel costs included $437,887 for the use of Air Force One and Air Force Two, $369,838 for EOP officials' travel, and $66,794 for travel by Treasury and SSA officials. EOP reported $62,388 in other direct costs to support its public speaking events. Treasury reported an additional $222,608 in other initiative costs to establish and operate its SSIC and Strengthening Social Security Web site, bringing the total reported costs to $2,810,975.

In addition to reporting the scope limitation imposed by EOP which prevents us from providing reasonable assurance that the costs reported to us are complete and fully supported, we are reporting a deficiency we found in how Treasury handled its interagency agreements with EOP. Treasury did not have supporting documentation for amounts it reimbursed EOP under the interagency agreements to pay for staging costs associated with Social Security reform events. We are making a recommendation to Treasury that it strengthen its guidance on obtaining, reviewing, and retaining supporting documentation for reimbursements under interagency agreements.

We requested comments on a draft of this report from the Director, Office of Administration, EOP; the Secretary of the Treasury; the Commissioner of Social Security; and the Secretary of Defense. EOP did not provide comments but did provide certain data we requested, which was incorporated into the report as appropriate. Treasury provided oral comments in which it agreed with our facts but would not say whether it agreed or disagreed with our recommendation. Instead, Treasury said it would review its procedures with respect to the processing of interagency agreements. We received written comments from SSA in which it requested that we modify our report to emphasize its role in educating the public about solvency issues rather than promoting any particular plan to achieve solvency. We did not incorporate any changes based upon this comment as GAO does not believe such a distinction is warranted. SSA also provided minor technical corrections, which were incorporated into the report as appropriate. The Department of Defense stated that it agreed with the facts contained in the report.

BACKGROUND

Social Security provides protection against the loss of earnings due to retirement, death, or disability. According to the 2007 Social Security Board of Trustees Report (Trustees Report), there were 49 million beneficiaries at the end of 2006. Total benefits paid during 2006 amounted to $546 billion. The Trustees Report goes on to state that under current law, the cost of Social Security will soon begin to increase faster than the program's income, because of the aging baby boom generation, expected low fertility, and increasing life expectancy. The Board of Trustees projected a long-range (75 year) funding shortfall in the Social Security Trust Funds of $4.7 trillion in present value, absent program reforms. For the infinite future, the Board projects a funding shortfall of $13.6 trillion in present value dollars.

In 2005, the President began promoting Social Security reform, including hundreds of public speaking events by administration officials across the country to educate the public about the Social Security solvency issues and gain popular support for his plan to reform Social Security. A large part of the costs of this initiative were paid by Treasury, HHS, and Labor through reimbursements to EOP, under interagency agreements covering event staging costs for many of the President's and Vice President's public speaking events around the country. Interagency agreements like those entered into by Treasury and EOP are permitted by the Economy Act,[5] which allows one department or agency to use the materials, supplies, facilities, and personnel of another. Under this authority, the agency requesting the goods or services (the ordering agency, or Treasury in this case) agrees to reimburse the agency providing the goods or services (the performing agency, or EOP in this case) the actual costs incurred by the performing agency, including both direct and indirect costs. The ordering agency is accountable to the Congress for expenses it incurs against appropriations made to it, and the performing agency is accountable for the proper use of the ordering agency's funds.

SOCIAL SECURITY REFORM PUBLIC SPEAKING EVENTS AND OTHER PROMOTION INITIATIVES

On the basis of information obtained from Treasury, SSA, and EOP, including information obtained from their Web sites, we identified 228 public speaking events conducted by eight agencies.[6] Table 1 summarizes the 228 identified public speaking events attended by agency and EOP officials. These events were primarily town hall meetings conducted across the country before various groups. Enclosure II provides the date and location of each event and the name of the administration official who was a primary speaker.

In addition to these 228 public speaking events, the President, Vice President, and agency officials also conducted radio addresses, television and radio interviews, and Internet question-and-answer sessions to promote Social Security reform. As part of these other promotion initiatives, Treasury established and staffed the Social Security Information Center

(SSIC) in February 2005, which administered the Strengthening Social Security Web site and coordinated many of the activities to promote reform, including identifying administration officials who were available to speak at reform events and posting summaries of the events to the Web site. According to Treasury officials, SSIC was shut down at the end of August 2005, and its staff was assigned to other duties within Treasury.[7] Enclosure III lists the other promotion initiatives we identified, including the date and type of initiative and the key administration officials involved.

Table 1. Number and Percentage of Social Security Reform Agenda Public Speaking

Agency	Number of events	Percentage of all disclosed events
Social Security Administration	73	32.0%
Executive Office of the President	57	25.0
Department of the Treasury	39	17.1
Department of Labor	16	7.0
Small Business Administration	16	7.0
Department of Commerce	13	5.7
Department of Health and Human Services	8	3.5
Department of Housing and Urban Development	6	2.7
Total	**228**	**100.0%**

Source: GAO analysis of Treasury, SSA, and EOP data.

Table 2. Reported Social Security Reform Costs

Cost category	Amount (in dollars)
EOP event staging costs reimbursed through interagency agreements with	$1,651,460
Treasury, HHS, and Labor	
Air Force One and Air Force Two costs for	437,887
presidential and vice presidential travel[a]	
EOP travel costs	369,838
SSA travel costs	45,898
Treasury travel costs	20,896
EOP other direct costs	62,388
Subtotal: reported public speaking event costs	**2,588,367**
Treasury's Social Security Information Center (SSIC) and Strengthening	222,608
Social Security Web site costs	
Total	**$2,810,975**

Sources: SSA, Treasury, EOP, Labor, HSS, and the Air Force.

[a] Reported fiscal year 2005 fuel costs, which accounted for nearly 90 percent of the Air Force's total reported costs, were $6,462 per flight hour for the VC-25 (the Boeing 747 used to transport the President to most of the Social Security reform events) and $1,325 per flight hour for the C-32A (the Boeing 757 that was primarily used to transport the Vice President).

Identified Costs of Promoting Social Security Reform

As agreed with your office, our review focused on EOP, Treasury, and SSA, as officials from these agencies participated in 169, or almost 75 percent, of the 228 Social Security reform public speaking events. Of these 169 events, 40 featured the President, 7 featured the Vice President, and 122 featured officials from EOP, SSA, or Treasury. As shown in table 2, the direct and incremental costs to the U.S. government reported to us totaled $2,810,975, of which $2,588,367 was reported as expenses related to the public speaking events. Reimbursements to EOP from Treasury, HHS, and Labor for event staging costs totaled $1,651,460. Travel costs were the next largest category totaling a reported $874,519, including $437,887 reported by the Air Force for the use of Air Force One and Air Force Two to transport the President and Vice President to and from the Social Security reform events. EOP reported an additional $369,838 in travel costs, with SSA and Treasury reporting a combined $66,794 in travel costs. EOP also reported $62,388 in other direct costs to support its public speaking events. Finally, Treasury reported $222,608 in costs to establish and operate its SSIC and Web site. The costs are discussed in greater detail below, including limitations on the data. Also, as discussed previously, the costs we identified do not include Secret Service and other security costs or the salaries of administration officials participating in the events within the context of performing their larger duties, which we view as fixed costs. Finally, SSA and Treasury officials told us that when officials from their agencies were invited to speak at events hosted by private sector organizations, the agencies only paid for travel expenses.

Costs Related to EOP Participation

We have identified staging, travel, and other direct costs for the public speaking events with EOP participation. The staging costs were reimbursed to EOP by Treasury, HHS, and Labor pursuant to interagency agreements. Air Force incurred direct travel costs for the use of Air Force One and Air Force Two in transporting the President and Vice President to and from their public speaking events. In addition to the amounts reported by the Air Force, EOP reported its own travel costs. Finally, EOP reported having other direct costs to support its public speaking events.

We determined that EOP had interagency agreements with Treasury, HHS, and Labor. In accordance with the agreements, these agencies agreed to reimburse EOP for staging costs associated with 36 events in which the President or Vice President participated. The agreements authorized a transfer of funds to EOP of up to $1,871,625. Respectively, Treasury, HHS, and Labor disbursed $703,177, $440,688, and $507,595 for a total of $1,651,460 to EOP for these events. Enclosure IV provides additional details on the costs reimbursed through these interagency agreements. In order to confirm the interagency agreement cost data submitted by EOP, we asked Treasury, Labor, and HHS to report on the amounts transferred by those agencies. However, we could not determine whether the transferred funds were actually used to pay for the costs of staging the events as stated in the agreements.[8]

Although we requested detailed source records (i.e., invoices, receipts, etc.) that would show what was purchased with these transferred funds, EOP withheld this documentation and Treasury officials said they did not receive supporting documentation from EOP and, therefore, could not provide the information. EOP stated in its April 25, 2007, letter that "much of the underlying data (such as the requested receipts, invoices, and travel vouchers) contains personal information for Executive Office of the President personnel (such as social security numbers, personal contact information, and credit card numbers), as well as certain information that could represent security concerns (such as travel patterns, the identities of vendors used, and names/pseudonyms used for arranging White House- related travel and supplies)," and, therefore, it would not provide the source documents. We disagree with EOP's decision to withhold this information and believe that it is inconsistent with current law. GAO has a statutory right of access to this information[9] and our work often involves reviewing information that is sensitive or classified and we have procedures for handling and protecting such information. However, given the nature of this request and the amounts involved, GAO decided not to pursue this records access issue.

Further, because Treasury was party to the interagency agreements, we expected that Treasury would possess or have immediate access to such documentation as a normal course of doing business. The Economy Act, under which Treasury entered into the agreements to reimburse EOP for its staging costs, requires that the reimbursement be based upon the actual cost of goods or services provided.[10] When coupled with Office of Management and Budget Circular No. A-123, *Management's Responsibility for Internal Control,* and our *Standards for Internal Control in the Federal Government,*[11] which require that all transactions be clearly documented and that documentation be properly maintained and managed and readily available for examination,[12] we believe it would be prudent for Treasury to receive, review, and retain supporting documentation that would allow Treasury officials to ensure that the goods or services were received and that payments are properly certified in accordance with Treasury's own guidance.[13] Additional Treasury guidance, such as the Treasury Financial Management Service's *Federal Intragovernmental Transactions Accounting Policy Guide*,[14] states that each agency is responsible for documenting and supporting the information recorded in its accounting records related to intragovernmental transactions. Without the availability of adequate documentation, Treasury lacks reasonable assurance of its compliance with the Economy Act and that its appropriations are used for purposes authorized by law.

Reported travel costs associated with EOP's participation totaled $807,725, including $437,887 reported by the Air Force for direct, incremental mission costs incurred to fly the President and Vice President aboard Air Force One and Air Force Two. The Air Force reported that it flew 39 missions in support of the Social Security reform initiative. Mission costs included fuel, travel expenses of Air Force personnel, and miscellaneous mission expenses. As discussed previously, this figure does not include security costs or the salaries of the flight crews, as these were not incremental costs. Separately, EOP reported that its personnel incurred $369,838 in direct travel costs relating to 46 of the 57 EOP events. Finally, EOP reported $62,388 in other direct costs. We were unable to review the travel authorizations and travel vouchers for EOP's travel and the receipts for the miscellaneous costs because EOP withheld certain information, as described above. We also cannot provide reasonable assurance based on the information provided by EOP that its reported travel costs are complete since EOP stated for 7 events that we had identified that its records reflected no events and expenses on those particular days.[15] However, we identified these events from either Treasury or White House Web sites and, for most of these events, have transcripts or other support showing that the events did occur.

Costs Related to SSA Participation

For the 73 public speaking events in which an SSA official was a primary speaker, we identified $45,898 in travel costs.[16] According to an SSA official, SSA had no other costs related to the administration's promotion of Social Security reform. We reviewed all associated travel vouchers for proper approvals and to ensure the vouchers agreed with the reported amounts, and selected a statistical sample[17] of these vouchers to test travel authorizations and supporting documentation for proper approvals and support for claimed amounts. We found that these costs were adequately supported.

Costs Related to Treasury Participation

For the 39 public speaking events and other initiatives in which a Treasury official was a primary speaker, we identified $20,896 in travel costs.[18] We reviewed the associated travel authorizations and travel vouchers for proper approvals and support for claimed amounts, and found that these costs were adequately supported. Treasury officials indicated that Treasury also had costs associated with its SSIC and Web site totaling $222,608. These costs included the salaries of personnel[19] dedicated to the SSIC and information technology costs.

CONCLUSIONS AND RECOMMENDATION FOR EXECUTIVE ACTION

We identified hundreds of events geared toward educating the public about Social Security solvency issues and reform ideas as well as associated costs reported by Treasury, SSA, EOP, Labor, HHS, and the Air Force totaling about $2.8 million. We could not test the validity of some of those costs because EOP withheld certain key information and Treasury did not have supporting documentation for amounts it reimbursed EOP under the interagency agreements. We are, therefore, unable to provide reasonable assurance that the costs reported to us are complete and fully supported. While we continue to assert that we have a right to the supporting documentation denied us by EOP, we have decided to report the limitation without initiating the process to enforce our right to these documents because of the disproportionate amount of time and resources needed to pursue this matter and the limited amount of the funds involved.

To strengthen Treasury's oversight of its interagency agreements, GAO recommends that the Secretary of the Treasury direct the Chief Financial Officer of the department to strengthen the department's guidance to clarify that sufficient documentation to support reimbursements made through interagency agreements is to be obtained, reviewed, and retained.

AGENCY COMMENTS AND OUR EVALUATION

EOP did not provide comments but did provide certain data related to our August 2006 request. The information contained therein was incorporated into the report.

In oral comments, Treasury agreed with the facts contained in this report but did not say whether it agreed or disagreed with GAO's recommendation. Rather, Treasury stated that it would review its procedures with respect to the processing of interagency agreements.

In written comments on a draft of this report, which are reprinted in enclosure V, SSA stated that it strongly believes that the body of the report should be modified to indicate the involvement of SSA's representatives and the funds spent on those activities were to provide solvency education to the public rather than to promote any particular plan to achieve solvency. GAO does not believe such a distinction is warranted. Solvency issues are integral to any discussion of modifications to Social Security and the events identified in the report were, among other things, used to promote the President's reform agenda as evidenced by their inclusion on Treasury's Strengthening Social Security Web site. SSA's comments also included minor technical corrections, which were incorporated into the report as appropriate.

The Department of Defense orally commented that the agency agreed with the facts contained in the report.

Sincerely yours,

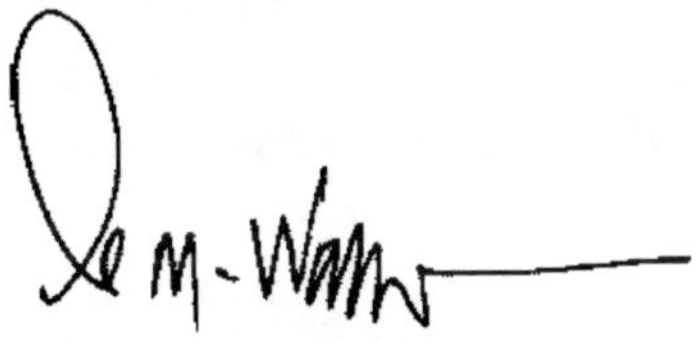

David M. Walker
Comptroller General of the United States

ENCLOSURE I

Scope and Methodology

To address your inquiry, we first identified the universe of public speaking events and other initiatives reported on the Department of the Treasury's (Treasury) Web site dedicated to the President's Social Security reform agenda, www.strengtheningsocialsecurity.gov, the general Treasury Web site, www.treas.gov, and the White House Web site, www.whitehouse.gov, and collected basic event data from these Web sites. Because the Social Security Administration (SSA), Treasury, and the Executive Office of the President (EOP) accounted for approximately 75 percent of all identified events,[20] we requested financial records and other documentation for the events attended by officials from SSA, Treasury, and EOP.[21] We requested additional information concerning EOP activities from the United States Air Force (Air Force) regarding the use of Air Force One and Air Force

Two, and asked the Departments of Labor (Labor) and Health and Human Services (HHS) to report on interagency agreement costs those agencies reimbursed to EOP for many of the President's and Vice President's speaking events. We received information from SSA, Treasury, EOP, Air Force, Labor, and HHS. We also conducted interviews with officials from SSA, Treasury, and the Air Force. We did not ask the agencies that participated in a minimal number of speaking engagements (like Labor and HHS) to report their events or to provide us with costs related to those agencies' speaking events. We also did not determine the costs of the Secret Service, other security, and the salaries of government officials who participated in the Social Security reform events within the context of performing their larger duties. Except as discussed below, salaries were considered fixed costs because they would have been incurred whether or not the officials participated in the Social Security reform events.

We reviewed information and documentation from SSA, Treasury, and EOP, which we used to compile the lists of public speaking events and other reform initiatives. See enclosures II and III, respectively. EOP was unable to fully verify the completeness and accuracy of our list of EOP public speaking events. It stated in its April 2007 submittal that it did not have records for some of the events we identified. For the events that EOP could not verify, we are including the ones we identified from data contained on either the White House or Treasury Web sites. For most of these events, we have transcripts or other support showing that these events did occur.

For the staging costs reimbursed to EOP through interagency agreements, we compared amounts reported by EOP with those reported by Treasury, Labor, and HHS. We reviewed Treasury's interagency agreements with EOP for Treasury approvals but could not test for adequate support because Treasury did not have support and EOP did not provide the requested support. EOP's decision to withhold the requested documentation hindered our ability to provide reasonable assurance that the reported costs are complete and fully supported. Although we did not perform detailed tests at Labor and HHS because any results from those tests would not have fully eliminated the records access limitation, we did ask Labor and HHS to report on the amounts transferred to EOP under the interagency agreements.

We reviewed SSA and Treasury travel authorizations and vouchers for proper approvals and support for claimed amounts. For SSA travel, we reviewed 100 percent of the travel vouchers for proper approvals and to ensure the vouchers supported the reported amounts. We also selected a statistical sample of 15 SSA travel vouchers totaling $11,510 from a population of 60 vouchers totaling $45,898[22] to test for proper travel authorizations and adequate support (i.e., hotel bills, airline tickets, etc.). We found no exceptions during testing.[23] For Treasury travel, we reviewed 100 percent of the trips for proper approvals and for adequate support.

In addition to SSA and Treasury travel cost data, we received information from the Air Force and EOP pertaining to EOP travel. The Air Force calculated and provided mission cost data for presidential and vice presidential events in which Air Force One and Air Force Two were used. To assess the reasonableness of the data, we applied analytic procedures and interviewed an Air Force official. For the travel and other miscellaneous costs reported by EOP, we could not perform tests because EOP withheld the requested records.

Finally, our review of Treasury costs related to the Social Security Information Center (SSIC) and Web site was limited to analytic procedures focusing on the salaries of Treasury employees dedicated to the SSIC, which constituted the majority of the SSIC costs. The salary expenses associated with the assignments to the SSIC were considered direct and incremental because newly hired employees were initially assigned full-time to the SSIC.

Except for the limitation related to EOP's withholding of detailed source records which affected our ability to provide reasonable assurance that the reported costs are complete and fully supported, we performed our work in accordance with generally accepted government auditing standards from June 2005 through June 2007 in Washington, D.C. This report reflects the information we were able to obtain from Treasury, SSA, EOP, the Air Force, Labor, and HHS. Through our review of supporting documentation, interviews, and analytical procedures, we found that the data provided by Treasury, SSA, EOP, the Air Force, Labor, and HHS were sufficiently reliable to substantially meet our objectives and therefore could be reported with disclosed limitations about the completeness of the costs and adequacy of the supporting documentation. While EOP provided certain cost information, it withheld from us the detailed source records showing how the funds transferred pursuant to the interagency agreements with Treasury, HHS, and Labor were spent as well as the travel documentation we requested. EOP provided some summary and other cost data on April 25, 2007, which was after the scheduled end of field work and about 3 weeks into the 30-day agency comment period in which the agencies involved in this review had the opportunity to comment on a draft of this report. The information EOP provided was in response to our written request for information first made in August 2006. We could not confirm whether the transferred funds were actually used to pay for costs of staging the events as stated in the agreements but we are reporting the interagency agreement reimbursements because Treasury, Labor, and HHS reported to us that they had reimbursed EOP for costs associated with Social Security reform events. Further, we are including EOP reported amounts for travel and miscellaneous costs although we were unable to review the supporting documentation.

We decided to report the limitation on our work without initiating the process to enforce our right of access to EOP financial and related information under 31 U.S.C. § 716(a) because of the disproportionate amount of time and resources needed to pursue this matter and the limited amount of the funds involved. Under the circumstances, we decided that it was appropriate to report that EOP withheld basic financial and related information and have the Congress decide whether to pursue this matter further as part of its own oversight and investigative agenda.

We requested comments on a draft of this report from the Director, Office of Administration at EOP; the Secretary of the Treasury; the Commissioner of Social Security; and the Secretary of Defense.

ENCLOSURE II: 228 IDENTIFIED SOCIAL SECURITY REFORM PUBLIC SPEAKING EVENTS

Date	Location of event	Administration official	Agency
1/11/2005	Washington, D.C.	George W. Bush	Executive Office of the President
1/13/2005	Washington, D.C.	Richard B. Cheney	Executive Office of the President
2/3/2005	Great Falls, Mont.	George W. Bush	Executive Office of the President
2/3/2005	Fargo, N.Dak.	George W. Bush	Executive Office of the President
2/4/2005	Omaha, Nebr.	George W. Bush	Executive Office of the President
2/4/2005	Little Rock, Ark.	George W. Bush	Executive Office of the President

(Continued)

Date	Location of event	Administration official	Agency
2/4/2005	Tampa, Fla.	George W. Bush	Executive Office of the President
2/8/2005	Detroit, Mich.	George W. Bush	Executive Office of the President
2/9/2005	Washington, D.C.	John W. Snow	Department of the Treasury
2/10/2005	Blue Bell, Pa.	George W. Bush	Executive Office of the President
2/10/2005	Raleigh, N.C.	George W. Bush	Executive Office of the President
2/16/2005	Portsmouth, N.H.	George W. Bush	Executive Office of the President
2/18/2005	New York, N.Y.	John W. Snow	Department of the Treasury
2/18/2005	Ft. Lauderdale, Fla.	Mark J. Warshawsky	Department of the Treasury
2/19/2005	Tucson, Ariz.	James B. Lockhart, III	Social Security Administration
2/21/2005	Atlanta, Ga.	Andrew Biggs	Social Security Administration
2/22/2005	Philadelphia, Pa.	James B. Lockhart, III	Social Security Administration
2/23/2005	Cincinnati, Ohio	James B. Lockhart, III	Social Security Administration
2/23/2005	Sharonville, Ohio	James B. Lockhart, III	Social Security Administration
2/24/2005	Tampa, Fla.	John W. Snow	Department of the Treasury
2/24/2005	Houston, Tex.	James B. Lockhart, III	Social Security Administration
2/25/2005	Jacksonville, Fla.	John W. Snow	Department of the Treasury
3/3/2005	Fayetteville, Ark.	John W. Snow	Department of the Treasury
3/4/2005	Notre Dame, Ind.	George W. Bush	Executive Office of the President
3/4/2005	Westfield, N.J.	George W. Bush	Executive Office of the President
3/4/2005	New Orleans, La.	John W. Snow	Department of the Treasury
3/4/2005	Allendale, Mich.	James B. Lockhart, III	Social Security Administration
3/4/2005	Muskegon, Mich.	James B. Lockhart, III	Social Security Administration
3/5/2005	Cadillac, Mich.	James B. Lockhart, III	Social Security Administration
3/5/2005	Manistee, Mich.	James B. Lockhart, III	Social Security Administration
3/5/2005	Ludington, Mich.	James B. Lockhart, III	Social Security Administration
3/7/2005	Westminster, Md.	Keith Hennessey	Executive Office of the President
3/8/2005	Washington, D.C.	John W. Snow	Department of the Treasury
3/8/2005	Fort Lauderdale, Fla.	Eric Stewart	Department of Commerce
3/8/2005	Boca Raton, Fla.	Eric Stewart	Department of Commerce
3/8/2005	New Orleans, La.	James B. Lockhart, III	Social Security Administration
3/9/2005	Washington, D.C.	John W. Snow	Department of the Treasury
3/9/2005	New Orleans, La.	James B. Lockhart, III	Social Security Administration
3/9/2005	New Orleans, La.	James B. Lockhart, III	Social Security Administration
3/10/2005	Albuquerque, N.Mex.	John W. Snow	Department of the Treasury
3/10/2005	Albuquerque, N.Mex.	John W. Snow	Department of the Treasury
3/10/2005	Montgomery, Ala.	George W. Bush	Executive Office of the President
3/10/2005	Louisville, Ky.	George W. Bush	Executive Office of the President
3/11/2005	San Antonio, Tex.	John W. Snow	Department of the Treasury
3/11/2005	Memphis, Tenn.	George W. Bush	Executive Office of the President
3/11/2005	Shreveport, La.	George W. Bush	Executive Office of the President
3/11/2005	London, England	Elaine L. Chao	Department of Labor
3/11/2005	Orlando, Fla.	James B. Lockhart, III	Social Security Administration
3/12/2005	Philadelphia, Pa.	Anna Escobedo Cabral	Department of the Treasury
3/15/2005	Washington, D.C.	Mark J. Warshawsky	Department of the Treasury
3/15/2005	Charlotte, N.C.	Eric Stewart	Department of Commerce
3/16/2005	Hickory, N.C.	Eric Stewart	Department of Commerce
3/16/2005	Gastonia, N.C.	Eric Stewart	Department of Commerce
3/18/2005	Pensacola, Fla.	George W. Bush	Executive Office of the President
3/18/2005	Orlando, Fla.	George W. Bush	Executive Office of the President

3/18/2005	Orlando, Fla.	George W. Bush	Executive Office of the President
3/21/2005	Columbia, S.C.	Melanie R. Sabelhaus	Small Business Administration
3/21/2005	Tucson, Ariz.	George W. Bush	Executive Office of the President
3/21/2005	Pasadena, Calif.	Hector V. Barreto	Small Business Administration
3/21/2005	Bakersfield, Calif.	Richard B. Cheney	Executive Office of the President
3/21/2005	Denver, Colo.	George W. Bush	Executive Office of the President
3/21/2005	Lakewood, Colo.	James B. Lockhart, III	Social Security Administration
3/21/2005	Lakewood, Colo.	James B. Lockhart, III	Social Security Administration
3/21/2005	Castle Rock, Colo.	James B. Lockhart, III	Social Security Administration
3/21/2005	Grand View, Colo.	James B. Lockhart, III	Social Security Administration
3/21/2005	Atlanta, Ga.	Timothy S. Bitsberger	Department of the Treasury
3/21/2005	Green Bay, Wis.	William H. Lash, III	Department of Commerce
3/21/2005	Edgefield, S.C.	Michel N. Korbey	Social Security Administration
3/21/2005	Aiken, S.C.	Michel N. Korbey	Social Security Administration
3/21/2005	North Augusta, S.C.	Michel N. Korbey	Social Security Administration
3/22/2005	Aurora, Colo.	James B. Lockhart, III	Social Security Administration
3/22/2005	Denver, Colo.	James B. Lockhart, III	Social Security Administration
3/22/2005	Reno, Nev.	Richard B. Cheney	Executive Office of the President
3/22/2005	Albuquerque, N.Mex.	George W. Bush	Executive Office of the President
3/22/2005	Albuquerque, N.Mex.	George W. Bush	Executive Office of the President
3/22/2005	Memphis, Tenn.	Melanie R. Sabelhaus	Small Business Administration
3/22/2005	San Dimas, Calif.	Hector V. Barreto	Small Business Administration
3/22/2005	Los Angeles, Calif.	Hector V. Barreto	Small Business Administration
3/22/2005	Abbeville, S.C.	Michel N. Korbey	Social Security Administration
3/22/2005	Greenwood, S.C.	Michel N. Korbey	Social Security Administration
3/22/2005	Oxford, Miss.	Timothy S. Bitsberger	Department of the Treasury
3/23/2005	Atlanta, Ga.	Michael O. Leavitt	Department of Health and Human Services
3/23/2005	Seneca, S.C.	Michel N. Korbey	Social Security Administration
3/23/2005	Anderson, S.C.	Michel N. Korbey	Social Security Administration
3/23/2005	Easley, S.C.	Michel N. Korbey	Social Security Administration
3/24/2005	Battle Creek, Mich.	Richard B. Cheney	Executive Office of the President
3/24/2005	Pittsburgh, Pa.	Richard B. Cheney	Executive Office of the President
3/24/2005	Stanton, Del.	Jo Anne B. Barnhart	Social Security Administration
3/24/2005	Wilmington, Del.	John W. Snow	Department of the Treasury
3/24/2005	Kennett Square, Pa.	John W. Snow	Department of the Treasury
3/24/2005	Little Rock, Ark.	Carlos M. Gutierrez	Department of Commerce
3/24/2005	St. Louis, Mo.	Carlos M. Gutierrez	Department of Commerce
3/24/2005	Springfield, Mo.	Allan B. Hubbard	Executive Office of the President
3/24/2005	Ozark, Mo.	Allan B. Hubbard	Executive Office of the President
3/24/2005	Mo.	Allan B. Hubbard	Executive Office of the President
3/24/2005	Mo.	Allan B. Hubbard	Executive Office of the President
3/24/2005	Clinton, S.C.	Michel N. Korbey	Social Security Administration
3/24/2005	Saluda, S.C.	Michel N. Korbey	Social Security Administration
3/24/2005	McCormick, S.C.	Michel N. Korbey	Social Security Administration
3/25/2005	Billings, Mont.	James B. Lockhart, III	Social Security Administration
3/28/2005	Portland, Ore.	John W. Snow	Department of the Treasury
3/28/2005	Noblesville, Ind.	Allan B. Hubbard	Executive Office of the President
3/29/2005	Bellevue, Wash.	Robert S. Nichols	Department of the Treasury
3/29/2005	Manhattan, Kans.	James B. Lockhart, III	Social Security Administration
3/29/2005	Topeka, Kans.	James B. Lockhart, III	Social Security Administration
3/30/2005	Bozeman, Mont.	John W. Snow	Department of the Treasury
3/30/2005	Cedar Rapids, Iowa	George W. Bush	Executive Office of the President

(Continued)

Date	Location of event	Administration official	Agency
3/30/2005	Colusa, Calif.	James B. Lockhart, III	Social Security Administration
3/30/2005	Willows, Calif.	James B. Lockhart, III	Social Security Administration
3/30/2005	Redding, Calif.	James B. Lockhart, III	Social Security Administration
3/30/2005	Red Bluff, Calif.	James B. Lockhart, III	Social Security Administration
3/30/2005	Woodstock, Ga.	Michel N. Korbey	Social Security Administration
3/30/2005	Charlotte, N.C.	Keith Hennessey	Executive Office of the President
3/30/2005	Portland, Maine	Michael O. Leavitt	Department of Health and Human Services
3/30/2005	Flagstaff, Ariz.	Steven J. Law	Department of Labor
3/30/2005	Flagstaff, Ariz.	Steven J. Law	Department of Labor
3/31/2005	Chico, Calif.	James B. Lockhart, III	Social Security Administration
3/31/2005	Magalia, Calif.	James B. Lockhart, III	Social Security Administration
3/31/2005	Yuba City, Calif.	James B. Lockhart, III	Social Security Administration
3/31/2005	Woodland, Calif.	James B. Lockhart, III	Social Security Administration
3/31/2005	Bismarck, N.Dak.	John W. Snow	Department of the Treasury
3/31/2005	Bismarck, N.Dak.	John W. Snow	Department of the Treasury
3/31/2005	West Palm Beach, Fla.	Alphonso R. Jackson	Department of Housing and Urban Development
3/31/2005	Delray Beach, Fla.	Melanie R. Sabelhaus	Small Business Administration
3/31/2005	Pittsburgh, Pa.	Elaine L. Chao	Department of Labor
3/31/2005	Baton Rouge, La.	Michel N. Korbey	Social Security Administration
3/31/2005	Roswell, Ga.	Michel N. Korbey	Social Security Administration
3/31/2005	Peachtree City, Ga.	James J. Courtney, Jr.	Social Security Administration
3/31/2005	Las Vegas, Nev.	Steven J. Law	Department of Labor
4/1/2005	Miami, Fla.	Carlos M. Gutierrez	Department of Commerce
4/1/2005	Jupiter, Fla.	Melanie R. Sabelhaus	Small Business Administration
4/1/2005	Newark, Del.	Jo Anne B. Barnhart	Social Security Administration
4/1/2005	Lake Charles, La.	Michel N. Korbey	Social Security Administration
4/1/2005	Las Vegas, Nev.	Hector V. Barreto	Small Business Administration
4/1/2005	San Antonio, Tex.	Anna Escobedo Cabral	Department of the Treasury
4/2/2005	Fairfield, Conn.	James B. Lockhart, III	Social Security Administration
4/2/2005	Baltimore, Md.	Noam Neusner	Executive Office of the President
4/3/2005	Darien, Conn.	James B. Lockhart, III	Social Security Administration
4/4/2005	Washington, D.C.	John W. Snow	Department of the Treasury
4/4/2005	Dallas, Tex.	Elaine L. Chao	Department of Labor
4/4/2005	Manchester, N.H.	Steven J. Law	Department of Labor
4/4/2005	Fairfax, Va.	Jo Anne B. Barnhart	Social Security Administration
4/4/2005	Waterbury, Conn.	Melanie R. Sabelhaus	Small Business Administration
4/4/2005	Dumont, N.J.	Joshua B. Bolten	Executive Office of the President
4/5/2005	Parkersburg, W.Va.	George W. Bush	Executive Office of the President
4/5/2005	Parkersburg, W.Va.	George W. Bush	Executive Office of the President
4/5/2005	Philadelphia, Pa.	Melanie R. Sabelhaus	Small Business Administration
4/6/2005	Richmond, Va.	Hector V. Barreto	Small Business Administration
4/6/2005	Orlando, Fla.	Michel N. Korbey	Social Security Administration
4/7/2005	Cleveland, Ohio	Alphonso R. Jackson	Department of Housing and Urban Development
4/11/2005	Cincinnati, Ohio	Elaine L. Chao	Department of Labor
4/11/2005	Philadelphia, Pa.	Michael O. Leavitt	Department of Health and Human Services
4/11/2005	Aiken, S.C.	Arnold Havens	Department of the Treasury
4/11/2005	Aiken, S.C.	Arnold Havens	Department of the Treasury

4/12/2005	Flagstaff, Ariz.	Eric Stewart	Department of Commerce
4/12/2005	Atlanta, Ga.	Hector V. Barreto	Small Business Administration
4/12/2005	Flagstaff, Ariz.	Eric Stewart	Department of Commerce
4/13/2005	Chicago, Ill.	Michael O. Leavitt	Department of Health and Human Services
4/13/2005	New Orleans, La.	Hector V. Barreto	Small Business Administration
4/13/2005	Providence, R.I.	Dominic "Dan" Iannicola, Jr.	Department of the Treasury
4/14/2005	Cartersville, Ga.	Anna Escobedo Cabral	Department of the Treasury
4/14/2005	Rome, Ga.	Anna Escobedo Cabral	Department of the Treasury
4/14/2005	Smyrna, Ga.	Anna Escobedo Cabral	Department of the Treasury
4/14/2005	Columbus, Ga.	Hector V. Barreto	Small Business Administration
4/15/2005	Kirtland, Ohio	George W. Bush	Executive Office of the President
4/15/2005	Pemberton, N.J.	Richard B. Cheney	Executive Office of the President
4/16/2005	Decatur, Ga.	James B. Lockhart, III	Social Security Administration
4/18/2005	Columbia, S.C.	George W. Bush	Executive Office of the President
4/18/2005	Charlotte, N.C.	Elaine L. Chao	Department of Labor
4/18/2005	Aurora, Colo.	Steven J. Law	Department of Labor
4/18/2005	Baltimore, Md.	Michel N. Korbey	Social Security Administration
4/18/2005	Yonkers, N.Y.	Thomas M. Sullivan	Small Business Administration
4/19/2005	St. Petersburg, Fla.	Elaine L. Chao	Department of Labor
4/19/2005	Denver, Colo.	Michael O. Leavitt	Department of Health and Human Services
4/20/2005	New York, N.Y.	John W. Snow	Department of the Treasury
4/20/2005	Seattle, Wash.	Michael O. Leavitt	Department of Health and Human Services
4/21/2005	Washington, D.C.	George W. Bush	Executive Office of the President
4/22/2005	Louisville, Ky.	Elaine L. Chao	Department of Labor
4/22/2005	Las Cruces, N.Mex.	Carlos M. Gutierrez	Department of Commerce
4/22/2005	Albuquerque, N.Mex.	Carlos M. Gutierrez	Department of Commerce
4/23/2005	Houston, Tex.	Alphonso R. Jackson	Department of Housing and Urban Development
4/25/2005	Mandeville, La.	James B. Lockhart, III	Social Security Administration
4/25/2005	Lancaster County, Pa.	Brian Reardon	Executive Office of the President
4/26/2005	Galveston, Tex.	George W. Bush	Executive Office of the President
4/26/2005	Philadelphia, Pa.	Mark J. Warshawsky	Department of the Treasury
4/27/2005	New Orleans, La.	Elaine L. Chao	Department of Labor
4/27/2005	St. Louis, Mo.	Alphonso R. Jackson	Department of Housing and Urban Development
4/27/2005	New Orleans, La.	James B. Lockhart, III	Social Security Administration
4/27/2005	New Orleans, La.	Elaine L. Chao	Department of Labor
4/28/2005	Kansas City, Mo.	Michael O. Leavitt	Department of Health and Human Services
4/28/2005	New York, N.Y.	James B. Lockhart, III	Social Security Administration
4/28/2005	Fort Washington, Md.	Michel N. Korbey	Social Security Administration
4/29/2005	Falls Church, Va.	George W. Bush	Executive Office of the President
4/29/2005	Bowling Green, Ky.	Elaine L. Chao	Department of Labor
4/29/2005	Dallas, Tex.	Michael O. Leavitt	Department of Health and Human Services
4/29/2005	Hartford, Conn.	Alphonso R. Jackson	Department of Housing and Urban Development
4/29/2005	Hartford, Conn.	James B. Lockhart, III	Social Security Administration
4/30/2005	New York, N.Y.	Alphonso R. Jackson	Department of Housing and Urban Development
5/2/2005	Smyrna, Ga.	Richard B. Cheney	Executive Office of the President
5/3/2005	Canton, Miss.	George W. Bush	Executive Office of the President
5/3/2005	Washington, D.C.	John W. Snow	Department of the Treasury
5/4/2005	Washington, D.C.	George W. Bush	Executive Office of the President

(Continued)

Date	Location of event	Administration official	Agency
5/4/2005	New Orleans, La.	Elaine L. Chao	Department of Labor
5/7/2005	Los Angeles, Calif.	James B. Lockhart, III	Social Security Administration
5/9/2005	Hartford, Conn.	John W. Snow	Department of the Treasury
5/11/2005	Orlando, Fla.	Michel N. Korbey	Social Security Administration
5/12/2005	Davis, Calif.	Anna Escobedo Cabral	Department of the Treasury
5/13/2005	Washington, D.C.	George W. Bush	Executive Office of the President
5/16/2005	Lakewood, Va.	James B. Lockhart, III	Social Security Administration
5/19/2005	Milwaukee, Wis.	George W. Bush	Executive Office of the President
5/20/2005	San Diego, Calif.	Hector V. Barreto	Small Business Administration
5/23/2005	Washington, D.C.	John W. Snow	Department of the Treasury
5/24/2005	Greece, N.Y.	George W. Bush	Executive Office of the President
6/1/2005	Orange, Va.	Jo Anne B. Barnhart	Social Security Administration
6/2/2005	Hopkinsville, Ky.	George W. Bush	Executive Office of the President
6/2/2005	Glen Allen, Va.	James B. Lockhart, III	Social Security Administration
6/6/2005	New York, N.Y.	James B. Lockhart, III	Social Security Administration
6/8/2005	Washington, D.C.	George W. Bush	Executive Office of the President
6/14/2005	University Park, Pa.	George W. Bush	Executive Office of the President
6/18/2005	Ann Arbor, Mich.	James B. Lockhart, III	Social Security Administration
6/18/2005	St. Petersburg, Fla.	Michel N. Korbey	Social Security Administration
6/21/2005	Boston, Mass.	James B. Lockhart, III	Social Security Administration
6/23/2005	Silver Spring, Md.	George W. Bush	Executive Office of the President
6/27/2005	Clifton Park, N.Y.	James B. Lockhart, III	Social Security Administration
6/27/2005	Trumbull, Conn.	John W. Snow	Department of the Treasury
6/29/2005	Kearney, Neb.	James B. Lockhart, III	Social Security Administration
6/30/2005	Medford, Ore.	James B. Lockhart, III	Social Security Administration
7/6/2005	Omaha, Neb.	John W. Snow	Department of the Treasury

Sources: Department of the Treasury, Social Security Administration, and the Executive Office of the President.

ENCLOSURE III: OTHER SOCIAL SECURITY REFORM PROMOTION INITIATIVES

Date	Type of initiative	Administration official	Agency
12/11/2004	Radio address	George W. Bush	Executive Office of the President
1/11/2005	Internet questions	Charles P. Blahous	Executive Office of the President
1/15/2005	Radio address	George W. Bush	Executive Office of the President
2/3/2005	Internet questions	John W. Snow	Department of the Treasury
2/5/2005	Radio address	George W. Bush	Executive Office of the President
2/12/2005	Radio address	George W. Bush	Executive Office of the President
2/26/2005	Radio address	George W. Bush	Executive Office of the President
3/3/2005	Various media interviews	John W. Snow	Department of the Treasury
3/7/2005	Internet questions	Charles P. Blahous	Executive Office of the President
3/8/2005	Radio interview	Richard B. Cheney	Executive Office of the President
3/10/2005	Radio interview	Joshua B. Bolten	Executive Office of the President
3/10/2005	Radio interview	Karl Rove	Executive Office of the President
2/14/2005 -	Social Security Information	Treasury Staff	Department of the Treasury

8/31/2006	Center		
3/12/2005	Radio address	George W. Bush	Executive Office of the President
3/16/2005	Radio interview	Nicolle Devenish	Executive Office of the President
3/18/2005	Radio interview	Daniel J. Bartlett	Executive Office of the President
3/23/2005	Social Security Trustees meeting	James B. Lockhart, III	Social Security Administration
3/23/2005	Social Security Trustees report speech	John W. Snow	Department of the Treasury
3/23/2005	23 Radio interviews	James B. Lockhart, III	Social Security Administration
3/30/2005	Radio interview	George W. Bush	Executive Office of the President
4/5/2005	Internet questions	Charles P. Blahous	Executive Office of the President
4/6/2005	Social Security Radio Day	Multiple officials	Various
4/7/2005	Radio interview	Richard B. Cheney	Executive Office of the President
4/13/2005	Radio interview	Hector V. Barreto	Small Business Administration
4/15/2005	Internet questions	John W. Snow	Department of the Treasury
4/26/2005	Teach Children to Save Day	23 officials	Department of the Treasury
4/29/2005	Internet questions	Catherine J. Martin	Executive Office of the President
4/30/2005	Radio address	George W. Bush	Executive Office of the President
5/2/2005	Anniversary of President's commission	John W. Snow	Department of the Treasury
5/9/2005	Various media interviews	James B. Lockhart, III	Social Security Administration
5/19/2005	Social Security Economic Roundtable	John W. Snow	Department of the Treasury
5/19/2005	Newspaper article	John W. Snow	Department of the Treasury
6/2/2005	Radio interview	Catherine J. Martin	Executive Office of the President
6/6/2005	Various media interviews	James B. Lockhart, III	Social Security Administration
6/8/2005	Internet questions	Charles P. Blahous	Executive Office of the President
6/14/2005	Radio interview	Allan B. Hubbard	Executive Office of the President

Sources: Department of the Treasury, Social Security Administration, and the Executive Office of the President.

ENCLOSURE IV: EOP EVENTS COVERED BY INTERAGENCY AGREEMENTS AND THE AMOUNTS REIMBURSED BY AGENCY

Event location	President (POTUS)/ Vice President (VP)	Event date	Reimbursed amount (dollars)			
			Department of the Treasury	Department of Health and Human Services	Department of Labor	Total
Washington, D.C.	POTUS	1/11/2005	$56,404.83	$0.00	$0.00	**$56,404.83**
Washington, D.C.	VP	1/13/2005	10,625.00	0.00	0.00	**10,625.00**
Great Falls, Mont.	POTUS	2/3/2005	0.00	19,613.18	84,974.97	**104,588.15**
Fargo, N.Dak.	POTUS	2/3/2005	77,621.20	0.00	3,464.07	**81,085.27**
Omaha, Neb.	POTUS	2/4/2005	79,536.86	0.00	0.00	**79,536.86**
Little Rock, Ark.	POTUS	2/4/2005	0.00	40,475.47	4,047.55	**44,523.02**
Tampa, Fla.	POTUS	2/4/2005	16,295.44	0.00	56,672.04	**72,967.48**

(Continued)

Event location	President (POTUS)/ Vice President (VP)	Eventdate	Reimbursed amount (dollars)			
			Department of the Treasury	Department of Health and Human Services	Department of Labor	Total
Blue Bell, Pa.	POTUS	2/10/2005	46,707.91	23,353.96	0.00	**70,061.87**
Raleigh, N.C.	POTUS	2/10/2005	0.00	0.00	22,588.27	**22,588.27**
Portsmouth, N.H.	POTUS	2/16/2005	25,000.00	15,000.00	15,000.00	**55,000.00**
Westfield, N.J.	POTUS	3/4/2005	65,000.00	5,000.00	0.00	**70,000.00**
Notre Dame, Ind.	POTUS	3/4/2005	0.00	25,000.00	15,000.00	**40,000.00**
Montgomery, Ala.	POTUS	3/10/2005	21,207.54	26,250.00	24,742.13	**72,199.67**
Louisville, Ky.	POTUS	3/10/2005	22,500.00	18,750.00	18,750.00	**60,000.00**
Memphis, Tenn.	POTUS	3/11/2005	22,500.00	2,991.32	3,250.00	**28,741.32**
Shreveport, La.	POTUS	3/11/2005	22,500.00	33,750.00	33,750.00	**90,000.00**
Pensacola, Fla.	POTUS	3/18/2005	17,500.00	20,000.00	17,500.00	**55,000.00**
Orlando, Fla.[a]	POTUS	3/18/2005	17,300.69	14,829.16	17,300.69	**49,430.54**
Tucson, Ariz.	POTUS	3/21/2005	14,161.93	14,161.93	14,161.93	**42,485.79**
Denver, Colo.	POTUS	3/21/2005	20,851.85	20,755.75	20,851.84	**62,459.44**
Bakersfield, Calif.	VP	3/21/2005	0.00	0.00	29,334.23	**29,334.23**
Albuquerque, N.Mex.[a]	POTUS	3/22/2005	13,400.00	13,400.00	13,200.00	**40,000.00**
Reno, Nev.	VP	3/22/2005	0.00	0.00	17,958.83	**17,958.83**
Battle Creek, Mich.	VP	3/24/2005	0.00	23,809.61	0.00	**23,809.61**
Pittsburgh, Pa.	VP	3/24/2005	0.00	27,817.27	0.00	**27,817.27**
Cedar Rapids, Iowa	POTUS	3/30/2005	19,290.96	19,290.96	19,290.96	**57,872.88**
Parkersburg, W.Va.[a]	POTUS	4/5/2005	13,500.00	13,000.00	13,500.00	**40,000.00**
Kirtland, Ohio	POTUS	4/15/2005	10,632.00	11,813.50	10,632.00	**33,077.50**
Pemberton, N.J.	VP	4/15/2005	28,116.67	0.00	0.00	**28,116.67**
Columbia, S.C.	POTUS	4/18/2005	532.89	532.89	532.89	**1,598.67**
Galveston, Tex.	POTUS	4/26/2005	844.50	844.50	844.50	**2,533.50**
Falls Church, Va.	POTUS	4/29/2005	14,495.85	14,495.85	14,495.85	**43,487.55**
Smyrna, Ga.	VP	5/2/2005	29,499.65	0.00	0.00	**29,499.65**
Canton, Miss.	POTUS	5/3/2005	19,036.22	18,170.98	18,170.98	**55,378.18**
Rochester, N.Y.	POTUS	5/24/2005	2,020.13	1,960.72	1,960.72	**5,941.57**
Hopkinsville, Ky.	POTUS	6/2/2005	16,094.38	15,621.02	15,621.02	**47,336.42**
Total			**$703,176.50**	**$440,688.07**	**$507,595.47**	**$1,651,460.04**

Sources: Executive Office of the President, Departments of the Treasury, Labor, and Health and Human Services.

[a] For each of these entries, there were two presidential events.

ENCLOSURE V: COMMENTS FROM THE SOCIAL SECURITY ADMINISTRATION

SOCIAL SECURITY
The Commissioner
May 02,2007

Mr. Robert E. Martin
Director, Financial Management and
Assurance
U.S. Government Accountability Office
Washington, D.C. 20548

Dear Mr. Martin:

Thank you for the opportunity to review and comment on the draft report, "SOCIAL SECURITY: Costs Associated with the Administration's Efforts to Promote Program Reforms" (GAO-07-621).

If you have any questions, please contact Candace Skurnik, Director, Audit Management and Liaison Staff, at (410) 965-4636.

Sincerely,

Michael J. Astrue

Enclosure

SOCIAL SECURITY ADMINISTRATION BALTIMORE MD 21235-0001

COMMENTS ON THE GOVERNMENT ACCOUNTABILITY OFFICE (GAO) DRAFT REPORT, "SOCIAL SECURITY: COSTS ASSOCIATED WITH THE ADMINISTRATION'S EFFORTS TO PROMOTE PROGRAM REFORMS" (GAO-07-621R)

Thank you for the opportunity to review and comment on the draft report. We appreciate the professionalism of your audit team during the course of this audit.

We pointed out at the entrance conference, in our written responses to GAO's requests for information, and again at the exit conference, that the Social Security Administration (SSA) strongly believes that the body of the report should clearly indicate that the role of SSA's representatives at the events constituted public education on the factors impacting the long-range solvency of the Social Security system and the range of options to address solvency. The funds spent on these activities were to promote solvency education and provide factual information, rather than to promote any particular plan to achieve solvency. Agency participation focused on the many factors affecting the solvency of the trust funds--including the rapid growth in the number of retirees, increasing life expectancy and lower birth rates, and the range of solutions to achieve sustainable solvency--including increasing taxes, slowing the growth of benefits and/or increasing the rate of return on investments.

Further, many of these events were congressional town hall meetings where SSA's participation was specifically requested by the sponsoring member of Congress. These included events sponsored by both Republicans and Democrats.

We believe that the report will be misleading if this information is not included in the body of the report. We request that the information be added to the section, "Costs Related to Social Security Administration Participation," beginning on page 12 of the draft report.

Other Comments

Page 1, sentences 2 and 3—change "revenues" to "tax revenues." These sentences should be revised to read, "As you know, the ...will exceed tax revenues. After that time, the gap between costs and tax revenues..."

Pages 5-6, under **BACKGROUND**, sentence 2, should be changed to two sentences that read, "According to the 2006 Social ...48 million beneficiaries at the end of 2005. Total benefits paid during 2005 amounted to $521 billion." Also, change last sentence of same paragraph, making two sentences which read, "The Board of Trustees projected a long-range (75-year) funding shortfall in the Social Security trust funds of $4.6 trillion in present value, absent program reforms. For the infinite future, the Board projects a funding shortfall of about $13 trillion in present value."

End Notes

[1] Officially, Social Security is called the Old-Age, Survivors, and Disability Insurance program.

[2] This is the name given to the administration's plan to schedule at least 60 events across the country over a 60-day period to promote Social Security reform.

[3] www.strengtheningsocialsecurity.gov' www.treas.gov' and www.whitehouse.gov

[4] Fixed costs are those costs which would have been incurred whether or not the officials participated in the Social Security reform events.

[5] 31 U.S.C. §§ 1535–1536.

[6] HHS identified 2 other events for which it stated it reimbursed $59,749.47 to EOP for costs associated with Social Security reform events, which are not included in the report totals. We could not obtain corroborating evidence that there were Social Security reform events in Cleveland, Ohio on January 27, 2005, and in Maple Grove, Minnesota on June 17, 2005.

[7] The Strengthening Social Security Web site was still available at www.strengtheningsocialsecurity.gov as of July 25, 2007.

[8] As discussed in enc. I, because Labor and HHS were not asked to report the costs associated with events with their agency officials based upon our decision to review the agencies with significant numbers of public speaking events and the fact that any additional information we might have obtained from Labor and HHS would not

fully remove the records access limitation imposed by EOP, we only asked that Labor and HHS confirm the amounts reported by EOP.

[9] 31 U.S.C. § 716(a).

[10] 31 U.S.C. § 1535(b).

[11] GAO, *Standards for Internal Control in the Federal Government*, GAO/AIMD-00-21.3.1 (Washington, D.C.: November 1999).

[12] See also chapter 2 of title VII of GAO's *Policy and Procedures Manual for Guidance of Federal Agencies*, which provides guidance on agencies' responsibilities with regard to reimbursements between agencies.

[13] Department of the Treasury, Procurement Services Division, *Customer's Guide To Processing Payable Interagency Agreements (IAA)* (January 2006), p. 9.

[14] Department of the Treasury, Financial Management Service, *Federal Intragovernmental Transactions Accounting Policy Guide* (Washington, D.C. August 2006).

[15] The EOP events with no reported expenses include the President's events on May 4 and 13, and June 8, 14, and 23, 2005; Noam Neusner's April 2, 2005 event; and Keith B. Hennessey's March 7, 2005, event. The reported expenses do include travel expenses for 8 events that EOP reported it could not tie to the specific Social Security reform events we identified based upon its review of travel expense files. Those events include Joshua B. Bolten's April 4, 2005, event, Allan B. Hubbard's events on March 24 and 28, 2005, Keith B. Hennessey's March 30, 2005, event, and Brian Reardon's April 25, 2005, event.

[16] SSA did not report costs for local travel.

[17] Refer to enc. I, Scope and Methodology, for details related to the statistical sample.

[18] Identified Treasury travel expenses included $3,063 for travel to "Teach Children to Save Day" events, which are listed in enclosure III. While not the primary focus of these events, Social Security reform was discussed. Many of the initiatives were conducted in Washington, D.C., or in conjunction with other events and therefore did not likely have significant additional travel expenses. Treasury did not report costs for local travel.

[19] The salary expenses associated with the assignments to the SSIC were considered direct and incremental because newly hired employees were initially assigned full-time to the SSIC.

[20] The remaining events were attended by officials from five other agencies including the Departments of Commerce, Health and Human Services (HHS), Housing and Urban Development, and Labor (Labor), and the Small Business Administration.

[21] In our request for EOP information and documentation, we asked EOP to report nontravel and nonstaging expenses if they amounted to more than $2,500.

[22] These vouchers represent 73 of the events attended by SSA officials in support of the Social Security reform initiative.

[23] We are 95-percent confident that the error rate associated with sampling error inherent in statistical sampling is less than or equal to 1 percent, plus or minus 5 percent.

In: Social Security Reform: Disability, Indexing and Financing ISBN: 978-1-61668-354-2
Editor: Janet U. Burlington

Chapter 3

SOCIAL SECURITY REFORM: POSSIBLE EFFECTS ON THE ELDERLY POOR AND MITIGATION OPTIONS*

Kathleen Romig

SUMMARY

Social Security has significantly reduced elderly poverty. The elderly poverty rate has fallen from 35% in 1959 to an all-time low of 9% in 2006, in large part because of Social Security. If Social Security benefits did not exist, an estimated 44% of the elderly would be poor today assuming no changes in behavior. The Supplemental Security Income (SSI) program, also provides benefits to the poorest elderly, many of whom do not qualify for Social Security benefits. However, despite these programs, about 3.4 million elderly individuals remained in poverty in 2006.

The Social Security system faces a long-term financing problem. The Social Security Trustees project cash-flow deficits beginning in 2017 and trust fund insolvency in 2041. Many recent proposals to improve system solvency would reduce Social Security benefits in the future. Benefit reductions could affect the low- income elderly, many of whom rely on Social Security benefits for almost all of their income. Such potential benefit reductions could lead to higher rates of poverty among the elderly compared to those projected under the current benefit formula. Because the low-income elderly are especially vulnerable to benefit reductions, many recent Social Security reform proposals have included minimum benefits or other provisions that would mitigate the effect of benefit cuts on the elderly poor.

This report analyzes the projected effects of four possible approaches to mitigating the effects of Social Security benefit reductions on elderly poverty in 2042, the first full year of projected trust fund insolvency. The options are compared to a *payable baseline*, which assumes current-law benefits would need to be cut across the board to balance Social Security's annual income and spending at the point of insolvency. The four options examined are (1) a poverty-line Social Security minimum benefit; (2) a sliding-scale Social Security

* This is an edited, reformatted and augmented version of a CRS Report for Congress publication dated April 2008.

minimum benefit; (3) a poverty- line SSI benefit; and (4) a poverty-line SSI benefit with liberalized eligibility.

Major findings include the following:

- Each of the four options would reduce elderly poverty compared to the payable baseline — ranging from a negligible reduction in the elderly poverty rate for the option to create a sliding-scale Social Security minimum benefit to a reduction of three percentage points for the poverty-line SSI benefit with liberalized eligibility.
- The elderly poverty rate under all of the options would be higher than under the current law *scheduled baseline*, which assumes the current benefit formula can be maintained with no reductions.
- The SSI options examined would target the additional spending more efficiently toward the poor elderly than would the Social Security options.
- The Social Security options examined would reduce the incomes of some elderly because of interaction effects; the SSI options would not create such interactions.

BACKGROUND

Historical Declines in Elderly Poverty, Uncertain Future

Elderly poverty has declined over time

Elderly poverty in the United States has declined dramatically over time, ultimately reaching an all-time low in 2006. In 1959, when the Census Bureau began to measure poverty, more than a third (3 5%) of the elderly — those age 65 or older — were in poverty. By 2006, less than one-tenth (9%) of the elderly were in poverty.[1] This reduction in elderly poverty was primarily due to two factors: legislative changes that made Social Security benefits (i.e., Old-Age, Survivors, and Disability Insurance, or OASDI) more generous and strong wage growth that led to higher initial benefits. If Social Security benefits did not exist, an estimated 44% of the elderly would be poor today, assuming no behavioral changes such as saving more or working longer.[2]

Elderly poverty is lower than child or working-age adult poverty

The poverty rate among the elderly is lower than that for children or for the working- age population.[3] In 2006, 9% of the elderly were poor, compared to 17% of children and 11% of working-age adults (i.e., ages 18 to 64). In 1969, the poverty rate among the elderly was more than double the rate among working-age adults.[4] By the early 1 990s, the elderly poverty rate had fallen below the rate for working-age adults and has remained lower since. Within each age group, poverty rates vary dramatically depending on race, sex, education levels, and other demographic characteristics.[5]

Elderly poverty is projected to decline under the scheduled benefit formula

Elderly poverty is projected to continue to decrease over time under Social Security's scheduled benefit formula. Most of the elderly (roughly 90%) receive Social Security benefits. Under current law, initial Social Security benefits will increase at the rate of wages, while the poverty thresholds will rise with prices. Since wage growth is expected to outpace price growth, the rate of poverty should decline among Social Security beneficiaries, all else being equal.[6] The elderly poverty rate is projected to fall to about 5% by 2042 under the *scheduled baseline*, which assumes no changes in the Social Security benefit formula.[7]

Lack of action could reverse historic declines in elderly poverty

Social Security's scheduled benefit formula is unsustainable with current revenues. Lawmakers could restore long-term system solvency by increasing revenue (e.g., raising taxes), cutting benefits, or some combination of the two. According to the Social Security Administration, if no changes are made to Social Security and the trust funds are allowed to become insolvent, scheduled benefits would be reduced and elderly poverty rates could double.[8] Under the *payable baseline*, which assumes no action until projected trust fund insolvency in 2041, an across-the-board benefit cut to achieve annual balance is projected to result in an 11% elderly poverty rate.[9] This figure is more than twice as high as the rate projected under the scheduled baseline, and higher than the elderly poverty rate today.

Future solvency changes could also increase elderly poverty

Many recent proposals to improve system solvency would reduce Social Security benefits in the future.[10] If Social Security benefits were cut across the board, the poverty rate among elderly Americans could be significantly higher than under the current-law benefit formula. Some of the most commonly discussed options to improve solvency could increase the elderly poverty rate to levels almost as high as doing nothing until the trust funds run out.

During the 2005 debate over Social Security reform, one frequently mentioned solvency option was the price indexing provision from Model 2 of the 2001 President's Commission to Strengthen Social Security.[11] If such a price indexing provision were implemented in 2008, the Dynasim model estimates that the elderly poverty rate would increase to 10% by 2042, assuming no other changes.[12] This figure is twice the poverty rate projected under the scheduled benefit formula (which would require additional funding to be sustainable). In addition, the 10% elderly poverty rate projected under price indexing in 2042 is almost as high as the 11% rate projected under the payable baseline.

Another frequently mentioned option was developed by Robert Pozen, one of the co-chairs of the 2001 commission, and endorsed by President George W. Bush.[13] Dubbed progressive price indexing, this option would implement the price-indexing formula from Commission Model 2 but would protect some low earners from benefit cuts.[14] However, unlike price indexing, progressive price indexing would not restore solvency to the system; it could reduce the solvency gap by about 70%.[15] If progressive price indexing were implemented in 2008, the Dynasim model estimates that elderly poverty rate would be 8% by 2042, assuming no other changes.[16] This is higher than the 5% poverty rate projected under the current law scheduled baseline (which assumes no benefit cuts) but lower than the 11% rate projected under the payable baseline.[17]

The Social Security and SSI Programs

Workers, and in some cases their families, receive Social Security benefits based on their contributions into the system. The Supplemental Security Income (S SI) program, in contrast, is a means-tested program that does not have work or contribution requirements, but restricts benefits to those who meet strict limitations on assets and income, as well as other criteria. Both programs are administered by the Social Security Administration (SSA). **Table 1** outlines some of the differences between Social Security and SSI.

Table 1. Social Security (OASDI) and Supplemental Security Income (SSI)

	Social Security (OASDI)	**Supplemental Security Income (SSI)**
Program Type	Federal	Federal and state
Federal Outlays	$581 billion (2007)	$36 billion (2007)
Funding Source	Funded primarily through payroll taxes	Funded through general revenues
Beneficiaries	Benefits paid to retired or disabled workers and their families, and to the survivors of deceased workers	Benefits paid to aged, blind, and disabled individuals and couples with very limited income and assets
Eligibility Age for Aged Benefits	62 (at reduced levels)	65
Benefit Levels	Benefit levels based on workers' earnings	Federal benefit rate in 2008 for noninstitutionalized recipients (less any applicable reductions); future rates indexed to inflation: — $637/month for individuals — $956/month for a couple
Income and Asset Limits	No income or asset limits for eligibility	Means-tested eligibility: — Countable income limited to the federal benefit rate[a] — Countable assets limited to $2,000 for individuals and $3,000 for couples (not indexed to inflation)
Growth Rate of Average Benefits	Average benefits increase with wage growth	Average benefits increase with price growth (i.e., inflation)
% of Elderly Receiving Benefits (12/05)	92% (34.0 million), of which 3% (1.1 million) also receive SSI	5% (2.0 million), of which more than half (1.1 million) also receive Social Security (OASDI)

Source: Congressional *Budget Office, Baseline Budget Projections,* January 23, 2008 [http://www.cbo.gov/budget/budproj.pdf] (for total outlays); Social Security Administration, *Annual Statistical Supplement,* 2006, June 2007, at [http://www.ssa.gov/policy/docs/statcomps/supplement/2006/] (for participation).

Notes: In addition to federal SSI benefits, most states provide supplemental SSI benefits. If state supplemental SSI benefits are federally administered, they are included in the SSI income limits.

[a] Plus federally administered state supplement, if applicable.

Social security receipt among the elderly has increased

About 92% of the elderly currently receive Social Security.[18] More people qualify for Social Security now than in the past because of legislative changes that expanded eligibility and increased workforce participation.[19] Reliance on Social Security benefits is also increasing. In 2006, about one-quarter of the elderly relied on Social Security for all of their income.[20]

SSI receipt among the elderly has declined.

In contrast to Social Security, only about 5% of the elderly currently receive SSI. Many poor elderly individuals do not receive SSI, either because they do not meet SSI's strict asset and income restrictions, or because they are eligible but have not enrolled in the program. The academic literature estimates that about one-half to two-thirds of qualifying elderly participate in SSI.[21] Substantially fewer people qualify for SSI now than in the past because SSI's income limits rise with inflation, while many potential SSI applicants receive Social Security benefits, which rise with wages. This means that all other things being equal, for each year in which wages rise faster than prices, fewer Social Security beneficiaries qualify for SSI. SSI's resource limits and income disregards are not indexed and thus do not rise at all. As a result, SSI's eligibility criteria become stricter over time.

Issues and Options Related to Elderly Poverty

Poverty Reduction under Current Law

Social security

Although Social Security has substantially reduced poverty among the elderly, its primary purpose is to replace earnings lost when a worker of any income level retires, dies, or becomes disabled — not to reduce poverty.[22] The Social Security benefit formula is progressive, so lower earners' benefits represent a greater proportion of their average lifetime earnings than do higher earners' benefits. However, not all of the elderly receive Social Security benefits, and those who do receive benefits do not necessarily receive enough to stay out of poverty. As a result, about 7% of elderly Social Security beneficiaries lived in poverty in 2006, while about 22% of elderly non-beneficiaries were poor.[23]

Some long-term low earners receive Social Security benefits that are less than the elderly poverty threshold. For example, a person born in 1943 who earned the minimum wage every year for 40 years and then retired at his or her full retirement age (66) would receive a Social Security benefit that is slightly less than the official poverty threshold for an elderly individual.[24] At age 62 (the age at which most individuals take up retirement benefits), the benefit for such a worker would be about three-quarters of the elderly poverty threshold. Individuals with limited working histories (for example, women who take time out of the labor force) also frequently receive Social Security benefits that are below poverty.

Social security's special minimum

One provision of the Social Security benefit formula that was intended to benefit poor individuals is the special minimum primary insurance amount (PIA).[25] The special minimum

PIA was enacted in 1972 to increase benefits for long-term low wage earners and their families. To qualify, a worker must have at least 11 years of Social Security-covered earnings above a specified threshold.[26] The amount of the special minimum PIA rises each year with inflation and varies depending on the number of years a person works. In 2008, the amounts range from $34.90 per month for workers with 11 years of qualifying earnings to $721.40 for workers with 30 years. Initial Social Security benefits rise at the rate of wage growth, while the special minimum PIA rises at the generally slower rate of price growth. Thus, the amount of the special minimum PIA has gradually become smaller relative to minimum PIA a person could receive under the ordinary Social Security rules. As a result, the special minimum is paid to a small and rapidly dwindling population.[27] SSA's actuaries project that it will be impossible for anyone who becomes eligible for benefits in 2013 or later to receive the special minimum PIA.[28]

The current law special minimum PIA affects very few Social Security beneficiaries and does not necessarily bring these people out of poverty.[29] In 2005, approximately 100,000 Social Security beneficiaries (less than 0.25%) received a special minimum PIA.[30] Among these beneficiaries, the average Social Security benefit amount ($710 per month) was less than the poverty threshold for an elderly individual ($781 per month in 2005).

Supplemental security income (SSI)

The Supplemental Security Income (SSI) program was designed explicitly to benefit the elderly poor, in addition to the low-income blind and disabled.[31] Its strict income and asset thresholds ensure that SSI benefits go only to the extremely poor. Unlike Social Security, SSI benefits and eligibility are not based on work, so SSI reaches many individuals with limited work histories who do not qualify for Social Security.

SSI benefits are typically not high enough to lift recipients out of poverty — about four in ten (39%) of SSI beneficiaries are poor.[32] The maximum federal benefit rates for SSI are less than the poverty thresholds for elderly individuals and couples, and SSI recipients may only receive limited income other than their SSI benefits.[33] Many poor elderly individuals do not receive SSI, either because they do not meet SSI's strict asset and income restrictions, or because they are eligible but have not enrolled in the program.

Some Basic Considerations

Poverty under the baselines

When discussing policy options to address elderly poverty, it is instructive to take a closer look at the poor elderly. **Figure 1** provides projected elderly poverty rates under both the scheduled and payable baselines in 2042, the first full year of projected trust fund insolvency.[34] These projections were produced by CRS using the Urban Institute's Dynasim microsimulation model. (For more details on the Dynasim model and its use in this analysis, please see the **Appendix**.)

The projected elderly poverty rate is 11% under the payable baseline and 5% under the scheduled baseline. Under the payable baseline, a few groups stand out as having poverty rates that are substantially above average. For example, racial and ethnic minority groups have higher-than-average projected poverty rates: 19% for black and Hispanic elderly, and

21% for Asian and Native American elderly (labeled as "other" in **Figure 1**). Elderly individuals with low levels of education are projected to have three times the overall poverty rate: 33%. Unmarried elderly individuals are projected to have high rates of poverty: 21% for never married individuals, 17% for divorced individuals, and 13% for widowed elderly individuals. Finally, women are projected to have higher poverty rates than men (13% compared to 9%, respectively).

Benefit receipt among poor elderly

When considering a policy change, it is also useful to consider what kinds of benefits (if any) the poor elderly receive.

Social security

About 70% of the poor elderly are projected to receive Social Security benefits under the payable baseline in 2042, compared to 97% of the non-poor elderly. The poverty rate among elderly individuals who receive Social Security benefits is projected to be 8% under the payable baseline in 2042, compared to 58% among individuals who do not receive Social Security benefits. Thus, even after accounting for potential across-the-board cuts, Social Security is projected to keep many elderly out of poverty and to provide income to most of those who remain poor.

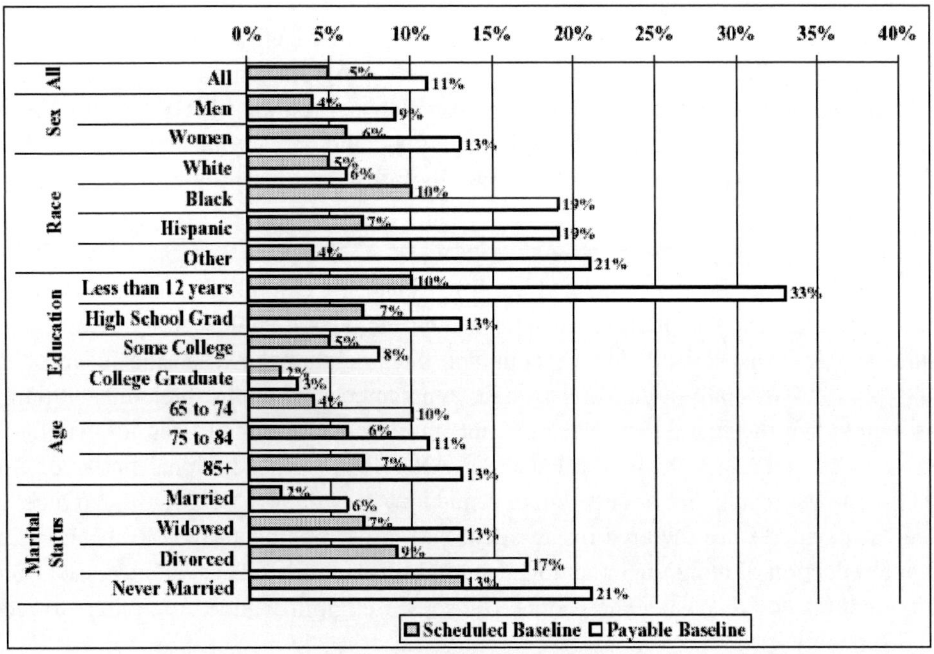

Source: CRS projections produced using the Urban Institute's Dynasim microsimulation model.

Figure 1. Projected Poverty Rates Among the Elderly in 2042, Assuming Scheduled and Payable Baselines

SSI

Fewer of the elderly poor receive SSI than Social Security. However, SSI recipients are much more likely to be poor than are Social Security beneficiaries. About 22% of the poor elderly are projected to receive SSI benefits under the payable baseline in 2042, compared to 1% of the non-poor elderly. The poverty rate among elderly individuals who receive SSI is projected to be about 75% under the payable baseline in 2042, compared to about 9% among elderly individuals who do not receive SSI benefits.

Interactions between policy options and low-income programs

When discussing changes to public policy, it is important to keep in mind the possible unintended consequences of a potential change. One of the advantages of a microsimulation model such as Dynasim is that it brings unexpected interactions between policy options and existing program rules to light. Social Security is a complex program, and changes to its structure could lead to unexpected results — both within the Social Security program and in the relationship of Social Security to SSI and other means-tested programs. The results presented here show only the interactions that occur within and between Social Security and SSI, as Dynasim does not model other low-income programs. Also, since the official poverty thresholds are based only on money income, policy interactions with in-kind or quasi-cash benefits such as Medicaid or food stamps would not affect people's poverty status.

Changes to Social Security could potentially affect eligibility and benefit levels for various government assistance programs. Any change to Social Security benefits could affect SSI eligibility and benefit levels. In turn, any change to SSI eligibility (direct or indirect) could affect eligibility for a number of low-income programs, including Medicaid, food stamps, and the Low-Income Home Energy Assistance Program (LIHEAP). In the most extreme cases, an increase in Social Security benefits could actually make some low-income beneficiaries worse off because they would lose eligibility for other programs as a result.

SSI

Changes to Social Security could affect SSI, since SSI eligibility and benefit levels are determined in part using applicants' income, which includes Social Security benefits.[35] The SSI rules stipulate that an individual's countable income cannot exceed the federal benefit amount (plus the federally-administered state supplements, if applicable). In addition, the rules stipulate that the first $20 of unearned income (including Social Security benefits) can be excluded from the SSI benefit calculation. After that, each additional dollar of Social Security benefits results in a one dollar reduction in federal SSI benefits. (Once state supplement payments are factored in, an additional dollar of Social Security benefits could result in a reduction of more than one dollar in total SSI benefits.) Thus, an increase in Social Security benefits could cause some people to lose SSI eligibility and cause others to receive less in SSI benefits.

Other means-tested programs

Changes to Social Security or SSI could also affect individuals' eligibility for other programs.[36] For example, an increase in Social Security benefits could raise some individuals' income above the qualifying thresholds for SSI, Medicaid, food stamps, and the Low Income Home Energy Assistance Program (LIHEAP). An increase in SSI enrollment (due to direct or indirect changes) could lead to more people qualifying for means-tested programs, because in many cases SSI recipients are considered categorically eligible for assistance. The following programs for low-income individuals could potentially be affected by changes to Social Security and SSI eligibility and benefits.

- **Medicaid.** States have three options for determining Medicaid eligibility for SSI recipients. As of 2008, in 32 states and the District of Columbia, individuals who are eligible for SSI are automatically eligible for Medicaid. SSI recipients in seven states and the Northern Mariana Islands are eligible for Medicaid but must complete a separate application. Eleven other states have the option to impose Medicaid eligibility requirements that are more restrictive than SSI criteria.
- **Food Stamps.** SSI recipients living alone or in a household where all members receive SSI benefits are automatically eligible for food stamps.
- **LIHEAP.** Households with a member receiving SSI are categorically eligible for LIHEAP, so changes to SSI eligibility would also affect LIHEAP eligibility.[37]

Effects of policy interactions on the cost of policy options

The interactions between changes to Social Security or SSI and low-income programs affect not just beneficiaries, but the total cost of an option as well. For example, increased SSI enrollment could lead to higher expenses not just for SSI, but also for Medicaid, the food stamp program, and LIHEAP. This is because a greater number of SSI recipients would mean a greater number of people who are categorically eligible for these programs, increasing their cost. Similarly, an increase in Social Security benefits could lead to higher expenses for Social Security, but lower expenses for SSI, Medicaid, the food stamp program, and LIHEAP. This is because higher Social Security benefits would increase the total income of some people enough so that they would lose eligibility for SSI and other means-tested programs.

Minimizing the effects of policy interactions

If one wanted to increase Social Security benefits while minimizing effects on SSI eligibility and benefit levels, one option would be raising SSI's $20 unearned income exclusion, which has not changed since 1981. This change would allow a greater proportion of Social Security benefit increases to be passed on to SSI recipients, and allow a greater number of recipients to maintain SSI eligibility. Raising the unearned income exclusion would also allow policymakers to increase Social Security benefits with fewer effects on beneficiaries' eligibility for Medicaid, food stamps, and LIHEAP.

It would also be possible to raise Social Security benefits while preserving current-law eligibility for Medicaid, food stamps, and/or LIHEAP for some SSI recipients without increasing SSI's unearned income exclusion. Legislation could deem current SSI recipients eligible for SSI for the purposes of qualifying for Medicaid, food stamps, and/or LIHEAP without actually paying them SSI benefits.[38] This way, SSI recipients who lost SSI eligibility after a change to Social Security would not lose their eligibility to the affected program(s). Such a deeming provision would only affect individuals who were already receiving SSI when the policy was implemented — not necessarily individuals in the future who could have received SSI under the old rules.

POLICY OPTIONS AND THEIR PROJECTED EFFECTS ON BENEFIT LEVELS AND ELDERLY POVERTY

The following section describes each of the four options CRS modeled. It also provides the projected effects of the options on Social Security and SSI benefit levels and eligibility in 2042, and the interaction between the two programs. These four options were chosen to illustrate different approaches to mitigating poverty in a benefit cut scenario, allowing policymakers to see the potential pros and cons of generic options. The details of each option could be modified or combined with other provisions. This analysis does not cover potential transition issues nor the cost of the options modeled.

Option 1: Poverty-Line Minimum Social Security Benefit

The first option would create a new minimum Social Security benefit equal to the elderly poverty line. Under this option, any individual who was insured for Social Security (i.e., who had enough credits to qualify for a worker benefit) would be guaranteed a primary insurance amount (PIA) at least equal to the single-person elderly poverty threshold.[39]

Some Social Security beneficiaries could receive this minimum and still be poor under the option. Since the PIA would be equal to the poverty threshold under this option, an individual would only get a poverty-level benefit if he or she claimed benefits at the full retirement age (at which unreduced benefits are paid). Most people, especially people with low incomes, claim benefits before their full retirement ages and are thus subject to a permanent reduction in monthly benefits. For example, claiming benefits at Social Security's earliest eligibility age (62) permanently reduces workers' PIAs by 30% if they were born in 1960 or later. Finally, poverty is a family measure, not an individual measure, so if a person receives a poverty-line benefit but other members of his/her family have little or no income, that person could still be considered poor.

In addition, some beneficiaries would not receive a minimum benefit under this option because they would not qualify for benefits based on their own work records, but would receive benefits based on others' work (e.g., spouse benefits, in which a person receives 50% of his/her spouse's PIA). These auxiliary beneficiaries do not have their own PIAs, and in some cases their benefits would be less than poverty.

Projected change in benefits

The mean change in Social Security benefits among all beneficiaries is projected to be about 2% under this option. Eligibility for Social Security would not change under the option, but the additional income received would disqualify some individuals from SSI. As a result, about 12% of individuals (307,000) who received SSI benefits under the baseline are projected to lose their entire SSI benefit. Among beneficiaries projected to retain eligibility for SSI, about 20% would receive lower benefits. This effect on SSI benefits dilutes the option's poverty reduction effect.

Projected change in elderly poverty

The poverty-line Social Security minimum benefit option is projected to reduce the elderly poverty rate by about one percentage point compared to the current law payable baseline, reducing the net number of elderly poor by about 494,000 individuals in 2042.

Figure 2 shows the projected effect of this option on the poverty status of elderly individuals living in poor families in 2042, by demographic characteristics. An estimated 7% (561,000) of the elderly poor would be moved out of poverty. The option is projected to have a bigger poverty-reduction effect on some subgroups within the elderly poor than others. For example, the option is projected to bring 23% of married poor elderly individuals out of poverty, but a only 1-2% of each non- married group. This result might seem counterintuitive since married individuals are less likely than non-married individuals to receive higher Social Security benefits under the option, but it reflects the fact that married people can potentially be brought out of poverty by a spouse's benefit increase. About 67,000 individuals are projected to fall into poverty under this option, increasing the number of elderly poor by about 1%. All of these individuals are projected to lose SSI benefits under the option.

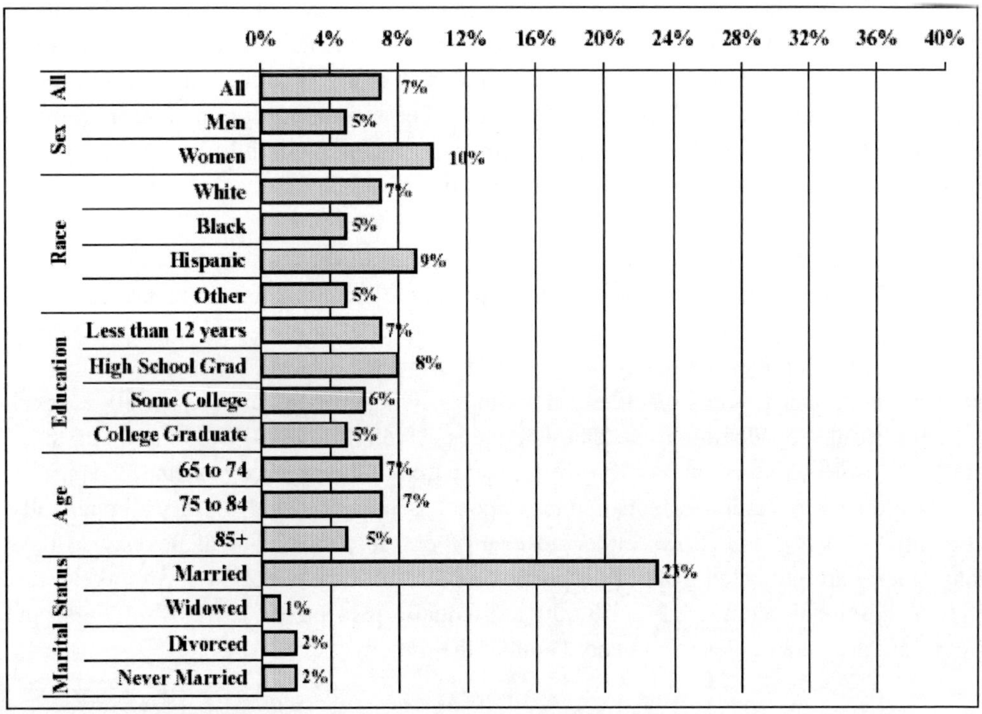

Source: CRS projections produced using the Urban Institute's Dynasim microsimulation model.

Figure 2. Percentage Reduction in the Number of Elderly Poor Projected Under Option #1 Compared to Payable Baseline, by Demographic Characteristics, 2042

Option 2: Sliding Scale Minimum Social Security Benefit

Some policymakers are interested in minimum benefit options targeted at longterm low earners, as a way of rewarding work and reinforcing Social Security's ties to earnings.[40] One such option is a provision in Senator Lindsay Graham's 2003 comprehensive Social Security reform bill that would create a sliding-scale minimum benefit that would vary depending on number of years of work.[41] Retired worker beneficiaries with at least 35 years of work would be guaranteed a PIA equal to 120% of the single elderly poverty threshold, which would gradually phase out for workers with 10 years of work (the minimum required to be insured for a retired worker benefit).[42] For people with 30 or fewer years of work, the minimum benefit guaranteed under this option would be less than poverty. Even individuals who qualify for a minimum PIA at the poverty line or higher could still be poor under this option, for the same reasons described for the previous option: they could be subject to benefit reductions, or other members of their families might not have enough income for the enhanced benefit to bring the entire unit out of poverty.

Projected change in benefits

Overall, there is projected to be no change in the mean amount of Social Security benefits under this option. Eligibility for Social Security would not change, but the additional Social Security benefits some individuals receive would disqualify them for SSI. As a result, about 2% of individuals (60,000) who would have received SSI benefits under the baseline are projected to lose eligibility. The model estimates that the option would disqualify more people for SSI than it would bring out of poverty after accounting for changes in both Social Security and SSI benefits. Among beneficiaries who retained eligibility for SSI, a projected 6% would have lower SSI benefits under the option.

Projected change in elderly poverty

The sliding-scale minimum benefit option is not projected to change the projected elderly poverty rate from the current law payable level of 11%. It is projected to have a negligible effect on the net number of elderly poor in 2042. **Figure 3** shows the projected effect of this option on the poverty status of elderly individuals living in poor families in 2042, breaking down the results by demographic characteristics. Overall, about 1% (58,000) of the poor elderly are projected to come out of poverty, compared to the payable baseline.

The poverty reduction effect of this proposal is not projected to vary dramatically by subgroup — each group shows either no change or 1% coming out of poverty. Almost as many elderly are projected to fall into poverty as a result of this option as are taken out of it (58,000 individuals compared to 53,000 individuals, respectively). Many of those put in poverty are projected to lose SSI benefits under the option.

Option 3: Poverty Line SSI Federal Benefit Rates

Under this option, SSI's federal benefit rates would be increased to the elderly poverty thresholds for individuals and couples.[43] The asset thresholds and income exclusions for SSI would remain the same as under current law (i.e., would not increase with inflation).

Increasing the federal benefit rate would effectively liberalize eligibility for SSI, since SSI's income eligibility thresholds are linked to federal benefit rates. Some SSI beneficiaries could still have benefits that are less than poverty under the option. A person could, for example, receive less than the full federal benefit rate because there is a dollar-for-dollar reduction in federal SSI benefits for unearned income above the thresholds. In addition, since poverty is determined for families and SSI benefits are paid to individuals or couples, a person could receive a poverty-line SSI benefit and still be considered poor if other family members have little or no income.

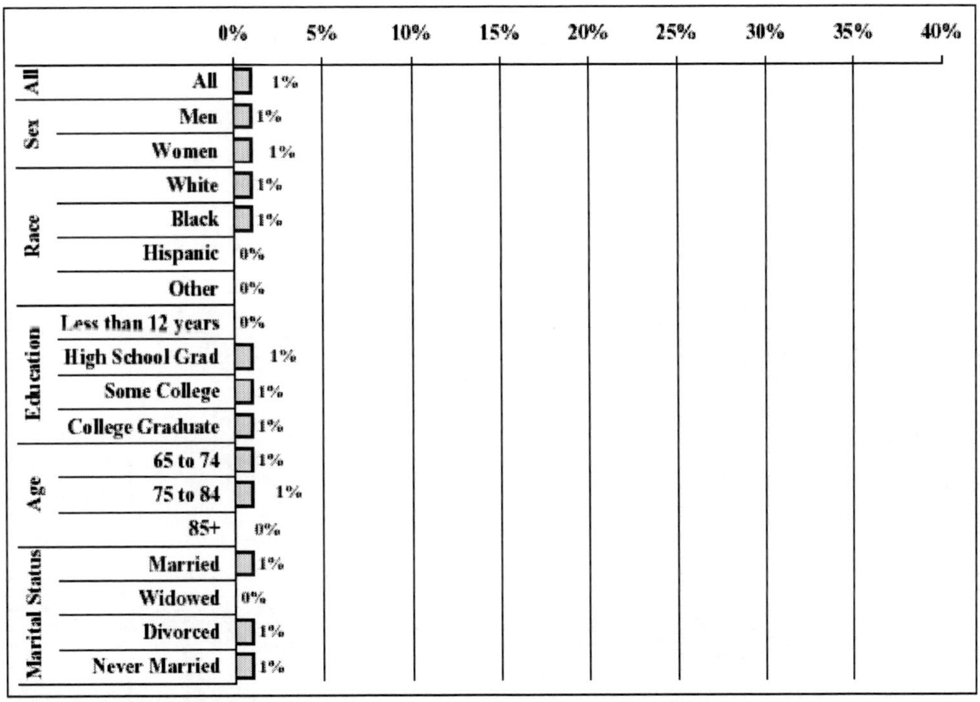

Source: CRS projections produced using the Urban Institute's Dynasim microsimulation model.

Figure 3. Percentage Reduction in the Number of Elderly Poor Projected Under Option #2 Compared to Payable Baseline, by Demographic Characteristics, 2042

Projected change in benefits

An additional 1% of the elderly (913,000 individuals) who did not receive SSI benefits under the baseline are projected to receive them under this option. This is projected to increase SSI participation by more than a third.[44] Among those who received SSI under the baseline, all are projected to receive higher SSI benefits, which would almost double on average. Changes in SSI receipt or benefit levels do not affect Social Security eligibility or benefit levels, so there would be no change in Social Security receipt or benefits under this option.

Projected change in elderly poverty

The poverty-line SSI option is projected to reduce the projected elderly poverty rate by about two percentage points compared to the payable baseline, reducing the number of elderly poor by about 395,000 individuals in 2042. **Figure 4** shows projections of the effect of this option on the poverty status of elderly individuals living in poor families in 2042, breaking down the results by demographic characteristics. Overall, the number of elderly in poverty is projected to be reduced by about 5% (395,000) under the option, in comparison with the current law payable baseline.

The poverty reduction effect of this option would vary depending on demographic characteristics. For example, it is projected to have a relatively small poverty-reduction effect on individuals with more than a high school education (3%) and married individuals (3%), both of whom are less likely than average to receive SSI benefits. On the other hand, this option would particularly help the oldest old (age 85 or older), 7% of whom are projected to be brought out of poverty. No one is projected to be put into poverty by this option.

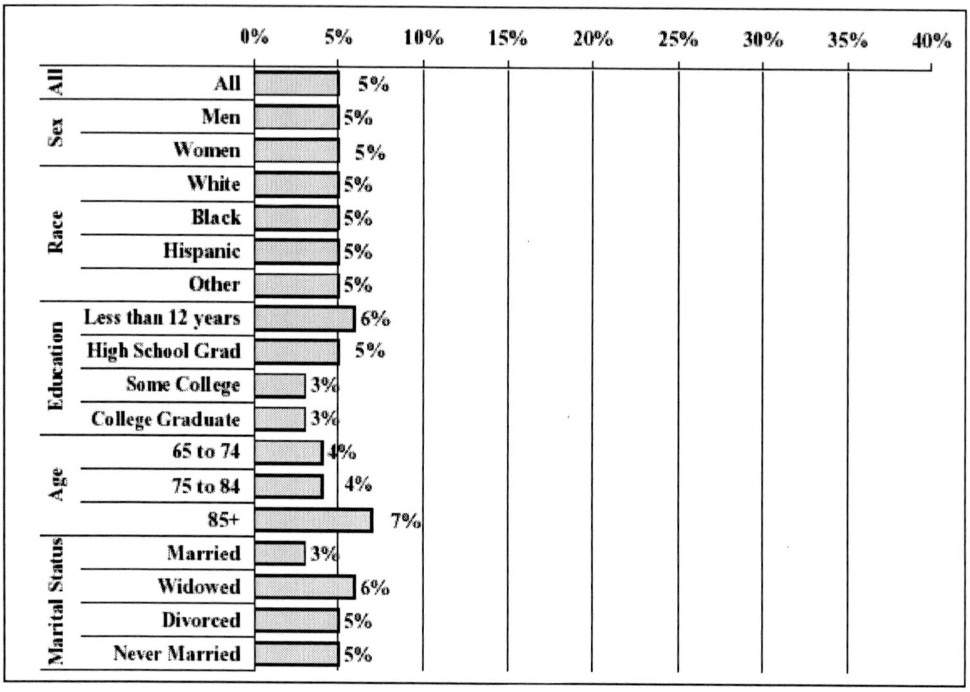

Source: CRS projections produced using the Urban Institute's Dynasim microsimulation model.

Figure 4. Percentage Reduction in the Number of Elderly Poor Projected Under Option #3 Compared to Payable Baseline, by Demographic Characteristics, 2042

Option 4: Poverty-Line SSI Benefits with Liberalized Eligibility

The final option modeled would build upon the previous option by retaining the poverty-line SSI federal benefit rates and adding on provisions to increase SSI' s asset limits and income exclusions and index them to inflation. Under current law, SSI's asset limits and income exclusions are very strict and do not rise with inflation.[45] The current unearned income exclusion ($20/month) and earned income exclusion ($65/month plus half of earnings above this amount) were set in 1981. The current asset exclusions ($2,000/individual and

$3,000/couple) were set in 1989.[46] The increased asset limits and income exclusions in this option are based on the SSI Modernization Act, introduced by Representative Benjamin Cardin, most recently in 2005.[47] This bill would have doubled the earned and unearned income exclusions (to $130/month and $40/month, respectively) and increased the asset thresholds by 50% (to $3,000/individual and $4,500/couple). The bill would also have automatically indexed these thresholds to inflation.

Projected change in benefits

An additional 3% of the elderly (2.0 million individuals) who did not receive SSI benefits under the baseline are projected to receive them under this option. This would almost double the number of the elderly who are projected to receive S SI.[48] Among beneficiaries who received SSI under the baseline, all are projected to receive higher SSI benefits, which would more than double on average. Changes in SSI receipt or benefit levels do not affect Social Security eligibility or benefit levels, so there would be no change in Social Security receipt or benefits under this option.

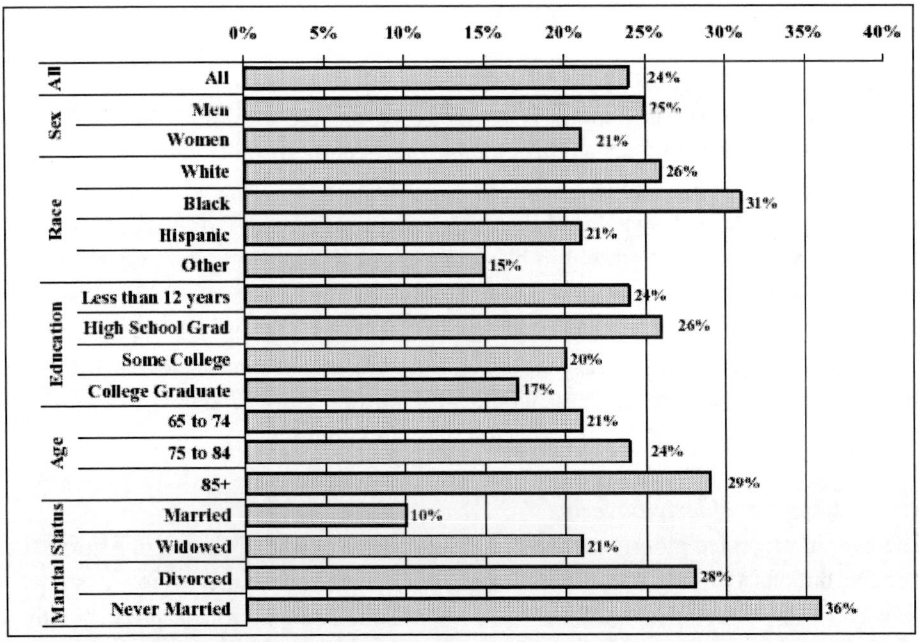

Source: CRS projections produced using the Urban Institute's Dynasim microsimulation model.

Figure 5. Percentage Reduction in the Number of the Elderly Poor Projected Under Option #4 Compared to Payable Baseline, by Demographic Characteristics, 2042

Projected change in elderly poverty

The option to create a poverty-line SSI benefit and liberalize eligibility is projected to reduce the elderly poverty rate by about three percentage points, compared to the payable baseline, reducing the number of elderly poor by about 1.9 million individuals in 2042. **Figure 5** shows the estimated effect of this option on the poverty status of elderly individuals living in poor families in 2042, breaking down the results by demographic characteristics.

Overall, the number of elderly poor is projected to be reduced by about 24% (1.9 million) under the option, compared to the current law payable baseline.

This option would have a bigger poverty-reduction effect on some subgroups of the elderly poor than others. For example, the Dynasim model estimates that the option would bring 36% of never-married individuals out of poverty, along with 31% of black elderly poor and 29% of the oldest elderly poor (age 85+). All of these groups would be relatively more likely to receive SSI. The option is projected to have a smaller poverty-reduction effect on the elderly poor who are married (10%), Asian or Native American (labeled "other" in the figure, 15%), and college graduates (17%). All of these groups would be relatively less likely to receive SSI. No one is projected to be put into poverty by this option.

Summary of Results

The following section summarizes the results described above, showing the projected effects of the options on Social Security and SSI eligibility, benefit levels, and poverty rates in 2042, and the interaction between the two programs.

Projected change in benefits

In summary, none of the options is projected to change eligibility for Social Security benefits, but Options #1 and #2 would change the benefit formula. Overall, Option #1 is projected to increase the average Social Security benefit by 2%, while Option #2 is not projected to change the average Social Security benefit received. As for SSI, Options #3 and #4 are projected to increase both eligibility and benefit levels. Both of these changes would dramatically affect the SSI program. Under Option #3, the number of SSI beneficiaries is projected to increase by more than a third, while under Option #4 the number of SSI beneficiaries is projected to increase by 80%. The change in benefit levels for those who would receive SSI under current law would also be dramatic. Under both Option #3 and Option #4, SSI benefit payments are projected to roughly double.

Projected change in elderly poverty

The overall projected elderly poverty rate under each option is shown in **Figure 6** below. Each of the options is modeled with a current law payable baseline, which is shown along with a current law scheduled baseline for comparison. Each option is projected to reduce poverty somewhat compared to the current law payable baseline — ranging from a negligible reduction in the elderly poverty rate for Option #2 (which would create a Social Security minimum benefit for long-term low earners) to a reduction of three percentage points for Option #4 (the poverty-line SSI benefit with liberalized eligibility). It is important to note that the projected elderly poverty rate under *all* of the options would be higher than under the current law scheduled baseline, which assumes no benefit cuts.

Both the number and demographic breakdown of individuals who are projected to come out of poverty under each of these options varies substantially. Overall, the number of elderly poor people brought out of poverty would vary dramatically, from 1% for Option #2 to 24% for Option #4. Option #1 is projected to bring 7% of the elderly poor out of poverty, compared to 5% for Option #3. As far as demographic breakdowns, Option #1 is projected to bring a greater proportion of married individuals out of poverty, which reflects the fact that married people can potentially be brought out of poverty by a spouse's benefit increase. The poverty-reduction effects of Option #2 would not vary much by subgroup, probably because the impact of the option would be small overall. Both of the SSI options (Options #3 and #4) are projected to bring a greater proportion of non-married individuals and the oldest elderly (age 85+) out of poverty, in part because these groups are more likely to receive SSI.

Program interactions

One of the most striking differences between the Social Security and SSI options is whether and how they interact with other programs. Both of the Social Security options reduce eligibility and benefit levels for SSI (which in turn can affect eligibility for other benefit programs). For Option #2 in particular, this interaction would offset the poverty reduction effect of the policy. Both of the SSI options are free of similar interaction effects. They each increase SSI benefits without affecting eligibility or benefits for Social Security. However, increased eligibility for SSI could affect participation in the food stamp program and other low-income programs for which SSI recipients are categorically eligible.

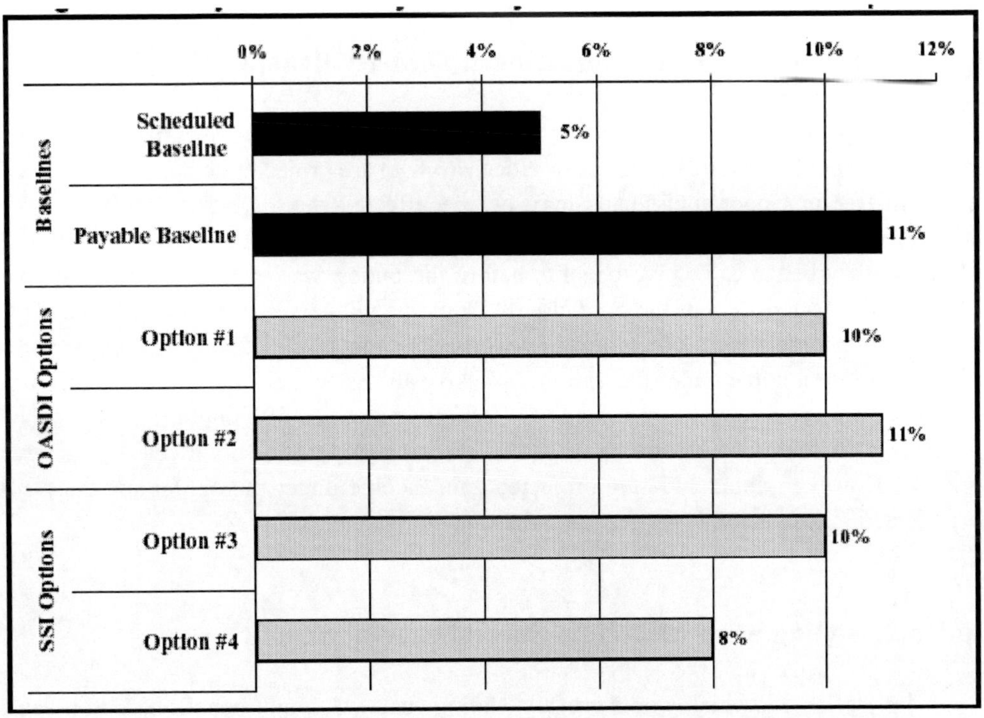

Source: CRS projections produced using the Urban Institute's Dynasim microsimulation model.
Note: The four policy options were modeled with a current law payable baseline.

Figure 6. Projected Elderly Poverty Rates in 2042 Across Options

TARGETING SPENDING TOWARD THE ELDERLY POOR

If one of the objectives of reforming Social Security were to mitigate the effect of possible benefit reductions on the elderly poor, targeting spending would become an important consideration. One way to measure such targeting is to compare the estimated effects of potential policy options on the elderly poor vs. the elderly non- poor. Other ways of analyzing the targeting of an option include measuring the poverty gap and looking at the proportion of people who fall below a given percentage of the poverty threshold (e.g., 150% or 200% of poverty). However, this report focuses on elderly people who are officially considered poor.

Figure 7 shows the elderly poor, the target group for the modeled policy options. For each option, it shows the proportion of individuals projected to gain income (labeled "winners"), lose income (labeled "losers"), or stay the same (labeled "no change"). The income measure shows the projected net change in income under each option, including both Social Security and SSI benefits, so these projections reflect the interaction between the two programs. **Figure 8** shows the same measures for the non-poor elderly.

Option 1: Poverty-Line Minimum Social Security Benefit

Under Option #1, which would create a new minimum Social Security benefit at the poverty line, about two-thirds of the poor elderly (6 8%) are projected to be unaffected. There are several reasons poor individuals may not be affected: because they don't qualify for Social Security benefits, because they receive benefits based on another person's work record, or because they began to receive benefits before the option was implemented. As shown in **Figure 7**, a projected 27% of the poor elderly would be winners, but most aren't projected to gain enough income to bring them out of poverty. The remaining 5% of the elderly poor are projected to lose income under the option. In nearly all cases, their increased Social Security benefits are projected to result in reduced SSI benefits or loss of SSI eligibility.

Among the non-poor elderly, most (84%) are projected not to be affected, as shown in **Figure 8**. However, about 11% are projected gain income under the option and another 5% are projected to lose income, for the same reasons outlined above.

Option 2: Sliding Scale Minimum Social Security Benefit

Under Option #2, which would create a sliding-scale minimum benefit based on years of work, about nine out of ten of the poor elderly (89%) are projected to be unaffected, for the same reasons mentioned in the previous option. About 8% of the poor elderly are projected to be winners under the option, but most don't gain enough income to bring them out of poverty. The remaining 3% of the elderly poor are projected to lose income under the option. Most of the individuals who lose income under the option would either have reduced SSI benefits or lose SSI eligibility.

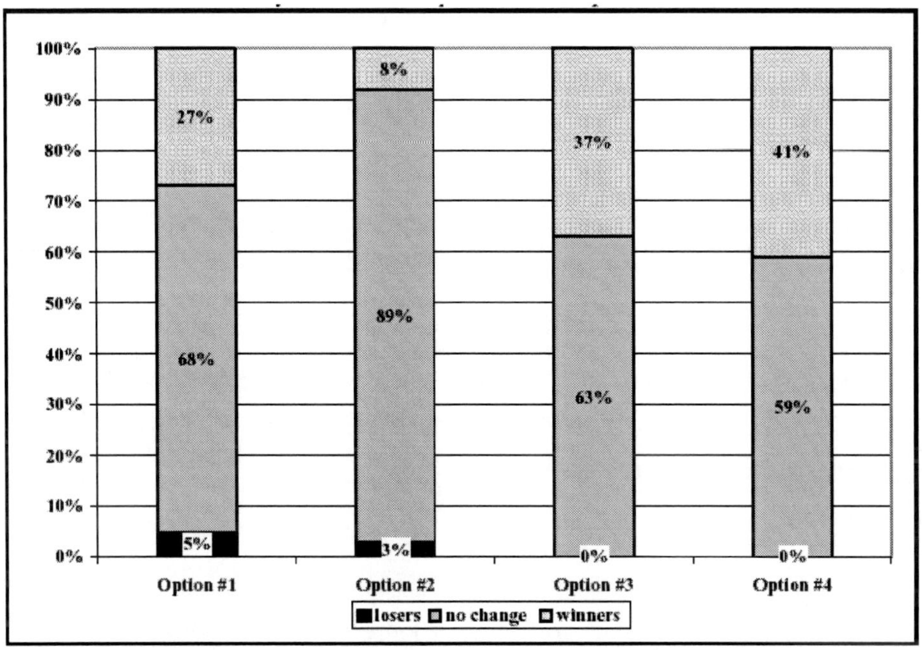

Source: CRS projections produced using the Urban Institute's Dynasim microsimulation model.

Figure 7. Proportion of the Poor Elderly Projected to Gain or Lose Income Under Options, Compared to Payable Baseline, 2042

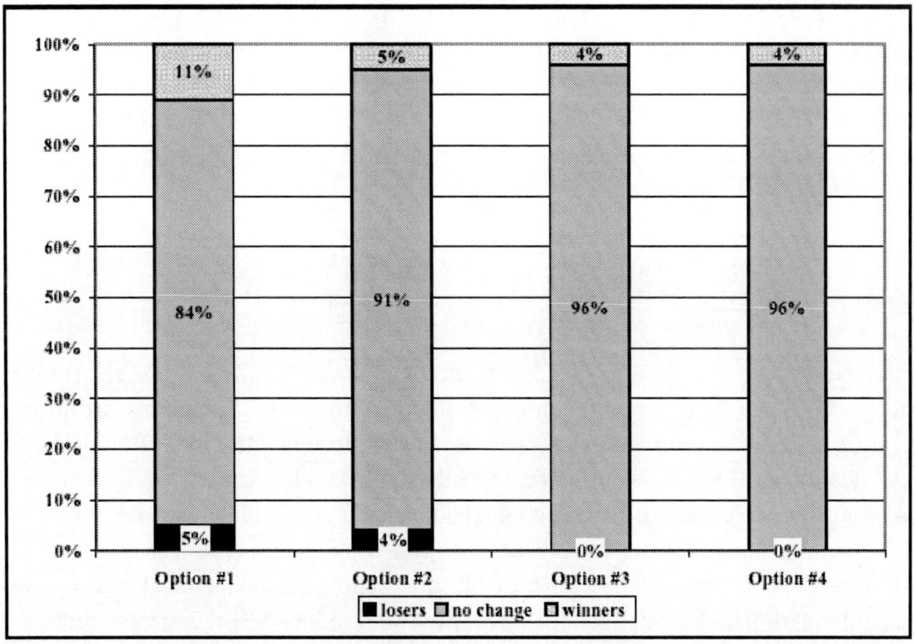

Source: CRS projections produced using the Urban Institute's Dynasim microsimulation model.

Figure 8. Proportion of the Non-Poor Elderly Projected to Gain or Lose Income Under Options, Compared to Payable Baseline, 2042

Among the non-poor elderly, most (91%) are projected not to be affected, as shown in **Figure 8**. However, about 5% are projected gain income under the option and another 4% are projected to lose income, for the same reasons outlined above.

Option 3: Poverty Line SSI Federal Benefit Rates

Under Option #3, which would raise the SSI federal benefit rates to the poverty line, about 63% of the poor elderly are projected to be unaffected, as shown in Figure 7. This is roughly the same proportion of the poor elderly who live in families where no elderly member receives SSI under the option. The remaining 37% of the poor elderly are projected to be winners under the option. None of the elderly poor is projected to lose income.

Among the non-poor elderly, most (96%) are projected not to be affected, as shown in **Figure 8**. About 4% are projected gain income under the option. None of the non-poor elderly is projected to lose income.

Option 4: Poverty-Line SSI Benefits with Liberalized Eligibility

Under Option #4, which would raise SSI federal benefit rates to the poverty line and also liberalize eligibility, about 59% of the poor elderly are projected to be unaffected, as shown in **Figure 7**. This is roughly the same proportion of the poor elderly who live in families where no elderly member receives SSI under the option. The remaining 41% of the poor elderly are projected to be winners under the option The remaining 41% of the poor elderly are projected to be winners under the option None of the elderly poor is projected to lose income.

Among the non-poor elderly, most (96%) are projected not to be affected, as shown in **Figure 8**. About 4% are projected gain income under the option. None of the non-poor elderly is projected to lose income.

Summary of Results

The SSI options analyzed in this report are better targeted toward the elderly poor than are the Social Security options. Among the elderly poor, the SSI options are projected to create more winners and no losers. This is because SSI recipients, by definition, are mostly poor, so any changes to SSI would affect mostly poor people. Among the non-poor, the SSI options change the incomes of fewer people, and cause no one to lose income.

The Social Security options are projected to cause some people to lose income, especially poor people. This is primarily because of the interaction between Social Security and SSI. Each additional dollar of Social Security benefits could reduce SSI recipients' benefits by one dollar (or more, after factoring in state supplements), and could disqualify some recipients for SSI altogether.

Other Considerations

In addition to considering benefit levels, poverty rates, and targeting, as examined above, policymakers examining the potential effects of Social Security reform on the elderly poor would likely consider other criteria when discussing policy changes to either Social Security or SSI. The following section briefly summarizes some of these other criteria. One important factor not explicitly addressed in this report is the cost of each option, which would vary substantially. The Dynasim model does not produce cost estimates, and current cost estimates for these options are not available from other sources.[49]

Program design and purpose

One possible subject for discussion if policy changes are considered is the original purpose of the programs that could be modified. For example, SSI was originally designed to benefit the poor and its strict income and asset limits restrict benefits to the poorest elderly. As such, expanding SSI eligibility or benefits would effectively target additional spending toward the elderly poor. Social Security, on the other hand, was not primarily intended to reduce poverty, but to replace the lost earnings of contributing workers of all income levels. Changing the Social Security benefit formula to mitigate the effects of changes on the elderly poor arguably would not target additional dollars as efficiently. It also might complicate the balance between adequacy and equity in the Social Security program.

Potential scope of changes

Another possible subject for discussion is the potential scope of policy changes — factors such as program participation rates and eligibility restrictions. Social Security participation among the elderly is nearly universal. SSI has strict eligibility criteria and its participation rates are far lower. As a result, changes to SSI would likely affect fewer of the elderly poor than would changes to Social Security. Some individuals prefer not to receive means-tested assistance and would not participate in SSI regardless of changes. Other individuals may not qualify even for a liberalized SSI program because of asset restrictions. This would be a particular problem for people with retirement savings, as defined contribution retirement plans (such as 401 (k)s and Individual Retirement Accounts) count toward SSI's asset test.[50]

Political and fiscal environment

Finally, another potential topic that could be discussed is the prevailing political and fiscal environment. In recent years, major changes to Social Security and SSI have been rare. For example, the last significant amendments to Social Security were in 1983. SSI's income disregards and asset tests have stayed the same since 1981 and 1989, respectively, and are not indexed to inflation. There are also fiscal constraints on additional spending. The federal budget is currently in deficit and is projected to remain so in the future.[51] In addition, Social Security faces long-term solvency problems.

Ultimately, future elderly poverty rates depend largely on how policymakers choose to address Social Security's looming solvency problems. Once those decisions are made, the tradeoffs between any options to mitigate the effects of potential benefit cuts would be judged based on their effectiveness, efficiency, cost, and on policymakers' judgments about a myriad of other factors.

APPENDIX: METHODOLOGY

This paper examines four possible policy options to reduce elderly poverty. The projections in the paper were prepared using the Urban Institute's Dynasim microsimulation model.[52] The Dynasim model projects future Social Security and SSI benefits by using a mix of historical data and projections. When interpreting the results of Dynasim or any other model, it is important to note that projections are inherently imprecise; the further into the future one looks, the wider the range of possible outcomes.

Population

The analysis focuses on all noninstitutionalized individuals who will be age 65 or older in 2042, including those who do not receive Social Security and/or SSI benefits.

Baseline

All of the options in this paper are compared to a current law payable baseline, which assumes that current law benefits are cut across the board to balance Social Security's annual income and spending at the point of insolvency, currently projected to occur in 2041. This baseline illustrates how such options could work in a benefit-cut scenario. Some of the most commonly discussed solvency options are projected to result in poverty rates similar to the current law payable baseline in the year of analysis, as discussed above. Using a different baseline or different solvency option would lead to different results.

Year of Analysis

This report focuses on the effects of policy changes in 2042, the first full year of projected trust fund insolvency. Analyzing this year shows how various poverty-reduction options could mitigate the effects of an across-the- board cut to Social Security benefits at the projected point of insolvency, assuming no action was taken before then. This reduction is assumed to bring annual cash- flow balance to the system, cutting benefits by about 25% in 2042.[53] The figures and accompanying analysis are essentially a snapshot of the projected beneficiary population in this single year. Focusing on a different year would lead to different results.

It is also important to recall that initial Social Security benefits rise with wages over time, while SSI benefits and income limits as well as the poverty thresholds rise with prices. Since wages are projected to rise faster than prices over time, this means that in general, the projected prevalence of SSI receipt decreases each year under current law, as does the number of people in poverty.

Start Year for Options

All of the options in this report are assumed to be implemented in 2008. The year 2008 was chosen so that the analysis could rely as much as possible on near-term projections, which are more reliable than long-term projections. In addition, choosing an earlier start year means that almost all of the elderly beneficiaries in the analysis year, 2042, will be subject to the options.

Measure of Income

Many of the results presented in this paper focus on changes in income. For the purposes of this paper, income includes Social Security benefits, SSI benefits, pension payments, earnings, and the annuitized value of financial assets. In modeling these options, Social Security benefits were calculated before SSI benefits. This sequence is intended to mimic program rules, in which SSI applicants must apply for all other benefits for which they may qualify before applying for SSI. As a result, the interactions between Social Security and SSI benefits can be seen. Income is calculated on a per capita basis, which means that for married couples the income of both spouses is averaged together. However, in showing poverty status, a measure of family income is used since the official poverty threshold is calculated on a family basis.[54]

Poverty Thresholds

In the U.S., poverty is officially defined using the Census Bureau's poverty thresholds. These thresholds reflect rough estimates of the amount of money individuals or families need per year to purchase a basket of goods and services deemed "minimally adequate," according to the living standards of the early 1 960s, when the poverty thresholds were developed. The thresholds are increased at the rate of inflation.[55] The 2007 annual poverty threshold was $9,944 for an elderly individual and $12,533 for an elderly couple.[56] A family is considered poor if its countable money income is less than the poverty threshold for its family type and size.[57] This report uses the official poverty thresholds appropriate for each individual's family type and size (including the thresholds for elderly individuals and couples). The thresholds are projected using the intermediate assumptions about future inflation from the 2005 Social Security Trustees Report.

Behavioral Changes

This analysis assumes that no behavioral changes result from the modification of the Social Security or SSI benefit rules. Thus, policy changes will not automatically alter an individual's work patterns or age at benefit take-up. However, it's likely that if policy changes were implemented, individuals' incentives and behavior could also change. The model assumes that roughly two- thirds of individuals who qualify for SSI take up benefits.[58]

For policies with liberalized eligibility criteria (such as the SSI options analyzed in this report), the same proportion of qualifying individuals is assumed to take up benefits. However, it is possible that a more generous SSI program would also change the proportion of qualifying individuals taking up benefits, which is not captured in these projections.[59] The analysis also assumes no changes in state policy as a result of policy changes at the federal level. However, it is possible that federal policy changes in SSI could result in adjustments to state supplements, for example.

End Notes

[1] U.S. Census Bureau, *Historical Poverty Tables*, Table 3. Poverty Status of People, by Age, Race, and Hispanic Origin: 1959 to 2006, at [http://www.census.gov/hhes/www/poverty/ histpov/hstpov3.html].

[2] CRS estimate produced using March 2007 Current Population Survey.

[3] See CRS Report RL33069, *Poverty in the United States: 2006,* by Thomas Gabe.

[4] See CRS Report 95-1024, *Trends in Poverty in the United States*, by Thomas Gabe.

[5] For a demographic breakdown of elderly poverty rates, see CRS Report RL3 2697, *Income and Poverty Among Older Americans in 2006*, by Patrick Purcell.

[6] See Seyda G. Wentworth and David Pattison, "Income Growth and Future Poverty Rates of the Aged," *Social Security Bulletin*, vol. 64 no. 3, January 2003, at [http://www.ssa.gov/ policy/docs/ssb/v64n3/v64n3p23 .pdf].

[7] CRS estimate produced using the Urban Institute's Dynasim microsmiluation model, which uses the intermediate assumptions about price and wage growth from the 2005 Social Security Trustees Report.

[8] Social Security Administration, "The Distributional Consequences of a 'No-Action' Scenario: Updated Results," Policy Brief No. 2005-01, available at [http://www.ssa.gov/ policy/docs/policybriefs/pb2005-0 1 .pdf]. Note that this paper focuses on the baby boomer Social Security beneficiary population (born between 1946 and 1964).

[9] Estimate produced using Dynasim. According to the 2007 Social Security Trustees Report, if no action were taken before projected trust fund exhaustion in 2041, benefits would need to be reduced by about 25% in 2041, rising to 30% by 2081, in order to balance annual income and spending. (Tax increases could also be used to achieve cash-flow balance.) If the changes were undertaken immediately, the benefit reductions would only need to be half the size of the projected 2041 cuts. (Social Security Administration, *2007 Annual Report of the Board of Trustees of the Federal Old-Age and Survivors Insurance and Disability Insurance Trust Funds*, April 23, 2007, at [http://www.ssa.gov/OACT/TR/TR07/tr07.pdf].)

[10] For examples, see CRS Report RL33544, *Social Security Reform: Current Issues and Legislation*, by Dawn Nuschler.

[11] See President's Commission to Strengthen Social Security, "Strengthening Social Security and Creating Personal Wealth for All Americans, the Final Report of the President's Commission to Strengthen Social Security," December 21, 2001, at [http://www.csss.gov/ reports/].

[12] Estimate produced using Dynasim.

[13] Press conference by President George W. Bush, April 28, 2005, at [http://www.white house.gov/news/releases/2005/04/20050428-9.html].

[14] See CRS Report RL32900, *Indexing Social Security Benefits: The Effects of Price and Wage Indexes*, by Patrick Purcell, Laura Haltzel, and Neela K. Ranade.

[15] Robert Pozen, testimony before Senate Finance Committee hearing, "Proposals To Achieve Sustainable Solvency, With and Without Personal Accounts," April 26, 2005, at [http://www.senate.gov/ ~finance/hearings/testimony/2005test/ptest042605 .pdf].

[16] Estimate produced using Dynasim.

[17] See also Wade D. Pfau, "Comparing the Impacts of Social Security Benefit Reductions on the Income Distribution of the Elderly," *National Tax Journal*, vol. LVIV, no. 2, June 2006.

[18] This estimate was calculated by dividing the number of elderly Social Security beneficiaries reported by SSA in the *2007 Statistical Supplement* by the number of elderly individuals in the Social Security area in the *2007 Trustees Report.*

[19] CRS Report RL32697, *Income and Poverty Among Older Americans in 2006*, by Patrick Purcell.

[20] Ibid.

[21] For example, see Paul S. Davies, et al., "Modeling SSI Financial Eligibility and Simulating the Effect of Policy Options," *Social Security Bulletin*, vol. 64 no. 2, September 2002, at [http://www.ssa.gov/ policy/docs/ssb/v64n2/v64n2p 1 6.pdf], and Todd E. Elder and Elizabeth T. Powers, "The Incredible

Shrinking Program: Trends in SSI Participation of the Aged," *Research on Aging*, vol. 28, no. 3, 2006. (Cited hereafter as Elder & Powers, 2006.)

[22] Poverty reduction was one of the goals of Social Security, but not its primary purpose. Upon signing the Social Security Act in 1935, President Franklin Roosevelt said, "we have tried to frame a law which will give some measure of protection to the average citizen and to his family against the loss of a job and *against poverty-ridden old age*" (emphasis added).

[23] Estimate produced using March 2007 Current Population Survey.

[24] The Urban Institute, *Minimum Benefits in Social Security*, by Melissa M. Favreault, et al., August 2006, at [http://www.urban.org/UploadedPDF/411 406_Minimum_Benefits.pdf]. The official poverty thresholds are determined by the U.S. Census Bureau. See "Poverty Thresholds 2007," at [http://www.census.gov/hhes/www/poverty/threshld/thresh07.html].

[25] Social Security's primary insurance amount (PIA) is the basic benefit amount before reductions and credits are applied; this is what beneficiaries would receive if they retired at their full retirement ages.

[26] Annual earnings must be at least 15% of the old-law contribution wage base to count toward special minimum PIA eligibility. In 2008, this level is $11,385, which is higher than what is required to earn four credits (one year) toward insured status ($4,200 in 2008).

[27] Social Security Administration, "Social Security's Special Minimum Benefit," *Social Security Bulletin*, vol. 64, no. 2, 2001/2002, by Kelly A. Olsen and Don Hoffmeyer. (Hereafter, SSA, "Special Minimum Benefit.")

[28] Social Security Administration, Office of the Chief Actuary, "Projected Demise of the Special Minimum PIA," Actuarial Note No. 143, October 2000, by Craig A. Feinstein, at [http://www.ssa.gov/OACT/NOTES/pdf_notes/note 143 .pdf].

[29] Some beneficiaries receive the special minimum because they are subject to the windfall elimination provision (WEP), which reduces Social Security benefits for those who also receive noncovered pensions. An estimated 12% of beneficiaries who received the special minimum in 2000 also had noncovered pension income (SSA, "Special Minimum Benefit").

[30] Social Security Administration, *Annual Statistical Supplement, 2006*, Table 5.A8, at [http://www.ssa.gov/policy/docs/statcomps/supplement/2006/].

[31] Upon signing the act that established SSI in 1972, President Richard Nixon said, "America has always cared for its aged poor, the blind, and the disabled — and this bill will move that concern to higher ground by providing better and more equitable benefits."

[32] Estimate for 2006 produced using March 2007 Current Population Survey.

[33] The 2007 federal benefit rate was $623 for individuals and $934 for couples, while the monthly poverty threshold was $829 for elderly individuals and $1044 for elderly couples.

[34] The scheduled baseline assumes the current benefit formula is maintained with no reductions; the payable baseline assumes current-law benefits are cut across the board to balance Social Security's annual income and spending at the point of insolvency.

[35] CRS Report RS20294, *SSI Income and Resource Limits: A Fact Sheet,* by Scott Szymendera.

[36] CRS Report RL32279, *Primer on Disability Benefits: Social Security Disability Insurance (SSDI) and Supplemental Security Income (SSI)*, by Scott Szymendera.

[37] Only 15% of federally eligible households received LIHEAP in 2005. (CRS Report RL3 1865, *The Low-Income Home Energy Assistance Program (LIHEAP): Program and Funding*, by Libby Perl.)

[38] On several occasions in the past, when changes to Social Security benefits would have made some beneficiaries ineligible for SSI, Congress has deemed such individuals eligible for SSI for the purpose of receiving Medicaid benefits.

[39] To be insured for a retirement benefit, an individual needs to have at least 40 credits, or 10 years of covered work. An individual would not have to be eligible for the current law special minimum to qualify for this alternative minimum benefit.

[40] In fact, creating a minimum benefit equal to the poverty line (as in Option #1) would also disproportionately benefit people with longer work histories. For example, about 8% of poor elderly with more than 40 years of work are projected to be brought out of poverty by the option, compared to about 4% of poor elderly with fewer than 20 years of work.

[41] S. 1878 in the 108th Congress; for more details, see the Social Security Administration memorandum to Stephen C. Goss, Chief Actuary, from Chris Chaplain, Actuary, and Alice H. Wade, Deputy Chief Actuary, "Estimated OASDI Financial Effects of 'Social Security Solvency and Modernization Act of 2003,' introduced by Senator Lindsey Graham," November 18, 2003, at [http://www.ssa.gov/OACT/solvency/LGraham_2003 111 8.html].

[42] For example, the PIA for an individual with 35 years of work would be 120% of the monthly single elderly poverty threshold in the year of eligibility. The option would not apply to individuals receiving Social Security disability (DI) benefits. However, when a DI beneficiary is converted to retired worker benefits at his or her full retirement age (as required by law), a modified sliding-scale minimum benefit formula would apply, which would reflect the number of years the disabled individual was able to work. The minimum benefit would be 120% of the poverty threshold for workers with at least 3.5 times as many Social Security credits as elapsed years, gradually scaling down to no minimum benefit for workers with credits equal to the number of

their elapsed years. This modified scale would also apply to survivor beneficiaries in cases where the worker died before age 62.

[43] In 2007, the monthly SSI federal benefit rate was $623 for individuals and $934 for couples; the monthly poverty thresholds were about $829 for elderly individuals and $1,044 for elderly couples. Both of these thresholds rise with inflation.

[44] About 2.5 million elderly are projected to receive SSI under the payable baseline in 2042. Though the model assumes that the proportion of qualifying individuals who take up SSI benefits would not change, it is likely that the proportion would increase if SSI were made more generous.

[45] The federal benefit amount, and thus income limits, rise each year with inflation.

[46] Social Security Administration, "Legislative History of the SSI Program," *Annual Statistical Supplement*, 2000, at [http://www.ssa.gov/history/pdf/ssi.pdf].

[47] H.R. 1682 in 1 09th Congress, also introduced in earlier Congresses.

[48] About 2.5 million elderly are projected to receive SSI under the payable baseline in 2042. Though the model assumes that the proportion of qualifying individuals who take up SSI benefits would not change, it is likely that the proportion would increase if SSI were made more generous.

[49] Dynasim is not a Social Security actuarial model and thus cannot estimate the solvency effect of a proposed policy change. The Dynasim model does not contain all of the information required to produce solvency estimates. For example, Dynasim does not calculate children's benefits and so a complete account of benefit payments cannot be calculated. In addition, Dynasim simulates the population between the years 1993 and 2050. The benefits received by individuals outside of this yearly range would not be included in the calculations. For these same reasons, long-term cost estimates cannot be calculated.

[50] Social Security Administration, *Defined Contribution Pension Plans and the Supplemental Security Income Program*, Policy Brief No. 2006-01, March 2006, at [http://www.ssa.gov/policy/docs/policybriefs/pb2006-0 1 .pdf].

[51] See CRS Report RL3 1414, *Baseline Budget Projections: A Discussion of Issues*, by Marc Labonte.

[52] For a more detailed explanation of the Dynasim model, please see Urban Institute, "A Primer on the Dynamic Simulation of Income Model (DYNASIM3)," by Melissa Favreault and Karen E. Smith, February 1, 2004, at [http://www.urban.org/url.cfm?ID=4 10961].

[53] According to the 2007 Social Security Trustees Report, if no action were taken before projected trust fund exhaustion in 2041, benefits would need to be reduced by about 25% in 2041, rising to 30% by 2081, in order to balance annual income and spending.

[54] The Dynasim model projects nuclear families, not households.

[55] The federal poverty thresholds are an absolute measure of income. Historically, since wages have risen faster than prices, the American standard of living has risen over time. Since the official poverty thresholds are increased with inflation, they measure the amount of income necessary to maintain a constant standard of living — not the amount of income needed to keep up with rising standards of living. Assuming wages continue to grow faster than prices, the disparity between rising real incomes and a fixed real poverty threshold will lead to a decreasing proportion of the population being in poverty.

[56] The poverty thresholds for the elderly are lower than those for the non-elderly. In 2007, the threshold for working-age people was $10,787 for an individual and $13,884 for a couple. (U.S. Census Bureau, "Poverty Thresholds 2007," at [http://www.census.gov/hhes/ www/poverty/threshld/thresh07.html].)

[57] The poverty measure counts most sources of pre-tax money income (e.g., earnings, Social Security, pensions, cash public assistance, interest and dividends, alimony and child support, among others). Noncash benefits (such as the value of Medicare and Medicaid, public housing, or employer-provided health care) and "near-cash" benefits (e.g., food stamps) are not counted as income, nor are tax payments subtracted from income, nor are tax credits added (e.g., Earned Income Tax Credit (EITC)).

[58] As described above, the academic literature estimates that about one-half to two-thirds of qualifying elderly participate in SSI.

[59] For example, see Elder & Powers, 2006.

In: Social Security Reform: Disability, Indexing and Financing ISBN: 978-1-61668-354-2
Editor: Janet U. Burlington

Chapter 4

SOCIAL SECURITY REFORM: CURRENT ISSUES AND LEGISLATION*

Dawn Nuschler

SUMMARY

In recent years, an initiative by former President Bush to restructure Social Security through the creation of individual accounts moved Social Security reform to the forefront of the political debate. While much attention has been focused on the issue, there has been no legislative action. In the *Fiscal Year 2010 President's Budget*, President Obama stated that he does not support the creation of individual accounts within the Social Security system.

The spectrum of ideas for reform range from relatively minor changes to the pay-as-you-go social insurance system enacted in the 1930s to a redesigned, "modernized" program based on personal savings and investments modeled after IRAs and 401(k)s. Proponents of the fundamentally different approaches to reform cite varying policy objectives that go beyond simply restoring long-term financial stability to the Social Security system. They cite objectives that focus on improving the adequacy and equity of benefits, as well as those that reflect different philosophical views about the role of the Social Security program and the federal government in providing retirement income. However, the system's projected long-range financial outlook provides a backdrop for much of the Social Security reform debate in terms of the timing and degree of recommended program changes.

Currently, the Social Security system is generating surplus tax revenues. However, its board of trustees projects that the trust funds will be depleted in 2037, at which point an estimated 76% of scheduled annual benefits will be payable with incoming receipts (under the intermediate projections). The primary reason is demographics. Between 2010 and 2030, the number of people aged 65 and older is projected to increase by 75%, while the number of workers supporting the system is projected to increase by 8%. In addition, the trustees project that the system will begin running cash flow deficits in 2016, at which point other federal

* This is an edited, reformatted and augmented version of a CRS Report for Congress publication dated May 2009.

receipts will be needed to meet benefit costs. If there are no other surplus governmental receipts, policymakers would have three options: raise taxes or other income, reduce spending, or borrow.

Public opinion polls show that fewer than 50% of respondents are confident that Social Security can meet its long-term commitments. There is also a public perception that Social Security may not be as good a value for future retirees. These concerns, and a belief that the nation must increase national savings, have led to proposals to redesign the system. At the same time, others suggest that the system's financial outlook is not a "crisis" in need of immediate action. Supporters of the current program structure point out that the system is now running surpluses, continues to have public support and could be affected adversely by the risk associated with some of the reform ideas. They contend that only modest changes are needed to restore long-range solvency to the Social Security system.

During the 110th Congress, six Social Security reform measures were introduced, five of which would have established individual accounts. None of the measures received congressional action. During the 111th Congress, two Social Security reform measures have been introduced. This report will be updated as legislative activity warrants.

Background

In recent years, an initiative by former President Bush to restructure Social Security through the creation of individual accounts moved Social Security reform to the forefront of the political debate. The former President advocated a pre-funded system in which benefits would be based increasingly on personal savings and investments through the creation of individual Social Security accounts. He pointed to the system's projected long-range funding shortfall as a driver for change in conjunction with his vision of an "ownership society." Most Democrats have supported maintaining the current program structure (i.e., a defined benefit system funded on a pay-as-you-go basis), pointing to the system's projected long-range financial outlook to support their view that the system is not in "crisis" and that only modest program changes may be needed. In the *Fiscal Year 2010 President's Budget*, President Obama stated that he does not support the creation of individual accounts within the Social Security system.[1]

Proponents of the fundamentally different approaches to reform (ranging from relatively minor changes to the current pay-as-you-go social insurance system to the creation of a "modernized" program based on personal savings and investments modeled after IRAs and 401 (k)s) cite varying policy objectives that go beyond simply restoring long-term financial stability to the system. They cite objectives that focus on improving the adequacy and equity of benefits, as well as those that reflect different philosophical views about the role of the Social Security program and the federal government in providing retirement income. However, the system's projected long-range financial outlook provides a backdrop for much of the Social Security reform debate in terms of the timing and degree of recommended program changes. For example, one of the key criteria used to evaluate any reform proposal is its projected impact on the Social Security trust funds. To place the discussion of Social Security reform issues into context, this report looks first at the long-range projections for the Social Security trust funds, then at the various objectives and proposals for reform.

Currently, Social Security income exceeds expenditures. However, the Social Security Board of Trustees[2] projects that Social Security expenditures will exceed income by 14% on average over the next 75 years.[3] In addition, the trustees project that the Social Security trust funds will be exhausted by 2037, at which point incoming receipts will cover an estimated 76% of scheduled annual benefits.[4] One of the primary reasons is demographics. The first wave of the post-World War II baby boom generation began retiring in 2008 and projected increases in life expectancy will contribute to an older society. Between 2010 and 2030, the number of people aged 65 and older is projected to increase by 75%, while the number of workers whose taxes will finance future benefits is projected to increase by 8%. As a result, the number of workers supporting each Social Security recipient is projected to decline from 3.1 today to 2.1 in 2035.[5] In addition, program design features contribute to the projected growth in program spending. For example, elements of the Social Security benefit formula are indexed to wage growth, resulting in a projected increase in the value of benefits for future retirees.

Social Security revenues are paid into the U.S. Treasury and most of the proceeds are used to pay benefits. Surplus revenues are invested in federal securities recorded to the Old-Age, Survivors, and Disability Insurance (OASDI) trust funds maintained by the Treasury Department.[6] Social Security benefits and administrative costs are paid out of the Treasury and a corresponding amount of trust fund securities are redeemed. When current Social Security taxes are insufficient to pay benefits, the trust fund's securities are redeemed and Treasury makes up the difference with other receipts.

Currently, Social Security tax revenues exceed what is needed to pay benefits and administrative costs. Surplus tax revenues and interest credited to the trust funds in the form of government bonds appear as growing trust fund balances. Beginning in 2024, however, program expenditures are projected to exceed total income (tax revenues plus interest income), and trust fund assets will begin to be drawn down. By 2037, the trust funds are projected to be exhausted and technically insolvent (see **Table 1** and **Figure 1**).

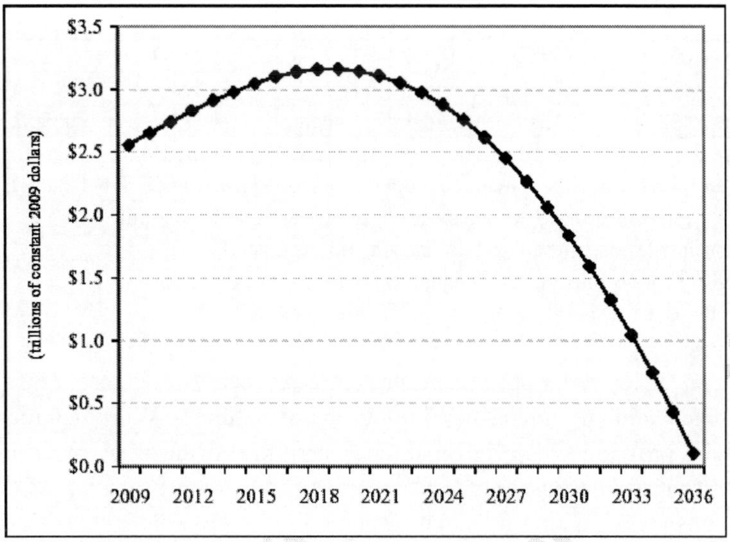

Figure 1. Projected Social Security Surpluses/Deficits, Under Intermediate Assumptions of the 2009 Trustees Report, Calendar Years 2009-2036

Table 1. Projected Income and Outgo of the Social Security Trust Funds, Under Intermediate Assumptions, Calendar Years 2009-2036 (in billions of constant 2009 dollars)

	Tax Revenues	Interest Income	Total Income	Cost	Annual Surplus/ Deficita	Cash Flow Surplus/ Deficitb	Trust Fund Balance
2009	701.3	118.1	819.4	682.5	136.9	18.8	2,555.5
2010	715.8	118.1	833.9	697.8	136.1	18.0	2,650.1
2011	733.9	121.5	855.4	706.6	148.8	27.3	2,738.2
2012	758.5	127.4	885.9	722.9	163.0	35.6	2,829.1
2013	776.8	134.7	911.5	747.0	164.5	29.8	2,909.2
2014	791.6	141.9	933.5	775.5	158.0	16.1	2,980.7
2015	808.5	147.7	956.2	806.6	149.6	1.9	3,049.0
2016	822.3	152.7	974.9	838.0	136.9	-15.7	3,102.9
2017	836.3	157.5	993.9	871.1	122.8	-34.8	3,141.2
2018	849.5	162.1	1,011.6	905.1	106.5	-55.6	3,162.1
2019	863.4	165.6	1,029.0	940.8	88.2	-77.4	3,164.1
2020	877.4	168.0	1,045.4	976.9	68.5	-99.5	3,146.4
2021	891.5	169.3	1,060.8	1,012.3	48.5	-120.8	3,109.2
2022	905.8	169.4	1,075.2	1,047.0	28.2	-141.2	3,052.7
2023	920.4	168.2	1,088.5	1,081.5	7.0	-161.1	2,976.6
2024	935.1	163.4	1,098.5	1,115.7	-17.2	-180.6	2,878.3
2025	950.1	157.3	1,107.4	1,149.4	-42.0	-199.3	2,757.9
2026	965.1	150.1	1,115.2	1,182.3	-67.1	-217.2	2,615.6
2027	980.5	141.6	1,122.1	1,214.9	-92.8	-234.4	2,451.6
2028	996.0	132.0	1,128.0	1,247.0	-119.0	-251.0	2,265.8
2029	1,012.0	121.1	1,133.1	1,277.6	-144.5	-265.6	2,059.6
2030	1,028.3	109.1	1,137.4	1,307.8	-170.4	-279.5	1,833.2
2031	1,045.0	96.1	1,141.0	1,336.8	-195.8	-291.8	1,587.5
2032	1,062.0	81.9	1,143.9	1,364.9	-221.0	-302.9	1,323.2
2033	1,079.2	66.8	1,146.0	1,391.8	-245.8	-312.6	1,041.4
2034	1,096.7	50.8	1,147.4	1,417.3	-269.9	-320.6	743.2
2035	1,114.4	33.8	1,148.2	1,441.8	-293.6	-327.4	429.4
2036c	1,132.4	16.0	1,148.4	1,465.6	-317.2	-333.2	100.5

Source: CRS, on the basis of data from The 2009 Annual Report of the Board of Trustees of the Federal Old- Age and Survivors Insurance and Federal Disability Insurance Trust Funds, May 12, 2009, table VI.F7, available at http://www.ssa.gov/OACT/TR/2009/lr6f7.html.

a. The annual surplus/deficit is equal to total income minus cost.

b. The annual *cash flow* surplus/deficit is equal to tax revenues minus cost.

c. The Social Security trust fund is projected to be exhausted in 2037.

Beginning in 2016, program expenditures are projected to exceed Social Security tax revenues (income excluding interest credited to the trust funds). With the emergence of *cash flow* deficits, the program will rely on interest credited to the trust funds to meet annual expenditures. Because interest credited to the trust funds is an exchange of credits between Treasury accounts (rather than a financial resource for the government from outside sources), other federal receipts will be needed to meet the program's costs. If there are no other surplus governmental receipts, policymakers would have three options: raise taxes, reduce spending, or borrow the money from the public (i.e., replace bonds held by the trust funds with bonds held by the public). The program's reliance on general revenues is projected to be about $100 billion by 2020 and $280 billion by 2030 (in constant 2009 dollars). Projected annual Social Security surpluses and deficits, as well as projected annual *cash flow* surpluses and deficits, are shown in **Table 1** and **Figure 2**.

In 2009, the cost of the Social Security program is estimated to be $682.5 billion, an amount equal to 12.35% of workers' pay subject to Social Security payroll taxes (or taxable payroll).[7] The trustees project that program costs will increase sharply between 2010 and 2030 as the baby boom generation moves into retirement. As a share of taxable payroll, the cost of the program is projected to reach 12.88% in 2015, 14.50% in 2020, and 16.76% in 2030. Program costs are then projected to increase at a slower rate for about five years, reaching 17.10% of taxable payroll in 2035. Beyond 2035, program costs as a share of taxable payroll are projected to remain relatively stable for several decades before gradually increasing to 17.68% of taxable payroll in 2083 (the end of the projection period). By comparison, projections show relatively small increases in income rates over the period. As a percentage of taxable payroll, program income is projected to increase from 12.83% in 2009 to 13.34% in 2083. Income rates are projected to remain relatively stable over the period because the Social Security payroll tax rate (12.4%) is fixed under current law, and income from the taxation of Social Security benefits is projected to increase gradually as the proportion of beneficiaries who must pay income taxes on part of their benefits increases gradually over time.[8] As shown in **Table 2**, the gap between income and expenditures is projected to increase over the 75-year projection period. By 2083, program costs are projected to exceed income by 33% (an amount equal to 4.34% of taxable payroll). Over the 75-year period, *on average*, the cost of the program is projected to exceed income by 14% (an amount equal to 2.00% of taxable payroll).

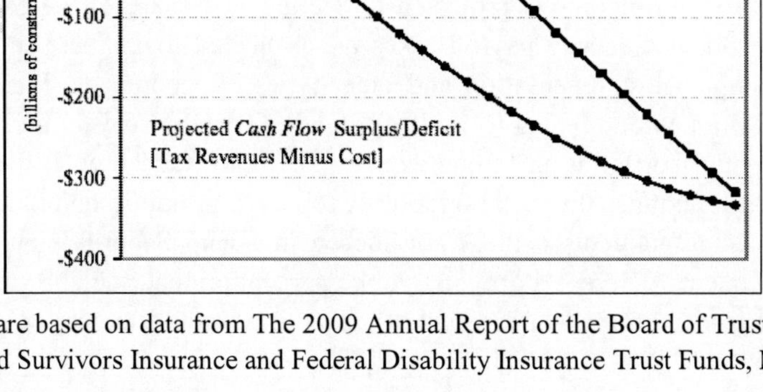

Source: Figures are based on data from The 2009 Annual Report of the Board of Trustees of the Federal Old-Age and Survivors Insurance and Federal Disability Insurance Trust Funds, May 12, 2009.

Figure 2. Projected Social Security Surpluses/Deficits, Under Intermediate Assumptions of the 2009 Trustees Report, Calendar Years 2009-2036

Table 2. Projected Social Security Income Rate, Cost Rate, and Balance as a Percentage of Taxable Payroll, Selected CalendarYears 2009-2085 (under the intermediate assumptions of the 2009 trustees report)

	Income Rate	Cost Rate	Balance
2009	12.83	12.35	0.48
2010	12.87	12.50	0.37
2015	12.94	12.88	0.06
2020	13.04	14.50	-1.46
2025	13.13	15.86	-2.73
2030	13.20	16.76	-3.56
2035	13.24	17.10	-3.86
2040	13.25	16.99	-3.74
2045	13.25	16.75	-3.50
2050	13.25	16.61	-3.36
2055	13.26	16.62	-3.36
2060	13.27	16.73	-3.45
2065	13.28	16.86	-3.57
2070	13.30	17.05	-3.75
2075	13.32	17.27	-3.96
2080	13.33	17.53	-4.19
2085	13.35	17.78	-4.43
75 years: 2009-2083	14.02	16.02	-2.00

Source: The 2009 Annual Report of the Board of Trustees of the Federal Old-Age and Survivors Insurance and Federal Disability Insurance Trust Funds, May 12, 2009, table VI.F2, p. 179, and table VI.F3, p. 181.

Program costs and income are also evaluated relative to the size of the economy. As a percentage of Gross Domestic Product (GDP), program costs are projected to increase from 4.84% in 2009 to a peak of 6.17% in 2034. Program costs are then projected to decline slightly as a share of GDP before stabilizing at about 5.8% during the 205 0-2083 period. By comparison, program income is projected to remain relatively stable over the projection period, declining gradually as a percentage of GDP from 4.98% in 2009 to 4.76% in 2035 and 4.41% in 2083. Program income is projected to decline as a share of the economy because wages subject to Social Security payroll taxes are projected to increase more slowly than other forms of employee compensation and other types of income. In 2083, the projected funding shortfall is an amount equal to 1.45% of GDP. Over the 75-year period, *on average*, the projected funding shortfall is an amount equal to 0.72% of GDP (see **Table 3**).

The projected long-range financial outlook is reflected in public opinion polls that show fewer than 50% of respondents express confidence in Social Security's ability to meet its long-term commitments. There is a growing public perception that Social Security may not be as good a value in the future. Until recent years, retirees could expect to receive more in benefits than they paid in Social Security taxes. However, because Social Security tax rates have increased to cover the costs of the maturing "pay-as-you-go" system, these ratios have become less favorable. Such concerns, and a belief that the nation must increase national savings to meet the needs of an aging society, are among the factors behind reform efforts.

Table 3. Projected Social Security Income, Cost, and Balance as a Percentage of Gross Domestic Product (GDP), Selected Calendar Years 2009-2085 (under the intermediate assumptions of the 2009 trustees report)

	Income	Cost	Balance
2009	4.98	4.84	0.13
2010	4.99	4.86	0.13
2015	4.90	4.89	0.01
2020	4.87	5.42	-0.55
2025	4.84	5.85	-1.01
2030	4.80	6.11	-1.30
2035	4.76	6.16	-1.40
2040	4.72	6.06	-1.34
2045	4.68	5.92	-1.25
2050	4.64	5.82	-1.18
2055	4.60	5.77	-1.17
2060	4.57	5.76	-1.20
2065	4.53	5.76	-1.23
2070	4.50	5.78	-1.28
2075	4.47	5.80	-1.34
2080	4.43	5.84	-1.40
2085	4.40	5.87	-1.47
75 years: 2009-2083	5.03	5.75	-0.72

Source: The 2009 Annual Report of the Board of Trustees of the Federal Old-Age and Survivors Insurance and Federal Disability Insurance Trust Funds, May 12, 2009, table VI.F4, p. 184.

Supporters of the current program structure suggest that the issues confronting the system are not as serious as sometimes portrayed and believe there is no imminent crisis. They point out that the system is now running surpluses, that there continues to be public support for the program, and there would be considerable risk in some of the reform ideas. They contend that relatively modest changes could restore long-range solvency to the system.

Basic Debate

The Social Security system has faced funding shortfalls in the past. In 1977 and 1983, Congress enacted a variety of measures to address the system's financial imbalance. These measures include constraints on the growth of initial benefit levels, a gradual increase in the full retirement age from 65 to 67 (i.e., the age at which unreduced benefits are payable), payroll tax increases, taxation of benefits for higher-income recipients, and extension of Social Security coverage to federal and nonprofit workers. Subsequently, projections showed the re-emergence of long-term deficits as a result of changes in actuarial methods and assumptions, and because program changes had been evaluated with respect to their effect on the *average* 75-year deficit. That is, while program changes were projected to restore trust fund solvency on average over the 75-year period, a period of surpluses was followed by a period of deficits.

Some policymakers believe that some type of action should be taken sooner rather than later. This view has been shared by the Social Security trustees and other panels and commissions that have examined the issue. In recent years, a wide range of interest groups have echoed this view in testimony before Congress. However, there is no consensus on whether the projections represent a "crisis." In 1977 and 1983, the trust fund balances were projected to fall to zero within a very short period (within months of the 1983 reforms). Today, the problem is perceived to be as few as 8 or as many as 29 years away. Lacking a "crisis," the pressure to compromise is diffused and the issues and the divergent views about them have led to myriad complex proposals. In 1977 and 1983, the debate was not about fundamental reform. Rather, it revolved around how to raise the system's income and constrain costs. Today, the ideas range from restoring the system's solvency with as few alterations as possible to replacing it entirely with something modeled after IRAs or 401(k)s. This broad spectrum was reflected in the 1997 Social Security Advisory Council report, which presented three different reform plans. None of the plans was supported by a majority of the 13-member council. Similar diversity is reflected in the Social Security reform bills introduced in recent Congresses.

Push for Major Reform

Advocates of reform view Social Security as an anachronism, built on depression-era concerns about high unemployment and widespread "dependency" among the aged. They see the prospect of reform today as an opportunity to "modernize" the way society saves for retirement. They maintain that the vast economic, social and demographic changes that have transpired over the past 70 years require the system to change, and they point to changes made in other countries that now use market-based individual accounts to strengthen retirement incomes and bolster their economies by spurring savings and investments. They believe government-run, pay-as-you-go systems are unsustainable in aging societies. They prefer a system that allows workers to acquire wealth and provide for their retirement by investing in individual accounts.

Reform advocates also view it as a way to counter skepticism about the current system by giving workers a greater sense of "ownership" of their retirement savings. They contend that private investments would yield larger retirement incomes because stocks and bonds historically have provided higher returns than are projected from the current system. Some believe that individual accounts would address what they view as the system's contradictory mix of insurance and social welfare goals (although benefits are not based strictly on a worker's contributions, many of its social benefits go to financially well-off individuals in the absence of a means test). Others maintain that creating a system of individual accounts would prevent the government from using surplus Social Security taxes for other government spending. Recent stock market declines, however, may make investment-based proposals less popular among some policymakers in the near term.

Some, who do not necessarily seek a new system, view enactment of long-range Social Security constraints as one way to curb federal entitlement spending. The aging of society means that the cost of entitlement programs that aid the elderly will increase greatly in the future. The costs of the largest entitlement programs (Social Security, Medicare and Medicaid) are directly linked to an aging population. Proponents of imposing constraints on these programs express concern that, if left unchecked, their costs would place pressure on the federal budget far into the future, consuming resources that could be used for other priorities and forcing future generations to bear a much higher tax burden.

As a matter of fairness, it has been pointed out that many current recipients get back more than the value of their Social Security contributions, and far more than the baby boom generation will receive. They believe that to delay making changes to the program is unfair to current workers, who must pay for "transfer" payments that they characterize as "overgenerous" and unrelated to need, while facing the prospect that their own benefits may have to be scaled back severely. Others emphasize the system's projected long-range funding shortfall and contend that steps should be taken soon (e.g., raising the full retirement age, constraining the growth of initial monthly benefits for future retirees, reducing COLAs, raising taxes) so that changes can be phased in, allowing workers more time to adjust their retirement expectations and plans to reflect what the program will be able to provide in the future. They maintain that more abrupt changes in taxes and benefits would be required otherwise.

Arguments for Retaining the Existing System

Those who favor a more restrained approach believe that the issues facing the system can be resolved with modest tax and spending changes, and that the program's critics are raising the specter that Social Security will "bankrupt the nation" to undermine public support and provide an excuse to incorporate individual accounts into the system. They contend that individual savings accounts would erode the social insurance nature of the current system that favors low- income workers, survivors and the disabled.

Others are concerned that switching to a new system of individual accounts would pose large transition problems by requiring younger workers to save for their own retirement while paying taxes to cover benefits for current retirees. Some doubt that it would increase national savings, arguing that higher government debt (resulting from the redirection of current payroll taxes to individual accounts) would offset the increased individual account savings. They also contend that the capital markets' inflow created by the accounts would make the markets difficult to regulate and potentially distort equity valuations. They point out that some of the countries that have moved to individual accounts did so to create capital markets. Such markets, they argue, are already well developed in the United States.

Some believe that a system of individual accounts would expose participants to excessive market risk for an income source that has become essential to many of the nation's elderly. They say that the nation has a three-tiered retirement system (consisting of Social Security, private pensions and personal assets) that already includes private savings and investment components. They contend that while people may be willing and able to undertake some "risk" in the latter two tiers, Social Security (as the tier that provides a basic floor of protection) should be more stable. They further contend that the administrative costs of maintaining individual accounts could be very large and significantly erode the value of the accounts.

Some say that concerns about the future growth of entitlement spending are overblown, arguing that as people live longer, they will work longer as labor markets tighten and employers offer inducements for them to remain on the job. They state that a projected low ratio of workers to dependents is not unprecedented, as it existed when the baby boomers were in their youth.

SPECIFIC AREAS OF CONTENTION

System's Financial Outlook

There are conflicting views about the severity of Social Security's projected funding shortfall. Some maintain that the problem is more acute than portrayed under the traditional 75-year projections that show an average 75-year deficit equal to 2.00% of taxable payroll ($5.3 trillion in present value terms). They believe this view is supported by an alternative portrayal in the trustees' report that extends the projections indefinitely into the future. On an "infinite horizon" basis, the projected funding shortfall is equal to 3.4% of taxable payroll ($15.1 trillion in present value terms). They also point out that, in 2030, the cost of the system is projected to exceed income by 3.56% of taxable payroll (costs are projected to exceed income by 27%) and that, in 2083, the cost of the system is projected to exceed income by 4.34% of taxable payroll (costs are projected to exceed income by 33%). Therefore, on a pay-as-you-go basis, the system would require more than a 14% change in taxes or expenditures over the next 75 years to cover projected program costs (over the next 75 years, on average, the cost of the system is projected to exceed income by 14%).

They maintain that viewing the problem as 29 years away (the trust funds are projected to have a balance until 2037) does not take into account the pressure Social Security will exert on the federal budget beginning in 2016 when annual cash flow deficits are projected to emerge and the system begins to rely on interest credited to the trust funds to meet annual expenditures. At that point, the government would have to rely on other resources to help cover program costs, resources that could be used to finance other governmental functions.[9]

Others express concern that the problem is being exaggerated. They maintain that, in contrast to earlier episodes of financial imbalance, the system has no immediate problem: surplus tax receipts are projected for 7 years and the trust funds are projected to have a positive balance for 28 years. They state that projections for the next 75 years, let alone the indefinite future, cannot be viewed with any significant degree of confidence and that Congress should respond to the projections with caution. They point out that, even if the 75-year projections hold, the average imbalance could be eliminated by increasing the combined payroll tax rate immediately by 2.01 percentage points. While acknowledging that the cost of the system is projected to represent a notably larger share of GDP in the future (increasing from 4.84% of GDP today to a peak of 6.17% of GDP in 2034), they point out that GDP itself would have risen substantially in real terms. Moreover, while the ratio of workers to recipients is projected to decline, they believe that employers are likely to respond with inducements for older workers to stay on the job longer. Phased-in retirements are becoming more prevalent, and some older workers are viewing retirement increasingly as more than an all-or-nothing decision.

Public Confidence

In recent years, public opinion polls have shown that a majority of Americans lack confidence in the system's ability to meet its future commitments. Although skepticism abated following enactment of legislation in 1983 to shore up the system, it has risen again with just over half of the public expressing a lack of confidence (*CBS News/New York Times Poll*, June 2005). Younger workers are particularly skeptical. For example, 62% of persons aged 18-34, 56% of persons aged 35-44, and 49% of persons aged 45-54 expressed a lack of confidence in the system's ability to pay benefits scheduled under current law in the future, compared with 16% of persons aged 55 and older (*Newsweek Poll*, February 2005). In a more recent poll in which respondents were asked to describe the current financial situation of Social Security, 66% said the system is in "crisis" (30%) or in "serious trouble" (36%). Another 26% said the system is in "some trouble," 5% said the system is "not in trouble," and 3% said they are "unsure" (CBS News Poll, October 2007).[10]

Some observers express caution about inferring too much from polling data, arguing that public understanding of Social Security is limited and often inaccurate. They maintain that a major reason confidence is highest among older persons is that they have learned more about Social Security because they are more immediately affected by the program. Some believe that the annual statements provided by the Social Security Administration will make workers more aware of their estimated future benefits scheduled under current law and thus more trusting of the system. Others, however, suggest that the skepticism is justified by the system's repeated financial difficulties and diminished "money's worth" for younger workers.

Doubts about Money's Worth

Until recent years, Social Security recipients received more, often far more, than the value of the Social Security taxes they paid. However, because Social Security tax rates have increased over the years and the full retirement age (the age at which unreduced benefits are payable) is being increased gradually, it is becoming more apparent that Social Security will be less of a good deal for many future retirees. For example, for workers who earned average wages and retired in 1980 at age 65, it took 2.8 years to recover the value of the retirement portion of the combined employee and employer shares of their Social Security taxes plus interest. For their counterparts who retired at age 65 in 2003, it will take 17.4 years. For those retiring in 2020, it will take 21.6 years. Some observers believe these discrepancies are inequitable and cite them as evidence that the system needs to be substantially restructured.

Others discount this phenomenon, viewing Social Security as a *social insurance* program serving social ends that transcend questions of whether some individuals fare better than others. For example, the program's anti-poverty features replace a higher proportion of earnings for lower- paid workers and provide additional benefits for workers with families. In addition, current workers, who will receive less direct value from their taxes compared to current retirees, have in large part been relieved from having to support their parents, and many elderly are able to live independently and with dignity. These observers contend that the value of these aspects of the program is not reflected in comparisons of taxes and benefits.

Debate over Individual Accounts

Social Security's projected long-range financial outlook, skepticism about the sustainability of the current system, and a belief that economic growth could be bolstered through increased savings have led to a number of proposals to incorporate individual accounts into the Social Security system, reviving a debate that dates back to the creation of the program in 1935. All three plans presented by the 1994-1996 Social Security Advisory Council featured program involvement in the financial markets. The first called upon Congress to consider authorizing investment of part of the Social Security trust funds in equities (on the assumption that stocks would produce a higher return to the system). The second would require workers to contribute an extra 1.6% of pay to individual accounts to make up for Social Security benefit reductions called for under the plan to restore the system's long-range solvency. The third would redesign the system by gradually replacing Social Security retirement benefits with flat-rate benefits based on length of service and individual accounts (funded with 5 percentage points of the current Social Security tax rate).[11]

The reform that Chile enacted in 1981, which replaced a troubled pay-as-you-go system with one requiring workers to invest part of their earnings in individual accounts through government-approved pension funds, has been reflected in a number of reform bills introduced in recent Congresses.[12] These measures would permit or require workers to invest some or all of their Social Security payroll taxes in individual accounts. Most call for future Social Security benefits to be reduced or forfeited. Similarly, the three options presented by the Social Security reform commission appointed by former President Bush in 2001 would allow workers to participate in individual accounts and would reduce their future Social Security benefit by the projected value of the account based on an assumed (rather than the actual) rate of return.[13]

Another approach is reflected in bills that would require any budget surpluses to be used to finance individual accounts to supplement Social Security benefits for those who pay Social Security payroll taxes. Former President Clinton's January 1999 reform plan would have allocated a portion of budget surpluses to individual accounts, supplemented by a worker's own contributions and a government match (scaled to income). In addition, the plan would have redirected a portion of budget surpluses, or the interest savings resulting therefrom, to the Social Security trust funds. Some of the funds would have been used to acquire stocks, similar to the approach suggested in one of the Advisory Council plans and some past legislation. Most of these approaches would require establishment of an independent board to invest some of the funds in stocks or corporate bonds and the remaining funds in federal securities.

Some individual account proponents believe that individual accounts would reduce future financial demands on government and reassure workers by giving them a sense of "ownership" of their retirement savings. Others believe that individual accounts would enhance workers' retirement income because stocks and bonds generally have provided higher rates of return than are projected from Social Security. In conjunction with this, they maintain that individual accounts would increase national savings and promote economic growth. Others maintain that individual accounts would prevent the government from using surplus Social Security revenues to "mask" public borrowing, or for other spending or tax reductions. Generally, proponents of individual accounts express concern that "collective" investment of the Social Security trust funds in the markets would concentrate too much economic power in a government-appointed board.[14]

Opponents of individual accounts maintain that Social Security's projected long-range funding shortfall could be resolved without altering the fundamental nature of the program. They express concern that replacing Social Security with individual accounts would erode the social insurance aspects of the system that favor low-wage earners, survivors and the disabled. Others are concerned that individual accounts would pose large transition problems by requiring younger workers to save for their own retirement while simultaneously paying taxes to support current retirees, and would further exacerbate current budget deficits. Some doubt that individual accounts would increase national savings, maintaining that any increase in private savings would be offset by increased government borrowing. They also point out that the investment pool created by the accounts could be difficult to regulate and distort capital markets and equity valuations. Still others view it as exposing participants to excessive market risk for something as essential as core retirement benefits and, unlike Social Security, as providing poor protection against inflation. Many prefer "collective" investment of the Social Security trust funds in the markets to potentially bolster their returns and spread the risks of poor performance broadly.[15]

Retirement Age Issue

Raising the Social Security retirement age is often considered as a way to help restore long-range solvency to the system. Much of the projected growth in Social Security's costs is a result of projected increases in life expectancy. Since benefits were first paid in 1940, life expectancy for 65-year-old men and women has increased from 12.7 and 14.7 years, respectively, to 17.7 and 20.0 years, respectively. By 2030, life expectancy at age 65 is projected to reach 19.2 years for men and 21.4 years for women.[16] This trend bolstered arguments for increasing the full retirement age as a way to achieve savings when the system was facing major financial problems in the early 1 980s. Congress raised the "full benefit" age from 65 to 67 as part of the Social Security Amendments of 1983 (P.L. 98-2 1). The increase in the full retirement age enacted in 1983 is currently being phased in starting with persons born in 1938, with the full two-year increase affecting persons born in 1960 or later. The 1983 amendments did not raise the early retirement age (age 62). However, the benefit reduction for persons who retire at age 62 will increase from 20% to 30%. Proponents of increasing the early and/or full retirement age view it as reasonable in light of projected increases in life expectancy. Opponents believe it will penalize workers who already get a worse deal from Social Security compared to current retirees, persons who work in arduous occupations, and racial minorities and others who have shorter life expectancies.

Cost-of-Living Adjustments (COLA)

Social Security benefits are adjusted annually to reflect inflation as measured by the Bureau of Labor Statistics' (BLS) Consumer Price Index (CPI), which measures price increases for selected goods and services. The CPI has been criticized for overstating the effects of inflation, primarily because the index's market basket of goods and services was not revised regularly to reflect changes in consumer buying habits or improvements in quality. A BLS analysis in 1993 found that the annual overstatement may be as much as 0.6 percentage point. CBO estimated in 1994 that the overstatement ranged from 0.2 to 0.8 percentage point. A 1996 panel that studied the issue for the Senate Finance Committee argued that it may be 1.1 percentage points.[17] In response to its own analysis as well as outside criticisms, the BLS has since made various revisions to the CPI. To some extent, these revisions may account for part of the slower CPI growth in recent years. However, calls for adjustments continue.[18]

According to the Social Security Administration, a COLA reduction of 0.5 percentage point annually (beginning December 2009) would improve the system's long-range actuarial balance by an estimated 44%. Similarly, a COLA reduction of 1 percentage point annually would improve the long-range actuarial balance by an estimated 84%.[19] While some view further CPI changes as necessary to help keep Social Security and other entitlement spending under control, others view such changes as a backdoor way of reducing benefits. They maintain that the market basket of goods and services purchased by the elderly is different from that of the general population around whom the CPI is constructed. It is more heavily weighted with healthcare expenditures, which rise notably faster than the overall CPI, and thus they contend that the cost of living for the elderly is higher than reflected by the CPI.[20]

Social Security and the Budget

By law, Social Security is considered "off budget" for many aspects of developing and enforcing annual budget goals. However, it is a federal program and its income and outgo help shape the year-to-year financial condition of the federal government. As a result, policymakers often focus on "unified" (or overall) budget totals that include Social Security. When former President Clinton urged that the unified budget surpluses projected at the time be reserved until Social Security's projected long-range funding issues were resolved, and proposed using a portion of those surpluses to shore up the system, Social Security's budget treatment became a major issue. Congressional views about what to do with the surpluses were diverse, ranging from "buying down" publicly-held federal debt to cutting taxes to increasing spending. However, there was substantial support for setting aside a portion equal to the annual Social Security trust fund surpluses.

Although budget deficits have re-emerged, some congressional interest remains in the concept of a Social Security "lock box." For example, in the 109th Congress, H.R. 3435 (Savings for Seniors Act of 2005 introduced by Representative Blackburn) would have established a Social Security Surplus Protection Account in the OASI trust fund for the purpose of "holding" surplus Social Security tax revenues and would have established a Social Security Investment Commission to recommend alternative investment options for surplus Social Security funds. Under the measure, investment of funds held in the account would have been suspended pending enactment of legislation providing for trust fund investment in nongovernmental assets. S. 1730 (Truth in Budgeting Act of 2005 introduced in the 109th Congress by Senator Voinovich) would have established a Trust Fund Administration within the Treasury Department for the purpose of investing all federal trust fund revenues in nongovernmental debt instruments (such as municipal and corporate bonds) upon the issuance of special rate Treasury obligations to the trust funds (investment in stocks would have been prohibited). Under the measure, investment fund assets would have been used to redeem outstanding special rate Treasury obligations.

In the 109th Congress, Senator DeMint offered an amendment to the Senate budget resolution for FY2007 (S.Con.Res. 83) that would have allowed for the creation of a reserve fund for surplus Social Security tax revenues, provided that the Senate Finance Committee approve Social Security legislation that meets certain requirements. For example, the amendment (S.Amdt. 3087) specified that such legislation make no changes to Social Security benefits scheduled under current law for individuals born before 1950 and provide individuals with "the option to voluntarily obtain legally binding ownership of at least some portion of each participant's benefits." The amendment was defeated by a vote of 46-53.

In the 110th Congress, the FY2008 budget resolution (S.Con.Res. 21) passed by the Senate on March 23, 2007, included provisions aimed at "protecting" annual Social Security surpluses. The Senate-passed version of the budget resolution included a provision that would have created a new "Point of Order to Save Social Security First." The provision would have allowed a floor objection to be raised in the Senate against consideration of any legislation that would increase the *on-budget* deficit in any fiscal year (i.e., a deficit in the part of the federal budget that excludes Social Security and the Postal Service). The point of order could be raised against such legislation until the President submits legislation to Congress, and Congress enacts legislation, that would restore long-range solvency to the Social Security system (as scored by the Social Security Administration). The point of order could be waived with a three-fifths majority vote in the Senate. The Senate-passed version also included a provision ("Circuit Breaker to Protect Social Security") that would have provided a point of order against any budget resolution that does not achieve an *on-budget* balance within five years, with exceptions provided for periods of war or low economic growth. The point of order could be waived with a three-fifths majority vote in the Senate. These provisions, however, were not included in the FY2008 budget resolution conference report (S.Con.Res. 21, H.Rept. 110-153) passed by the House and Senate on May 17, 2007.[21]

INITIATIVES FOR CHANGE

The 1994-1996 Social Security Advisory Council presented three different approaches to restore long-range solvency to the system, none of which was endorsed by a majority of council members. The first (the "maintain benefits" plan) would maintain the system's current benefit structure by increasing revenues (including an eventual increase in the payroll tax) and making minor benefit reductions. It was also suggested that a portion of the Social Security trust funds be invested in stocks. The second (the "individual account" plan) addressed the problem mostly with benefit reductions, and would require workers to make an extra 1.6% of pay contribution to individual accounts. The third (the "personal security account" plan) proposed a major redesign of the system that would gradually replace the current earnings-related retirement benefit with a flat-rate benefit based on length of service and establish individual accounts funded by redirecting 5 percentage points of the current payroll tax. It would cover transition costs with an increase in payroll taxes of 1.52% of pay and government borrowing. The conceptual approaches incorporated in the three plans are reflected in many of the reform bills introduced in recent years.

During his last three years in office, former President Clinton repeatedly called for using Social Security's share of budget surpluses projected at the time to reduce publicly held federal debt and crediting the trust funds for the reduction.[22] In the 1999 State of the Union address, he proposed crediting $2.8 trillion of some $4.9 trillion in budget surpluses projected for the next 15 years to the trust funds—nearly $0.6 trillion was to be invested in stocks, the rest in federal securities. The plan was estimated to keep the system solvent until 2059. Concerns were raised that the plan would be crediting the Social Security trust funds twice for its surpluses, and that the plan would lead to government ownership of private companies. Former President Clinton further proposed that $0.5 trillion of the budget surpluses be used to create new Universal Savings Accounts— 401(k)-type accounts intended to supplement Social Security benefits. In June 1999, he revised the plan by calling for general fund infusions to the trust funds equal to the interest savings achieved by using Social Security's share of the budget surpluses to reduce federal debt. The infusions were to be invested in stocks until the stock portion of the trust funds' holdings reached 15%. In October 1999, former President Clinton revised the plan again by dropping the stock investment idea and calling for all the infusions to be invested in federal bonds. Former President Clinton's last plan, offered in January 2000, was similar but again called for investing up to 15% of the trust funds in stock.

During his first term, former President Bush appointed a commission to make recommendations to reform Social Security. As principles for reform, he stated that any reform plan must preserve the benefits of current retirees and older workers, return Social Security to a firm financial footing, and allow younger workers to invest in individual savings accounts. The commission's final report, which was issued on December 21, 2001, included three reform options. Each option would allow workers to participate in individual accounts on a voluntary basis and reduce their future Social Security benefit by the projected value of the account based on an assumed (rather than the actual) rate of return.

The first option would allow workers to redirect 2% of taxable earnings to individual accounts and would make no other changes. The second option would allow workers to redirect 4% of taxable earnings, up to an annual limit of $1,000, to individual accounts; reduce initial benefits for future retirees by indexing the growth of initial benefits to prices rather than wages; and increase benefits for lower-wage workers and widow(er)s. The third option would allow workers to contribute an additional 1% of taxable earnings to individual accounts and receive a government match of 2.5% of taxable earnings, up to an annual limit of $1,000; reduce initial benefits for future retirees by slowing the growth of initial benefits to reflect projected increases in life expectancy, and, for higher-wage workers, by modifying the benefit formula; and increase benefits for lower-wage workers and widow(er)s.[23]

During his second term, former President Bush continued efforts to build support for Social Security reform. Although the former President did not present a detailed plan for reform, he put forth guidelines for Congress to consider in the development of legislation to create individual accounts within a program that he described as in need of "wise and effective reform." During the 2005 State of the Union address, former President Bush offered the following guidelines for reform: (1) workers born before 1950 (aged 55 and older in 2005) would not be affected by individual accounts or other components of reform; (2) participation in individual accounts would be voluntary; (3) eligible workers would be allowed to redirect up to 4% of covered earnings to an individual account, initially up to $1,000 per year; (4) accounts would be administered by a centralized government entity; and (5) workers would be required to annuitize the portion of the account balance needed to provide at least a poverty-level stream of life-long income, with any remaining balance available as a lump sum.

In addition to restating support for individual accounts as part of the creation of an "ownership society," former President Bush acknowledged that other changes would be needed to address the system's projected long-range funding shortfall. He cited potential program changes that would be on the table for consideration, including (1) raising the full retirement age; (2) reducing benefits for wealthy recipients; and (3) modifying the benefit formula. At the time, the only approach ruled out by former President Bush was an increase in the payroll tax rate.

On April 28, 2005, during a television news conference, former President Bush proposed a change in the Social Security benefit formula in which future "benefits for low-income workers [would] grow faster than benefits for people who are better off." Although details of the proposal were not released, a White House press statement indicated that the President was referring to a proposal similar to one put forth by Robert Pozen, a member of the 2001 *President's Commission to Strengthen Social Security* appointed by former President Bush. Mr. Pozen's proposal, known as "progressive indexing," would constrain the growth of initial benefits for future retirees by using a combination of wage indexing and price indexing mechanisms in the benefit formula (rather than wage indexing only) to apply differing degrees of benefit reduction based on the worker's level of earnings.[24] Under progressive indexing, lower-wage workers would receive a benefit that is indexed closer to wage growth (as under current law) and higher-wage workers would receive a benefit that is indexed closer to price growth (or inflation). Based on current wage and price growth projections, a shift from wage indexing toward price indexing would result in lower initial benefits for many future retirees compared to current law.[25]

As the first session of the 109th Congress came to a close at the end of 2005, the reform debate focused on legislation introduced by Senator DeMint (S. 1302) that would have established voluntary individual accounts funded with surplus Social Security tax revenues and reduced Social Security benefits to reflect account assets (S. 1302 is described in the following section of the report). On November 15, 2005, Senator Santorum made unanimous consent requests to discharge S. 1302 and a second measure (S. 1750, 109th Congress) from the Senate Finance Committee and bring those measures to the Senate floor for consideration. S. 1750, introduced by Senator Santorum, would have provided for the issuance of Social Security "benefit guarantee certificates" to persons born before 1950 for the stated purpose of "guaranteeing their right to receive Social Security benefits ... in full with an accurate annual cost-of-living adjustment." The unanimous consent requests provided for 10 hours of debate on each measure followed by a vote on passage, with no amendments. Objections raised against the unanimous consent requests prevented further action on the measures.[26]

During the 2006 State of the Union address, former President Bush expressed concern regarding the level of federal spending for entitlement programs, citing projections that Social Security, Medicare, and Medicaid would account for almost 60% of the federal budget by 2030. The former President called for the creation of a commission, that would include Members of Congress from both parties, to "examine the full impact of baby boom retirements on Social Security, Medicare, and Medicaid." In addition, former President Bush included in his *Fiscal Year 2007 Budget* a proposal for voluntary individual accounts funded with a portion of current payroll taxes similar to the one he outlined in the 2005 State of the Union address. The *Fiscal Year 2007 Budget* also restated the former President's support for a change in the Social Security benefit formula known as "progressive indexing" to constrain the growth of initial benefits for future retirees as a cost-saving measure.

Immediately following the November 2006 congressional elections, in which Democrats gained a majority in both the House and the Senate, former President Bush and Administration officials publicly expressed interest in resuming discussions with congressional leaders on the issue of Social Security reform. In the *Fiscal Year 2009 Budget*, former President Bush restated support for voluntary individual accounts funded with a portion of current payroll taxes. Under his proposal, starting in 2013, individual accounts would be funded with 4% of taxable earnings, up to a limit of $1,400 (the contribution limit would increase by $100 more than average wage growth each year through 2018). The former President also restated support for "progressive indexing" of initial Social Security benefits for future retirees.

The *Fiscal Year 2010 President's Budget*, published on February 26, 2009, indicates that President Obama "is strongly opposed to privatizing Social Security and looks forward to working in a bipartisan way to preserve it for future generations."[27]

LEGISLATION INTRODUCED IN THE 109TH CONGRESS

During the past several Congresses, a number of Social Security reform bills have been introduced, many of which would have established individual accounts within the Social Security system either on a voluntary or mandatory basis. In the 109th Congress, 10 Social Security reform measures were introduced: H.R. 440 (Kolbe and Boyd), H.R. 530 (Johnson), H.R. 750 (Shaw), H.R. 1776 (Ryan), H.R. 2472 (Wexler), H.R. 3304 (McCrery), S. 540 (Hagel), S. 857 (Sununu), S. 1302 (DeMint), and S. 2427 (Bennett). All but two of the measures (H.R. 2472 and S. 2427) would have established individual accounts to supplement or replace traditional Social Security benefits, among other changes. This section provides a summary of Social Security reform legislation introduced in the 109th Congress, with the exception of H.R. 530, H.R. 750, S. 540 and H.R. 2472. These measures, which were re-introduced in the 110th Congress, are included in the section that follows ("Legislation Introduced in the 110th Congress"). Despite intense debate on the issue of Social Security reform in the 109th Congress, there was no congressional action on Social Security reform legislation.[28]

H.R. 440. Representatives Jim Kolbe and Allen Boyd introduced H.R. 440 (Bipartisan Retirement Security Act of 2005) on February 1, 2005. For workers under age 55, the measure would have redirected 3% of the first $10,000 of covered earnings (indexed to wage growth) and 2% of remaining covered earnings to mandatory individual accounts. Workers would have been allowed to make additional contributions of up to $5,000 annually (indexed to inflation), and lower-wage workers would have been eligible for an additional credit of up to $600 toward their account.

With respect to traditional Social Security benefits, the measure would have made a number of benefit computation changes, including several adjustments to the "replacement factors" used in the benefit formula. It would have constrained the growth of initial monthly benefits for future retirees by indexing initial benefits to increases in life expectancy, a provision known as "longevity indexing" of benefits. The measure would have modified the calculation of the worker's "average indexed monthly earnings" (AIME) for benefit computation purposes. In the future, the worker's AIME would have been based on the worker's average career earnings— counting all years of earnings divided by a 40-year computation period (rather than the worker's average career earnings, counting the 35 years of highest earnings divided by a 35-year computation period).

In addition, the measure would have accelerated the increase in the full retirement age from 65 to 67 scheduled under current law, so that it would have reached age 67 for persons born in 1956 or later (four years earlier than under current law). It would have modified the early retirement reduction factors and delayed retirement credits; set widow(er)s' benefits equal to 75% of the couple's combined pre-death benefit (rather than 50%-67%); limited benefits for aged spouses of higher earners; provided a minimum benefit tied to the poverty level for workers who meet specified coverage requirements; and reduced cost-of-living adjustments.

With respect to tax changes, the measure would have increased the taxable wage base gradually so that 87% of covered earnings would be taxable. It would have credited all revenues from the taxation of Social Security benefits to the Social Security trust funds (instead of crediting part to the Medicare Hospital Insurance trust fund).

H.R. 440 would have established a central authority to administer the accounts and provided initial investment options similar to those available under the Thrift Savings Plan for federal employees. Once the account balance reached $7,500 (indexed to inflation), the worker would have been allowed to choose among a broader range of centrally-managed investment options. The account would have become available at retirement, or earlier if the account balance were sufficient to provide a payment at least equal to 185% of the poverty level. The worker would have been required to annuitize the portion of the account balance needed to provide a combined monthly payment (traditional benefit plus annuity) at least equal to 185% of the poverty level. Any remaining balance could have been taken as a lump sum.

H.R. 3304. Representative Jim McCrery introduced H.R. 3304 (Growing Real Ownership for Workers Act of 2005) on July 14, 2005. The measure, which is similar to S. 1302, would have established voluntary individual accounts for workers born after 1949 (workers would have been enrolled automatically in the individual account system and given the option to disenroll). Individual accounts would have been funded with general revenues in amounts equal to surplus Social Security tax revenues from 2006 to 2016, the period during which surplus tax revenues are projected under current law.

H.R. 3304 would have established a central authority to administer the accounts. Initially, funds would have been invested in long-term Treasury bonds. Beginning in 2009, additional investment options may have been made available. The account would have become available at retirement, or in the event of the worker's death. At retirement, the worker would have been required to annuitize the portion of the account balance needed to provide a combined monthly payment (traditional benefit plus annuity) at least equal to the poverty level. Any remaining balance could have been taken as a lump sum. For account participants, traditional Social Security benefits would have been offset by an amount equal to the annuity value of a hypothetical (or "shadow") account assumed to have earned, on average, a 2.7% real rate of return. (The assumed rate of return for the hypothetical account was based on the projected ultimate real rate of return for the Social Security trust funds (3% on average) minus 0.3 percentage point to reflect administrative expenses.) The measure would have made no other changes to traditional Social Security benefits.

S. 857/H.R. 1776. Senator John Sununu introduced S. 857 (Social Security Personal Savings Guarantee and Prosperity Act of 2005) on April 20, 2005. Representative Paul Ryan introduced a companion measure (H.R. 1776) on April 21, 2005. The measures would have allowed workers under age 55 to redirect a portion of payroll taxes to voluntary individual accounts (workers would have been enrolled automatically in the individual account system and given the option to disenroll). From 2006 to 2015, workers would have been allowed to redirect 5% of covered earnings up to a base amount ($10,000 in 2006, indexed to wage growth thereafter) and 2.5% of remaining covered earnings to individual accounts. Beginning in 2016, workers would have been allowed to redirect 10% of covered earnings up to the base amount and 5% of remaining covered earnings to the accounts. Workers participating in individual accounts would have been issued a "benefit credit certificate" (or recognition bond) to reflect the value of benefits accrued under the traditional system. The recognition bond would have been redeemable at retirement, though the value of accrued benefits would have been reduced to reflect the payroll taxes redirected to the worker's account. The measures would have provided account participants a combined monthly payment (traditional benefit plus annuity) at least equal to benefits scheduled under current law. Workers choosing not to participate in individual accounts would have received traditional Social Security benefits.

The measures would have provided 6 indexed investment accounts, including a default "lifecycle investment account" with an expected average investment mix of 65% equities/35% fixed income instruments. Once the worker's account balance reached $25,000 (indexed to inflation), additional investment options would have become available. At retirement, the worker would have been required to annuitize the portion of the account balance needed to provide a combined monthly payment (traditional benefit plus inflation-indexed annuity) at least equal to benefits scheduled under current law. Any excess balance could have been withdrawn in a manner chosen by the worker. Pre-retirement distribution would have been allowed if the account balance were sufficient to provide an annuity at least equal to a required minimum payment. The measures also included several financing provisions that would have constrained future growth rates for federal spending and dedicated the savings to Social Security; "reserved" annual Social Security cash flow surpluses for Social Security purposes; and dedicated a portion of projected corporate tax revenue increases to Social Security.

S. 1302. Senator Jim DeMint introduced S. 1302 (Stop the Raid on Social Security Act of 2005) on June 23, 2005. The measure would have established voluntary individual accounts for workers born after 1949 (workers would have been enrolled automatically in the individual account system and given the option to disenroll). Individual accounts would have been funded with surplus Social Security tax revenues from 2006 to 2016, the period during which surplus tax revenues are projected under current law. Given the redirection of surplus Social Security tax revenues to individual accounts, the measure would have provided for general revenue transfers to the trust funds in amounts needed to maintain trust fund solvency based on current-law projections.

S. 1302 would have established a central authority to administer the accounts. Initially, funds would have been invested in long-term Treasury bonds. Beginning in 2008, additional investment options may have been made available. The account would have become available at retirement, or in the event of the worker's death. At retirement, the worker would have been required to annuitize the portion of the account balance needed to provide a combined monthly payment (traditional benefit plus annuity) at least equal to the poverty level. Any remaining balance could have been taken as a lump sum. For account participants, traditional Social Security benefits would have been offset by an amount equal to the annuity value of a hypothetical (or "shadow") account assumed to have earned, on average, a 2.7% real rate of return. (The assumed rate of return for the hypothetical account was based on the projected ultimate real rate of return for the Social Security trust funds (3% on average) minus 0.3 percentage point to reflect administrative expenses.) The measure would have made no other changes to traditional Social Security benefits.

S. 2427. Senator Robert Bennett introduced S. 2427 (Sustainable Solvency First for Social Security Act of 2006) on March 16, 2006. The measure would have modified the benefit formula to provide "progressive indexing" of initial Social Security benefits for future retirees.

Progressive indexing applies a combination of wage indexing and price indexing to the benefit formula that, under current projections, would result in lower benefits for workers with earnings above a certain level (with larger reductions for relatively higher earners) compared to current law. The measure would have further constrained the growth of initial Social Security benefits for future retirees by indexing initial benefits to increases in life expectancy, a provision known as "longevity indexing" of benefits. It would have accelerated the increase in the full retirement age (from 65 to 67) being phased-in under current law so that the full retirement age would have reached 67 for persons born in 1955 or later (five years earlier than under current law). The measure would have provided general revenue transfers to the Social Security trust funds as needed to maintain adequate trust fund balances.

LEGISLATION INTRODUCED IN THE 110TH CONGRESS

During the 110th Congress, six Social Security reform bills were introduced: H.R. 1090 (Lewis), H.R. 2002 (Johnson), H.R. 4181 (Flake), S. 2765 (Hagel), H.R. 5779 (Wexler) and H.R. 6110 (Ryan). H.R. 1090 (which is similar to H.R. 750 in the 109th Congress[29]) would have established voluntary individual accounts funded with general revenues, among other program changes. H.R. 2002 (which is similar to H.R. 530 in the 109th Congress), H.R. 4181, S. 2765 (which is similar to S. 540 in the 109th Congress) and H.R. 6110 would have established individual accounts funded with a redirection of current payroll taxes, among other program changes. H.R. 5779 (which is similar to H.R. 2472 in the 109th Congress) would have increased Social Security revenues by requiring workers and employers each to contribute 3% of earnings above the Social Security taxable wage base (in addition to current-law payroll tax contributions). This section provides a summary of Social Security reform legislation introduced in the 110th Congress, with the exception of H.R. 4181. H.R. 4181 has been re-introduced in the 111th Congress and is included in the section that follows (see H.R. 107 in "Legislation Introduced in the 111th Congress"). There was no congressional action on these measures during the 110th Congress.

H.R. 1090. Representative Ron Lewis introduced H.R. 1090 (Social Security Guarantee Plus Act of 2007) on February 15, 2007. The measure would have allowed workers aged 18 and older (who have been assigned a Social Security Number) to participate in voluntary individual accounts funded with general revenues. Account contributions would have been equal to 4% of taxable earnings, up to a limit of $1,000 (the limit would have been indexed to wage growth).

With respect to traditional Social Security benefits, the measure would have provided up to five years of earnings credits for workers who stay at home to care for a child under age seven and eliminated the earnings test for recipients below the full retirement age. In addition, it would have set widow(er) 's benefits equal to 75% of the couple's combined pre-death benefit (compared to 50%-67% under current law); allowed widow(er)s to qualify for benefits based on a disability regardless of age and the time frame in which the disability occurred; and lowered the Social Security spousal/widow(er)'s benefit reduction under the Government Pension Offset from two- thirds to one-third of the individual's pension from noncovered employment.

Under H.R. 1090, accounts would have been administered by private financial institutions selected by the government. The measure would have provided three initial investment options with specified allocations in equities and corporate bonds (60/40, 65/35, 70/30). The account would have become available upon the worker's entitlement to retirement or disability benefits, or upon the worker's death. Upon benefit entitlement, the worker would have received a lump sum equal to 5% of the account balance. The remaining balance would have been used to finance all or part of the worker's benefit. The account balance would have been withdrawn gradually and transferred to the trust funds for the payment of monthly benefits. In addition to the 5% lump sum, the measure would have provided a monthly payment equal to the higher of a benefit scheduled under current law and an annuity based on 95% of the account balance.

H.R. 2002. Representative Sam Johnson introduced H.R. 2002 (Individual Social Security Investment Program Act of 2007) on April 23, 2007. The measure would have established individual accounts funded with 6.2 percentage points of the current Social Security payroll tax. Participation in the individual account system would have been voluntary for workers aged 22 to 54 (in 2007) and mandatory for younger individuals. Workers participating in the individual account system would no longer have accrued benefits under the current system and would have been issued a marketable "recognition bond" equal to the value of benefits already accrued. The measure would have provided workers participating in the individual account system a minimum benefit equal to a specified percentage of the poverty level, up to 100% for workers who have at least 35 years of earnings.

Workers choosing not to participate in the individual account system would have remained in the current system, however, initial monthly benefits would have been lower than those scheduled under current law. The measure would have constrained the growth of initial monthly benefits for future retirees by indexing initial benefits to price growth (rather than wage growth), a provision known as "price indexing" of benefits.

H.R. 2002 would have established a central authority to administer the accounts and provided at least three initial investment options with specified allocations in equities and fixed income instruments (government bonds and corporate bonds), including a default 60/40 investment mix. Once the account balance reached $10,000 (indexed to inflation), the worker would have been allowed to transfer the balance to a private financial institution. The account would have become available at retirement (i.e., at the Social Security full retirement age), or earlier if the account balance were sufficient to provide an annuity at least equal to 100% of the poverty level. In the case of pre-retirement account distribution, the worker would have received an annual rebate of future payroll tax contributions (the employer share of the payroll tax would not have been subject to rebate). The worker would have been required to annuitize the portion of the account balance needed to provide an annuity at least equal to 100% of the poverty level. Any remaining balance could have been taken as a lump sum. At retirement, if the account balance were not sufficient to provide the prescribed minimum payment, a supplemental payment would have been made to the account from general revenues.

S. 2765. Senator Chuck Hagel introduced S. 2765 (Saving Social Security Act of 2008) on March 13, 2008. The measure would have allowed workers born in 1963 or later (workers aged 45 or younger in 2008) to redirect 4 percentage points of the current Social Security payroll tax to an individual account (a SAFE account). Eligible workers would have been enrolled automatically in the individual account system and allowed to waive their eligibility for a SAFE account.

With respect to traditional Social Security benefits, the measure would have constrained the growth of initial benefits for future retirees by indexing initial benefits to increases in life expectancy, a provision known as "longevity indexing" of benefits. In addition, the measure would have increased the full retirement age from 67 to 68 for persons born in 1963 or later and increased the early retirement reduction factors. For workers participating in the individual account system, traditional Social Security benefits would have been offset by an amount equal to the annuity value of a hypothetical (or "shadow") account assumed to earn a 3% real rate of return. The measure would have provided a minimum "primary insurance amount" (basic benefit amount before any adjustments for early or delayed retirement) up to 135% of the poverty level for workers with 35 years of Social Security-covered employment (lower percentages would have applied to workers with fewer years of coverage).

The bill would have established a central authority to administer the individual accounts and provided initial investment options such as those offered by the Thrift Savings Plan for federal employees. The individual account would have become available at retirement, or in the event of the worker's death. Upon entitlement to benefits, the worker would have been required to annuitize the portion of the account balance needed to provide a combined monthly payment (traditional benefit plus annuity) at least equal to 135% of the poverty level. Any remaining balance could have been withdrawn in a manner chosen by the worker.

H.R. 5779. Representative Robert Wexler introduced H.R. 5779 (Social Security Forever Act of 2008) on April 10, 2008. The measure would have increased Social Security revenues by requiring workers and employers each to contribute 3% of earnings above the Social Security taxable wage base, in addition to payroll tax contributions paid under current law. Under current law, workers and employers each contribute 6.2% of covered earnings, up to a limit (the Social Security taxable wage base). The Social Security taxable wage base, which increases each year according to average wage growth, is $106,800 in 2009. Earnings up to the taxable wage base (i.e., earnings on which contributions are paid) are credited for benefit computation purposes.

Under the measure, workers and employers each would have been required to contribute 3% of earnings *above* the taxable wage base, in addition to the 6.2% of earnings *up to* the taxable wage base payable under current law. Earnings above the taxable wage base taxed at the 3% rate would not have been credited for benefit computation purposes.

H.R. 6110. Representative Paul Ryan introduced H.R. 6110 (Roadmap for America's Future Act of 2008) on May 21, 2008, to provide for the reform of health care, the Social Security system, the tax code for individuals and businesses, and the budget process.[30] Title IV of the bill (Social Security Personal Savings Guarantee and Prosperity Act of 2008) would have allowed workers born in 1954 or later (workers under age 55 in 2008) to redirect a portion of payroll taxes to voluntary individual accounts (workers would have been enrolled automatically in the individual account system and given the option to disenroll). From 2011 to 2020, workers would have been allowed to redirect 2% of covered earnings up to a base amount ($10,000 in 2011, indexed to wage growth thereafter) and 1% of remaining covered earnings to an individual account. The amount of Social Security contributions that could be redirected to an individual account would have increased over time. From 2021 to 2030, workers would have been allowed to redirect 4% of covered earnings up to the base amount and 2% of remaining covered earnings. From 2031 to 2040, workers would have been allowed to redirect 6% of covered earnings up to the base amount and 3% of remaining covered earnings. For calendar years after 2040, workers would have been allowed to redirect 8 %of covered earnings up to the base amount and 4% of remaining covered earnings to an individual account.

Workers participating in individual accounts would have been issued a "benefit credit certificate" to reflect the value of benefits accrued under the traditional system. The benefit credit certificate would have been redeemable at retirement, though the value of accrued benefits would have been reduced to reflect the payroll taxes redirected to the worker's individual account. The measure would have provided account participants a monthly payment at least equal to the minimum level of benefits they would have received under the traditional system (subject to changes to the system). Workers choosing not to participate in the individual account system would have received traditional benefits.

The measure would have provided six indexed investment accounts, including a default "lifecycle investment account." Once the worker's account balance reached a specified threshold ($25,000 in 2011, indexed to inflation thereafter), additional investment options would have become available. The account would have become available at retirement, or earlier if the account balance were sufficient to provide an annuity at least equal to 150% of the poverty line. At retirement, the worker would have been required to annuitize the portion of the account balance needed to provide a monthly payment at least equal to 150% of the poverty line, and any excess balance could have been withdrawn in a manner chosen by the worker. If the account balance were not sufficient to provide the minimum level of benefit payments guaranteed under the proposal, the government would have made up the difference. Any funds remaining in the account at the time of the individual's death would have been payable to designated beneficiaries or to the individual's estate.

Among other changes, the measure would have modified the benefit formula to provide "progressive price indexing" of initial Social Security benefits for future retirees (the change would have applied to workers under age 55 in 2008). Progressive price indexing applies a combination of wage indexing and price indexing to the benefit formula that results in lower projected benefits for workers with earnings above a certain level (with larger benefit reductions for relatively higher earners) compared to current law. In addition, the measure would have accelerated the increase in the full retirement age (FRA) scheduled under current law so that the FRA would have reached 67 for persons born in 1959 (one year earlier than under current law) and further increased the FRA for persons born in subsequent years to reflect projected increases in life expectancy.

LEGISLATION INTRODUCED IN THE 111TH CONGRESS

During the 111th Congress, two Social Security reform bills have been introduced: H.R. 107 (Flake) and S. 426 (Bennett). This section provides a summary of these measures, which have received no congressional action to date.

H.R. 107. Representative Jeff Flake introduced H.R. 107 (Securing Medicare and Retirement for Tomorrow Act of 2009) on January 6, 2009.[31] Among other provisions, the measure would establish individual accounts funded with 6.2 percentage points of the current Social Security payroll tax. Participation in the individual account system would be mandatory for workers below the Social Security full retirement age. At retirement, workers would be allowed to choose between a Social Security retirement benefit (Part A retirement benefit payable to workers and spouses) and a retirement distribution from the individual account (Part B benefit). Part A retirement benefits would be phased-out over time. Individuals reaching retirement age after a period of 42 calendar years following enactment of the bill would not have the option of choosing Part A retirement benefits.[32]

The worker's individual account would be maintained by the employer and contributions would be invested in a qualified Social Security mutual fund. Workers would designate an investment fund from among five qualified Social Security mutual funds selected by the employer.

H.R. 107 would establish a Social Security Escrow Fund within the U.S. Treasury. The fund would include securities held by the Social Security trust fund (the combined Old-Age and Survivors Insurance and the Disability Insurance trust funds), 6.2 percentage points of the current Social Security payroll tax, Medicare Hospital Insurance (HI) payroll taxes, and amounts appropriated for the Supplemental Security Income (S SI) program, among other funding sources.[33] Amounts held in the Social Security Escrow Fund would be available for the payment of various types of Social Security benefits—including Part A retirement benefits, benefits payable to a worker's family members (such as children and surviving spouses), disability benefits, and lump-sum death benefits—as well as for the payment of SSI benefits. In addition, transfers would be made from the fund to the Medicare HI trust fund in the amount of Medicare Part A benefits.

The measure would establish the Personal Accounts Management and Review Board as an independent agency within the executive branch of the government. Among other duties, the board would operate the Social Security Escrow Fund and designate and regulate qualified Social Security mutual funds. The Secretary of the Treasury would serve as managing trustee of the Social Security Escrow Fund.

S. 426. Senator Robert Bennett introduced S. 426 (Social Security Solvency Act of 2009) on February 12, 2009.[34] The measure would modify the benefit formula to provide "progressive indexing" of initial Social Security benefits for future retirees. Progressive indexing applies a combination of wage indexing and price indexing to the benefit formula that, under current projections, would result in lower benefits for workers with earnings above a certain level (with larger reductions for relatively higher earners) compared to current law. The measure would further constrain the growth of initial benefits for future retirees by indexing initial benefits to increases in life expectancy, a provision known as "longevity indexing" of benefits. In addition, it would accelerate the increase in the full retirement age (from 65 to 67) being phased-in under current law so that the full retirement age would reach 67 for persons born in 1955 or later (five years earlier than under current law). The measure would provide general revenue transfers to the Social Security trust funds as needed to maintain adequate trust fund balances.

End Notes

[1] *A New Era of Responsibility: Renewing America's Promise*, published on February 26, 2009, available at http://www.whitehouse.gov/omb/assets/fy2010_new_era/A_New_Era_of_Responsibility2.pdf.

[2] The Social Security Board of Trustees is composed of three officers of the President's Cabinet (the Secretary of the Treasury, the Secretary of Labor, and the Secretary of Health and Human Services), the Commissioner of Social Security, and two public representatives who are appointed by the President and subject to confirmation by the Senate. Currently, the public trustee positions are vacant.

[3] The 2009 Annual Report of the Board of Trustees of the Federal Old-Age and Survivors Insurance and Federal Disability Insurance Trust Funds, May 12, 2009, available at http://www.ssa.gov/OACT/TR/2009/. Trust fund projections cited in this CRS report are based on the trustees' 2009 intermediate (or mid-range) assumptions.

[4] The current long-range projections for the Social Security trust funds are less favorable than the projections in the 2008 trustees report. The trustees cite the recent economic downturn, slightly lower estimates for real GDP after the economy recovers and faster reductions in mortality rates as the primary reasons for the changes in the long-range projections for the Social Security system.

[5] See CRS Report RL3298 1, *Age Dependency Ratios and Social Security Solvency*, by Laura B. Shrestha.

[6] OASDI is the formal name for Social Security.

[7] Program costs and income are evaluated as a percentage of taxable payroll because Social Security payroll taxes are the main source of funding for the program

[8] For more information on the taxation of Social Security benefits, please refer to CRS Report RL32552, *Social Security: Calculation and History of Taxing Benefits*, by Janemarie Mulvey and Christine Scott.

[9] The trust fund projections cited in this CRS report are based on the 2009 annual report of the Social Security Board of Trustees released on May 12, 2009. Projections released by the Congressional Budget Office (CBO)

in August 2008 reflect a similar long-range outlook for the Social Security trust funds. CBO projects that the trust funds will be exhausted in 2046, and that Social Security expenditures will exceed tax revenues beginning in 2019. For more information, please refer to CBO, *Updated Long-Term Projections for Social Security*, August 2008, available at http://cbo.gov/ftpdocs/96xx/doc9649/08-20-SocialSecurityUpdate.pdf.

[10] Polling results are from PollingReport.com at http://www.pollingreport.com/social.htm.

[11] *Report of the 1994-1996 Advisory Council on Social Security, Volume I: Findings and Recommendations*, Wash., DC, January 1997.

[12] For more information on the reforms in Chile and other countries, please refer to Congressional Budget Office, *Social Security Privatization: Experiences Abroad*, January 1999, available at http://www.cbo.gov/ftpdocs/10xx/ doc1065/ssabroad.pdf; and CRS Report RL34006, *Social Security: The Chilean Approach to Retirement*, by Christopher Tamborini.

[13] *Strengthening Social Security and Creating Personal Wealth for All Americans*, Final Report of the President's Commission to Strengthen Social Security, December 21, 2001, available at http://www.csss.gov/reports/Final_report.pdf.

[14] For examples of arguments in support of individual accounts, please refer to *Strengthening Social Security and Creating Personal Wealth for All Americans*, Final Report of the President's Commission to Strengthen Social Security, December 21, 2001, available at http://www.csss.gov/reports/Final_report.pdf, and a variety of sources available from the Cato Institute at http://www.socialsecurity.org/.

[15] For examples of arguments against individual accounts, please refer to the compilation of sources provided in *Social Security Issue Guide*, Economic Policy Institute, May 2005, available at http://www.epinet.org/issueguides/ socialsecurity/socialsecurityissueguide.pdf.

[16] Projections of cohort life expectancy are based on the intermediate assumptions of the 2009 trustees report.

[17] *Toward a More Accurate Measure of the Cost of Living*, Final Report to the Senate Finance Committee from the Advisory Commission to Study the Consumer Price Index, December 4, 1996.

[18] For more information, please refer to CRS Report RL3 0074, *The Consumer Price Index: A Brief Overview*, by Brian W. Cashell, and CRS Report RL34168, *Automatic Cost of Living Adjustments: Some Economic and Practical Considerations*, by Brian W. Cashell.

[19] Social Security Administration, *Summary of Provisions That Would Change the Social Security Program*, dated July 16, 2008, available at http://www.ssa.gov/OACT/solvency/provisions/cola_summary.html. Estimates are based on the intermediate assumptions of the 2008 trustees report.

[20] For more information, please refer to CRS Report RS20060, *A Separate Consumer Price Index for the Elderly?*, by Brian W. Cashell.

[21] During Senate floor consideration of S.Con.Res. 21 in March 2007, Senator DeMint offered an amendment (S.Amdt. 489) that would have allowed for the creation of a reserve fund for Social Security reform, provided that the Senate Finance Committee approve legislation that meets certain requirements. Among other requirements, the amendment specified that such legislation must ensure "that there is no change to current law scheduled benefits for individuals born before January 1, 1951" and must provide "participants with the benefits of savings and investment while permitting the pre-funding of at least some portion of future benefits." The amendment was defeated by a vote of 45 to 52. Senator DeMint offered a similar amendment to the FY2009 budget resolution (S.Con.Res. 70) on March 13, 2008. The amendment (S.Amdt. 4328) was defeated by a vote of 41 to 57.

[22] For more information, please refer to U.S. Congress, House Committee on Ways and Means, *The President's Social Security Framework*, hearing, 106th Cong., 1st sess., February 23, 1999, Serial 106-32 (Washington: GPO, 2000).

[23] For more information, please refer to CRS Report RL32006, *Social Security Reform: Effect on Benefits and the Federal Budget of Plans Proposed by the President's Commission to Strengthen Social Security*, by Dawn Nuschler and Geoffrey C. Kollmann.

[24] For more information, please refer to *Testimony on Progressive Indexing* before the Senate Finance Committee, April 26, 2005, by Robert C. Pozen, available at http://finance.senate.gov/hearings/testimony/2005test/ptest042605.pdf, and CRS Report RL32900, *Indexing Social Security Benefits: The Effects of Price and Wage Indexes*, by Patrick Purcell, Laura Haltzel, and Neela K. Ranade.

[25] Under the trustees' 2009 intermediate projections, wages are projected to increase at an average annual rate of 3.9% over the 75-year projection period. By comparison, prices are projected to increase at an average annual rate of 2. 8% over the period.

[26] For more information on S. 1302, please refer to CRS Report RS22278, *Social Security Reform: Growing Real Ownership for Workers (GROW) Act of 2005, H.R. 3304*, by Kathleen Romig. For more information on S. 1750, please refer to CRS Report RL32822, *Social Security Reform: Legal Analysis of Social Security Benefit Entitlement Issues*, by Kathleen S. Swendiman and Thomas J. Nicola.

[27] *A New Era of Responsibility: Renewing America's Promise*, page 109, available at http://www.whitehouse.gov/omb/ assets/fy2010_new_era/A_New_Era_of_Responsibility2.pdf.

[28] More detailed descriptions and estimates of the financial effects of these proposals are available from the Social Security Administration, Office of the Chief Actuary, at http://www.ssa.gov/OACT/solvency/index.html.

[29] In the 109th Congress, H.R. 750 was introduced by Representative Shaw.

[30] H.R. 6110 included provisions similar to H.R. 1776 introduced by Representative Ryan in the 109th Congress.

[31] H.R. 107 is similar to H.R. 4181 introduced by Representative Flake in the 1 10th Congress.

[32] The measure also would make changes to the Medicare program in connection with the establishment of Social Security individual accounts.

[33] If an individual elects to receive Part A retirement benefits (in lieu of Part B benefits), the qualified Social Security mutual fund in which the individual's account contributions are invested would be required to transfer the amount of the individual's Part B benefits to the Social Security Escrow Fund.

[34] S. 426 is similar to S. 2427 introduced by Senator Bennett in the 109th Congress.

In: Social Security Reform: Disability, Indexing and Financing ISBN: 978-1-61668-354-2
Editor: Janet U. Burlington

Chapter 5

SOCIAL SECURITY REFORM: LEGAL ANALYSIS OF SOCIAL SECURITY BENEFIT ENTITLEMENT ISSUES*

Kathleen S. Swendiman and Thomas J. Nicola

SUMMARY

Calculations indicating that in the long run the Social Security program will not be financially sustainable under the present statutory scheme have fueled the current debate regarding Social Security reform. This report addresses selected legal issues which may be raised regarding entitlement to Social Security benefits as Congress considers possible changes to the Social Security program, and in view of projected long-range shortfalls in the Social Security Trust Funds.

Social Security is a statutory entitlement program. Beneficiaries have a legal entitlement to receive Social Security benefits as set forth under the Social Security Act. However, the fact that Social Security benefits are financed by taxes on an employee's wages does not limit Congress's power to fix the levels of benefits under the Social Security Act, or the conditions upon which they may be paid. Congress's authority to modify provisions of the Social Security program was affirmed in the 1960 Supreme Court decision in *Flemming v. Nestor,* wherein the Court held that an individual does not have an accrued "property right" in his or her Social Security benefits. The Court has made clear in subsequent court decisions that the payment of Social Security taxes conveys no contractual rights to Social Security benefits.

Congress has the power to legislatively promise to pay individuals a certain level of Social Security benefits, and to provide legal evidence of Congress's "guarantee" of the obligation of the federal government to provide for the payment of such benefits in the future. While Congress may decide to take whatever measures necessary to fulfill such a obligation, courts would be unlikely to find that Congress's unilateral promise constitutes a contract which could not be modified in the future. In addition, a congressional promise not to reduce a specific level of Social Security benefits payable to certain eligible individuals would likely

* This is an edited, reformatted and augmented version of a CRS Report for Congress publication dated May 2009.

not overcome the constitutional principle, subject to due process considerations, that one Congress may not bind a subsequent Congress to legislative action or inaction.

The calculations concerning the possible future insolvency of the Social Security Trust Funds raise a question whether that result would affect the legal right of beneficiaries to receive full Social Security benefits. While an entitlement by definition legally obligates the United States to make payments to any person who meets the eligibility requirements established in the statute that creates the entitlement, a provision of the Antideficiency Act prevents an agency from paying more in benefits than the amount available in the source of funds available to pay the benefits. The Social Security Act states that Social Security benefits shall be paid only from the Social Security Trust Funds and the act appropriates all payroll taxes to pay benefits. Although the legal right of beneficiaries to receive full benefits would not be extinguished by an insufficient amount of funds in the Social Security Trust funds, it appears that beneficiaries would have to wait until the Trust Funds receive an amount sufficient to pay full benefits in the case of a shortfall, unless Congress amends applicable laws.

Calculations indicating that in the long run the current Social Security program will not be financially sustainable under the present statutory scheme have fueled the current debate regarding Social Security reform.[1] This report addresses selected legal issues which may be raised regarding entitlement to Social Security benefits as Congress considers possible changes to the Social Security program and in view of projected long-range shortfalls in the Social Security Trust Funds.[2]

Social Security benefits are administered pursuant to Title II of the Social Security Act, known as the *Old Age, Survivors and Disability Insurance (OASDI)* program.[3] Title II is part of a larger social insurance program in which Congress uses its power to tax and spend for the general welfare to promote the social goals of aiding the aged, survivors of workers, disabled persons and persons of limited means. Beneficiaries under title II have a legal entitlement to receive Social Security benefits as set forth by the Social Security Act and as administered by the Social Security Administration (SSA), an independent agency in the executive branch.

An individual's right to Social Security benefits is in a sense "earned," since there is a general relationship between OASDI benefits and wages earned and the tax paid thereon. However, benefits are not directly measured by the amount of payments made through the years into the system. Thus, the fact that Social Security benefits are financed by taxes on an employee's wages does not provide a limit on Congress's power to fix the levels of benefits under the Social Security Act, or the conditions upon which they may be paid.[4]

Congressional Authority to Modify Entitlements

The Supreme Court's landmark decision in *Flemming v. Nestor*,[5] provided an analysis of the relationship between a beneficiary's legal entitlement to receive Social Security benefits and the power of Congress to change that entitlement by amending the underlying statute. The Court in that case upheld a provision, section 202(a) of the Social Security Act, 42 U.S.C. §402(a), that terminated Social Security benefits to a person deported for membership in the Communist Party. Nestor had, at one time, been a member of the Communist Party. Later he began receiving Social Security benefits which were cut off when he was deported to his native Bulgaria. Nestor argued that he had a "property right" in his Social Security benefits and that, by cutting off those benefits, the government had made an unlawful "taking" of his benefits under the Fifth Amendment.[6]

The Court, however, disagreed. Justice Harlan wrote:

> To engraft upon the Social Security system a concept of "accrued property rights" would deprive it of the flexibility and boldness in adjustment to everchanging conditions which it demands.... It was doubtless out of an awareness of the need for such flexibility that Congress included in the original Act, and has since retained, a clause expressly reserving to it "[t]he right to alter, amend, or repeal any provision" of the act. § 1104, 49 Stat. 648, 42 U.S.C. § 1304. That provision makes express what is implicit in the institutional needs of the program... We must conclude that a person covered by the act has not such a right in benefit payments as would make every defeasance of "accrued" interests violative of the Due Process Clause of the Fifth Amendment.
>
> *Flemming* at 610-611.

The inherent ability of Congress to modify the provisions of Title II of the Social Security Act, even to the extent of affecting the benefits an individual is currently receiving, is thus well established.[7] The same principle that current benefit amounts may be modified has been applied to other, similar programs involving pensions, such as Federal Civil Service Retirement. One significant example is the Supreme Court affirmance, without opinion, of a decision of a three- judge district court in *National Association of Retired Federal Employees v. Horner.*[8] The district court in that case upheld a provision of the Balanced Budget and Emergency Deficit Control Act,[9] which suspended paying a scheduled cost-of-living adjustment (COLA) for federal retirees, saying that it did not violate the Takings Clause of the Fifth Amendment, which states that private property shall not be taken for public use without just compensation.

The dispute centered on whether the provision of the act, signed by the President on December 12, 1985, which suspended any automatic spending increase that first would be paid during the period beginning with the date of enactment, constituted a taking of private property of the retirees. The section providing for the COLA, 5 U.S.C. §8340(b), provided that it would take effect on December 1 of each year. While section 8340(b) made the COLA effective on December 1, it was not scheduled to be paid until January 2, 1986. The retirees argued that the COLA for the twelve months after December 1, 1985, became their private property on December 1, 1985, and, consequently, that the suspension signed on December 12, 1985 took their property which had accrued between December 1 and 12 without compensation in violation of the Takings Clause.

The court rejected their claim, asserting that, "It is utterly clear, however, that the statute [section 8340(b)] cannot be read as plaintiffs wish."[10] *Horner* at 514. It cited an earlier case, *Stouper v. Jones,* 284 F.2d 240 (D.C. Cir. 1960), as dispositive. The appellant in the *Stouper* case retired in 1953 and began receiving disability annuity payments pursuant to the law then in force. In 1956, Congress amended the law to discontinue benefits to recipients whose earning capacity was restored to a level fairly comparable to the current rate of pay for the position held immediately prior to retirement. After the Retirement Division of the Civil Service Commission determined that the appellant had been restored to that earning capacity, her disability annuity was terminated.

The appellant asserted that the 1956 amendment could not constitutionally be applied in her case because at the time she retired she acquired a vested right to an annuity that could not be taken from her by subsequent legislation. *Stouper* at 242. The U.S. Court of Appeals for the District of Columbia in *Stouper* said that "(i)t is well settled that a pension granted by the government confers no right which cannot be revised, modified, or recalled by subsequent legislation. *United States ex rel. Burnett v. Teller,* 107 U.S. 64 (1882)." The court in the *Stouper* case added that benefits under the Civil Service Retirement Act are similar to those under the Social Security Act: they are not based on an employee's contributions to the retirement fund, but instead on the employee's earnings record and years of service. It was noted that the Retirement Act pays higher benefits when a deceased employee is survived by a widow or widower and children, than when he or she is survived only by a widow or widower even though the employee's contribution to the Civil Service Retirement and Disability Fund had been the same in either case. "We conclude that an employee has no right under the Retirement Act based on contractual annuity principles, and hold that the appellant had no vested right to the disability annuity which was terminated." *Id.*

The U.S. Supreme Court has also made clear that the payment of Social Security taxes conveys no contractual rights to Social Security benefits. In 1937 the High Court upheld the constitutionality of the Social Security Act in *Helvering v. Davis*.[11] In doing so, the Court held that the Social Security program was not an insurance program. The court noted, "The proceeds of both employee and employer taxes are to be paid into the treasury like any other internal revenue generally, and are not earmarked in any way."[12] The Court, in essence, deferred to Congress on the question of which welfare schemes fall within the ambit of the Constitution's General Welfare Clause. Later, in *Flemming*, the Court rejected any comparison of Social Security with insurance or an annuity:[13]

> It is apparent that the noncontractual interest of an employee covered by the act cannot be soundly analogized to that of the holder of an annuity, whose right to benefits is bottomed on his contractual premium payments.

The absence of contractual rights extends to government pensions in general. In *Dodge v. Board Education,* 302 U.S. 74 (1937) a retired school teacher challenged the constitutionality of a state statute that reduced her retirement annuity from $1500 to $500. The statute in effect when she retired said that, "Each person so retired ... shall be paid the sum of fifteen hundred ($1500) annually and for life from the date of such retirement." The Supreme Court did not interpret this mandatory language ("shall," "annually and for life") to supersede a subsequent state statute that reduced the amount of the annual annuity, saying that, "The presumption is that a law is not intended to create private contractual or vested rights but merely declares a policy until the legislature shall ordain otherwise."[14]

The presumption that pension statutes do not preclude Congress from decreasing or eliminating benefits at a future time rests on the recognition that legislative bodies require flexibility in public welfare matters.[15] "[O]ur cases are clear that legislation readjusting rights and burdens is not unlawful solely because it upsets otherwise settled expectations." *Usery v. Turner Elkhorn Mining Co.,* 428 U.S. 1, 15-16. While acknowledging this latitude, the Supreme Court in *Flemming* nonetheless indicated that congressional action may be subject to some constitutional restraint:[16]

> "Whether wisdom or unwisdom resides in the scheme of benefits set forth in Title II [of the Social Security Act], it is not for us to say. The answer for such inquires must come from Congress, not the courts. Our concern here, as often, is with power, not with wisdom." *Helvering v. Davis,* [301 U.S. 619] *supra,* at 644 [1937]. Particularly when we deal with a withholding of a noncontractual benefit under a social welfare program such as this, we must recognize that the Due Process Clause can be thought to interpose a bar only if the statute manifests a patently arbitrary classification, utterly lacking in rational justification.

Thus, only if Congress were to act in a totally irrational and arbitrary manner would due process considerations invalidate a subsequent amendment.[17] The Court reiterated this view in *United States Railroad Retirement Board v. Fritz,* 449 U.S. 166 (1980), wherein it upheld congressional amendments to railroad retirement benefits that reduced benefits for some beneficiaries and eliminated benefits for others. These changes were challenged under the Due Process Clause on the ground that they irrationally distinguished between classes of annuitants. However, the Court held that because Congress could have eliminated benefits for all classes of employees, it was not constitutionally impermissible to draw lines between groups of employees for the purpose of phasing out the benefits. The Court said: "Where, as here, there are plausible reasons for Congress' action, our inquiry is at an end." The Court added that drawing lines between categories of beneficiaries "is a matter for legislative, rather than judicial, consideration." *Id.* at 179-180.[18]

Congressional Guarantee of Social Security Benefit Payments

The Social Security program has faced funding shortfalls in the past and Congress has enacted a variety of measures to deal with financial imbalances.[19] Given the clear judicial precedents to the effect that Social Security benefits under title II are not property rights and cannot be categorized as contractual in nature, the question may be raised whether Congress could legislatively create a new, legally enforceable right to the receipt of a certain level of benefits by individuals eligible for Social Security benefits.[20] A legislative guarantee of a certain level of Social Security benefit payments with a corresponding obligation upon future Congresses for payment of such benefits would require either a finding of a contractual relationship between the federal government and individual certificate holders, the modification or repeal of which would be constitutionally impermissible, or a right stemming from Congress's implied promise not to enact legislation in the future that would bind a future Congress in the sense that the legislative enactment guaranteeing Social Security benefit payments could not be repealed or altered.

Congressional Power to Modify Its Own Contracts

A legally enforceable guarantee of a certain level of Social Security benefits set forth in legislation may be argued to create a contract between the federal government and individual Social Security recipients. It may be argued further that such a contract constitutionally protects an individual's right to continue to receive full benefits, and prohibits the federal government from abrogating such a contract by reducing or otherwise modifying the full payment of benefits an individual is entitled to receive.

Under Article I, § 10, cl. 1, known as the Contracts Clause, the states are forbidden to pass laws impairing the obligation of contracts. Even as applied to the states, since *Home Building & Loan Assn. v. Blaisdell,* 290 U.S. 398 (1934), this stricture is not very severe, save for state efforts to avoid their own contracts. *United States Trust Co. v. New Jersey,* 431 U.S. 1 (1977). As for the federal government, there is no such clause, the right being subsumed under the Fifth Amendment's due process clause. And that right, as in the case of any economic right under the due process clause, is subject to standards that are not considered rigorous. *PBGC v. R.A. Gray & Co.,* 467 U.S. 717. 732-33 (1984). Even insofar as the Government's own contracts are concerned, the usual rule is that they too may be subject to alteration, especially when the right to alter laws is reserved. Thus, Congress, in *Legal Tender Cases (Knox v. Lee),* 12 Wall. (79 U.S.) 457 (1871), was held to have the authority to make Treasury notes legal tender in payment of debts previously contracted for payment in gold, and in *Norman v. Baltimore & Ohio R. R.,* 294 U.S. 240 (1935), Congress was held to have the authority to invalidate provisions in private contracts calling for payment in gold coin. But when the federal government seeks to abrogate its own contracts in order to serve its own financial purposes or to increase the public fisc, a more searching scrutiny, and usually invalidation, follows. *Perry v. United States,* 294 U.S. 330 (1935) (law purporting to abrogate a clause in government bonds calling for payment in gold coin was invalid); *Lynch v. United States,* 292 U.S. 571 (1931) (statute abrogating contracts of war risk insurance held invalid as applied to outstanding policies).[21]

The relevant distinction here is that the federal government acting as sovereign, and the federal government acting as contractor, constitute two separate roles. When the government acts as sovereign, in its legislative or executive capacity, rendering impossible the performance of its obligations, it cannot be held responsible in its capacity as a contractor. *Horowitz v. United States,* 267 U.S. 458 (1925); *Deming v. United States*, 1 Ct. Cl. 190 (1865). *See United States v. Winstar Corp. 518* U.S. 839, 894-910 (1996) (plurality opinion of Justice Souter); and *id.*, 932-935 (Chief Justice Rehnquist dissenting). In *Horowitz,* the federal government had contracted with the claimant for silk products and for the shipment of silk within a certain time. But the United States Railroad Administration placed an embargo on shipments of silk by freight, and by the time the silk reached Horowitz the price had fallen, rendering the deal unprofitable. The Court barred any damages award against the United States for the delay. "It has long been held by the Court of Claims that the United States as a contractor cannot be held liable for an obstruction to the performance of the particular contract resulting from its public and general acts as sovereign." Supra, 267 U.S., 461.[22]

If a recipient's right under law to a certain level of Social Security benefits is to be viewed as a contract between the recipient and the federal government, this contract is arguably not in the class of contracts that the federal government enters into in its proprietary capacity as a contractor. Title II recipients, whether receiving old age, survivors, or disability insurance benefits, have not, by virtue of the receipt of this promise, paid any money, provided any service or thing of value in exchange for the government's guarantee not to reduce the recipient's payments in the future. The government's commitment is unilateral, and it arguably remains subject to §1104 of the Social Security Act, which reserves the right of Congress to revise or modify the Social Security Act by subsequent legislation. While congressional modification of the express terms of the promise in law not to reduce benefits is limited by due process considerations, such constitutional concerns impose a bar only upon the enactment of an arbitrary modification that has no rational justification.

Congressional Power to Promise Future Deference

It may be argued that Congress, by giving eligible individuals a legislative guarantee of a certain level of Social Security benefits can legally bind itself in the future to pay the full amount of such Social Security benefits plus COLAs to certificate holders. There is no doubt that Congress may validly enact such a provision, and promise to pay full Social Security benefits in the future. Congress may also provide for a funding mechanism and judicial recourse for non-compliance. Thereafter, Congress may decide to take whatever measures necessary to fulfill such a promise. The undeniably strong moral duty to do so, however, would not trump the underlying constitutional principle that a legislative enactment such as this cannot bind a future Congress in the sense that the legislative enactment cannot be repealed or altered.[23] "The principle asserted is, that one legislature is competent to repeal any act which a former legislature was competent to pass; and that one legislature cannot abridge the powers of a succeeding legislature. The correctness of this principle, so far as respects general legislation, can never be controverted." *Fletcher v. Peck,* 6 Cr. (10 U.S.) 87, 135 (1810) (Chief Justice Marshall).

To be sure, some congressional enactments, by their nature, are irrevocable. If Congress should admit a territory as a State, it could not subsequently repeal the law and make that State something else. And, as discussed above, constitutional protection is accorded contracts when the federal government incurs financial obligations while acting in its proprietary capacity. In such cases federal efforts to avoid liabilities arising out of its own contracts have been found to deny due process. *Perry v. United States, Lynch v. United States, Sinking Fund Cases, discussed, supra.* However, where the federal government acts as lawmaker exercising its sovereign powers to provide for the general welfare, it cannot give up such powers by a binding contract. "Contractual arrangements, including those to which a sovereign itself is party, remain subject to subsequent legislation by the sovereign." *Bowen v. Public Agencies Opposed to Social Security Entrapment,* 477 U.S. 41, 52 (1986) (internal quotation marks omitted).

Illustrating this principle is the Supreme Court's holding in *Stone v. Mississippi*, 101 U.S. 814 (1880), in which the legislature entered into a contract with a company to operate a lottery within the State. The following year a constitutional amendment was adopted by the State's voters abolishing lotteries. Quoting a state case, the Court stated:

> Irrevocable grants of property and franchise may be made if they do not impair the supreme authority to make laws for the right government of the State; but no legislature can curtail the power of its successors to make such laws as they may deem proper in matters of police. Id., 817-818.

These and other cases that might be cited[24] demonstrate the limited role contract principles play in matters affecting the governmental functions, rather than the proprietary functions, of the states and the federal government. In essence, absent the kind of promise involving the essence of contracts covered by the Contracts Clause, say, a guarantee of the "full faith and credit" of the United States in backing bonds, a statute, which in fact promises future congressional action or inaction, would likely not be held to constitute a contract enforceable by the courts. Legislative language that obligates the federal government to provide a guaranteed level of Social Security benefits to recipients purports to preclude the possibility that a recipient's benefits may be reduced in the future by either a repeal of the underlying law or by an amendment of the statutory provisions in title II. However, the weight of judicial authority suggests that Congress may not so bind itself, and that neither concepts of property rights nor contract would disable a future Congress from changing the benefits provided under title II of the Social Security Act.

Payment of Social Security Benefits from the Trust Fund in Case of Exhaustion

The projected exhaustion of the Social Security Trust Funds, formally known as the Federal Old Age and Survivors Insurance (OASI) Trust Fund and the Disability Insurance (DI) Trust Fund, raises a question whether that possibility would affect the legal right of beneficiaries to receive full Social Security benefits.[25] On May 12, 2009, the Trustees of the Social Security Trust Funds stated that [26]

> Under the long-range intermediate assumptions, ... [t]he combined funds are ... projected to become exhausted and thus unable to pay scheduled benefits in full on a timely basis in 2037.... Based on the Trustees' best estimate, program cost will exceed tax revenues starting in 2016 and throughout the remainder of the 75-year projection period. Social Security's combined trust funds are projected to allow full payment of benefits until they become exhausted in 2037. At that time, annual tax income to the trust funds is projected to equal about 76 percent of program costs. By 2083, annual tax income is projected to be about 74 percent as large as the annual cost of the OASDI program....
>
> Separately, the OASI and DI funds are projected to have sufficient funds to pay full benefits on time until 2039 and 2020, respectively.

The OASDI Trust Funds are accounts maintained on the books of the U.S. Treasury. The system operates on a "pay-as-you-go" basis. Current workers and their employers and the self-employed pay taxes on wages and self-employment income under the Federal Insurance Contributions Act (FICA) and the Self-Employed Contributions Act (SECA), respectively. Taxes paid now finance benefits for today's beneficiaries. A full 100% of these payroll taxes is appropriated to the Social Security Trust Funds.[27] Interest on and proceeds from the sale or redemption of government securities held in these funds are credited to and form a part of them.[28] Moreover, amounts credited to the funds are the only source of funds to pay benefits.[29]

Social Security is a statutory entitlement program.[30] Entitlement authority has been defined as "authority to make payments (including loans and grants) for which budget authority is not provided in advance by appropriation acts to any person or government if, under the provisions of the law containing such authority, the government is obligated to make the payments to persons or governments who meet the requirements established by law."[31] Budget authority is the authority provided by law to enter into obligations that will result in immediate or future outlays involving federal government funds.[32]

According to a publication of the Government Accountability Office, formerly the General Accounting Office,[33]

> Congress occasionally legislates in such a manner as to restrict its own subsequent funding options.... An example ... is entitlement legislation not contingent upon the availability of appropriations. A well known example here is Social Security benefits. Where legislation creates, or authorizes the administrative creation of, binding legal obligations without regard to the availability of appropriations, a funding shortfall may delay actual payment but does not authorize the administering agency to alter or reduce the "entitlement." ... Even under an entitlement program, an agency could presumably meet a funding shortfall by such measures as making prorated payments, but such actions would be only temporary pending receipt of sufficient funds to honor the underlying obligation. The recipient would remain legally entitled to the balance.

While an entitlement by definition legally obligates the United States to make payments to any person who meets the eligibility requirements established in the statute that creates the entitlement, a provision of the Antideficiency Act, 31 U.S.C. § 1341, prevents an agency from paying more in benefits than the amount available in the source of funds available to pay the benefits, in this case the Old Age and Survivors Insurance Trust Fund and the Disability Insurance Trust Fund. Section 1341, in relevant part, provides that:

> An officer or employee of the United States government or of the District of Columbia government may not—
>
> (A) make or authorize an expenditure or obligation exceeding an amount available in an appropriation or fund for the expenditure or obligation;
>
> (B) involve either government in a contract or obligation for the payment of money before an appropriation is made unless authorized by law; ....

The Antideficiency Act prohibits making expenditures either in excess of an amount available in a fund or before an appropriation is made. It would appear to bar paying more money in benefits than the amount of the balance in the Social Security Trust Funds primarily because, as noted earlier, disability and old-age and survivor benefit payments shall be made "only" from the Disability Insurance Trust Fund and the Old Age and Survivors Insurance Trust Fund, respectively.[34]

Violations of the Antideficiency Act are punishable by administrative and criminal penalties. An officer or employee who violates the act's prohibitions is subject to appropriate administrative discipline, including, when circumstances warrant, suspension from duty without pay or removal from office.[35] An officer or employee who knowingly and willfully violates the act can be fined not more than $5000, imprisoned for not more than two years, or both.[36]

After the Social Security Trust Funds become insolvent (i.e., unable to pay scheduled benefits in full on a timely basis), it appears that beneficiaries who would file suit to be paid the difference between the amount that receipts allow paying and the full benefit amount to which they are entitled would not be likely to succeed in getting the difference. The Supreme Court in *Reeside* v. *Walker*, 53 U.S. (11 How.) 272, 275 (1850), held that no officer of the government is authorized to pay any debt due from the United States, whether reduced to a court judgment or not, unless an appropriation has been made for that purpose. To support its holding, the Court cited Article I, Section 9, clause 7 of the Constitution, which states that, "No money shall be drawn from the Treasury, but in consequence of appropriations made by law; ...." The Court reaffirmed this principle in *Office of Personnel Management* v. *Richmond*, 496 U.S. 414, 424-426 (1990). Consequently, unless Congress amends applicable laws, it appears that beneficiaries would have to wait until the Trust Funds receive an amount sufficient to pay full benefits to receive the difference between the amount that can be paid from the Trust Funds and the full benefit amount.

CONCLUSION

The Old Age, Survivors and Disability Insurance program is a statutory entitlement program. Beneficiaries have a legal right to receive benefits if they meet the Social Security Act's eligibility requirements. Congress has, however, reserved the "right to alter, amend, or repeal any provision of this (Social Security) Act" and the U.S. Supreme Court has affirmed Congress's power to modify provisions of the Social Security Act in *Flemming v. Nestor*, 363 U.S. 603 (1960), and in subsequent court decisions. The Social Security program does not accord individuals either vested property rights or contractual rights with regard to future benefits. Congress may modify provisions of the Social Security Act as it exercises its constitutional power to provide for the general welfare.

Congress has the power to legislatively guarantee to pay eligible individuals a certain level of Social Security benefits, and not to reduce that level of benefits to such individuals in the future. While Congress may decide to take whatever measures necessary to fulfill such a obligation, courts would be unlikely to find Congress's unilateral promise to constitute a contract that could not be modified or abrogated in the future. Congressional modification of the terms of a guarantee to pay a certain level of benefits would be limited by due process considerations, however such constitutional concerns would impose a bar only upon the enactment of an arbitrary modification that has no rational justification. In addition, a congressional promise not to reduce a specific level of Social Security benefits payable to certain eligible individuals would not overcome the constitutional principle that a legislative enactment in a social welfare program cannot bind a future Congress in the sense that the legislative enactment cannot be repealed or altered.

The Trustees of the Old Age and Survivors Insurance Trust Fund and the Disability Insurance Trust Fund have projected that these funds on a combined basis will be exhausted (i.e., unable to pay full benefits on time, in 2040). The Social Security Administration would not be able to pay beneficiaries full benefits at that time because the Social Security Act states that benefits shall be paid only from the Social Security Trust Funds. Social Security Administration officials are bound by the Antideficiency Act, which prohibits paying amounts that exceed the amount available in the source of funds available to pay them. Although the legal right of beneficiaries to receive full benefits would not be extinguished by the insufficient amount of funds in the Social Security Trust funds, a court suit to obtain the difference between the amount in the Social Security Trust Funds available to pay partial benefits and the full benefit amount would not be likely to succeed in getting the difference.

The Supreme Court has held that no officer of the government may pay a debt whether reduced to a court judgment or not, unless Congress has appropriated funds to pay it. Consequently, unless Congress amends applicable laws, it appears that beneficiaries would have to wait until the Trust Funds receive an amount sufficient to pay full benefits to receive the difference between the amount that can be paid from the Trust Funds and the full benefit amount.

End Notes

[1] See CRS Report RL33514, *Social Security: What Would Happen If the Trust Funds Ran Out?*, by Kathleen Romig.

[2] For more information, CRS Report RL33544, *Social Security Reform: Current Issues and Legislation*, by Dawn Nuschler.

[3] Section 201 *et seq.* of the Social Security Act, 42 U.S.C. § 401 et seq.

[4] *Richardson v. Belcher*, 404 U.S. 78 (1971). In addition, Section 1104, 42 U.S.C. § 1304 explicitly states "The right to alter, amend, or repeal any provision of this Act is hereby reserved to the Congress."

[5] 363 U.S. 603 (1960).

[6] The Fifth Amendment, in relevant part, states that, "No person shall ... be deprived of life, liberty, or property, without due process of law; nor shall private property be taken for public use without just compensation." Language preceding the semicolon is referred to as the Due Process Clause; language following the semicolon is referred to as the Takings Clause.

[7] *See Richardson v. Belcher*, 404 U.S. 78 (1971), where the Supreme Court upheld an amendment that reduced monthly Social Security disability benefits from $330 to $225 to reflect receipt of state workmen's compensation benefits. See Also Milner v. Apfel, 148 F. 3d 812 (7th Cir. 1998) upholding suspension of Social Security benefits payable to certain persons in public institutions found not guilty by reason of insanity of offenses punishable by imprisonment for more than one year.

[8] 633 F. Supp. 511 (D.D.C. 1986), *aff'd.* 479 U.S. 878 (1986).

[9] P.L. 99-177, known as the Gramm-Rudmann-Hollings Act.

[10] *See also Zucker v. United States,* 578 F. Supp. 1239 (S.D.N.Y.1984), *appeal dismissed on proced. grounds.* 751 F.2d 373 (2d Cir. 1984), *aff'd.* 758 F. 2d 637 (Fed. Cir. 1985), *cert. denied*, 474 U.S. 842 (1985). The court there upheld a modification of a Civil Service retirement COLA saying that, although retirees may have a protected property interest when they are entitled to immediate payment under pre-existing law, their entitlement to any post-retirement increases in an annuity stems from the underlying statute which may be adjusted at any time. Id. at 758 F.2d 638.

[11] 301 U.S. 619 (1937).

[12] *Id.* at 635.

[13] *Flemming* at 610.

[14] *Id.* at 79.

[15] In *Bowen v. Public Agencies Opposed to Social Security Entrapment*, 477 U.S. 41 (1986), the argument was advanced that agreements between Congress and states regarding Social Security coverage of state and local employees conferred contractual rights upon the state and local governments. When Congress revoked the state's right to withdraw from its coverage agreement, California claimed a "taking of private property" under the Fifth Amendment. However, the Court disagreed. "The provision simply cannot be viewed as conferring any sort of 'vested right' in the face of precedent concerning the effect of Congress' reserved power on agreements entered into under a statute containing the language of reservation [to alter, amend or repeal the underlying statutory provisions]... Rather, the provision simply was part of a regulatory program over which Congress retained authority to amend in the exercise of its power to provide for the general welfare." *Id.* at 55.

[16] *Flemming* at 611. Note, however, that once a beneficiary receives an actual benefit payment, the government cannot take it back. "Pension payments actually made to retirees become their property and are protected against takings, even if and where the payments are unquestionably a gift." *National Education Association-Rhode Island v. Retirement Board of Rhode Island Employees' Retirement System*, 172 F. 3d 22, 30 (1st Cir. 1999).

[17] "[T]he strong deference accorded legislation in the field of national economic policy is no less applicable when that legislation is applied retroactively. Provided that the retroactive application of a statute is supported by a legitimate legislative purpose furthered by rational means, judgments about the wisdom of such legislation remain within the exclusive province of the legislative and executive branches." *PBGC v, R.. A. Gray & Co.*, 467 U.S. 717, 729(1984).

[18] *See Steinberg v. United States*, 163 F. Supp. 590 (Ct. Cl. 1958), for a case which held that a provision of the Federal Civil Service Retirement Act terminating annuity payments to any person who invoked his Fifth Amendment privilege against self-incrimination was arbitrary and discriminatory in violation of the Due Process Clause and also a bill of attainder, i.e., a legislative punishment, in violation of Art. I, §6, cl. 3 of the Constitution.

[19] See CRS Report RL33544, *Social Security Reform: Current Issues and Legislation*, by Dawn Nuschler.

[20] Examples of this may be found in two 109th Congress bills: S. 1750 which proposed to create a legally enforceable guarantee for current retirees and workers born before 1950 to receive the level of their monthly Social Security benefits as determined on the date of entitlement plus applicable cost-of-living increases for the rest of their lives, and a related bill, H.R. 1164, which would have provided the same guarantee for all individuals eligible for Social Security benefits under title II. Current retirees, and workers upon being approved to receive benefits, would, under these proposals, have received certificates guaranteeing the level of benefits that were in effect at the time of retirement. Certificates would have constituted budget authority in advance of appropriations acts, and would have represented the obligation of the federal government to provide for the payment of Social Security benefits to individuals to whom certificates were issued in amounts in accordance with the guarantee as set forth in the certificates. No similar bills have been introduced in the 11 1th Congress as of the date of this report.

[21] The subject of the *Lynch case*, war risk term insurance policies for which the insured, former military personnel, had paid monthly premiums, were found to be contracts that were property and created vested rights. The Court contrasted these insurance policies with pensions, noting that "Pensions, compensation allowances and privileges are gratuities. They involve no agreement of parties; and the grant of them creates no vested right. The benefits conferred by gratuities may be redistributed or withdrawn at any time in the discretion of Congress." *Lynch*, at 577.

[22] *See also Flemming v. Rhodes*, 331 U.S. 100, 107 (1947) where the Court upheld a district court injunction against the eviction of tenants stating "So long as the Constitution authorizes the subsequently enacted legislation, the fact that its provisions limit or interfere with previously acquired rights does not condemn it. *Immunity from federal regulation is not gained through forehanded contracts*. Were it otherwise the paramount powers of congress could be nullified by 'prophetic discernment.'" (Emphasis supplied; footnote citation omitted).

[23] For an extensive treatment of this principle, see Eule, *Temporal Limits on the Legislative Mandate: Entrenchment and Retroactivity*, 1987 AM. B. FOUND. RES. J. 379.

[24] *See, United States v. Will,* 449 U.S. 200 (1980) involving congressional suspensions of automatic cost-of-living adjustments to the salaries of high-level federal officials. The Supreme Court held that Congress could legislate to revoke the salary increases, even though previously authorized in legislation. Whenever congress decides to suspend or repeal a statute in effect, "[t]here can be no doubt that ... it could accomplish its purpose by an amendment to an appropriation bill, or otherwise."

[25] See CRS Report RL33514, *Social Security: What Would Happen If the Trust Funds Ran Out?,* by Kathleen Romig.

[26] Board of Trustees, Federal Old-Age and Survivors Insurance and Disability Insurance Trust Funds, *The 2009 Annual Report of the Board of Trustees of the Federal Old-Age and Survivors Insurance and Disability Insurance Trust Funds* 3 and 19 (2009). The Annual Report is available at http://www.socialsecurity.gov/ OACT/TR/2009/tr09.pdf.

[27] Section 201(a) and (d) of the Social Security Act, 42 U.S.C. § 401(a) and (b).

[28] Section 201(f) of the Social Security Act, 42 U.S.C. § 401(f).

[29] Section 201(h) of the Social Security Act, 42 U.S.C. § 401(h).

[30] See sections 202 and 223 of the Social Security Act, 42 U.S.C. §§ 402 and 423, which state that every individual who meets the eligibility requirements set forth therein "shall be entitled" to an old age benefit or disability benefit, respectively.

[31] 2 U.S.C. §§ 622(9) and 651(c)(2)(C).

[32] 2 U.S.C. § 622(2).

[33] Office of the General Counsel, General Accounting Office, I *Principles of Appropriations Law* 3-49 and 3-49, n. 40. (3d ed. 2004).

[34] Section 201(h) of the Social Security Act, 42 U.S.C. § 401(h).

[35] 31 U.S.C. § 1349.

[36] 31 U.S.C. § 1350.

In: Social Security Reform: Disability, Indexing and Financing ISBN: 978-1-61668-354-2
Editor: Janet U. Burlington

Chapter 6

ISSUES FOR DISABILITY AND DEPENDENT BENEFITS*

United States Government Accountability Office

WHY GAO DID THIS STUDY

Many recent Social Security reform proposals to improve program solvency include elements that would reduce benefits currently scheduled for future recipients. To date, debate has focused primarily on the potential impact on retirees, with less attention to the effects on other Social Security recipients, such as disabled workers and dependents. As these beneficiaries may have fewer alternative sources of income than traditional retirees, there has been interest in considering various options to protect the benefits of disabled workers and certain dependents.

This report examines (1) how certain elements of Social Security reform proposals could affect disability and dependent benefits, (2) options for protecting these benefits and how they might affect disabled workers and dependents, and (3) how protecting benefits could affect the Social Security program. To conduct this study, GAO used a microsimulation model to simulate benefits under various reform scenarios. GAO also interviewed experts and reviewed various reform plans, current literature, and GAO's past work.

WHAT GAO RECOMMENDS

Congress should consider the potential implications of reform on disability and dependent beneficiaries.

GAO received general and technical comments from SSA and the Department of the Treasury, which were incorporated as appropriate.

* This is an edited, reformatted and augmented version of a U. S. Government Accountability Office publication dated October 2007.

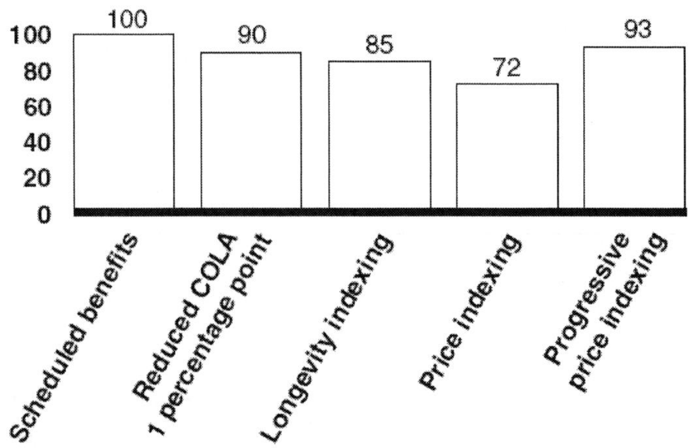

Source: GAO analysis of GEMINI data.
Note: Currently scheduled benefits are not attainable under current funding levels.

Simulated Median Lifetime Benefits for Disabled Workers (1985 Cohort) Percentage of scheduled benefits

WHAT GAO FOUND

We considered several reform elements that could improve Social Security Trust Fund solvency by reducing the initial benefits received or the growth of individual benefits over time. According to our simulations, these reform elements would reduce median lifetime benefits for disabled workers by up to 27 percent (see graph) and dependents by up to 30 percent of currently scheduled levels. While the size of the benefit reduction could vary across individuals, it could be substantial for the vast majority of these beneficiaries, depending upon the reform element.

Options for protecting the benefits of disabled workers and dependents from the impact of reform elements include, among others, a partial exemption, whereby currently scheduled benefits are maintained until retirement age. For example, while simulations showed that one reform element could decrease median lifetime benefits of disabled workers to about 89 percent of currently scheduled levels, a partial exemption could restore them to about 96 percent. Further, these protections could be more targeted. For example, a larger cost of living adjustment would result in more rapid benefit growth for those disabled workers who receive benefits for a prolonged period of time. Some protections for dependent benefits could be targeted to a single group of dependents, such as widows, while others could affect multiple groups. For example, increasing the maximum benefit a family can receive could protect a wider group of beneficiaries, including children and spouses of disabled workers, and disabled adult children.

While it may be desirable to protect the benefits of disabled workers and certain dependents, such protections would come at a cost to Social Security. Protecting benefits could lessen the impact that a reform element would have on solvency. In addition, such protections could create incentives to apply for Disability Insurance, if disability benefits remained stable while retirement benefits were reduced.

ABBREVIATIONS

AIME	Average Indexed Monthly Earnings
COLA	cost-of-living adjustment
CPI	Consumer Price Index
CPI-U	consumer price index for urban consumers
CPI-W	consumer price index for urban wage earners and clerical workers
CSSS	Commission to Strengthen Social Security
DAC	disabled adult children
DI	Disability Insurance
FRA	full retirement age
GEMINI	Genuine Microsimulation of Social Security Accounts
MINT3	Modeling Income in the Near Term
OASDI	Old Age, Survivors, and Disability Insurance
OCACT	Office of the Chief Actuary
PENSIM	Pension Simulator
PIA	primary insurance amount
PSG	Policy Simulation Group
SI	Survivors' Insurance
SSAB	Social Security Advisory Board
SSASIM	Social Security and Accounts Simulator

October 26, 2007

The Honorable Charles B. Rangel
Chairman
The Honorable Jim McCrery
Ranking Member
Committee on Ways and Means
House of Representatives

The Honorable Michael R. McNulty
Chairman
The Honorable Sam Johnson
Ranking Member
Subcommittee on Social Security
Committee on Ways and Means
House of Representatives

The Honorable Sander M. Levin
House of Representatives

Social Security forms the foundation of retirement income, providing old age benefits to millions of Americans. However, Social Security is more than a retirement program; it provides benefits to survivors and other dependents as well as to disabled workers. For all these recipients, benefits are determined through a common formula. Therefore, the prospect of altering the benefit formula to address Social Security's financial shortfall would affect all beneficiaries, not just retired workers. Moreover, changes to the benefit formula could have a large impact on those beneficiaries who are least able to compensate for any reduction in benefits. For example, disabled workers may have fewer alternative sources of income—especially earnings-related income—than do retired workers, to offset any planned reduction in benefits. In addition, certain dependents, such as older widows, may rely more heavily on Social Security benefits and may not have the means to offset reductions caused by reform. Hence, benefit reductions related to reform could potentially affect the welfare of disabled workers and dependent beneficiaries more substantially than those of retired workers.

Nonetheless, the debate over Social Security reform has focused primarily on the effects proposed reforms would have on retirees—with little discussion of how they might affect disabled workers and dependents. Given interest in protecting these beneficiaries, this report discusses (1) how certain elements of Social Security reform plans would affect disability and dependent benefits, (2) some options for protecting these benefits and how these options might affect disabled workers and dependents, and (3) how protecting these benefits could affect the Social Security program itself.

To determine how certain elements of reform would affect disability and dependent benefits,[1] we first selected reforms by reviewing a number of reform plans, current literature, and our past work to identify reform elements that would have an impact on benefits. We then estimated the percentage of disabled workers and dependents whose benefits would be affected by certain reform elements by simulating the outcome for a sample of workers born in 1985, using a microsimulation model.[2] We also used data from this model to analyze the difference in both median and total lifetime benefits between currently scheduled benefits and those under each reform element.[3] Rather than consider the distribution of benefits across recipients, we show the impact of reform and protections on median benefits. This approach provides a snapshot of how the reforms would affect individuals in each target group (disabled workers and dependents). In addition, when we consider total lifetime benefits, we are able to examine the extent to which individuals are affected. While scheduled benefits are not attainable under current funding levels, they nevertheless provide us with a point of comparison in examining the impact of various reform elements. To identify options for protecting disabled worker and dependent benefits, we reviewed the current literature and our past work and interviewed relevant experts. To determine how these protections would affect both disability and dependent benefits, we analyzed the change in median lifetime benefits given various reform elements and different protections, using the microsimulation model, as well as some qualitative analysis. Finally, to determine the impact that protecting benefits could have on the Social Security program itself, we interviewed relevant experts, reviewed the literature, and conducted a qualitative analysis of the issues involved. Throughout our analysis, we assume that the Disability Insurance (DI) program maintains its current operational structure in terms of disability determination, although GAO has recommended certain measures that Social Security should take to modernize the program and its administration. For more details on our approach to this study and on the microsimulation model, please see appendix I.

Throughout this report, the term "dependents" refers to those beneficiaries who receive some or all of their Social Security benefits based on a family member's earnings record. Our dependent category includes survivors— such as widow(er)s and surviving children—as well as spouses and children of both retirees and individuals receiving disability benefits. Specifically, dependents need not demonstrate financial dependence, but rather familial relationships such as those listed above. Also, throughout the report, "disabled worker benefits" refers to the type of benefit that an individual with disabilities who qualifies for the DI program would receive based on his or her own earnings record. Further, those individuals who receive disabled worker benefits are referred to as "disabled workers." While we understand the sensitivity associated with this terminology, our use of this term is consistent with the Social Security Administration's terminology and aims to precisely represent such beneficiaries and their benefits.

We conducted our work between October 2006 and October 2007 in accordance with generally accepted government auditing standards.

RESULTS IN BRIEF

Most of the elements for reforming Social Security that we considered would reduce future benefits from currently scheduled levels for Social Security recipients, including the great majority of disabled workers and dependents. These reform elements include longevity indexing (changing benefits to reflect increased life expectancies), price indexing (adjusting benefits so they grow at the rate of inflation rather than wages), progressive price indexing (a graduated form of price indexing), and changes to the cost-of-living adjustment. According to our simulations, most such changes would reduce benefits for at least three-quarters of disabled workers and dependent beneficiaries in the 1985 cohort. For example, progressive price indexing would affect more than 75 percent of these beneficiaries, while other reform elements we analyzed would affect virtually all beneficiaries. In addition, most reform elements would reduce the median lifetime benefits of disabled workers and dependents to between 70 and 93 percent of currently scheduled levels, with price indexing resulting in the largest reduction. These reform elements would not affect individuals uniformly. For example, longevity indexing would reduce the lifetime benefits of 86 percent of disabled workers by between 10 to 25 percent; the other 14 percent would generally face reductions of 10 percent or less.

There are many options for protecting both disabled worker and dependent benefits. Some of these options can be targeted to particular groups of beneficiaries. The options include, among others, a partial exemption—by which the beneficiary receives currently scheduled benefits until retirement age—and a full exemption—by which the beneficiary receives benefits at the currently scheduled level throughout the remainder of his or her life. Through our simulation of reform elements and various protections, for example, we found that a one percentage point reduction in the cost-of-living adjustment would reduce the median lifetime benefits of disabled workers to about 89 percent of their currently scheduled level, but a partial exemption could restore them to about 96 percent. Options for protecting the benefits of disabled workers could also be structured to mitigate benefit reductions that result from changes to the initial benefit calculation. For example, disabled workers who receive benefits for a prolonged period of time could be given a "super COLA" that would allow their benefits to grow more rapidly. In terms of dependent benefits, protections could cover a single group, such as widows, or multiple groups. For example, increasing the maximum family benefits could protect the benefits of child survivors, widowed parents, children and spouses of disabled workers, and disabled adult children.

In general, although it may be desirable to protect the benefits of certain disabled workers and dependents, such protections would come at a cost to the program and could create unintended incentives that would negatively affect Social Security's finances. While the reforms we considered were aimed at improving the solvency of Social Security, protecting the benefits of these populations would lessen the effect of each of these reforms. In addition, certain protections may create incentives for individuals who might not otherwise apply for Disability Insurance to do so. For example, those nearing retirement may apply for the Disability Insurance program if disability insurance benefits remained stable while retirement benefits fell.

The Department of the Treasury provided technical comments. The Social Security Administration (SSA) provided general and technical comments. We incorporated the comments throughout our report as appropriate.

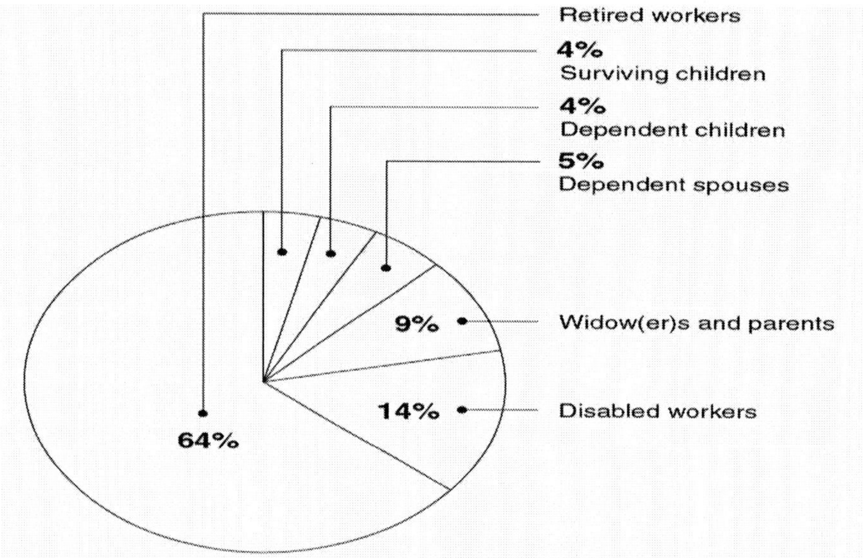

Source: GAO analysis of July 2007 SSA data.

Notes: Some Social Security beneficiaries are entitled to more than one type of benefit. If both benefits are financed from the same trust fund, the beneficiary is usually counted only once in the statistics, as a retired-worker or a disabled-worker beneficiary, and the benefit amount recorded is the larger amount associated with the auxiliary benefit. If the benefits are paid from different trust funds, the beneficiary is counted twice and the respective benefit amounts are recorded for each type of benefit. Accessed from http://www.ssa.gov/policy/docs/quickfacts/stat_snapshot/ on August 29, 2007.

Figure 1. Social Security Beneficiaries by Beneficiary Status, 2007

BACKGROUND

Social Security is one the largest federal programs in the United States, providing about $546 billion in benefits in 2006 to over 49 million beneficiaries. Although the majority of

Social Security benefits are paid to retirees, Social Security does much more than provide retirement income. Social Security Disability Insurance (DI) pays monthly cash benefits to nearly 7 million workers who, due to a severe long-term disability, can no longer remain in the workforce. Additionally, Social Security provides benefits to over 11 million dependents,[4] including payments to widows and widowers as well as surviving parents and children under Survivors' Insurance (SI), plus benefits to dependent spouses and children of retired and disabled workers paid from the Old Age Insurance (or Old Age) and DI trust funds. Social Security benefits often represent a significant source of income for their recipients, providing an average of $1,051 a month (as of July 2007) to retired workers, $995 a month to widows and widowers, and $979 a month to disabled workers. Although disabled workers and dependents receive slightly lower average monthly benefits than retired workers, benefits could be particularly important to these individuals. These beneficiaries may face considerable hardships; for example, a disabling condition may make work and other activities of daily living more difficult. As a result, these beneficiaries may have financial difficulties planning and preparing for death or disability in the way one might plan for retirement. Social Security was never intended to provide an adequate income by itself, but instead serves as an income base on which to build. In fact, the Social Security program balances the goals of income adequacy with individual equity, i.e., that lower income beneficiaries should receive higher benefits relative to wages than higher income beneficiaries (adequacy), and beneficiaries with higher lifetime income receive higher benefits in accordance with their income/lifetime contributions (equity).

History and Development of DI and Dependents' Benefits

Although Social Security had originally been envisioned to include disability and survivors' insurance, the 1935 Social Security Act created only a retirement program.[5] Over the next 40 years, the program expanded both the size and type of its benefits, introducing benefits for dependents and disabled workers (figure 2). The first new type of benefits went to dependents, as the 1939 amendments offered payments to elderly dependent wives and widows, as well as dependent children. (Some husbands and widowers were allowed to receive these same benefits after 1950[6]). Creating these benefits was not only seen as socially desirable, but also offered additional protections for workers and their families from risk and spent down surpluses created by the system. Disability Insurance, which had been recommended by the 1938 and 1948 advisory councils, was established in 1956 to provide cash benefits to permanently disabled workers over the age of 50. The DI program was later expanded to include disabled workers under the age of 50 as well. In 1961, widows benefits increased from 75 to 85 percent of their deceased spouse's benefits, and then to 100 percent in 1972. In addition, eligibility was extended to divorced spouses as well as to the spouses and children of disabled workers. Furthermore, benefit levels for retirees, dependents, and disabled worker beneficiaries grew during this time period. However, facing solvency crises, legislative efforts to control the size of the Social Security program were made in the mid 1970s and early 1980s.

In order to maintain trust fund solvency, major changes were enacted to reduce the growth of Social Security benefit levels from the mid1970s to the early 1980s. Additionally, a number of legislative changes to the DI and dependents' programs eliminated or reduced certain benefits and tightened the eligibility standards for receiving other benefits. However, despite ongoing fiscal concerns, eligibility for a few dependents' and disability benefits has been expanded since 1975, suggesting an interest in protecting some vulnerable populations who may rely on Social Security for a significant portion of their monthly income. Although recent reform proposals have focused on elements intended to improve solvency, there continues to be some interest in protecting some or all DI and dependents' benefits from potential benefit reductions. Figure 3 shows how Old Age, Survivors, and Disability Insurance (OASDI) has grown financially and in terms of beneficiaries over time.

Date	Benefits
1935	Social Security Act establishes retirement benefits.
1939	Benefits established for wives, widows, and dependent children.
1950	Benefits expanded to husbands, widowers, and some divorced widows.
1954	Disability Freeze enacted to exempt years an individual is unable to work due to disability from benefit calculation for disabled workers.
1956	Social Security Disability Insurance (DI) established.
1958	Benefits established for dependents of disabled workers.
1960	Age requirement for DI benefits eliminated.
1965	Benefits established for divorced wives under certain conditions.
1972	Automatic indexing implemented. Divorced wives' benefits liberalized.
1977	Indexing formula corrected, causing reductions in scheduled benefits.
1980	Continuing disability reviews become mandatory.
1981	Benefits for post-secondary students eliminated.
1983	Major reform permanently delayed COLA, resulting in lifetime benefit reductions in all programs. Full retirement age raised from 65 to 67, between 2003 and 2027.
1984	Medical Improvement Standard implemented for continuing disability reviews.
1990	The definition of a disabled widow(er) liberalized.
1999	Ticket to Work Act aimed to reintroduce disabled workers into labor force.

Source: GAO analysis.

Figure 2. Disabled Worker and Dependent Benefits Timeline

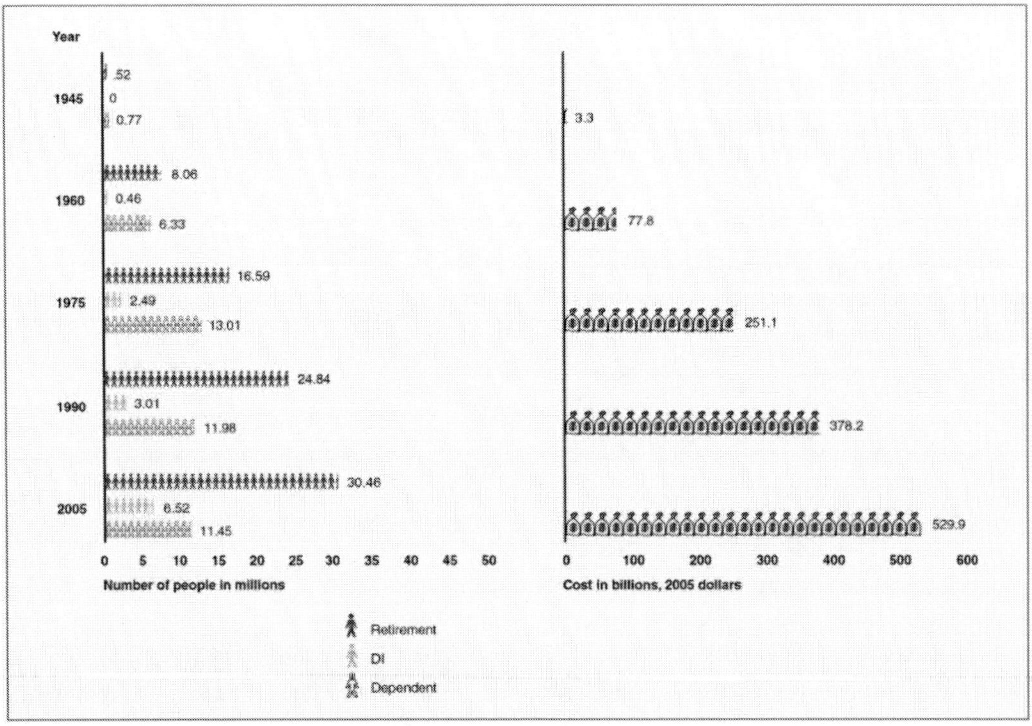

Source: GAO analysis of SSA data; Art Explosion, images.

Figure 3. Evolution of the OASDI Program

Development of a Single Benefit Formula

Although the 1935 act did not provide for disability and dependents' benefits, those benefits were later built upon the existing Social Security structure, and today all benefits continue to be calculated from a common formula. Dependents' benefit levels were set as fractions of the benefits owed to the person upon whom beneficiaries depended. For example, under the 1939 legislation, a widow would receive 75 percent of her deceased husband's benefits, and dependent children or spouses would receive 50 percent of the retired worker's benefits. When Congress created the DI program in 1956, it provided a lower retirement age (50) for those who were permanently and totally disabled. The same benefit formula used in computing OASI benefits was adopted for disability benefits because the original DI program treated disabled workers as being forced into premature retirement. In 1960, when Congress expanded the DI program by eliminating the requirement that disabled workers had to be 50 years old, the same benefit formula applied. Because benefit types shared a common formula, automatic indexing provisions implemented in 1972 and 1977 applied across the board.

The OASDI programs are tightly linked in other ways as well. These programs are financed through a common mechanism—payroll taxes; receipts from the payroll tax are deposited into the OASI and DI trust funds which, like the two programs, are separate but often combined in discussion and analysis of Social Security's solvency and sustainability.[7] Furthermore, beneficiaries can receive multiple types of benefits over their lifetimes, moving into, out of, and among Social Security programs at different life stages. When disabled workers reach the full retirement age (FRA), for example, they begin to receive retirement benefits from the Old Age program, in place of DI benefits; the common benefit formula keeps such individuals' benefit levels stable.[8] In another case, a recent widow(er) might have her (or his) retirement or spousal benefits replaced with survivors' benefits based on the relative earnings of the deceased spouse. Because parents, children, or spouses may be eligible for dependents' benefits through the Old Age, Survivors, and Disability Insurance programs, a person can collect several types of Social Security benefits over a lifetime, although generally not simultaneously.[9] The many linked pieces of Social Security could make developing a single, comprehensive reform package challenging because such a package would need to take into account all of these pieces.

Benefits under Current Law

Under current law, Old Age benefits are generally calculated through a four-step process in which a progressive yet earnings-based formula is applied to an earnings history, and then updated annually through a costof-living adjustment (COLA).[10] For those who receive retirement benefits, this earnings history is generally based on the 40 years in which credited earnings were highest, with the 5 lowest-earning years dropped out (leaving the highest 35 years of indexed earnings to be included in the initial benefit calculation).[11] Dependents' benefit levels are determined as a given percentage of Old Age benefit levels. Eligible children and spouses can receive up to 50 percent of a worker's benefit; widow(er)s can be given up to 100 percent; and surviving parents or children can collect up to 75 percent, subject to a family maximum.

DI benefits are calculated similarly to Old Age benefits, but are generally based upon a shortened work history. (For more detail on how benefits are calculated, refer to app. II.) To be eligible for benefits, individuals must have a specified number of recent work credits under Social Security when they first become disabled. Individuals must also demonstrate the inability to engage in substantial gainful activity by reason of a physical or mental impairment that has lasted or is expected to last for twelve continuous months or to result in death. If not eligible on medical grounds, SSA must also consider age, education and past work history. In particular, medical eligibility criteria for DI are less stringent for applicants over the age of 55.

Based on prior work, GAO has designated modernizing federal disability programs (including the DI program) as a high risk area because of challenges that continue today.[12] For example, GAO found that federal disability programs remain grounded in outmoded concepts that equate medical conditions with work incapacity. While SSA has taken some actions in response to prior GAO recommendations, GAO continues to believe that SSA should continue to take a lead role in examining the fundamental causes of program problems and seek the regulatory and legislative solutions needed to modernize its programs so that they are aligned with the current state of science, medicine, technology, and labor market conditions. Moreover, SSA should continue to develop and implement strategies to better manage the programs' accuracy, timeliness, and consistency of decision making.

Social Security's Financing

Social Security is currently financed primarily on a pay-as-you-go basis, in which payroll tax contributions of current workers are used primarily to pay for current benefits. Since the mid1980s, the Social Security program has collected more in taxes than it has paid out in benefits. However, because of the retirement of the baby boomers coupled with increases in life expectancy, and decreases in the fertility rate, this situation will soon reverse itself. According to the Social Security Administration's 2007 intermediate assumptions,[13] annual cash surpluses are predicted to turn into ever-growing cash deficits beginning in 2017. Absent changes to the program, these deficits are projected to deplete the Social Security DI trust fund in 2026 and the OASI trust fund in 2042, leaving the combined system unable to pay full benefits by 2041. Reductions in benefits, increases in revenues, or a combination of both will likely be needed to restore longterm solvency. A number of proposals have been made to restore fiscal solvency to the program, and many include revenue enhancements, benefit reductions, or structural changes such as the introduction of individual accounts as a part of Social Security. Because many reforms to the benefit side of the equation would reduce benefits through changes in the benefit formula, they could affect DI and dependents' benefits as well as Old Age benefits. Unless accompanied by offsets or protections, these reforms might reduce the income of disabled workers and dependents. This situation could be challenging for these beneficiaries as they may have relatively low incomes or higher health care costs and rely heavily on Social Security income. Many disabled workers and dependents may also have trouble taking on additional work and accumulating more savings and, thus, have difficulty preparing for Social Security benefit reductions.

CERTAIN BENEFIT-REDUCING REFORM ELEMENTS COULD HAVE A SUBSTANTIAL IMPACTON DISABLED WORKERS AND DEPENDENTS

Certain Benefit-Reducing ReformElements Could Havea Substantial Impacton Disabled Workersand Dependents Many reform elements could have a substantial impact on the benefits of Social Security recipients, including those of disabled workers and dependents. We considered six such elements that have been included in reform proposals to improve trust fund solvency. These reform elements take a variety of forms and would change either the initial benefit calculation or the growth of individual benefits over time. Our projections indicated that most of these elements would reduce benefits from currently scheduled levels[14] for the majority of both disabled workers and dependents. That is, most would reduce median lifetime benefits for these beneficiary types—some more substantially than others. Many of these beneficiaries would also experience a reduction in total lifetime benefits; the extent of which would depend on the reform element and individual.

Benefit-Reducing Reform Elements Take Different Forms

We considered six different reform elements that could help control costs and improve Social Security solvency by reducing benefits.[15] Five would change how initial benefits are calculated, and one would limit the growth of an individual's benefits over time.

We considered several ways to improve solvency:[16]

- Longevity indexing would lower the amount of the initial benefit in order to reflect projected increases in life expectancy. Such indexing would maintain relatively comparable levels of lifetime benefits across birth years by proportionally reducing the replacement factors in the initial benefit formula.
- Price indexing would maintain purchasing power while slowing the growth of initial benefits. This would be accomplished by indexing initial benefits to the growth in prices rather than wages, as wages tend to increase faster than prices.
- Progressive price indexing, a form of price indexing, would control costs while protecting the benefits of those beneficiaries at the lowest earnings levels (in terms of career average earnings). It would continue to index initial benefit levels to wages for those below a certain earnings threshold and employ a graduated combination of price indexing and wage indexing for those above this threshold.
- Increasing the number of years used in the benefit calculation would also control program costs. For example, initial benefits could be based on the highest 40, rather than 35, years of indexed earnings. This could be done either by eliminating the 5 years normally excluded from the calculation or by increasing the total number of years factored in from 40 to 45 years. In either of these cases, the initial Old Age benefit would be calculated using the highest 40 years of indexed earnings.[17] (For more information on these reform elements and how we incorporated them into our microsimulation model, see app. I.)
- Raising the age at which people are eligible for full retirement benefits could change the amount and/or the timing of initial benefits. Increasing the full retirement age would improve solvency by generally increasing the number of years worked, reducing the number of years benefits are received and increasing revenue to the system through payroll taxes in the additional years worked. Further, those who retire early would have their benefits actuarially reduced.
- Though it would not generally affect initial benefit amounts, a change to Social Security's cost-of-living adjustment (COLA) could also control costs and improve solvency by limiting the growth of an individual's benefits over time. The COLA adjusts benefits to account for inflation by indexing benefits to price growth annually, using the Consumer Price Index (CPI).[18] Setting the COLA below the CPI would limit the nominal growth of an individual's benefits over time,[19] and as such those who receive benefits for a prolonged period of time would see the largest reductions.

Most of the Social Security Reform Elements We Considered Would Reduce Benefits for Virtually All Beneficiaries

According to our projections for the 1985 cohort, four of the five reform elements that we analyzed would reduce total lifetime benefits for more than three-quarters of disabled workers and dependents, relative to currently scheduled benefits.[20] Table 1 shows the proportions of disabled workers and dependents affected by each of the reform elements. For three of the elements—reducing the COLA by one percentage point, price indexing and progressive price indexing—the percentage of disabled workers affected is very similar to the percentage of dependents affected. Moreover, for these three reform elements, more than 99 percent, or virtually all, disabled workers and dependents would see their benefits reduced. In contrast, progressive price indexing differs from other reform elements in its impact: fewer beneficiaries are affected, and the percentage of disabled workers affected varies from that of dependents. While an estimated 87 percent of dependents would experience a reduction in lifetime benefits under progressive price indexing, an estimated 77 percent of disabled workers would do so.

While the COLA reduction, longevity indexing and price indexing are all designed in such a way that they affect virtually all beneficiaries, the COLA, which has a greater impact on solvency than longevity indexing,[21] affects relatively fewer disabled workers and dependents. This is because the COLA reduction would first affect benefits one year after the initial benefit payment was made, whereas both longevity indexing and price indexing affect the initial benefit amount. Our simulations indicated that 1.11 percent of disabled workers died within the first year of receiving benefits, while only 0.35 percent of dependents did so. Most such beneficiaries would not have received a COLA.

Reform Elements Reduce Median Lifetime Benefits for Disabled Workers and Dependents to Varying Degrees

According to our simulations each of the reform elements we selected would reduce median lifetime benefits for both disabled workers and dependents relative to currently scheduled benefits (figures 4 and 5).[22] However, our projections also indicated that these reductions would vary by reform element. Price indexing would have the largest impact on disabled workers and dependents, reducing median lifetime benefits by more than 25 percent. Median lifetime benefits would fall from $473,960 to $343,350 for disabled workers and from $351,910 to $244,745 for dependents. Progressive price indexing, on the other hand, would create the smallest reduction in median lifetime benefits, with median lifetime benefits falling by 7 percent for disabled workers and 8 percent for dependents.[23]

Additionally, increasing the full retirement age and increasing the number of computation years would likely reduce median lifetime benefits for dependents.[24] Since dependent benefits are linked to those of the primary worker, an increase in the full retirement age could shorten the period of time over which they both receive benefits. Alternatively, some workers may decide not to adjust their retirement plans in response to the increase in the FRA. Those who maintain their original retirement plans, retiring prior to the new FRA, will also receive reduced benefits relative to current law. (See app. II for a discussion of how benefits are adjusted for early retirement.) Thus, under both scenarios, total lifetime benefits would be reduced, and so, too, would median lifetime benefits. A similar outcome results from increasing the number of computation years by which initial benefits are calculated. By increasing the number of computation years, a worker's earnings history is expanded to include years of possibly lower indexed earnings. As a result, total benefits for some retired workers, and therefore, their dependents, would likely be reduced, as would median lifetime benefits.

Table 1. Reform Elements, Their Solvency Impacts, and the Percentage of Disabled Workers and Dependents with Reduced Total Lifetime Benefit Levels for the 1985 Cohort

Element[a]	Solvency impact[b] (actuarial scoring)[c]	Percentage of disabled workers with reduced total lifetime benefits (1985 Cohort)	Percentage of dependents with reduced total lifetime benefits (1985 Cohort)
COLA reduction –1percentage point[d]	1.49	99.15	99.87
Increase the number of computation years—from 35 to 40[d]	0.46	n/a[e]	99.99
Longevity Indexing—reducing formula factors by 0.5%[f]	1.17	99.89	99.98
Price indexing[d]	2.38	99.95	99.97
Progressive price indexing[d,g]	1.43	76.78	86.90

Source: GAO analysis of GEMINI data and SSA OCACT.

[a] Because of modeling constraints, we were unable to analyze the effects of a change in the FRA. However, Social Security actuaries have estimated the solvency impact of increasing the FRA to age 68. This reform would improve actuarial balance by 0.62 percent of taxable payroll.

[b] Solvency impacts come from SSA's Office of the Chief Actuary (OCACT). Taken individually, each of the reform elements would improve Social Security solvency. For more on how the reform elements were scored for solvency, see appendix I.

[c] Actuarial balance as a percentage of taxable payroll.

[d] OCACT Score based on 2005 Trustees Report intermediate assumptions.

[e] We were also unable to analyze the effects of increasing the number of computation years for disabled workers.

[f] OCACT Score based on 2001 Trustees Report intermediate assumptions.

[g] In the microsimulation model, approximately 80 percent of all beneficiaries were affected by the progressive price indexing reform. Some disabled workers also received benefits as dependents at some point in their life, and if those workers are excluded then the percentage of disabled workers affected would fall.

Note: Using the 1985 cohort, we also projected the percentage of workers with reduced total lifetime benefits for Social Security beneficiaries who were never disabled. 99.68% of Social Security beneficiaries who were never disabled would see benefit reductions if the COLA were reduced by 1 percentage point, and 100% would see benefit reductions if the number of computation years was increased from 35 to 40. Under longevity indexing, price indexing, and progressive price indexing the percentage of beneficiaries affected would be 99.99%, 99.99%, and 80.97%, respectively.

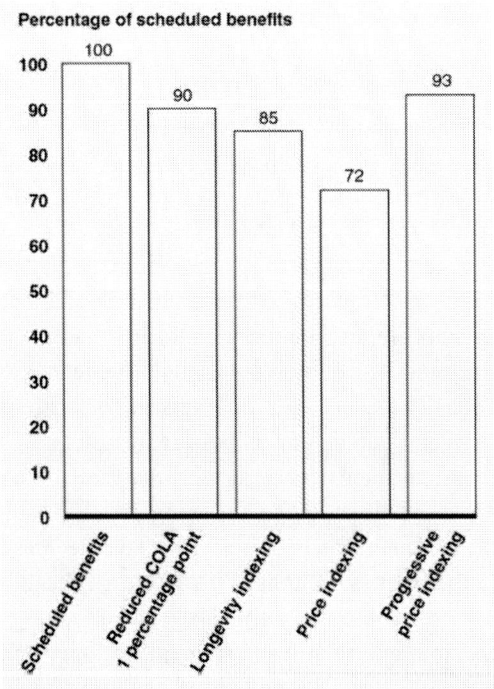

Source: GAO analysis of GEMINI data.

Figure 4. Projected Median Lifetime Benefits for Disabled Workers (1985 Cohort)

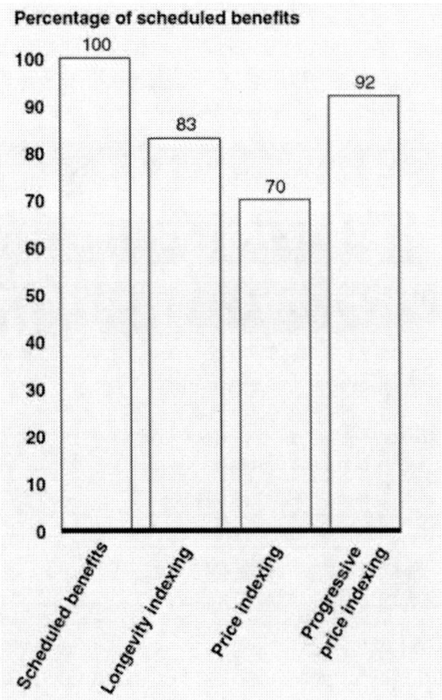

Source: GAO analysis of GEMINI data.

Figure 5. Projected Median Lifetime Benefits for Those Who Have Ever Received Dependent Benefits (1985 Cohort)

Disabled and Dependent Beneficiaries Are Not Uniformly Affected by Reform Elements

Our projections suggest that, while lifetime benefits would be reduced for virtually all disabled workers and dependents, such reductions would not be uniform across individuals. Figures 6 and 7 compare beneficiaries' total lifetime benefit reductions by each reform element, for disabled workers and dependents, respectively. If the COLA were reduced by one percentage point, our projections show that approximately 58 percent of disabled workers experienced lifetime benefit reductions of 10 percent or less,25 while about 42 percent of disabled workers experienced lifetime benefits reduced by 10 to 25 percent. Almost no disabled workers would see benefits fall by more than 25 percent.

Certain reform elements would create reductions in total lifetime benefits for the vast majority of disabled workers and dependents. These reductions may create new hardships for certain beneficiaries, such as disabled workers, who may not be able to easily replace lost income. According to our projections, price indexing would result in the greatest benefit reductions for the largest percentage of beneficiaries, with decreases in lifetime benefits of between 25 percent and 50 percent for almost 70 percent of disabled workers and about 90 percent of dependents. Both price indexing and longevity indexing have a greater effect on initial benefit amounts the longer the reform is in place. As such, people who leave the workforce early may experience a smaller reduction in lifetime benefits than those who leave at full retirement age.[26] For example, as shown in figures 6 and 7, longevity indexing could reduce lifetime benefits for about 86 percent of disabled workers and about 96 percent of dependents by 10 to 25 percent.[27]

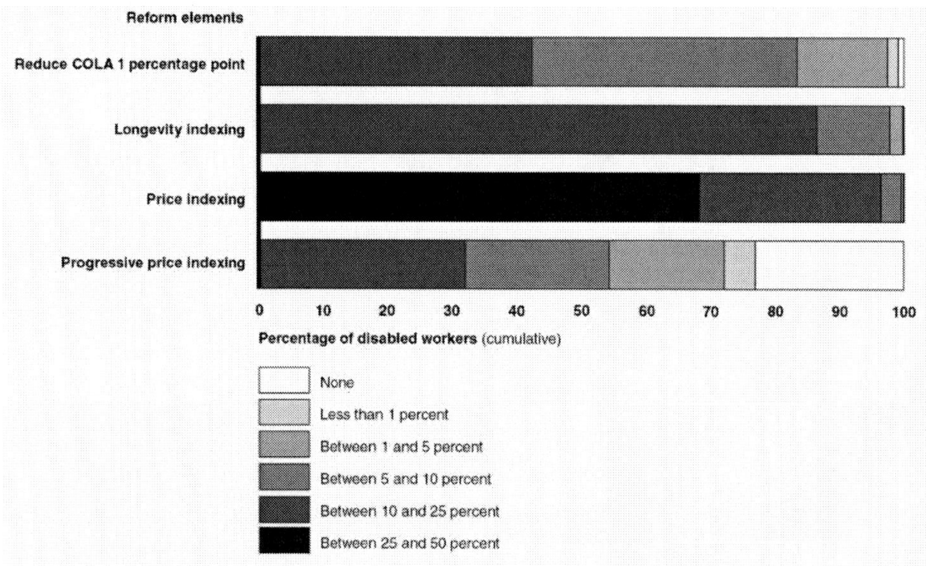

Source: GAO analysis of GEMINI data.

Note: The above intervals include the upper endpoint. For example "Between 1 and 5 percent" includes 5, but not 1. No disabled workers had total lifetime benefit reductions of more than 50 percent.

Figure 6. Percentage Range of Projected Reductions in Total Lifetime Benefits for Disabled Workers (1985 Cohort)

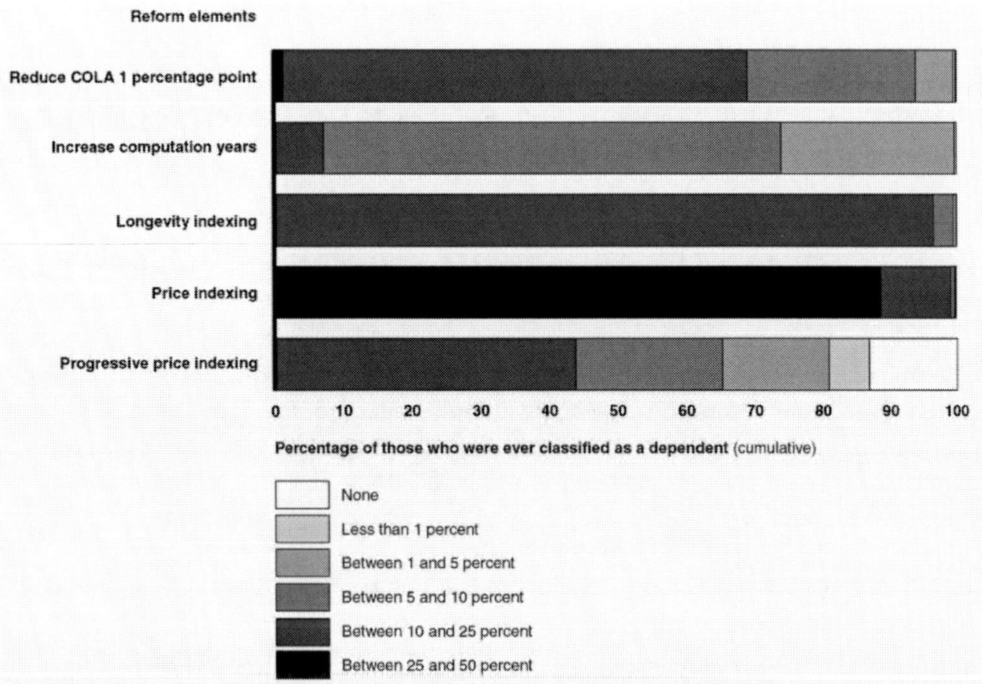

Source: GAO analysis of GEMINI data.

Note: The above intervals include the upper endpoint. For example "Between 1 and 5 percent" includes 5, but not 1. For those who were ever classified as a dependent, only a very few individuals had total lifetime benefit reductions of more than 50 percent. Four individuals experienced a benefit reduction of more than 50 percent under the COLA reduction, 21 individuals under increasing the number of computation years, 13 under longevity indexing, 34 under price indexing, and 5 under progressive price indexing.

Figure 7. Percentage Range of Projected Reductions in Total Lifetime Benefits for Individuals Who Have Ever Received Dependent Benefits (1985 Cohort)

Progressive price indexing may have a more moderate effect on the benefits of disabled workers and certain dependents because it is designed to protect benefit levels for low earners and gradually apply benefit reductions to beneficiaries with higher earnings. Because of shorter earnings histories, some disabled workers would be in the low end of the earnings distribution.[28] Thus, under progressive price indexing, a greater proportion of disabled workers would be likely to have benefits adjusted by wage indexing. According to our projections, progressive price indexing would reduce total lifetime benefits by 5 percent or less for 46 percent of disabled workers and 35 percent of dependents.

Options Protecting the Benefits of Disabled Workers and Dependents Could Mitigate the Effects of Benefit-Reducing Reform Elements

Various options are available to protect benefits in different ways, including accelerating the growth of an individual's benefits, modifying current constraints on benefit levels, and exempting certain populations from reforms. Options can also target certain types of beneficiaries. We analyzed some of these protections and found they could be structured to mitigate the effects of benefit reductions for varying lengths of time. In addition, we found that specific options to protect dependent benefits could be targeted to certain vulnerable beneficiaries, such as widows and dependent children.

Many Options Exist for Protecting Social Security Benefits, Including Full and Partial Exemptions

We found a wide range of options exist for protecting disabled workers and dependents from benefit-reducing reforms. Table 2 provides a summary of the options.[29] The protection options may be very specific in terms of whom they protect and how, or broader in scope. For example, while two protection options focus specifically on disabled adult children (DAC), others, such as partial exemptions could apply to any vulnerable population. In addition to each option having its own strengths and weaknesses, the options could interact with each other and with the various reform elements. When implementing a protection option, all of these factors could influence its impact.

There are several protection options that could be applied to all disabled workers and dependents. Under a full exemption, beneficiaries would not be subject to a reform and their benefits would remain unchanged. Under a partial exemption, beneficiaries would not be subject to a reform until a certain point in time. For example, disabled workers could be exempt from benefit changes until they are converted to the Old Age program at the full retirement age. At this point, their benefit amount would be recalculated to reflect the reform in proportion to the years they spent working. In addition, a super COLA could help protect the benefits of disabled workers and dependents. A super COLA would mitigate some of the effects of a benefit-reducing reform by annually increasing benefits at a rate above the consumer price index—which is currently used to index benefits.

Some protection options could cover all dependents by increasing the percentage of the worker's benefit that the dependent receives. (See app. II for more detail on how dependent benefits are calculated.) For example, a number of proposals have called for increasing the percentage of the worker's benefit that widow(er)s receive. Another option that could protect the benefits of a wide range of dependents would be to raise the maximum benefit that families can receive based on one worker's earnings record. Other protection options, such as caregiver credits, could focus on protecting particular groups of dependents. Several reform proposals have, in fact, called for providing caregiver credits to individuals who spend time out of the workforce to care for their dependents or to those with reduced or low earnings while attending to care-giving responsibilities. Some proposals assign caregivers a specified level of earnings for each year the caregiver received zero or low earnings compared to prior years. Other proposals exclude zero-earning care years from the initial benefit calculation.[30] Another option specific to a certain type of dependent would be to increase benefits for aged survivors, since they are more likely to rely on Social Security to stay out of poverty and could have fewer opportunities, such as returning to work, to respond to benefit-reducing reforms.

Table 2. Options for Protecting Disabled Worker and Dependent Benefits from Social Security Reform

Protection option available for	Protection option	Given a specific reform, the protection option could affect the:				
		Initial benefit amount	Growth of individual benefits	Maximum family benefit available	Eligibility for benefits	Conversion at the full etirement age
Any beneficiary type	Full exemption	✓	✓			
	Partial exemption	✓	✓			✓
	Minimum benefit	✓				
	Super COLA		✓			
	Age-indexed super COLA		✓			
Children and families of disabled workers	Increase the percentage of the worker's benefit that the dependent family member receives as his/her benefit	✓				
	Increase the family maximum benefit level for DI			✓		
	Increase the percentage of the worker's benefit that a dependent child or a disabled adult child (DAC) receives as his/her benefit in combination with increasing the family maximum benefit	✓		✓		
	Decouple DAC benefits from other family benefits			✓		
	Hold initial benefit amount harmless for family benefits	✓				
Children and families of retired workers	Expand eligibility rules for divorced spouses				✓	
	Increase the percentage of the worker's benefit that the dependent family member receives as his/her benefit	✓				
	Increase the percentage of the worker's benefit that a dependent child or DAC receives as his/her benefit in combination with increasing the family maximum benefit	✓		✓		
	Decouple DAC benefits from other family benefits			✓		
Spouses	Increase the percentage of the worker's benefit that the spouse receives as his/her benefit	✓				
	Implement a child/family care credit[a]	✓				
Survivors	Hold initial benefit amount harmless for family benefits	✓				
	Hold early survivors (young children or young widow(er)s) harmless	✓	✓			
	Increase the surviving spouse benefit to 2/3 or 3/4 of the combined couples' benefit	✓				
	Increase benefits for aged survivors	✓				
	Increase the early retirement age[b]	✓				

Source: GAO.

[a] If the spouse is eligible for retirement benefits based on his or her own earnings record, Social Security will pay that amount first. However, if the spouse benefit (based on his or her husband's earnings record) would be a higher amount, Social Security will combine the benefits and pay the higher amount. A spouse receiving such a benefit may also be eligible for a care credit for his or her own earnings record. This care credit could change the initial benefit amount.

b While an increase in the early retirement age could increase the initial benefit amounts for those who retire at the new early retirement age, others who may need to stop working at 62 may have no Social Security payments for the elapsed time.

Increasing the early retirement age could offer some protection for survivors. If the early retirement age were raised—for example, from 62 to 64—then workers who take early retirement would receive actuarially adjusted benefits for a shorter period of time under the new early retirement age, and thus their monthly benefits would be relatively higher than the monthly benefits they would have received if they had retired at the current early retirement age.[31] Since a dependent's benefit is linked to the worker's initial benefit amount, an increase in the worker's benefit would also increase the dependent's benefit, mitigating some of the negative effects of other reforms. Similarly, raising the FRA coupled with a partial exemption from a benefit reduction could offer some additional protection for disabled worker benefits. With an increase in the FRA, disabled workers would receive (exempted) DI benefits for a longer period of time because the age at which their disability benefits are converted to retiree benefits would rise with the new FRA.

Some Benefit Protections Could Restore Benefits to Levels near Those Scheduled under Current Law

In general, the reform elements we examined reduce median lifetime benefits for disabled workers and dependents. Because disabled workers may not have the financial resources—especially earnings related income—to adjust to benefit reductions, we explored the interaction of reform elements and certain options to offset them.

According to our projections, protections from a reduction in the COLA could restore benefits of disabled workers to levels close to those scheduled under current law. Reducing the COLA by one percentage point would result in about a 10 percent decrease in median lifetime benefits for workers who become disabled before age 60. To offset such a decrease, they could be partially or fully exempted. With a COLA reduction, a partial exemption would mean that the Social Security Administration would increase a disabled worker's benefits annually as scheduled under current law (i.e., using the full COLA) until the worker reached the full retirement age. At that point, the disabled worker's benefits would grow annually by the reduced COLA (1 percentage point lower than what it would be under current law). Our projections showed that a partial exemption as described above would raise median lifetime benefits from their reduced levels by 7 percent (up to 96 percent of scheduled levels under current law). In contrast, a full exemption would allow annual COLA adjustments in line with current law until death (figure 8).[32]

In addition to a decrease in the COLA, we analyzed options for protecting the benefits of disabled workers under three reform elements that have an impact on the initial benefit amount a disabled worker receives—price indexing, longevity indexing, and progressive price indexing. There are several protection options for mitigating the effects of these reform elements, including full and partial exemptions. In the case of price indexing initial benefits, we projected that the median lifetime benefits of disabled workers would be about 75 percent of the median benefits under current law (figure 9). A full exemption for disabled workers would raise the benefits of those disabled workers who exclusively receive DI benefits to the currently scheduled levels. However, a partial exemption from price indexing would restore the median lifetime benefit to 89 to 90 percent of scheduled levels, depending on how the partial exemption is implemented.[33] One type of partial exemption (Type I) uses price indexing to calculate the portion of the benefits based on the years a person is out of the workforce and receiving DI benefits. In contrast, the other type of partial exemption (Type II) uses wage indexing to cover the same time period. (For more details, please see app. I.) The difference between the two partial exemptions becomes more substantial the earlier one becomes disabled, as the difference between wages and prices increases over time. While offering some protection from benefit reductions, both types of partial exemptions involve a recalculation of benefits at the full retirement age. This recalculation would result in lower benefits for the DI recipient and could create a potential problem if that individual relied on the prior benefit amount and had limited options for replacing the lost income. (See figures. 10 and 11 for longevity indexing and progressive price indexing, respectively.)

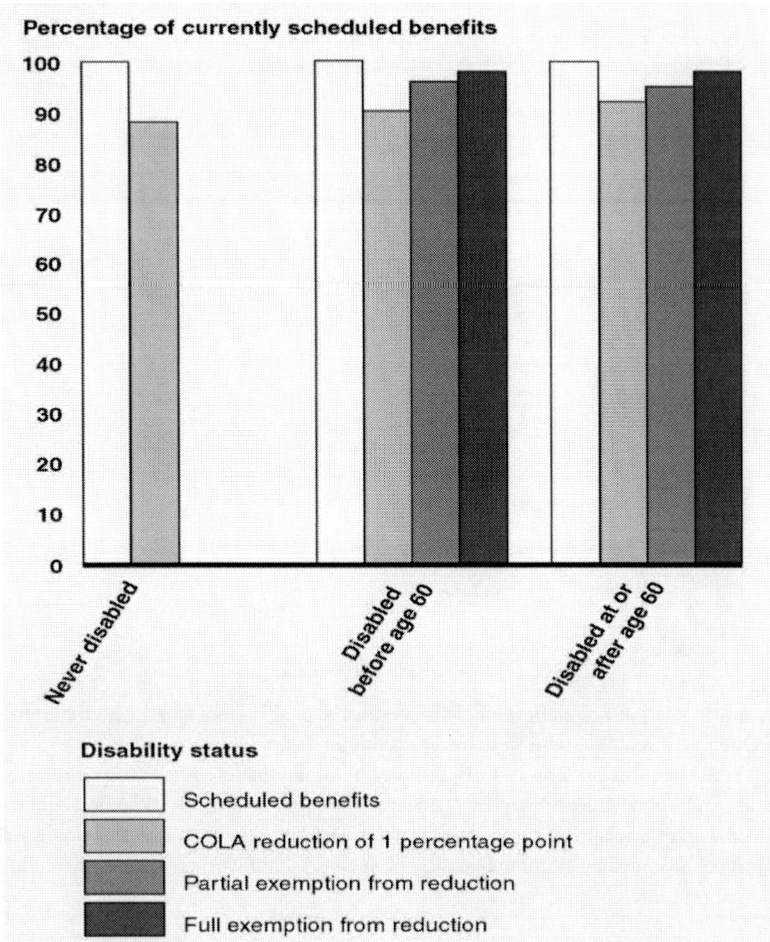

Source: GAO analysis of GEMINI data.

Notes: In figures 8 to 11, the population labeled "Never disabled" refers to all beneficiaries—dependent or retirees on their own record—who were never disabled.

In figures 8 to 11, the benefits under a full exemption do not completely return to pre-reform levels. This is because some individuals receiving disabled worker benefits also received some benefits as dependents from another worker's record at some point in their lifetime. As those benefits would not be subject to the same protections, median lifetime benefits for such disabled workers may remain slightly lower than those under current law.

Figure 8. Projected Median Lifetime Benefits under a COLA Reduction of 1 Percentage Point (1985 Cohort)

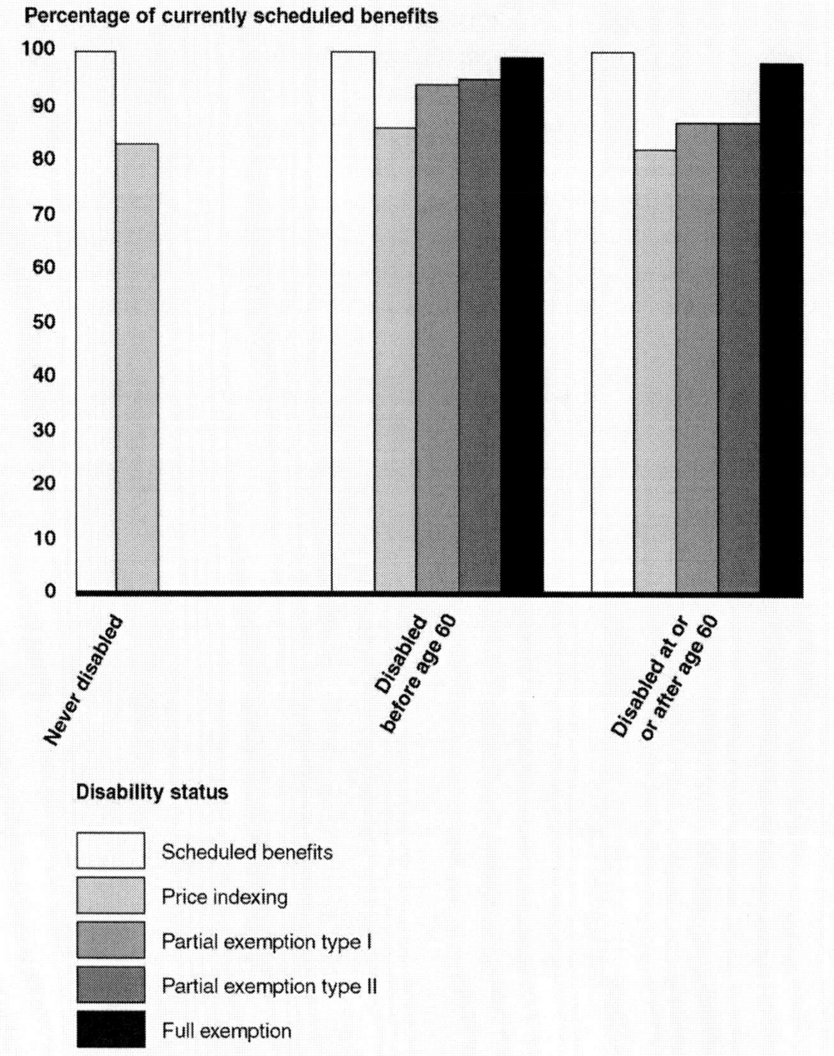

Source: GAO analysis of GEMINI data.

Notes: In figures 8 to 11, the population labeled "Never disabled" refers to all beneficiaries—dependent or retirees on their own record—who were never disabled.

In figures 8 to 11, the benefits under a full exemption do not completely return to pre-reform levels. This is because some individuals receiving disabled worker benefits also received some benefits as dependents from another worker's record at some point in their lifetime. As those benefits would not be subject to the same protections, median lifetime benefits for such disabled workers may remain slightly lower than those under current law.

Figure 9. Projected Median Lifetime Benefits under Price Indexing (1985 Cohort)

Another protection option would be to allow disability benefits to grow at a greater rate than other benefits. For example, disabled workers could be explicitly included in the scope of the reform, and receive reduced initial benefits. However, instead of receiving annual increases based on the current-law COLA, disabled workers could have their benefits increased by a "super COLA"—one that is set above the Consumer Price Index. In this case, benefits for the disabled would grow at a faster rate than they would under current law and could approach or even exceed current law levels. Variations on the super-COLA could include an "age-indexed super COLA" which would be greater for those disabled at younger ages. For those workers who become disabled near the full retirement age the COLA would be closer to that used for retirees. These protections could be particularly beneficial for disabled workers who receive benefits for a prolonged period of time.

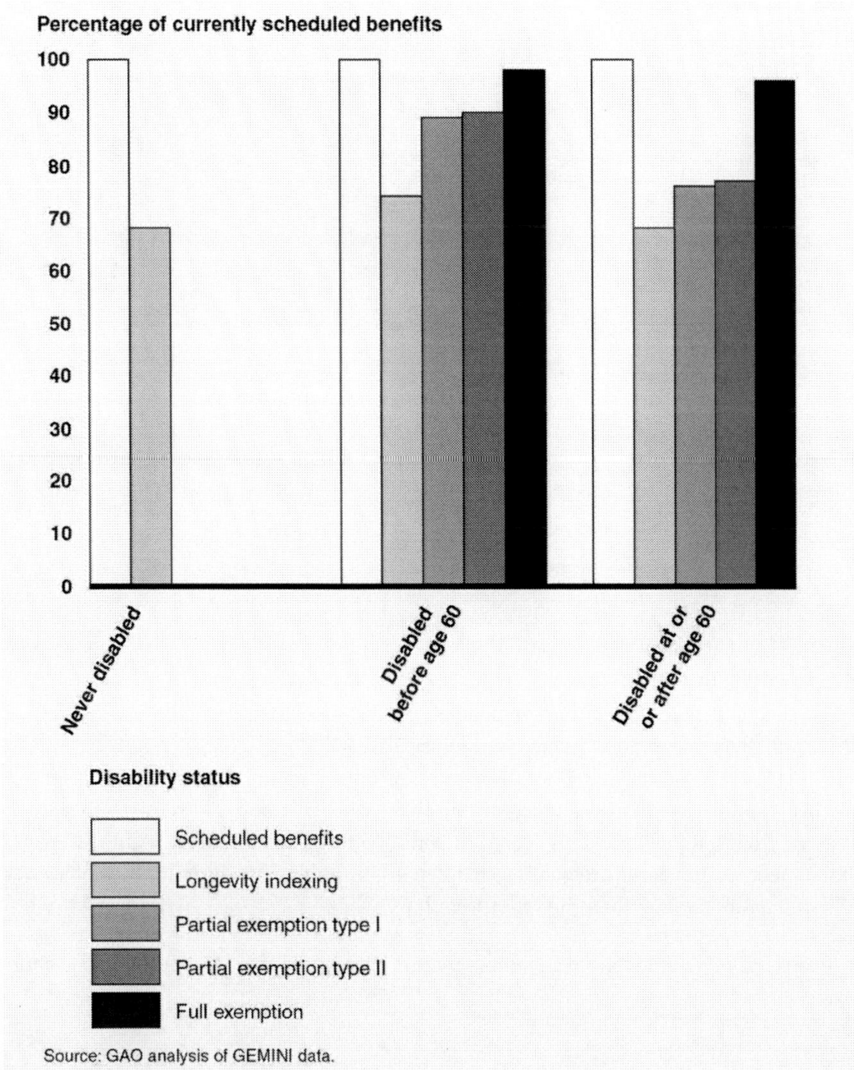

Source: GAO analysis of GEMINI data.

Notes: In figures 8 to11, the population labeled "Never disabled" refers to all beneficiaries—dependent or retirees on their own record—who were never disabled.

In figures 8 to 11, the benefits under a full exemption do not completely return to pre-reform levels. This is because some individuals receiving disabled worker benefits also received some benefits as dependents from another worker's record at some point in their lifetime. As those benefits would not be subject to the same protections, median lifetime benefits for such disabled workers may remain slightly lower than those under current law.

Figure 10. Projected Median Lifetime Benefits under Longevity Indexing (1985 Cohort)

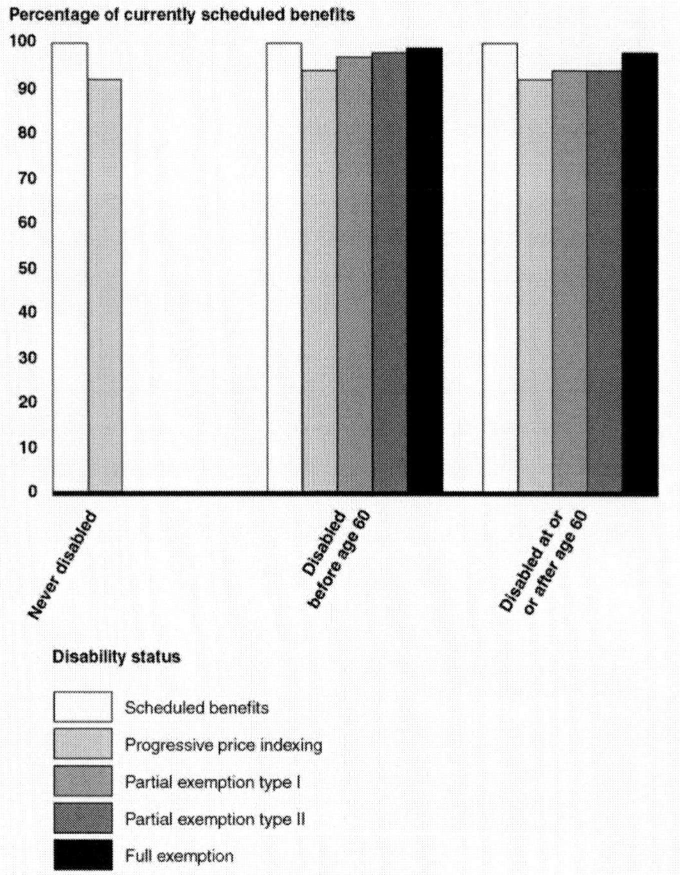

Source: GAO analysis of GEMINI data.

Notes: In figures 8 to 11, the population labeled "Never disabled" refers to all beneficiaries—dependent or retirees on their own record—who were never disabled.

In figures 8 to 11, the benefits under a full exemption do not completely return to pre-reform levels. This is because some individuals receiving disabled worker benefits also received some benefits as dependents from another worker's record at some point in their lifetime. As those benefits would not be subject to the same protections, median lifetime benefits for such disabled workers may remain slightly lower than those under current law.

Figure 11. Projected Median Lifetime Benefits under Progressive Price Indexing (1985 Cohort)

Protections for Dependent Benefits Could Be Targeted to Certain Vulnerable Beneficiaries, Including Survivors

While protections for disabled workers would generally cover all such beneficiaries, the options for protecting dependent benefits could be more targeted to specific dependents and not necessarily applied to the full range of dependents, which includes spouses, divorcees, widow(er)s, and child survivors. The circumstances around which a person becomes a dependent vary greatly, as does the role of Social Security benefits in their lives. For some,

Social Security may be the primary source of support; for others, it may be only a small proportion of their income.

Table 3. Child Beneficiaries

Program	Number of children receiving benefits (thousands)	Children as a percentage of program beneficiaries	Total monthly benefit children receive (in millions of dollars)	Average monthly benefit (in dollars)
All	3959	8.0	1993	503
Old Age	485	1.4	253	522
Survivors	1850	28.6	1269	686
Disability	1624	18.6	471	290

Source: GAO analysis. of Social Security data.

Note: Data accessed from http://www.ssa.gov/policy/docs/quickfacts/stat_snapshot/ on August 29, 2007. The children referred to in this chart receive benefits off someone else's work record – generally a parent. For example, the 1,624,000 children receiving benefits from the DI program have a parent/guardian who is disabled.

Protections could target children, who make up about 8 percent of Social Security beneficiaries, receiving benefits as the survivors or dependents of disabled or retired workers. Table 3 shows the number of children who receive benefits in each category and the average monthly benefit for these children. One way to protect the benefits of children would be to exempt them from any reform, keeping their benefit calculation tied to current law. Another way to protect their benefits to some degree would be to raise the maximum benefit a family could receive on a single worker's earnings record.[34]

The majority of experts with whom we spoke told us that increasing the maximum amount that a family could receive from one worker's earnings record could help protect child and other dependent benefits. Such an increase could help those dependents who are constrained by the family maximum. A family may have several people receiving benefits based on one worker's record. The sum of the family members' benefits may exceed the specified maximum, which is calculated as a percentage of the worker's benefit amount. Thus, any reform that would result in a decrease in the primary benefit amount would also result in a decrease in the amount that each eligible family member would receive and a corresponding decrease in the total amount a family would receive.

Certain options, including increased allowable benefits for widows or partial exemptions, could be designed to protect the benefits of widow(er)s or others who may have fewer resources available to them. Under current law, widows and widowers can collect 100 percent of their deceased spouse's benefits (or their own benefit—whichever is greater); a "widow's boost" would allow them to receive up to 75 percent of the couple's combined benefits. Widow(er)s may rely on Social Security for a large percentage of their retirement income, in part because they may live many years beyond the exhaustion of other financial resources, may find it difficult to work, or may incur large health expenses that deplete their other resources.

A reduction in the COLA may be particularly detrimental to the lifetime benefits of those who live long lives, because the effect of reducing the COLA is compounded over time. As such, it may be desirable to protect older widow(er)s—along with other individuals who receive benefits for a prolonged period of time—from the effect of a COLA reduction. For example, in our projections for the COLA reduction, we found that for the group of widows who received some benefits and who died before age 75, median lifetime benefits would be approximately 93 percent of those under current law. In contrast for those who lived past age 95, median lifetime benefits would be only 83 percent of currently scheduled levels.

Some Protection Options May Create New Costs and Unintended Incentives for the Social Security Program

The options for protecting the benefits of disabled workers and those of dependents come at a cost to the Social Security program in terms of its solvency. In addition, some protections options may create incentives for people to apply to the Disability Insurance program if DI benefits increase while retirement benefits stay stable. Further, protection options could provide disincentives for some to return to work.

Protecting the Benefits of Disabled Workers and Dependents Would Increase Costs for the Social Security Program

The Social Security reform elements we examined were designed primarily to improve program solvency. These reform elements would generally reduce benefits from their currently scheduled but underfunded levels.[35] While protecting the benefits of disabled workers and dependents may be socially desirable, such protection would come at some cost to the Social Security program. In particular, the protections lessen the degree to which the potential reforms could restore solvency. One could counter these costs with further benefit reductions to beneficiaries considered less vulnerable than those recipients whose benefits are specifically protected. That is, reform packages with certain benefit protections for vulnerable populations may necessitate further reductions in the benefits of retired workers or increases in revenues to achieve the intended solvency effect. In addition to the effects on solvency, some of the protections discussed may also have administrative costs associated with them.

Certain Protections May Create Incentives for Individuals to Apply for Disability Benefits

Protecting the benefits of disabled workers may increase the number of people who apply for disability benefits. This may also be relevant to certain reform elements. An increase in the full retirement age coupled with the reduction in benefits for early retirement could motivate some individuals approaching the early retirement age to apply for disability benefits, if they believed that they could qualify for the now greater DI benefits.[36] For example, before a change in the retirement age a worker who is a year away from the full retirement age, and who would qualify for DI but is unsure of that outcome, may choose to wait and only receive Old Age benefits. Once the full retirement age is raised, this worker may choose to apply for DI, rather than waiting to receive retirement benefits. The greater the benefit disparity between the two programs, the more likely it may be that DI applications and enrollment will increase. Thus, the potential for an increase in DI program costs exists with any reform elements that decrease the generosity of the Old Age component of OASDI without a corresponding decrease in that of the DI component.[37]

Under current law, there may already be an incentive for older workers to apply for DI rather than retire early. Using individual level data from the simulation model, we analyzed the benefits of two similar individuals under current law and under price indexing with and without full and partial exemptions. Both of the simulated individuals had similar lifetime earnings, close to the median for the simulated 1985 cohort, and both would have received initial benefits at age 62. However, they differed in two significant ways: one retired at age 62, while the other was disabled at age 62, and the retiree had lower lifetime benefits under current law.[38] The retiree, who died at age 84, had lifetime benefits of about $433,000, while the disabled worker, who died at age 82, had lifetime benefits of about $505,000—about 16 percent higher than those of the retired worker.

A full exemption for disabled workers from certain reform elements could similarly create discrepancies between the two programs, resulting in incentives to apply for the DI program. Under price indexing, the lifetime benefits of both individuals would be reduced, but the relative difference would remain at about 16 percent. However, if disabled workers were fully exempted from price indexing, the simulated disabled worker's lifetime benefits would be back to the initial amount of $505,000, or 72 percent greater than those of the retired worker. This difference in potential benefits would likely increase the incentive to apply for the DI program. Figure 12 and table 4 show the total lifetime benefits and the average monthly benefits of these two simulated individuals under current law, price indexing, and with exemptions.

However, partial rather than full exemptions or other protections, such as an age-indexed super COLA, could provide benefit protections without substantially increasing the disparity between the programs for people approaching the early or full retirement ages. Under a partial exemption, in which the disabled worker would be exempted from the reform until full retirement age, the added incentive that could be created by a full exemption would be reduced. Such a partial exemption for the disabled worker in our example would result in lifetime benefits that are about 33 percent higher than those of the retired worker under price indexing.

Certain Protections May Affect the Work Decisions of Beneficiaries

The family maximum limits the amount that can be received off of a worker's record. This limit is compatible with the incentive for individuals to work. Changing such a limit could affect beneficiaries' work decisions. For example, protecting benefits of dependents by increasing the family maximum could affect an individual's work decisions. Under the current family maximum with a benefit reduction in place, if a person chooses to work 30 hours a week, an increase in the total amount a family (or individual dependents) could receive might affect this decision and decrease the person's time in the workforce. In such a case, the individual may find that the increase in the benefits received would allow for fewer weekly hours of work without a change in total income. In addition, protections that increase the benefits of disabled workers, such as the super COLA, can also create disincentives for such beneficiaries to return to work. As such, some individuals may continue to rely on the DI program, rather than finding a way to re-enter the workforce.

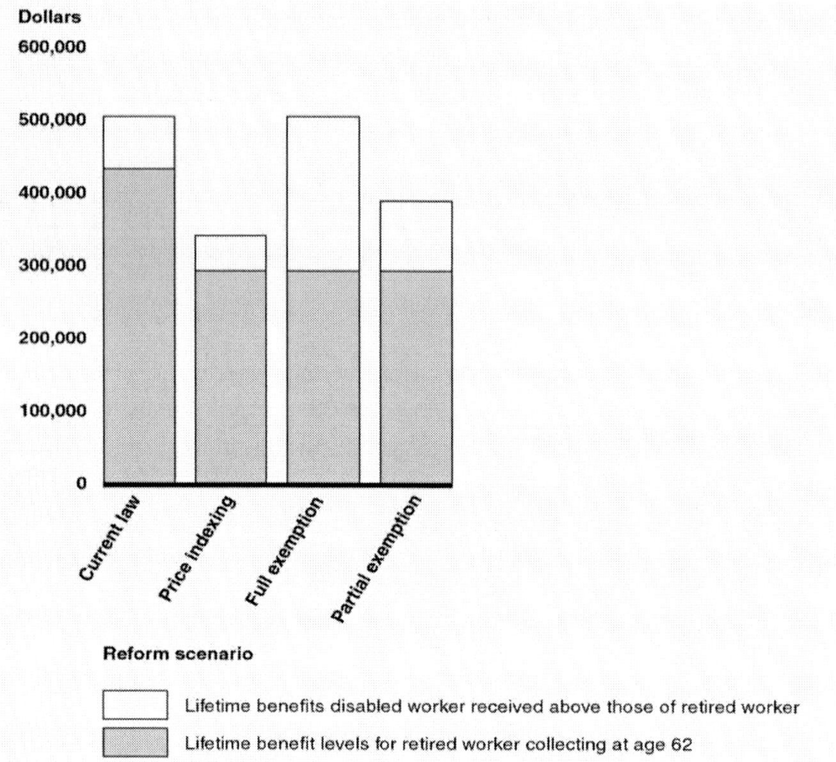

Source: GAO analysis of GEMINI data.

Figure 12. Simulated Total Lifetime Benefits for Two Similar Individuals Who Began Receiving Benefits at Age 62, Exemptions Apply to Disabled Workers (1985 Cohort)

Table 4. Total Lifetime and Average Monthly Benefits of Two Simulated Individuals Who Began Receiving Benefits at Age 62, Exemptions Apply to Disabled Workers (1985 Cohort)

	Total lifetime benefits			Average monthly benefits		
	Retired worker	**Disabled worker**	**Difference as a percentage of the retired worker's benefits**	**Retired worker**	**Disabled worker**	**Difference as a percentage of the retired worker's benefits**
Current law	$433,000	$505,000	16.63%	$1,640	$2,104	28.29%
Price indexing	$293,000	$341,000	16.38%	$1,110	$1,421	28.02%
Full exemption	$293,000	$505,000	72.35%	$1,110	$2,104	89.59%
Partial exemption	$293,000	$389,380	32.89%	$1,110	$1,622	46.18%

Source: GAO analysis of GEMINI data.

CONCLUSIONS

Social Security's financial challenges may result in program modifications that may include benefit reductions. These benefit reductions will likely affect all beneficiaries, including vulnerable individuals who may not be able to adjust to these reductions or who rely on Social Security as their primary source of income. While protecting the benefits of vulnerable populations may be desirable, such action does come at a cost. Further benefit reductions or revenue increases would be needed to achieve program solvency. These offsets, in turn, may create new financial vulnerabilities among other beneficiaries who would bear the burden of these protections.

Few reform proposals consider the impact that benefit reductions would have on all beneficiary types, instead treating all beneficiaries similarly. However, some special consideration should be given to the effects of the reform on the benefits of the most vulnerable, especially when these individuals are disproportionately affected. If the solution to Social Security's financing problems includes benefit reductions, then the equal treatment of all beneficiaries may need to be reconsidered, and the complex interactions of benefit reductions, protections, and direct and indirect costs to the system and to other retirees will need to be weighed carefully. Benefit protections can be a part of a comprehensive reform package and the reform debate should consider the design, inclusion, and implications of such measures to assure income adequacy. Likewise, to the extent that Social Security aligns the disability program with the current state of science, medicine, technology, and labor market conditions, such modernization should also be considered.

MATTER FOR CONGRESSIONAL CONSIDERATION

Accordingly, in light of potential reform, Congress should consider the potential implications of reform on disability and dependent beneficiaries. Such a review might usefully be coordinated with any modernization of the Social Security disability program.

AGENCY COMMENTS

We provided a draft of this report to SSA and the Department of the Treasury, which generally agreed with our findings. Both provided technical comments, and SSA also provided general comments, which appear in appendix III. We incorporated the comments throughout our report as appropriate.

In general, SSA concurred with the methodology, overall findings, and conclusions of the report. However, SSA felt that the report could benefit from a more direct comparison of disabled beneficiaries and retired beneficiaries (and a similar construct for dependents). While such a comparison could be beneficial and give context to the reform discussion, this report was premised on the notion that certain beneficiaries would be less able to offset benefit reductions, rather than a comparison of relative welfare.

Finally, GAO agrees that one could better assess the degree to which a reform element or protection option support the program's goal of adequacy if benefits were compared to a standard of adequacy; however such a comparison was beyond the scope of the current study.

Barbara D. Bovbjerg
Director, Education, Workforce,
and Income Security Issues

APPENDIX I: METHODOLOGY

Microsimulation Model

To analyze the effects of individual reform elements and certain protections from these reforms on Social Security benefit levels for disabled workers and dependents, we simulated their benefits using the Policy Simulation Group's (PSG) microsimulation models. We based our analysis on projected lifetime benefits for a simulated 1985 birth cohort. Inorder to have a point of comparison, we also used the microsimulation models to simulate Social Security benefits of retirees who receive

Description

For our simulations, we used the PSG's Social Security and Accounts Simulator (SSASIM) and Genuine Microsimulation of Social Security Accounts (GEMINI) simulation models. GEMINI simulates Social Security benefits and taxes for large representative samples of people born in the same year. GEMINI simulates all types of Social Security benefits including retired workers', spouses', survivors', and disability benefits. It can be used to model a variety of Social Security reforms. GEMINI uses inputs from SSASIM, which has been used in numerous GAO reports,[39] and from the Pension Simulator (PENSIM), which was developed for the Department of Labor. GEMINI relies on SSASIM for economic and demographic projections and relies on PENSIM for simulated life histories of large representative samples of people born in the same year and their spouses.[40] Life histories include educational attainment, labor force participation, earnings, job mobility, marriage, disability, childbirth, retirement, and death. Life histories are validated by PSG against data from the Survey of Income and Program Participation, the Current Population Survey, Modeling Income in the Near Term (MINT3),[41] and the Panel Study of Income Dynamics. Additionally, any projected statistics (such as life expectancy, employment patterns, and marital status at age 60) are, where possible, consistent with intermediate cost projections from Social Security Administration's Office of the Chief Actuary (OCACT). At their best, such models can provide only very rough estimates of future incomes. However, these estimates may be useful for comparing future incomes across alternative policy scenarios and over time.

For this report, we used the Genuine Microsimulation of Social Security Accounts (GEMINI) to estimate Social Security benefits for a sample of approximately 2 percent of individuals born in the 1985 cohort. This consisted of just over 97,000 individuals, with positive benefit levels for just over 83,400 individuals.

For our baseline, benefits were simulated under current law. These simulations are based on the Social Security Trustees' 2007 intermediate economic and actuarial assumptions. While our simulations provide projections of future retirement income, as promised under current law, there is a considerable amount of uncertainty involved with these estimates. Since these estimates could change significantly, depending on assumptions used and behavior responses, they should not be considered predictions. In addition, because simulations are sensitive to economic and demographic assumptions, it is more appropriate to compare benefits across the scenarios than to focus on the actual estimates themselves.

Evaluating reform proposals

In general, GAO has suggested that policy makers should consider three basic criteria when evaluating reform proposals[42]

- the extent to which the proposal achieves sustainable solvency and how the proposal would affect the economy and the federal budget;
- the balance struck between the goals of individual equity[43] (rates of return on individual contributions) and income adequacy[44] (level and certainty of monthly benefits); and
- how readily such changes could be implemented, administered, and explained to the public.

Moreover, reform proposals should be evaluated as packages that strike a balance among the individual elements of the proposal and the interactions among these elements. The overall evaluation of any particular reform proposal depends on the weight individual policy makers place on each of the above criteria.

However, for the purposes of this study, we did evaluate individual reform elements and individual protection options. We looked at specific elements of solvency-improving reform proposals to analyze their effects on our populations of interest—disabled workers and dependents. In particular, we wanted to isolate each element in order to project the magnitude of their effects on these populations and in order to model certain protection options. Nevertheless, we recognize that there would be important interactive effects with any set of reforms and maintain the importance of considering all possible effects of any reform package as a whole.

Assumptions and limitations

Simulating retirement income almost 50 years into the future requires many assumptions and simplifications and, consequently, our simulations have a number of limitations. A primary limitation of our analysis is that our simulations do not include important components of retirement income, such as personal savings, earnings in retirement, health benefits, and other public assistance programs such as SSI. These sources could also be used to offset benefit reductions. In addition, the model is structured such that changes in Social

Security benefits have no behavioral consequences in terms of decisions regarding work, disability, or retirement. As a result, the individuals would not change their work decisions (earnings/retirement) based on the reforms.

2007 social security trustees' assumptions

The simulations are based on economic and demographic assumptions from the 2007 Social Security Trustees' report.[45] We used Trustees' intermediate assumptions for inflation, real wage growth, mortality decline, immigration, labor force participation, and interest rates.

Specification of disabledworkers and dependents

For the purpose of this analysis:

Disabled Workers consisted of those individuals who had a valid disability onset age and who received a positive amount of benefits from Disability Insurance. This includes any disabled workers who were dependents at some point in time.

Dependents consisted of those individuals who received benefits based on someone else's earnings record, at any point. Specifically, dependents excluded those who only received benefits based on their own record as retirees or as disabled workers.

Description of Social Security Reform Elements

Longevity indexing

To simulate longevity indexing, which links the growth of initial benefits to changes in life expectancy, we successively modified the PIA formula replacement factors (90, 32, 15) beginning in 2009, reducing them annually by multiplying them by 0.995. This specification mimics provision 1 of Model 3 of the President's Commission to Strengthen Social Security (CSSS).[46] The CSSS solvency memorandum notes that the 0.995 successive reductions "reduces monthly benefit levels by an amount equivalent to increasing the normal retirement age (NRA) for retired workers by enough to maintain a constant life expectancy at NRA, for any fixed age of benefit entitlement."[47] This provision as specified and scored—using the intermediate assumptions of the 2001 Trustees' report—in the CSSS memo by SSA's Office of the Chief Actuary would improve the long-range OASDI actuarial balance (reduce the actuarial deficit) by an estimated1.17 percent of taxable payroll.

Price indexing

We also simulated the effects of price indexing, where initial benefits would be indexed to the consumer price index (CPI) in order to limit thegrowth of benefits. We successively modified the primary insurance amount (PIA) formula replacement factors (90, 32, and 15) beginning in 2012, reducing them successively by real wage growth in the second prioryear. This specification mimics provision B6 of the August 10, 2005, memorandum to SSA's Chief Actuary regarding the provision requested bythe Social Security Advisory Board (SSAB), which is an update of provision 1 of Model 2 of the CSSS.[48] As noted in the CSSS's solvency memorandum from SSA's Chief Actuary, "[t]his provision would result in increasing benefit levels for individuals with equivalent lifetime earnings across generations (relative to the average wage level) at the rate of pricegrowth (increase in the CPI), rather than at the rate of growth in the average wage level as in current law." This provision as specified

Progressive price indexing

To simulate the effects of implementing a progressive price index, we mimicked provision B7 of the August 10, 2005, memorandum to SSA's Chief Actuary.[49] We created a new bend point at the 30th percentile of earnings, beginning in 2012. We maintained current-law benefits for earners at the 30th percentile and below. We also maintained the lower two PIA formula replacement factors (90 and 32). We reduced the upper two PIA formula replacement factors (32 and 15) so that maximum worker benefits from one generation to the next grew by inflation rather than the growth in average wages. This provision as specified and scored by OCACT would improve the long-range OASDI actuarial balance (reduce the actuarial deficit) by an estimated 1.43 percent of taxable payroll.

Increase the number of computation years used in the initial benefit calculation

In our modeling of this reform element, we gradually reduced the number of drop out years from 5 to 0, thereby extending the number of computation years from 35 to 40. The number of computation years would increase to 36 in 2007, 37 in 2008, 38 in 2010, 39 in 2012, and 40 in 2014. This specification mimics provision B2 of the August 10, 2005memorandum to SSA's Chief Actuary.[50] This provision as specified and scored by OCACT would improve the long-range OASDI actuarial balance (reduce the actuarial deficit) by an estimated 0.46 percent of taxable payroll.

Reduction in the cost-ofliving adjustment

We also simulated a reduction in the cost-of-living adjustment (COLA) of one percentage point, beginning in 2012. This specification mimics provision A2 of the August 10, 2005, memorandum to SSA's Chief Actuary.[51] This provision as specified and scored by OCACT would improve the long-range OASDI actuarial balance (reduce the actuarial deficit) by an estimated 1.49 percent of taxable payroll. Some reform proposals have called for reducing the COLA by about 0.2 percent to 0.4 percent, in response to methodological concerns that the CPI for urban wage earners and clerical workers, the current CPI measure used to adjust benefits, overstates inflation. The intent of these proposals is to implement a COLA that may more accurately reflect inflation.

Description of Protection Options

Table 5. Options for Protecting Disabled Worker and Dependent Benefits from Social Security Reform

Protection option available for	Protection option	How the protection option could work
Any beneficiary type	Full exemption	The beneficiary would not be subject to reform. Benefits would be unchanged.

Table 5. (Continued)

Protection option available for	Protection option	How the protection option could work
	Partial exemption	Benefits would not be subject to reform until a certain point in time. At this point in time, benefits would be adjusted to reflect reform.
	Minimum benefit	Beneficiaries would be guaranteed a specified minimum benefit level.
	Super COLA	A larger COLA would be applied to benefits to partially mitigate reductions.
	Age-indexed super COLA	Works similarly to the super COLA. However, this COLA would vary in size, with younger beneficiaries receiving larger adjustments.
Children and families of disabled workers	Increase the percentage of the worker's benefit that the dependent family member receives as his/her benefit	Children and spouses receiving benefits from a parent's or spouse's earnings record receive a set percentage of their parent's or spouse's benefits as their benefit. This option would increase the size of this percentage.
	Increase the family maximum benefit level for DI	Families would be subject to a higher family maximum benefit level if they receive benefits off the earnings record of a disabled worker.
	Increase the percentage of the worker's benefit that a dependent child or a disabled adult child (DAC) receives as his/her benefit in combination with increasing the family maximum benefit	This option would increase the percentage used to determine a dependent child or DAC's benefit level while also increasing the family maximum benefit level.
	Decouple DAC benefits from other family benefits	This option would exclude DAC benefits from the family benefit calculation. While a DAC would continue to receive benefits based from his/her parent's earnings record, DAC benefits would not be included in the calculation of total family benefits when determining whether family benefits have exceeded the maximum family benefit.
	Hold initial benefit amount harmless for family benefits	If reform adjusts the initial benefit amount for a disabled worker, the amount used for calculating the benefits for any dependent of a disabled worker would be unchanged.
Children and families of retired workers	Expand eligibility rules for divorced spouses	This option would alter eligibility rules for divorced spouses (e.g. shorten the duration of marriage requirement for the divorced spouse to receive benefits from his/her spouse's earnings record).
	Increase the percentage of the worker's benefit that the dependent family member receives as his/her benefit	Children and spouses receiving benefits from a parent's or spouse's earnings record receive a set percentage of their parent's or spouse's benefits as their benefit. This option would increase the size of this percentage.

	Increase the percentage of the worker's benefit that a dependent child or DAC receives as his/her benefit in combination with increasing the family maximum benefit	This option would increase the percentage used to determine a dependent child or DAC's benefit level while also increasing the family maximum benefit level.
	Decouple DAC benefits from other family benefits	This option would exclude DAC benefits from the family benefit calculation. While a DAC would continue to receive benefits based from his/her parent's earnings record, DAC benefits would not be included in the calculation of total family benefits when determining whether family benefits have exceeded the maximum family benefit.
Spouses	Increase the percentage of the worker's benefit that the spouse receives as his/her benefit	Husbands and wives receiving benefits from their spouses' earnings records receive a set percentage of their spouses' benefits as their benefit. This option would increase the size of this percentage.
	Implement a child/family care credit	A child/family care credit could be work in one of three ways: Reduce the number of computation years for caregivers: A certain number of years would be "dropped" from the initial benefit level calculation to credit years an individual spent caring for children or other dependent family members. Credit caregivers a particular dollar amount for years spent out of the labor force providing care to children: Earnings used to calculate an individual's initial benefit level would be adjusted upward for a particular number of years. Provide caregivers with a credit equal to 1/2 of median worker earnings for the years spent working part-time or earning low incomes because caring for children or other family members: Replaces years with no or low earnings, up to a certain number of years. Alternatively, instead of using 1/2 of median worker earnings as the replacement, could use 1/2 of the median earnings from a caregiver's remaining work years.
Survivors	Hold initial benefit amount harmless for family benefits	If a reform adjusts the initial benefit amount for a primary beneficiary, the amount for calculating the benefits for any survivor of a worker would be unchanged.
	Hold early survivors (young children or young widow(er)s) harmless	Early survivors would not be subject to any benefit change resulting from reform.
	Increase the surviving spouse benefit to 2/3 or 3/4 of the combined couples' benefit	This option would increase the size of the benefit a surviving spouse receives to 2/3 or 3/4 of what the couples' combined benefit would have been.
	Increase benefits for aged survivors Increase the early retirement age	This option increases the size of benefits older survivors receive. This option would increase the early retirement age. Survivors' benefits are based on workers' benefit. If a worker takes benefits during the

Table 5. (Continued)

Protection option available for	Protection option	How the protection option could work
		early retirement period, then the monthly benefit level is reduced. By increasing the early retirement age, a worker wouldn't be able to receive as large a reduced monthly benefit or receive benefits for as long a period of time. Accordingly, any survivor's benefit would be larger.

Source: GAO.

Options Modeled to Protect Benefits of Disabled Workers

Full exemption

To simulate the effects of fully exempting disabled workers from the various reform elements, we modified the simulation to exclude the benefits of disabled workers from the reform elements. As such, there would be no recalculation of benefits when the exempted beneficiary reached full retirement age.

Partial Exemptions

We defined partial exemptions for disabled workers to mean that their benefit would be exempted from any simulated reform until the FRA and then would be recalculated. For the COLA reduction, we simply startedthe one percentage point reduction at the FRA for disabled workers. However, for the reforms that involved a change in the initial benefit amount (longevity indexing, price indexing, and progressive priceindexing), we simulated the recalculation of benefits at the FRA in two different ways.

Partial exemption type I— kolbe-stenholm

The first partial exemption, which we refer to as Partial Exemption Type I, followed the Kolbe-Stenholm model of converting benefits at the FRA. The Kolbe-Stenholm model reduces benefits in proportion to the difference in the disabled-worker PIA and the retired-worker PIA at the DI-onset age. This OASI benefit amount would be indexed by the COLA to for the years between the disability onset age and age 62.

Partial exemption type II—graham

The second partial exemption, or Partial Exemption Type II, followed the Graham model of converting benefits at the FRA. The mechanism for converting from DI to Old Age benefits is as follows::

$$\frac{DI_c * Y_D}{40} + \frac{OASI_{62} * (40 - Y_D)}{40}$$

where:

DI_C is the promised DI benefit level under current law

Y_D is the number of years (ages 21 to 62) that the disabled worker received DI benefits

$OASI_{62}$ is the OASI benefit level, calculated by computing the PIA under the reform using the formula applicable for newly eligible retired workers in the year the converting worker reached age 62. In this case, earnings from the years prior to disability would be wage indexed. The disability freeze years[52] would apply in computing the AIME

Data Reliability

To assess the reliability of simulated data from GEMINI, we reviewed PSG's published validation checks and examined the data for reasonableness and consistency.

PSG has published a number of validation checks of its simulated life histories. For example, simulated life expectancy is compared with projections from the Social Security Trustees; simulated benefits at age 62 are compared with administrative data from SSA; and simulated educational attainment, labor force participation rates, and job tenure are compared with values from the Current Population Survey. We found that simulated statistics for the life histories were reasonably close to the validation targets.

Appendix II: Calculating OASDI Benefits

Social Security offers a variety of types of benefits, and although they are all based upon the same formula, they are calculated in different ways. The methods for calculating the different types of benefits are outlined below[53].

Calculating Old-Age Benefits

Old Age benefits are calculated through a four-step process in order to provide retirees with progressive yet wage-based cash payments (see figure 13).

First a worker's Average Indexed Monthly Earnings (AIME) is calculated by indexing the worker's past earnings to changes in average wage levels over the worker's lifetime and then averaging them. The AIME formula considers all years in which a worker earned covered earnings.[54] It then uses the number of elapsed years from 1950 or attainment of age 21 through the age of 62 (or death) and allows for 5 "drop-out years" so that the worker's highest 35 years of covered indexed earnings are used in the calculation.[55] Once the AIME is determined, a progressive formula is applied to the AIME to yield a worker's Primary Insurance Amount (PIA). In 2007, the PIA formula had the following bend points: 90 percent of the first \$680 of AIME, plus 32 percent of the next \$3,420, and 15 percent of any earnings above that level (fig. 13). For example, the PIA of a worker whose AIME was \$1000, the equivalent of at \$12,000 annual salary, would be the sum of \$612 (90 percent of \$680) and \$102.40 (32 percent of \$320), yielding a total initial monthly benefit of around \$715. Similarly, the PIA of a worker with an \$8,000 AIME (the equivalent of a \$96,000 annual salary) would be the sum of \$612 (90 percent of \$680), \$1094.40 (32 percent of \$3420), and \$585 (15 percent of \$3,900), for a total of just under \$2,292. Because the formula is both wage-based and progressive, the second worker receives a much higher actual benefit than the first worker ($2,292 versus $715), but his benefits are a much lower proportion of his past earnings than the first worker's benefits (28.6 percent versus 71.4 percent).

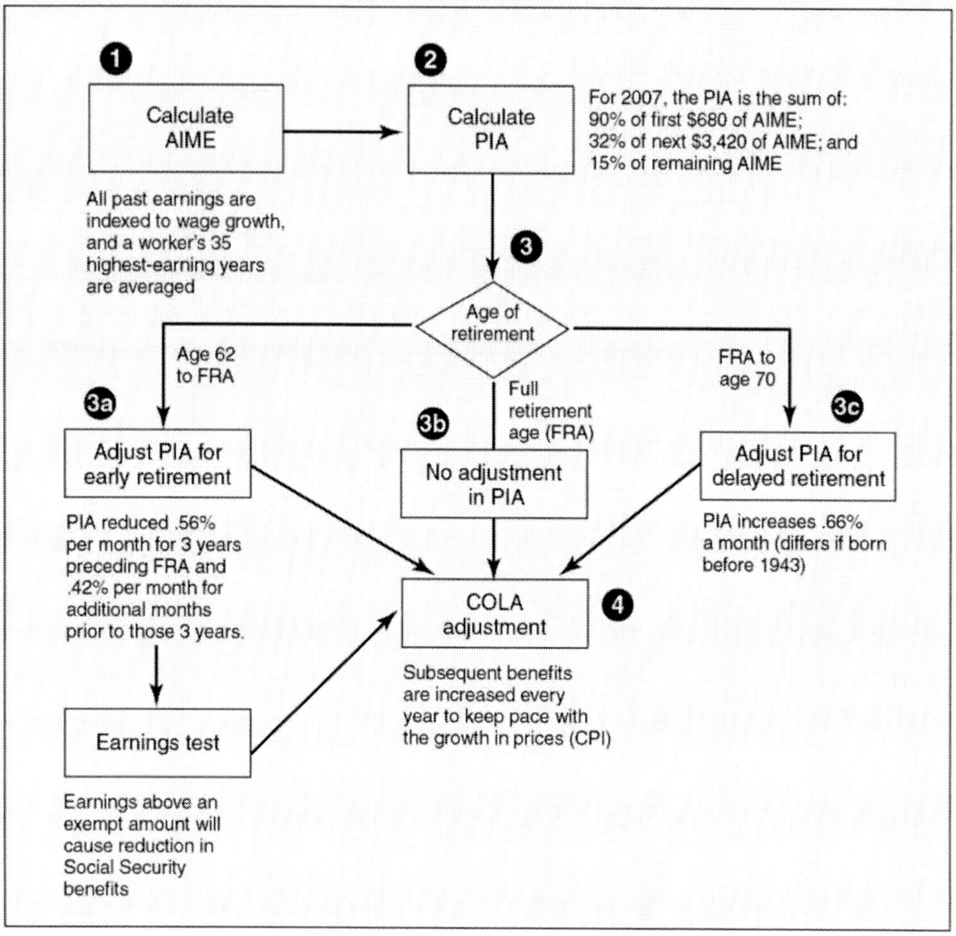

Source: GAO.

Notes: Specifically, Social Security's COLAs are based on the consumer price index for urban wage earners and clerical workers (CPI-W), as opposed to the CPI series for all urban consumers (CPI-U).

Also the PIA numbers in step 2 refer to workers attaining age 62 in 2007.

Figure 13. Calculating Benefits for Retirees

If a worker retires at the full retirement age, which is currently between ages 65 and 66, and legislated to reach 67 in 2027, this PIA represents the first year's benefit (although it is adjusted for inflation through a cost-ofliving adjustment (COLA)). However, workers can begin receiving reduced benefits at 62; benefits are progressively larger for each month workers postpone drawing them, up to age 70.[56] In general, benefits are actuarially neutral to the Social Security program; that is, the reduction for starting benefits before full retirement age and the credit for starting after full retirement age are such that the total value of benefits received over one's lifetime is approximately equivalent for the average individual.[57] Those receiving benefits before the full retirement age will also be subject to an earnings test. If earned income is above a certain threshold, Social Security withholds one dollar of benefits for every two dollars of earning above the threshold. Each year, benefits receive a COLA to keep pace with inflation.

Calculating Disability Benefits

Similarly to Old Age benefits, disability benefits are determined by calculating a worker's AIME, applying the progressive PIA formula to it, and then adjusting benefit levels through yearly COLAs (figure 14).

However, because disabled workers are likely to have shorter work histories, their benefits calculation relies on fewer years of earnings. In general, the number of years of earnings used to calculate the AIME is based on the total number of years between when a worker turns 21 and when he applies for DI. If this number of years is 25 or more, a worker's 5 lowest (or zero) earnings years will be dropped from the calculation. The number of drop-out years gradually declines as a worker applies for disability earlier in life. If the disabled worker is 60 at the time of application, for example, 38 years would have elapsed since age 21. He will receive 5 drop out years, and his AIME will be calculated based upon his 33 highest-earning years. In contrast, if a worker applies for DI at 32, he would have only had 10 elapsed years since age 21, and only be eligible for 2 drop-out years; his AIME would be calculated based upon his top 8 years. At the full retirement age, disabled workers begin receiving retirement benefits, instead of disability benefits; however, benefit levels remain the same and continue to grow through annual COLAs.

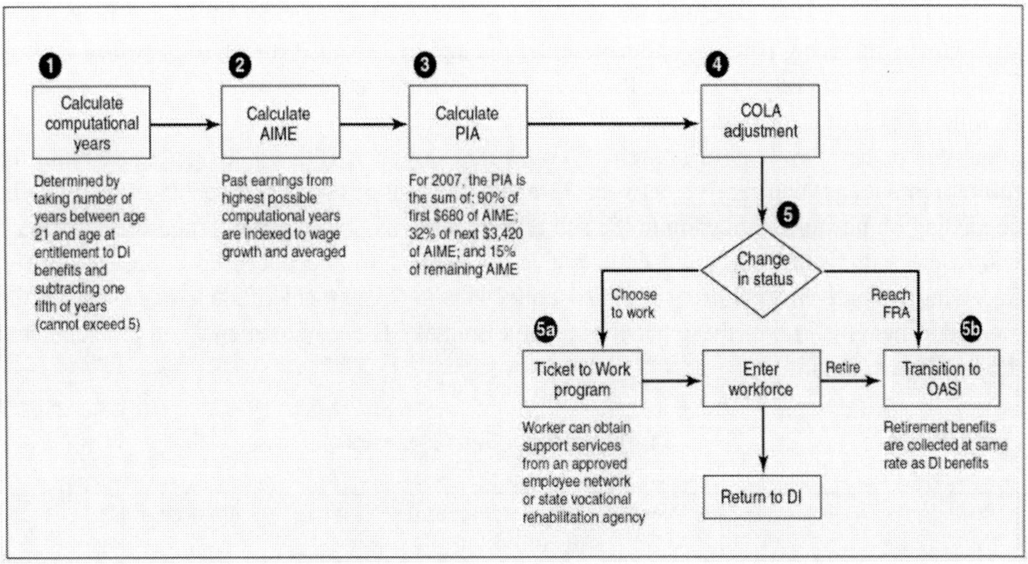

Source: GAO.

Note: The PIA numbers in step three refer to workers qualify for receiving DI benefits in 2007.

Figure 14. Calculating Benefits for Disabled Workers

Calculating Benefits for Dependents of Retired and Disabled Workers

- **Spouses:** In addition to being eligible to receive retirement benefits on their own earnings records as early as age 62, individuals can also receive dependents' benefits at age 62, based on their spouse's benefit amount or, in some cases, that of an ex-spouse (table 5). These individuals can collect these benefits regardless of whether their spouse is concurrently receiving retired or disabled worker benefits. If collection begins at full retirement age, these individuals are eligible for either one-half of their spouse's benefit amount, or the benefits based on their own earnings record; whichever is greater. As with Old Age benefits, adjustments are made if these individuals chooses to take early retirement.

- **Dependent Children:** Dependent children may also qualify for one- half of their retired or disabled parent's benefit amount. This benefit is available for disabled adult children who are not working on a regular basis, children under age 18, or children still in high school and under age 19.

Like other benefits, dependents' benefits receive annual COLAs. Dependent benefits are subject to a family maximum, whereby a family is limited in the total amount of benefits that can be received from a single individual's earnings record. The size of the family maximum is currently between 150 percent and 188 percent of the primary beneficiary's benefit.[58]

Calculating Survivors'Benefits

Widow(er)s may be eligible to receive a one-time death benefit of $255. In addition, widow(er)s, surviving parents, children under the age of 18 (19 if the child is still in school) and disabled adult children can collect benefits off of the deceased person's earnings record. A widow(er) at full retirement age will receive 100 percent of his or her spouse's benefits, unless his or her own benefit is higher. Younger widow(er)s (those between age 60 and the full retirement age) can receive between 71 and99 percent of their deceased spouses' benefits depending on how close they are to the full retirement age.[59] Furthermore, regardless of age, a widow(er) with young children, can receive 75 percent of the deceased spouse's benefit. Surviving parents and children can also collect up to 75 percent of their deceased family members' benefits. All of these benefits receive annual COLA adjustments and are subject to the family maximum.

Table 6. Dependent Benefits

	Worker retires or becomes disabled	Worker dies
Child of worker	Can collect 50% of worker's benefits if under 18, in high school, or disabled	Can collect 75% of worker's benefits if under 18, in high school, or disabled

Spouse of worker	Can collect 50% of worker's benefits at FRA or reduced amount at age 62	Can collect 100% of worker's benefit at FRA or reduced amount at age 60
Spouse taking care of young or disabled child	Can collect 50% of worker's benefits at any age	Can collect 75% of worker's benefits if not eligible for more through other provisions
Disabled spouse	No special provision	Can collect 100% of worker's benefits at age 50
Ex-Spouse of worker	Can collect normal spousal benefits if marriage lasted longer than 10 years and dependent is unmarried	Can collect normal spousal benefits if marriage lasted longer than 10 years and survivor is unmarried
Parent of worker	No special provision	Can collect 75% or 82.5% (if only one parent is entitled) of worker's benefits if parent is age 62 or above, and dependent on worker for over half of income

Source: GAO.

Note: All benefits, except those for divorcees, are subject to the family maximum. A spouse can collect benefits on his own earnings record, if this amount is greater than the corresponding dependent benefits.

APPENDIX III: COMMENTS FROM THE SOCIAL SECURITY ADMINISTRATION

SOCIAL SECURITY

The Commissioner

October 17, 2007

Ms. Barbara D. Bovbjerg
Director, Education, Workforce, and
Income Security Issues
U.S. Government Accountability Office
Washington, D.C. 20548

Dear Ms. Bovbjerg:

Thank you for the opportunity to review and comment on the draft report, "Social Security Reform: Issues for Disability and Dependent Benefits" (GAO-08-26).

If you have any questions, please contact Ms. Candace Skurnik, Director, Audit Management and Liaison Staff, at (410) 965-4636.

Sincerely,

Michael J. Astrue

Enclosure

COMMENTS ON THE GOVERNMENT ACCOUNTABILITY OFFICE (GAO) DRAFT REPORT, "SOCIAL SECURITY REFORM: ISSUES FOR DISABILITY AND DEPENDENT BENEFITS" (GAO-08-26)

Thank you for the opportunity to review and comment on the draft report. This report is very complete and gives a good overview of the potential effects of various reforms. However, the report would benefit from a better framing of the discussion with some context. While we would not expect an exhaustive analysis of the disability/dependent population, the following questions could be addressed:

- Are the current disabled beneficiaries worse off than the current retired beneficiaries?
- How about dependents? Where do dependents rank economically as compared to the general population?

General and Technical Comments

The GAO methodology involves compiling data from different sources and performing simulations, computations, and analyses. It would require a considerable amount of time, with complete access to GAO's data, mathematical derivations, and detailed computer logic, in order to determine whether or not the GAO results are technically correct. It would be helpful if the report provided information on the magnitude of estimation errors (e.g., upper bounds) for the benefit reduction estimates computed under the respective proposals.

In considering the options used to protect the benefits of disabled and dependent individuals, GAO should consider whether such options (especially if they distinguish between classes of persons based on age, disability, or other protected class) could violate the due process or equal rights of any particular class members.

There are several references to (and/or explanations of) how various benefits are calculated under the Social Security Act, and how individuals qualify for such benefits. However, there are no citations to the relevant, controlling authorities; i.e., the Social Security Act and Title 20 of the Code of Federal Regulations. This report would benefit from citations to the applicable source when such issues are discussed.

In describing the provision that reduces the cost-of-living adjustment, the phrase "one percent reduction" is used throughout this report. We suggest that this phrase be replaced with "one percentage point reduction."

Page 5, the last sentence, "...the Social Security program balances the goals of income adequacy with individual equity..." given the importance of benefit adequacy and equity, it seems that not much consideration was given to these issues while evaluating how disabled beneficiaries and their dependents would fare under different reform elements. Instead, the report evaluates six reform elements by measuring the benefit reductions individuals may incur. The reader could better assess the degree to which a reform option supports the disability insurance (DI) adequacy goal if GAO compared reform benefits to a standard of adequacy (i.e., the Census poverty standard). This would gauge whether or not disabled persons and their dependents would be able to meet their basic needs with reduced benefits. Secondly, readers could better gauge the equity of reform elements if the report illustrated the distribution of benefit reductions among all disabled beneficiaries and dependents, and persons differentiated by the number of years since their date of disability onset, gender, and earnings history.

Related GAO Products

Retirement Security: Women Face Challenges in Ensuring Financial Security in Retirement. GAO-08-105. Washington, D.C.: October 11, 2007.

Retirement Decisions: Federal Policies Offer Mixed Signals about When to Retire. GAO-07-753. Washington, D.C.: July 11, 2007.

Social Security Reform: Implications of Different Indexing Choice. GAO-06-804. Washington, D.C.: Sept ember 14, 2006.

Social Security: Societal Changes Add Challenges to Program Protections. GAO-05-706T. Washington, D.C.: May 17, 2005.

Options for Social Security Reform. GAO-05-649R. Washington, D.C.: May 6, 2005.

Social Security Reform: Answers to Key Questions. GAO-05-193SP. Washington, D.C.: May 2, 2005.

Social Security Reform: Early Action Would Be Prudent. GAO-05-397T. Washington, D.C.: March 9, 2005.

Long Term Fiscal Issues: The Need for Social Security Reform. GAO-05-318T. Washington, D.C. February 9, 2005.

Social Security: Distribution of Benefits and Taxes Relative to Earnings Level. GAO-04-747. Washington, D.C.: June 15, 2004.

Social Security: Program's Role in Helping Ensure Income Adequacy. GAO-02-62. Washington, D.C.: November 30, 2001.

Social Security Reform: Potential Effects on SSA's Disability Programs and Beneficiaries. GAO-01-35. Washington, D.C.: January 24, 2001.

Social Security: Evaluating Reform Proposals. GAO/AIMD/HEHS-00-29. Washington, D.C.: November 4, 1999.

Social Security Reform: Implications of Raising the Retirement Age. GAO/HEHS-99-112. Washington, D.C.: August 27, 1999.

Social Security: Issues in Comparing Rates of Return with Market Investments. GAO/HEHS-99-110. Washington, D.C.: August 5, 1999.

Social Security: Criteria for Evaluating Social Security Reform Proposals. GA0/T-HEHS-99-94. Washington, D.C.: March 25, 1999.

End Notes

[1] Our approach to the analysis is based on the premise that, under benefit reducing reforms, disabled workers and certain dependents would likely have limited options for alternative sources of income to make up for the loss in benefits. In particular, comparisons of the relative welfare of disabled workers, dependents, and retirees are beyond the scope of this job.

[2] We used the Genuine Microsimulation of Social Security (GEMINI) microsimulation model under a license from the Policy Simulation Group, a private contractor. GEMINI estimates individual effects of policy scenarios for a representative sample of future beneficiaries. GEMINI can simulate different reform features for their effects on the level and distribution of benefits. See appendix I for more detail on the modeling analysis, including a discussion of our assessment of the data reliability of the model.

[3] We analyzed the impact of each reform element individually. We did not simulate a scenario in which reform elements were combined and implemented simultaneously. It is important to note that the individual reform elements can interact with one another and that the impact of one reform element, taken on its own, may change when combined with other reform elements in a proposal. Moreover, each reform element has pluses

and minuses. As a result, Social Security reform proposals should be evaluated as a package of reform options designed to meet certain stated objectives.

[4] For the purpose of this report, dependents will encompass benefits to survivors as well as all dependent spouses and children.

[5] The Social Security Act of 1935 also included aid to states for programs which are no longer considered to be part of Social Security.

[6] In order to receive these benefits, husbands and widowers needed to be currently and fully insured at the time of their wives' retirement or death. In addition, the husband (or widower) had to prove he was financially dependent on his wife. In 1983, virtually all gender-based distinctions were eliminated.

[7] Payroll tax rates are specified separately for each program and receipts deposited into two separate accounts in the United States Treasury. However, over the years, there have been tax rate reallocations and loans between the two trust funds.

[8] When a person is converted from the DI program to the Old Age programs, there is no recalculation of his benefits, which continue to receive annual COLAs; however, the benefits will be paid from the OASI trust fund instead of the DI trust fund.

[9] Some beneficiaries may be dually entitled and receive benefits based on their own record and on that of their spouse.

[10] 42 U.S.C. § 415.

[11] The total number of years to be counted in the work history is the number of elapsed years from the latter of 1950 or the year in which the worker attains age 21 and before the worker becomes disabled, dies, or attains age 62 (thus the 40 years in the text above)— whichever comes first—excluding any years in which the worker is in a period of disability.

[12] See GAO, *High Risk Series, An Update,* GAO-07-310 (Washington, D.C.: January 2007).

[13] Because the future is uncertain, the Trustees use three alternative sets of assumptions to show a range of possible outcomes. The intermediate assumptions represent the Social Security Administration's best estimate of the trust funds' future financial outlook. The Trustees also present estimates using low cost and high cost sets of assumptions. In addition, the Trustees Report describes a range of possible outcomes using stochastic modeling techniques.

[14] While currently scheduled benefits are not attainable under current funding levels, they nonetheless provide a point of comparison in examining the impact of various reform elements.

[15] These reform elements have been proposed as part of recent larger reform proposals.

[16] See appendix II for a full explanation of how benefits are currently calculated.

[17] Changing the number of drop-out years would have less of an effect (or no effect) on disabled workers because their drop-out years are calculated differently. For more on how initial benefits are calculated for disabled workers, see appendix II.

[18] Specifically, Social Security's COLAs are based on the consumer price index for urban wage earners and clerical workers (CPI-W), as opposed to the CPI series for all urban consumers (CPI-U).

[19] We identified two options for modifying the COLA. The first option, which we analyzed in this report, would reduce the COLA by 1 percentage point to improve solvency. The second option, which we did not analyze, would reduce the COLA by 0.2 to 0.4 percentage points in response to methodological concerns that the CPI overstates the true rate of inflation.

[20] We did not analyze the simulated change in the FRA for both disabled workers and dependents because of modeling constraints nor did we analyze the increase in the number of computation years for disabled workers.

[21] A 1 percentage point decrease in the COLA may have a greater effect on solvency than longevity indexing as we've modeled it. In part because while the effects of both reforms are compounded over time, the COLA would affect all beneficiaries once it is implemented and continue over a longer horizon—until death. In contrast, longevity indexing would not affect those who have already retired, nor would it have a great impact on those who retire close to the implementation date. Its effects would be greater on the benefits of those individuals who retire further out from the implementation date.

[22] While this report focuses on the impact of certain reforms on disabled worker and dependent benefits, the reforms would affect the benefits of other Social Security recipients as well.

[23] Additionally, according to our simulations, disabled workers experienced greater absolute reductions in median lifetime benefits than did beneficiaries who were never disabled for each of the reform elements considered. However, disabled workers also experienced a smaller percentage change in median lifetime benefits than those who were never disabled. Under current law, disabled workers would have higher lifetime benefits (since they may receive benefits for a longer period of time); therefore, the reduction in benefits represents a smaller share of current law benefits.

[24] Increasing the FRA would not affect disabled workers because the initial benefits calculation for disabled workers does not involve the FRA. However, it would change the age of conversion to retirement benefits. Similarly, changing the number of drop-out years would have less of an effect (or no effect) on disabled workers because drop-out years are calculated differently for disabled workers. For more on how initial benefits are calculated for disabled workers, see appendix II.

[25] In particular, under the COLA reduction, less than 1 percent of disabled workers had no change in lifetime benefits; about 2 percent of disabled workers had a change of 1 percent or less; about 14 percent had a change of more than 1 and up to 5 percent; and about 41 percent had lifetime benefits change by more than 5 and up to 10 percent.

[26] Many disabled workers leave the workforce in their fifties.

[27] The other 14 percent generally had reductions of 10 percent or less, and very few disabled workers had reductions in lifetime benefits of more than 25 percent under longevity indexing.

[28] Many people have lower relative earnings in their first years of work.

[29] This table results from our discussions with knowledgeable experts and relevant officials as well as a review of the current literature on Social Security reform. For more information on how these options could work, see appendix I.

[30] For more information on caregiver credits and other program modifications, see GAO, *Retirement Security: Women Face Challenges in Ensuring Financial Security in Retirement,* GAO-08-105 (Washington, D.C.: Oct. 11, 2007).

[31] This would not be the case if at age 62 a worker could no longer remain in the workforce. In such a case, a person may have to apply for DI or may be unemployed (and have low income) for the 2 years prior to taking early retirement.

[32] In figures 8 to 11, the benefits under a full exemption do not completely return to pre- reform levels. This is because some individuals receiving disabled worker benefits also received some benefits as dependents from another worker's record. As those benefits would not be subject to the same protections, median lifetime benefits for such disabled workers may remain slightly lower than those under current law.

[33] We modeled two different ways of partially exempting disabled workers from the various indexing reforms—one follows the methods outlined in the Kolbe-Stenholm (2001) proposal, which we refer to as Type I . The other partial exemption follows the methods outlined in the Graham (2003) proposal, which we refer to as Type II. For more details on the difference, please see appendix I.

[34] Rather than being an absolute amount, the family maximum is defined as a percentage of the primary worker's benefit. Therefore, if a reform reduces benefits, the maximum amount a family could receive would also decrease. See appendix II for more details on the family maximum.

[35] As mentioned earlier, solvency could also be improved by increasing revenues (taxes).

[36] Some research has been done on whether there is a link between the increase in the FRA and the recent increase in the number and percentage of people applying for DI. For example, Duggan, Singleton, and Song (2005) find that the 1985 increase in the FRA had an important effect on the percent of people applying for DI.

[37] Besides incentive-related costs, increasing the FRA would create other costs for the DI program by expanding the size of the DI-eligible population. Workers who remain in the workforce past the old FRA and become injured prior to the new FRA may enroll in the DI program.

[38] In part, this may be because the retired individual chose to retire early (at age 62) and thus his benefits were actuarially reduced. In addition, while the present value of the individuals' lifetime earnings were similar, the distribution of these earnings could have been different and as such, the average indexed monthly earnings used as the basis for determining benefit amounts could be different.

[39] See GAO-08-105; GAO, *Social Security Reform: Implications of Different Indexing Choices*, GAO-06-804 (Washington, D.C.: Sept. 14, 2005); and GAO, *Distribution of Benefits and Taxes Relative to Earnings Level*, GAO-04-747 (Washington, D.C.: June 15, 2004).

[40] While these models use sample data, our report, like others using these models, does not address the issue of sampling errors. The results of the analysis reflect outcomes for individuals in the simulated populations and do not attempt to estimate outcomes for an actual population.

[41] MINT3 is a detailed microsimulation model developed jointly by the Social Security Administration, the Brookings Institution, RAND, and the Urban Institute to project the distribution of income in retirement for the 1931 to 1960 birth cohorts.

[42] See GAO, *Social Security: Criteria for Evaluating Reform Proposals,* GAO/T-HEHS-99-94 (Washington, D.C.: Mar. 25, 1999) and GAO, *Social Security: Evaluating Reform Proposals,* GAO/AIMD/HEHS-00-29 (Washington, D.C.: Nov. 4, 1999).

[43] For a discussion of individual equity issues, see GAO, *Social Security: Issues in Comparing Rates of Return with Market Investments,* GAO/HEHS-99-110 (Washington, D.C.: Aug. 5, 1999).

[44] See GAO, *Social Security: Program's Role in Helping Ensure Income Adequacy,* GAO-02-62 (Washington, D.C.: Nov. 30, 2001).

[45] The Board of Trustees, Federal Old-Age and Survivors Insurance and Disability Insurance Trust Funds, *The 2007 Annual Report of the Board of Trustees of the Federal Old-Age and Survivors Insurance and Disability Insurance Trust Funds* (Washington, D.C.: Apr. 23, 2007).

[46] For more information on provision 1 or Model 3, see page 8 of the CSSS proposal at http://www.ssa.gov/OACT/solvency/PresComm_20020131.pdf.

[47] We chose the CSSS specification because it was already scored and readily available. Other constructions or interpretations of a longevity index are certainly possible. For example, life expectancy at birth or some other

age could be used. Further, life expectancy could be defined as period or cohort. A period life table represents the mortality conditions at a specific point in time, whereas a cohort table depicts the mortality conditions of a specific group of individuals born in the same year or series of years.

[48] See page 3 of http://www.ssab.gov/documents/advisoryboardmemo—2005tr— 08102005.pdf for description of the provision. For the original provision from the President's Commission to Strengthen Social Security, see page 4 of http://www.ssa.gov/OACT/solvency/PresComm_20020131.pdf.

[49] See the August 10, 2005, memorandum to SSA's Chief Actuary, page 3 of http://www.ssab.gov/documents/advisoryboardmemo—2005tr—08102005.pdf, for a description of the provision.

[50] See the August 10, 2005, memorandum to SSA's Chief Actuary, page 3 of http://www.ssab.gov/documents/advisoryboardmemo—2005tr—08102005.pdf, for description of the provision.

[51] See page 3 of http://www.ssab.gov/documents/advisoryboardmemo—2005tr— 08102005.pdf for description of the provision. We did make one adjustment to this provision. We modeled the change beginning in 2012 so that the simulation start date was consistent with the start date for price indexing and progressive price indexing.

[52] The disability freeze is a special rule that helps increase retirement or disability benefits. People who have a disability or are legally blind, not on DI, and working may have lower earnings because of the disability or blindness. In such a case, SSA can exclude those years when calculating retirement or disability benefits. Because Social Security benefits are based on average lifetime earnings, the exclusion of those years increases benefits.

[53] To summarize the calculation of benefits, we relied on several Social Security publications, including the Social Security Handbook and a variety of resources available on SSA's website, www.ssa.gov.

[54] Years with wages greater than those earned from 21 to 62 would also be considered as long as the worker had "credited" earnings.

[55] For example, if a worker had some of his or her highest covered earnings between the ages of 18 and 22, these would be counted. The 40 years between age 22 and 62 simply give the formula the number of years to consider when picking the top earning years.

[56] SSA reduces retired worker benefits by 5/9 of 1 percent per month for the first 36 months and 5/12 of one percent for each additional month that a worker elects to start benefits in advance of full retirement age. Conversely, delayed retirement credits increase benefits for each month the worker delays the start of benefits after full retirement age until they reach age 70. The factor used to calculate these credits varies by birth year. For workers born in1943 or later the increase is 2/3 of 1 percent each month (8 percent per year).

[57] This is the case if lifetime benefits are calculated on a present value basis with a discount rate equal to the expected return for the Social Security trust fund—that is, 2.9 percentage points above the rate of inflation after 2015, according to the intermediate assumptions in the Trustees' 2007 report—The Board of Trustees, Federal Old Age and Survivors Insurance and Federal Disability Insurance Trust Funds, *The 2007 Annual Report of the Board of Trustees of the Federal Old Age and Survivors Insurance and Federal Disability Insurance Trust Funds* (Washington, D.C.: Apr. 23, 2007) 94.

[58] The formula used to compute the OASI family maximum is similar to that used to compute the PIA. It involves computing the sum of four separate percentages of portions of the worker's PIA. For 2007, these are 150 percent of the first $869, 272 percent of the amount between $869 and $1,255, 134 percent of the amount between $1,255 and $1,636, and 175 percent of the amount over $1,636. The disability family maximum is equal to 85 percent of the disabled worker's AIME, but cannot be less than his or her PIA, nor more than 150 percent of his or her PIA.

[59] Widow(er)s who begin collecting benefits at age 60 receive 71 percent of their deceased spouses' benefit amount, and this percentage increases for every year they delay collecting survivors benefit, reaching 100 percent at the FRA.

In: Social Security Reform: Disability, Indexing and Financing ISBN: 978-1-61668-354-2
Editor: Janet U. Burlington

Chapter 7

IMPLICATIONS OF DIFFERENT INDEXING CHOICES*

United States Government Accountability Office

WHY GAO DID THIS STUDY

The financing shortfall currently facing the Social Security program is significant. Without remedial action, program trust funds will be exhausted in 2040. Many recent reform proposals have included modifications of the indexing currently used in the Social Security program. Indexing is a way to link the growth of benefits and/or revenues to changes in an economic or demographic variable.

Given the recent attention focused on indexing, this report examines (1) the current use of indexing in the Social Security program and how reform proposals might modify that use, (2) the experiences of other developed nations that have modified indexing, (3) the effects of modifying the indexing on the distribution of benefits, and (4) the key considerations associated with modifying the indexing. To illustrate the effects of different forms of indexing on the distribution of benefits, we calculated benefit levels for a sample of workers born in 1985, using a microsimulation model. We have prepared this report under the Comptroller General's statutory authority to conduct evaluations on his own initiative as part of a continued effort to assist Congress in addressing the challenges facing Social Security. We provided a draft of this report to SSA and the Department of the Treasury. SSA provided technical comments, which we have incorporated as appropriate.

WHAT GAO FOUND

Indexing currently plays a key role in determining Social Security's benefits and revenues, and is a central element of many proposals to reform the program. The current indexing provisions that affect most workers and beneficiaries relate to (1) benefit

* This is an edited, reformatted and augmented version of a U. S. Government Accountability Office publication dated September 2006.

calculations for new beneficiaries, (2) the annual cost-of-living adjustment (COLA) for existing beneficiaries, and (3) the cap on taxable earnings. Some reform proposals would slow benefit growth by indexing the initial benefit formula to changes in prices or life expectancy rather than wages. Some would revise the COLA under the premise that it currently overstates inflation, and some would increase the cap on taxable earnings.

National pension reforms in other countries have used indexing in various ways. In countries with high contribution rates that need to address solvency issues, recent changes have generally focused on reducing benefits. Although most Organisation for Economic Co-operation and Development (OECD) countries compute retirement benefits using wage indexing, some have moved to price indexing, or a mix of both. Some countries reflect improvements in life expectancy in computing initial benefits. Reforms in other countries that include indexing changes sometimes affect both current and future retirees.

Indexing can have various distributional effects on benefits and revenues. Changing the indexing of initial benefits through the benefit formula typically results in the same percentage change in benefits across income levels regardless of the index used. However, indexing can also be designed to maintain benefits for lower earners while reducing or slowing the growth of benefits for higher earners. Indexing payroll tax rates would maintain scheduled benefit levels but reduce the ratio of benefits to contributions for younger cohorts. Finally, the effect of modifying the COLA would be greater the longer people collect benefits.

Indexing raises considerations about the program's role, the treatment of disabled workers, and other issues. For example, indexing initial benefits to prices instead of wages implies that benefit levels should maintain purchasing power rather than maintain relative standards of living across age groups (i.e., replacement rates). Also, as with other ways to change benefits, changing the indexing of the benefit formula to improve solvency could also result in benefit reductions for disabled workers as well as retirees.

ABBREVIATIONS

ABM	automatic balancing mechanism
AIME	average indexed monthly earnings
AWI	average wage index
COLA	cost-of-living adjustment
CPI	consumer price index
CPI-E	consumer price index for older Americans
CPI-U	consumer price index for all urban consumers
CPI-W	consumer price index for urban wage earners and clerical workers
DI	Disability Insurance
GDP	gross domestic product
GEMINI	Genuine Microsimulation of social Security and Accounts
OASDI	Old-Age, Survivors, and Disability Insurance
OASI	Old-Age and Survivors Insurance
OCACT	Office of the Chief Actuary
OECD	Organisation for Economic Co-operation and Development

PENSIM	Pension Simulator
PIA	primary insurance amount
PSG	Policy Simulation Group
SSA	Social Security Administration
SSASIM	Social Security and Accounts Simulator

September 14, 2006

The Honorable Charles E. Grassley
Chairman
The Honorable Max Baucus
Ranking Minority Member
Committee on Finance
United States Senate

The Honorable Jim McCrery
Chairman
The Honorable Sander M. Levin
Ranking Minority Member
Subcommittee on Social Security
Committee on Ways and Means
House of Representatives

The Honorable John Warner
United States Senate

The total long-term financing shortfall currently facing the Social Security program is significant and growing over time, thereby making system reform an important priority. Once the Social Security trust fund balances are exhausted in 2040, annual revenue will be sufficient only to pay about 74 percent of promised benefits, according to the Social Security trustees' 2006 intermediate assumptions. Benefit costs are projected to exceed income in 2017, and thus trust fund securities will need to be redeemed. This will require increased government revenue, increased borrowing from the public, reduced spending in the rest of the government, or some combination of these. Redeeming these securities will have an adverse impact on the federal budget much sooner than the 2040 trust fund exhaustion date.

Many recent reform proposals have proposed modifications to the indexing currently used in the Social Security program. Indexing is a way to link the growth of benefits and/or revenues to changes in economic or demographic variables. For example, initial benefits can be set to grow with changes in average wages or changes in prices. Modifications to indexing seek to slow the growth of benefits or increase the growth of revenues, either of which would improve solvency. However, indexing does not guarantee that the program will achieve and remain in long-term financial balance. Proposals that would modify Social Security's indexing implicitly pose the question of whether and how such adjustments could provide a mechanism to keep the program sustainably solvent and minimize the need for periodic rebalancing of the program's finances. At the same time, how it is done can affect the distribution of benefits between low and high earners and across generations of workers.

Given the recent attention focused on indexing as a critical component of reform, this report examines (1) the current use of indexing in the Social Security program and how reform proposals might modify that use, (2) the experiences of other developed nations that have modified indexing when reforming their public pension systems, (3) the effects of indexing modifications on the distribution of Social Security benefits, and (4) the key considerations associated with modifying Social Security's indexing.

To examine the use of indexing in the Social Security program and how reform proposals might modify the indexing, we conducted a literature review and reviewed recent Social Security reform proposals. To examine the experience of other developed nations that changed indexing when reforming their own national pension systems, we reviewed the academic literature and documentation on other countries' public pension systems. To analyze the effects of different forms of indexing on the distribution of benefits, we calculated benefit levels for a sample of workers using a microsimulation model (see app. I for a more detailed discussion of our scope and methodology).[1] For this analysis, we selected four well-known indexing approaches to illustrate the effects on the distribution of benefits.[2] To describe the distributional effects of the different indexing approaches, we used our model to simulate benefits for workers born in 1985.[3] Consistent with our past work on Social Security reform, and to illustrate a full range of possible outcomes, we used hypothetical benchmark policy scenarios that would achieve 75-year solvency either by only increasing payroll taxes (which simulated "promised benefits") or only reducing benefits (which simulated "funded benefits").[4] To determine the key considerations associated with various forms of indexing, we reviewed the literature and talked with relevant experts. We have prepared this report under the Comptroller General's statutory authority to conduct evaluations on his own initiative as part of a continued effort to assist Congress in addressing the challenges facing Social Security. We conducted our work between July 2005 and August 2006 in accordance with generally accepted government auditing standards.

RESULTS IN BRIEF

While the initial Social Security program did not use automatic indexing, it is now a key feature of the program's design, as well as a central element of many proposals to reform the program. Under the current system, the indexing provisions that affect most workers and beneficiaries relate to (1) the formula used to calculate initial benefits for new beneficiaries, (2) the cost-of-living adjustment (COLA) for existing beneficiaries, and (3) the cap on taxable earnings. The benefit indexing provisions help maintain relative standards of living across age groups and protect the purchasing power of benefits over time. Various reform proposals have suggested changes to all of these provisions. For example, for future beneficiaries, some proposals would index initial benefit levels to keep pace with price inflation rather than wages. This would result in gradually declining earnings replacement rates but maintain the purchasing power of current benefit levels across age groups, assuming wages grow faster than prices on average over time.[5] Other proposals accept slowing the growth of initial benefits, in general, but seek to protect benefit levels for the lowest earners, consistent with the program's goal of helping ensure income adequacy. Proposals to change the annual COLA for existing beneficiaries generally focus on making it reflect inflation levels more accurately, with the presumption that this would result in lower benefits. On the revenue side, proposals to increase the cap on taxable earnings generally seek to raise revenue from higher earners and avoid increasing tax rates for all workers.

Other countries' efforts to reform their national pension systems reveal a diversity of indexing approaches. Countries with relatively high contribution rates tend to focus on methods that reduce benefits to address the financial solvency of their pension systems. Although most Organisation for Economic Co-operation and Development (OECD) countries index past earnings to reflect wage growth in computing initial retirement benefits, some now use a price growth index (France, Belgium, and South Korea), or an index that blends price and wage growth (Portugal, Poland, and Finland). Some benefit formulas contain a measure of life expectancy that reduces payments to new retirees in accordance with increases in longevity (Sweden, Italy, and Poland). Changes to indexing approaches abroad sometimes affect both current and future retirees. Germany includes a "sustainability" factor that lowers pension amounts for both new and old retirees when the number of workers paying into the system declines relative to those drawing benefits. Similarly, other national systems rely on automatic balancing mechanisms that modify both the future benefits of workers and the benefits of current pensioners (Sweden, Japan).

Indexing can have different effects on the distribution of benefits and on the relationship between contributions and benefits, depending on how it is applied. Regardless of the index, adjusting the initial benefit level through the benefit formula typically would have a proportional effect, with constant percentage changes at all earnings levels, on the distribution of benefits. However, indexing can also be used to achieve specific distributional goals. For example, so-called progressive indexing applies different indexes at different earnings levels to adjust benefits of higher- income earners more than the benefits of lower-income earners. Indexing payroll tax rates would have distributional effects across generations, maintaining the existing distribution of benefits but instead affecting equity measures like the ratio of benefits to contributions across age cohorts. In this case, younger cohorts would have lower ratios, because they would receive lower benefits relative to their contributions. Finally, proposals that modify the indexing of annual COLAs for existing beneficiaries would have adverse distributional effects for groups with longer life expectancies, such as women, but these individuals would still receive higher lifetime benefits since they live longer. In addition, disabled worker beneficiaries, especially those who receive benefits for many years, would also experience lower benefits because such proposals would typically reduce future benefits, and this effect compounds over time.

Indexing raises other important considerations about the program's role, the stability of economic or demographic relationships underlying the index, and the treatment of disabled worker beneficiaries. The choice of the index implies certain assumptions about the appropriate level of benefits and taxes for the program. Thus, if the current indexing of initial benefits to wage growth was changed to track price growth, there is an implication that the appropriate level of benefits is one that maintains purchasing power over time rather than the current approach that maintains replacement rates. The solvency effects of an index are predicated upon the relative stability and historical trends of the underlying economic or demographic relationships implied by the index. For example, the 1970s were a period of economic instability in which actual inflation rates and earnings growth diverged markedly from past experience, with the result that benefits unexpectedly grew much faster than revenues. Finally, since the benefit formula for Social Security retirement and disability benefits are linked, an important consideration of any indexing proposal, as with any other change to benefits, is its effect on the benefits provided to disabled workers. Disabled worker beneficiaries typically become entitled to benefits much sooner than retired workers and under different eligibility criteria. An index that is designed to improve solvency, for example, by adjusting retirement benefits, could also result in large reductions to disabled workers, who often have fewer options to obtain additional income from other sources.

Background

Title II of the Social Security Act, as amended, establishes the Old-Age, Survivors, and Disability Insurance (OASDI) program, which is generally known as Social Security. The program provides cash benefits to retired and disabled workers and their eligible dependents and survivors. Congress designed Social Security benefits with an implicit focus on replacing lost wages. However, Social Security is not meant to be the sole source of retirement income; rather it forms a foundation for individuals to build upon. The program is financed on a modified pay-as-you-go basis in which payroll tax contributions of those currently working are largely transferred to current beneficiaries. Current beneficiaries include insured workers who are entitled to retirement or disability benefits, and their eligible dependents, as well as eligible survivors of deceased insured workers. The program's benefit structure is progressive, that is, it provides greater insurance protection relative to contributions for earners with lower wages than for high-wage earners. Workers qualify for benefits by earning Social Security credits when they work and pay Social Security taxes[6]; they and their employers pay payroll taxes on those earnings. In 2005, approximately 159 million people had earnings covered by Social Security, and 48 million people received approximately $521 billion in OASDI benefits.

Currently, the Social Security program collects more in taxes than it pays out in benefits. However, because of changing demographics, this situation will reverse itself, with the annual cash surplus beginning to decline in 2009 and turning negative in 2017. In addition, all of the accumulated Treasury obligations held by the trust funds are expected to be exhausted by 2040.[7] Social Security's long-term financing shortfall stems primarily from the fact that people are living longer and labor force growth has slowed.[8] As a result, the number of workers paying into the system for each beneficiary has been falling and is projected to decline from 3.3 today to about 2 by 2040. The projected long-term insolvency of the OASDI program necessitates system reform to restore its long-term solvency and assure its sustainability. Restoring solvency and assuring sustainability for the long term requires that either Social Security gets additional income (revenue increases), reduces costs (benefit reductions), or undertakes some combination of the two.

To evaluate reform proposals, we have suggested that policy makers should consider three basic criteria:[9]

1. the extent to which the proposal achieves sustainable solvency and how the proposal would affect the economy and the federal budget;

2. the balance struck between the goals of individual equity[10] (rates of return on individual contributions) and income adequacy[11] (level and certainty of monthly benefits); and
3. how readily such changes could be implemented, administered, and explained to the public.

Moreover, reform proposals should be evaluated as packages that strike a balance among the individual elements of the proposal and the interactions among these elements. The overall evaluation of any particular reform proposal depends on the weight individual policy makers place on each of the above criteria.

Changing the indexing used by the OASDI program could be used to increase income or reduce costs. Indexing provides a form of regular adjustment of revenues or benefits that is pegged to a particular economic, demographic, or actuarial variable. An advantage of such indexing approaches is that they take some of the "politics" out of the system, allowing the system to move toward some agreed-upon objective; they may also be administratively simple. However, this "automatic pilot" aspect of indexing poses a challenge, as it may make policy makers hesitant to enact changes, even when problems arise.

Social Security Currently Indexes Both Benefits and Revenues

While Social Security did not use automatic indexing initially, it is now a key feature of the program's design, as well as a central element of many reform proposals. Under the current program, benefits for new beneficiaries are computed using wage indexing, benefits for existing beneficiaries are adjusted using price indexing, and on the revenue side, the cap on the amount of earnings subject to the payroll tax is also adjusted using wage indexing. Reform proposals have included provisions for modifying each of these indexing features.

Program Did Not Use Indexing until 1970s

Before the 1970s, the Social Security program did not use indexing to adjust benefits or taxes automatically. For both new and existing beneficiaries, benefit rates increased only when Congress voted to raise them. Benefit levels, when adjusted for inflation, fell and then jumped up with ad hoc increases, and these fluctuations were dramatic at times. Similarly, Congress made only ad hoc changes to the tax rate and the cap on the amount of workers' earnings that were subject to the payroll tax, which is also known as the maximum taxable earnings level. Adjusted for inflation, the maximum taxable earnings level also fluctuated dramatically, and as a result, the proportion of all wages subject to the payroll tax also fluctuated. (See app. II for more detail.)

For the first time, the 1972 amendments provided for automatic indexing. They provided for automatically increasing the maximum taxable earnings level based on increases in average earnings, and this approach is still in use today. However, the 1972 amendments provided an indexing approach for benefits that became widely viewed as flawed. In particular, the indexing approach in the 1972 amendments resulted in (1) a "double-indexing" of benefits to inflation for new beneficiaries though not for existing ones[12]; (2) a form of "bracket creep" based on the structure of the benefit formula that slowed benefit growth as earnings increased over time, which offset the double indexing to some degree; and (3) instability of program costs that was driven by the interaction of price and wage growth in benefit calculations. (See app. II for more detail.) Within a few years, problems with the 1972 amendments became apparent. Benefits were growing far faster than anticipated, especially since wage and price growth varied dramatically from previous historical experience. Addressing the instability of this indexing approach became a focus of policy makers' efforts to come up with a new approach. As a 1977 paper on the problem noted, "Clearly, it is a system that needs to be brought under greater control, so that the behavior of retirement benefits over time will stop reflecting the chance interaction of certain economic variables."[13]

1977 Amendments Created Indexing Approach of Current Social Security System

The 1977 amendments instituted a new approach to indexing benefits that remains in use today. The experience with the 1972 amendments and double indexing made clear the need to index benefits differently for new and existing beneficiaries, which was referred to as "decoupling" benefits. Indexing now applies to several distinct steps of the benefit computation process, including (1) indexing lifetime earnings for each worker to wage growth, (2) indexing the benefit formula for new beneficiaries to wage growth, and (3) indexing benefits for existing beneficiaries to price inflation.[14] Under this approach, benefit calculations for new beneficiaries are indexed differently than for existing beneficiaries, and earnings replacement rates have been fairly stable. The cap on taxable earnings is still indexed to wage growth as specified by the 1972 amendments.

Indexing lifetime earnings to wages

Social Security benefits are designed to partially replace earnings that workers lose when they retire, become disabled, or die. As a result, the first step of the benefit formula calculates a worker's average indexed monthly earnings (AIME), which is based on the worker's lifetime history of earnings covered by Social Security taxes. The formula adjusts these lifetime earnings by indexing them to changes in average wages.[15] Indexing the earnings to changes in wage levels ensures that the same relative value is accorded to each year's earnings, no matter when they were earned.

For example, consider a worker who earned $5,000 in 1965 and $40,000 in 2000. The worker's earnings increased by eight times, but much of that increase reflected changes in the average wage level in the economy, which increased by about seven times (690 percent) over the same period. The growth in average wages in turn partially reflects price inflation; however, wages may grow faster or slower than prices in any given year. Indexed to reflect wage growth, the $5,000 would become roughly $35,000, giving it greater weight in computing average earnings over time and making it more comparable to 2000 wage levels.

Indexing initial benefit formula to wages

Once the AIME is determined, it is applied to the formula used to calculate the worker's primary insurance amount (PIA). This formula applies different earnings replacement factors to different portions of the worker's average earnings. The different replacement factors make the formula progressive, meaning that the formula replaces a larger portion of earnings for lower earners than for higher earners. For workers who become eligible for benefits in 2006, the PIA equals

- 90 percent of the first $656 dollars of AIME plus
- 32 percent of the next $3,299 dollars of AIME plus
- 15 percent of AIME above $3,955.

For workers who do not collect benefits until after the year they first become eligible, the PIA is adjusted to reflect any COLAs since they became eligible. The PIA is used in turn to determine benefits for new beneficiaries and all types of benefits payable on the basis of an individual's earnings record. To determine the actual monthly benefit, adjustments are made reflecting various other provisions, such as those relating to early or delayed retirement, type of beneficiary, and maximum family benefit amounts. Figure 1 illustrates how the PIA formula works.

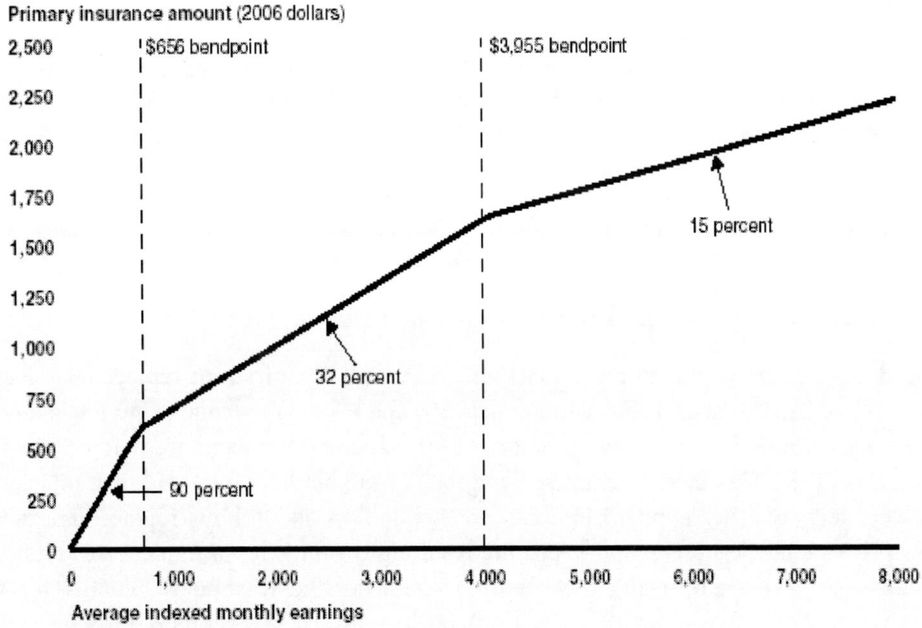

Source: Social Security Administration.

Figure 1. Social Security Benefit Formula Replaces Earnings at Different Rates

Source: SSA.

Note: Replacement rates are the annual retired worker benefits at age 65 divided by career-average earnings. Illustrative workers have career-average earnings equal to about 45, 100, and 160 percent of Social Security's Average Wage Index, respectively, for low, medium, and high earners. These three cases have earnings patterns that reflect differences by age in the probability of work and in average earnings levels. Taxable maximum earners have earnings equal to the maximum earnings taxable under OASDI in each year. Variations in these illustrative replacement rates result not only from program changes but also from short-term fluctuations in the growth rate of wages, which helps determine the earnings histories of the illustrative earners.

Figure 2. Social Security's Earnings Replacement Rates for Illustrative Workers

The dollar values in the formula that indicate where the different replacement factors apply are called bendpoints. These bendpoints ($656 and $3,955) are indexed to the change in average wages, while the replacement factors of 90, 32, and 15 percent are held constant. In contrast, under the 1972 amendments, the bendpoints were held constant and the replacement factors were indexed. (See app. II.) Indexing the bendpoints and holding replacement factors constant prevents bracket creep and keeps the resulting earnings replacement rates relatively level across birth years. Indexing the benefit formula in this way helps benefits for new retirees keep pace with wage growth, which reflects increases in the standard of living.

Figure 2, which shows earnings replacement rates for successive groups of illustrative workers, illustrates the program's history with indexing initial benefits.[16] Replacement rates declined before the first benefit increases were enacted in 1950 and then rose sharply as a result of those increases. From 1950 until the early 1970s, replacement rates fluctuated noticeably more from year to year than over other periods; this pattern reflects the ad hoc nature of benefit increases over that period. Between 1974 and 1979, replacement rates grew rapidly for new beneficiaries, reflecting the double indexing of the 1972 amendments. The

1977 amendments corrected for the unintended growth in benefits from double indexing, and replacement rates declined rapidly as a result. This pattern of increasing and then declining benefit levels is known as the notch.[17] Finally, replacement rates have been considerably more stable since the 1977 amendments took effect, a fact that has helped to stabilize program costs. (See app. II.)

Indexing benefits to prices for existing beneficiaries

After initial benefits have been set for the first year of entitlement, benefits in subsequent years increase with a COLA designed to keep pace with inflation and thereby help to maintain the purchasing power of those benefits. The COLA is based on the consumer price index (CPI), in contrast to the indexing of lifetime earnings and initial benefits, which are based on the national average wage index.[18]

Indexing maximum taxable earnings to wages

The cap on taxable earnings increases each year to keep pace with changes in average wages. As a result, in combination with a constant tax rate, total program revenues tend to keep pace with wage growth and therefore also with benefits to some degree. In 2006, the cap is set at $94,200. As the distribution of earnings in the economy changes, the percentage of total earnings that fall below the cap can also change. (See app. II.)

Table 1 summarizes the various indexing and automatic adjustment approaches that affect most workers and beneficiaries under the current program.

Table 1. Key Indexing Approaches under Current U.S. Social Security System

Approach	How it works	Comments
Benefit provisions		
Wage-indexing initial benefit calculation	Before averaging workers' earnings over their careers, AIME adjusts actual earnings using average wage index.	Maintains relative standards of living across age groups (that is, replacement rates), at time of retirement.
	Bendpoints of PIA formula rise over time according to wage growth.	Actuarial balance of the program is relatively insensitive to economic fluctuations because benefit levels and tax revenues are both linked to wages.
	Earnings replacement factors in PIA formula remain constant.	Initial benefits keep pace with standard of living, as reflected by wage levels.
Price-indexing post-entitlement benefits	Benefits rise yearly according to rise in the CPI.	Purchasing power of benefits remains constant over time, once benefits start.
Tax provisions		
Wage-indexing maximum taxable earnings	Earnings are only taxed on the first $94,200 per year in 2006. Limit rises every year according to average wage growth.	Share of earnings not taxed can change as income distribution changes.
Constant tax rate	Earnings are taxed yearly at 12.4 percent (6.2 percent from workers and 6.2 percent from employers).	Program revenue rises annually with the rise in wages.
		Constant tax rate maintains the same proportion of taxes for all workers earning less than maximum taxable earnings.

Source: GAO.

Various reform proposals include indexing provisions

Various reform proposals have suggested changes to most of the indexing features of the current Social Security system. Some proposals would use alternative indexes for initial benefits in order to slow their growth. Other proposals would take the same approach but would limit benefit reductions on workers with lower earnings. Some propose modifying the COLA in the belief that the CPI overstates the rate of inflation. Still others propose indexing revenue provisions in new ways.

Changes to the indexing of Social Security's initial benefits could be implemented by changing the indexing of lifetime earnings or the PIA formula's bendpoints.[19] However, they could also be implemented by adjusting the PIA formula's replacement factors, even though these factors are not now indexed. Under this approach, which is used in this report, the replacement factors are typically multiplied by a number that reflects the index being used. The replacement factors would be adjusted for each year in which benefits start, beginning with some future year. So such changes would not affect current beneficiaries. Indexing the replacement factors would reduce benefits at the same proportional rate across income levels, while changing the indexing of lifetime earnings or the bendpoints could alter the distribution of benefits across income levels. Recent reform proposals, as described by the Social Security Administration's (SSA) Office of the Chief Actuary in its evaluations, generally implement indexing changes as adjustments to the PIA formula's replacement factors.

Two indexing approaches—to reflect changes in the CPI or increasing longevity—have been proposed as alternatives to the average wage index for calculating initial benefits. Proponents of using CPI indexing for initial benefit calculations generally offer the rationale that wage indexing has never been fiscally sustainable and CPI indexing would slow the growth of benefits to an affordable level while maintaining the purchasing power of benefits. They say that maintaining the purchasing power of benefits should be the program's goal, as opposed to maintaining relative standards of living across age groups (that is, earnings replacement rates), which the current benefit formula accomplishes. Proponents of longevity indexing offer the rationale that increasing longevity is a key reason for the system's long-term insolvency. Since people are living longer on average, and are expected to continue to do so in the future, they will therefore collect benefits for more years on average. Using an index that reflects changes in life expectancy would maintain relatively comparable levels of lifetime benefits across birth years and thereby promote intergenerational equity. Also, longevity indexing could encourage people to work longer.

Some indexing proposals accept the need to slow the growth of initial benefits in general but seek to protect benefit levels for the lowest earnings levels, consistent with the program's goal of helping ensure income adequacy. Such proposals would modify how a new index would be applied to the formula for initial benefits so that the formula is still wage-indexed below a certain earnings level. As a result, they would maintain benefits promised under the current program for those with earnings below that level such as, for example, those in the bottom 30 percent of the earnings distribution. Such an approach has been called progressive price indexing.

A few proposals would alter the COLA used to adjust benefits for current retirees. Some proposals respond to methodological concerns that have been raised about how the CPI is calculated and would adjust the COLA in the interest of accuracy.[20] In general, such changes would slightly slow the growth of the program's benefit costs. However, other proposals call for creating a new CPI for older Americans (CPI-E) specifically tailored to reflect how inflation affects the elderly population and using the CPI-E for computing Social Security's COLA.[21] Depending on its construction, such a change could increase the program's benefit costs.

Table 2. Summary of Indexes and Automatic Adjustments Proposed in United States

Provision	How it works	Rationales offered by proponents
Provisions affecting initial benefit calculations for future beneficiaries		
Longevity indexing	Proportionally reduces replacement factors in PIA formula to reflect adjustments for increasing life expectancy.[a]	Increasing longevity is a key reason for the system's long-term solvency problem. People are living longer on average and therefore collecting benefits for more years on average. Would maintain comparable levels of lifetime benefits across birth years and thereby promote intergenerational equity.
Price indexing[b]	Proportionally reduces replacement factors in PIA formula to reflect changes in index.[a]	"Wage-indexing … has never been fiscally sustainable."[c] Would slow the growth of benefits to an affordable level. Would still maintain the purchasing power of benefits.
Progressive price indexing	Proportionally reduces replacement factors in PIA formula to reflect changes in index.[a] But no change to factors for earnings below a certain level. Effectively adds new bendpoint between two current ones.	Protects benefits for lower earnings to help ensure income adequacy.
Provisions affecting benefit COLAs for current and future beneficiaries		
Revise COLA to reflect more accurate calculation of CPI	Use more accurate CPI in determining COLA.	Greater accuracy.
Provisions affecting taxes for current and future workers		
Longevity indexing of payroll tax rates	Proportionally increase payroll tax rate to reflect changes in index.	Increasing longevity is a key reason for the system's long-term solvency problem.
Increase payroll tax rates to ensure maintaining ratio of trust fund assets to program costs	Use trustees' intermediate projections of trust fund ratios.	Ensure ongoing solvency.
Increase maximum taxable earnings to ensure a constant percentage of aggregate earnings are taxed	Use recent data on earnings distribution with trustees' intermediate projections of wage growth.	Promote intergenerational equity by ensuring consistent application of payroll tax.

Source: GAO.

[a] Average indexed monthly earnings would be computed as under present law.

[b] An implication of price indexing is that it would slow benefit growth to a greater degree if wages grow faster than projected, even as Social Security's financial situation would be improving.

[c] Commission to Strengthen Social Security. "Strengthening Social Security and Creating Personal Wealth for All Americans: Report of the President's Commission" p. 120, Washington, D.C.: Dec. 21, 2001.

Some proposals would index revenues in new ways. Some would apply a longevity index to payroll tax rates, again focused on the fact that increasing life expectancy is a primary source of the program's insolvency. Proponents of indexing tax rates feel that benefits are already fairly modest, so the adjustment for longevity should not come entirely from benefit reductions. Other proposals would institute other types of automatic revenue adjustments. Some would raise the maximum taxable earnings level gradually until some percentage of total earnings are covered and then maintain that percentage into the future. Implicitly, such proposals reflect a desire to hold constant the percentage of earnings subject to the payroll tax. Still another proposal would provide for automatically increasing the tax rate when the ratio of trust fund assets to annual program costs is projected to fall.

Table 2 summarizes the various indexing and automatic adjustment approaches that reform proposals have contained.

A Variety of Indexing Approaches Highlight International Reform Efforts

Faced with adverse demographic trends, many countries have enacted reforms in recent years to improve the long-term fiscal sustainability of their national pension systems. New indexing methods now appear in a variety of forms around the world in earnings-related national pension systems.[22] In general, they seek to contain pension costs associated with population aging. Some indexing methods affect both current and future retirees.

Retirement Indexing Approaches in Other Countries Generally Focus on Benefit Reductions instead of Increased Contributions

A number of reforms have focused on methods that primarily adjust benefits rather than taxes to address the fiscal solvency of national pension systems. There are two main reasons for this. First, contribution rates abroad are generally high already, making it politically difficult to raise them much further. For example, while in the United States total employer-employee Social Security contribution rates are 12.4 percent of taxable earnings, they are above 16 percent in Belgium and France, more than 18 percent in Sweden and Germany, above 25 percent in the Netherlands and the Czech Republic, and over 30 percent in Italy.[23] In fact, some countries have stipulated a ceiling on employee contribution rates in order to reassure the young—or current contributors—that the burden would be shared among generations. For example, Japan settled, with the 2004 Reform Law, its pension premium rates for the next 100 years with an increase of 0.35 percent per year until 2017, at which time premium levels are to be fixed at 18.3 percent of covered wages. Similarly, Canada chose to raise its combined employer-employee contribution rate more quickly than previously scheduled, from 5.6 percent to 9.9 percent between 1997 and 2003, and maintain it there until the end of the 75-year projection period.[24] This increase is meant to help Canada's pension system build a large reserve fund and spread the costs of financial sustainability across generations.[25] Germany's recent reforms set the workers' contribution rate at 20 percent until 2020 and at 22 percent from 2020 to 2030. Second, increasing employee contribution rates without significantly reducing benefit levels will tend to make continued employment less attractive compared to retirement. In the context of population aging and fiscally stressed national pension systems facing many countries, reform measures seek to do the opposite: encourage people to remain in the labor force longer to enhance the fiscal solvency of pension programs. Contribution rates that become too high are not likely to provide sufficient incentives to continue work.

Indexing Approaches Aim at Containing Costs

One commonly used means of reducing, or containing the growth of, promised benefits involves changing the method used to compute initial benefits. For example, France, Belgium, and South Korea now adjust past earnings in line with price growth rather than wage growth to determine the initial pension benefits of new retirees. In general, this shift to price indexation tends to significantly lower benefits relative to earnings, as over long periods prices tend to grow more slowly than wages.[26] Because of compounding, the effect of such a change is larger when benefits are based on earnings over a long period than when they reflect only the last few years of work, as in pension plans with benefits based on final salaries. In fact, the OECD estimates that, in the case of a full-career worker with 45 years of earnings, price indexation can lead to benefits 40 percent lower than with wage indexation.[27] In contrast to full price indexing, some nations use an index that is a mix of price growth and wage growth, which tends to produce higher benefits than those calculated using price indexation only, then adjust the relative weights of the two to cover program costs. Finland, for example, changed its indexation of initial benefits from 50 percent prices and 50 percent wages to 80 percent and 20 percent, respectively. Similarly, Portugal's index combines 75 percent price growth and 25 percent wage growth.[28]

A few countries have moved away from wage indexing but without necessarily adopting price indexation. Sweden, for instance, uses an index that reflects per capita wage growth to compute initial benefits, provided the system is in fiscal balance. However, when the system's obligations exceed its assets, a "brake" is applied automatically that allows the indexation to be temporarily abandoned.[29] This automatic balancing mechanism (ABM) ensures that the pension system remains financially stable.[30] In Germany and Japan, recent reforms changed benefit indexation from a gross-wage base to a net-wage base—i.e., gross wages minus contributions. In Italy, workers' benefit accounts rise in line with gross domestic product (GDP) growth so both the changes in the size of the labor force and in productivity dictate benefit levels.

Another approach countries have used is adding a longevity index to the formula determining pension payments. In Sweden, Poland, and Italy, for example, remaining life expectancy at the time of retirement inversely affects benefit levels. Thus, as life spans gradually increase, successive cohorts of retirees get smaller benefit payments unless they choose to begin receiving them later in life than those who retired before them. Also, people who retire earlier than their peers in a given cohort get significantly lower benefits throughout their remaining life than those who retire later. Longevity indexing helps ensure that improvements in life expectancy do not strain the system financially.[31]

Germany, on the other hand, now uses a sustainability factor that links initial benefits to the system's dependency ratio—i.e., the number of people drawing benefits relative to the number paying into the system. This dependency ratio captures variations in fertility, longevity, and immigration, and consequently makes the pension system self-stabilizing. For example, higher fertility and immigration, which raise labor force growth, will, other things equal, improve the dependency ratio, leading to higher pension benefits, while higher longevity or life expectancy will increase the dependency ratio, and hence cause benefits to decline.[32]

Indexing Approaches Affect Both Current and Future Beneficiaries

In some of the countries we studied, changes in indexing methods affect both current and future retirees. In Japan, for example, post-retirement benefits were indexed to wages net of taxes before 2000. However, reforms enacted that year altered the formula by linking post-retirement benefits to prices. As a result, retirees saw their subsequent benefits rise at a much slower pace. The 2004 reforms reduced retirees' purchasing power further by introducing a negative "automatic adjustment indexation" to the formula. With this provision, post-retirement benefits increase in line with prices minus the adjustment rate, currently fixed at 0.9 percent until about 2023. This rate is the sum of two demographic factors: the decline in the number of people contributing to the pension program (projected at 0.6 percent) plus the increase in the number of years people collect pensions (projected at 0.3 percent). This negative adjustment also enters the formula determining the benefit of new recipients as past earnings are indexed to net wages minus the same 0.9 percent adjustment rate.

Sweden's ABM modifies both the retirement accounts of workers—or future retirees—and the benefits paid to current pensioners. As explained earlier, this mechanism is triggered whenever system assets fall short of system liabilities. Moreover, post-retirement benefits in Sweden are indexed each year to an economic factor equal to prices plus the average rate of real wage increase minus 1.6 percent, which is the projected real long-term growth in wages. As a result, if average real wages grow annually at 1.6 percent, post-retirement benefits are adjusted for price increases. On the other hand, if real wage growth falls below 1.6 percent, benefits do not keep up with prices, leading to a decline in retiree purchasing power.[33]

Germany's sustainability factor affects those already retired, as it is included in the formula that adjusts their benefits each year. If, as projected, the number of contributors falls relative to that of pensioners, increasing the dependency ratio, all benefits are adjusted downward, so all cohorts share the burden of adverse demographic trends. This intergenerational burden sharing is also apparent in the indexation of all benefits to net wages—wages minus contributions, which affect workers and pensioners alike. Thus an increase in contributions, everything else equal, lowers both initial benefits and benefits already being paid.

Table 3 summarizes relevant characteristics of earnings-related public pension programs in selected countries.

Table 3. Characteristics of Earnings-Related Public Pension Programs–Selected Countries

	Remaining life expectancy at age 65[a] men-women	Normal retirement age (early retirement age)[b]	Average contribution rate (percentage of earnings)	Years of individual earnings considered in initial benefit calculation	Indexing of earnings for calculating initial benefits	Indexing of benefits in retirement
Belgium	15.8 19.7 (2002)	65 (60)	16.36	Lifetime average	Prices	100% prices
Canada	17.4 20.8	65 (60)	9.9	Lifetime average excluding worst 15% of years	Average earnings	100% prices
Czech Republic	13.9 17.3	Men: 63 Women: 59-63 (men: 60, women: 56-60)[c]	28	Since 1985 moving to 30	Average earnings	67% prices 33% real wage growth
France	17.1 21.4 (2002)	60	16.45	Lifetime average (public employees: best 20 moving to 25)	Prices	100% prices
Germany	16.1 19.6	65 (63)	19.5	Lifetime average	Average net earnings (subject to demographic adjustment)	100% wages net of contributions (subject to demographic adjustment)
Italy	16.7 20.7 (2001)	65 (60)	32.7	Lifetime average	5-year moving average of GDP growth (subject to demographic adjustment)	Between 75-100% prices depending on benefit level
Japan	18.2 23.3 (2004)	65 (60)	13.58	Lifetime average	Average earnings (subject to demographic adjustment)	100% prices (subject to demographic adjustment)
Sweden	17.4 20.6 (2004)	65 (61)	18.5	Lifetime average	Average earnings (subject to demographic and fiscal adjustments)	100% prices plus real wages less 1.6% (subject to demographic and fiscal adjustments)
United States	16.8 19.8	67 (62)	12.4	Best 35	Average earnings up to age 60	100% prices

Source: GAO

[a] In 2003 unless otherwise indicated.

[b] 2002 data, including legislated changes.

[c] Women's retirement ages (full and early) depend on the number of children.

INDEXING CAN BE USED TO ACHIEVE DESIRED DISTRIBUTIONAL EFFECT

In the U.S. Social Security program, indexing can have different effects on the distribution of benefits and on the relationship between contributions and benefits, depending on how it is applied to benefits or taxes. There are a variety of proposals that would change the current indexing of initial benefits, including a move to the CPI, to longevity or mortality measures, or to the dependency ratio.[34] When the index is implemented through the benefit formula, each will have a proportional effect, with constant percentage changes at all earnings levels, on the distribution of benefits (i.e., the progressivity of the current system is unchanged). However, indexing provisions can be modified to achieve other distributional effects. For example, so-called progressive indexing applies different indexes at different earnings levels in a manner that seeks to protect the benefits of low-income workers. Indexing payroll tax rates would also have distributional effects. Such changes maintain existing benefit levels but affect equity measures like the ratio of benefits to contributions across age cohorts, with younger cohorts having lower ratios because they receive lower benefits relative to their contributions. Finally, proposals that modify the indexing of COLAs for existing beneficiaries have important and adverse distributional effects for groups that have longer life expectancies, such as women and highly educated workers, because such proposals would typically reduce future benefits, and this effect compounds over time. In addition, disabled worker beneficiaries, especially those who receive benefits for many years, would also experience lower benefits.

Proposals to Index Initial Benefits Have a Proportional Effect on the Distribution of Benefits

There are a variety of proposals that would change the current indexing of initial benefits from the growth in average wages. These include a move to a measure of the change in prices like the CPI, to longevity measures that seek to capture the growth in population life expectancies, or to the dependency ratio that measures changes in the number of retirees compared to the workforce. We analyzed three indexing scenarios; the dependency ratio index, which links the growth of initial benefits to changes in the dependency ratio, the ratio of the number of retirees to workers; the CPI index, which links the growth of initial benefits to changes in the CPI; and the mortality index, which links the growth of initial benefits to changes in life expectancy to maintain a constant life expectancy at the normal retirement age.[35] Figure 3 illustrates the projected distribution of benefits for workers born in 1985 under three different indexing scenarios[36] (on the left side of the figure) and under a so-called benefit reduction benchmark that reduces benefits just enough to achieve program solvency over a 75-year projection period (on the far right).[37] Median benefits under the dependency ratio index and the CPI index are lower than the median benefit for the benchmark; they reduce benefits more than is needed to achieve 75-year solvency.[38] In contrast, the mortality index has a higher median benefit level than the benchmark, so without further modifications, it would not achieve 75-year solvency.

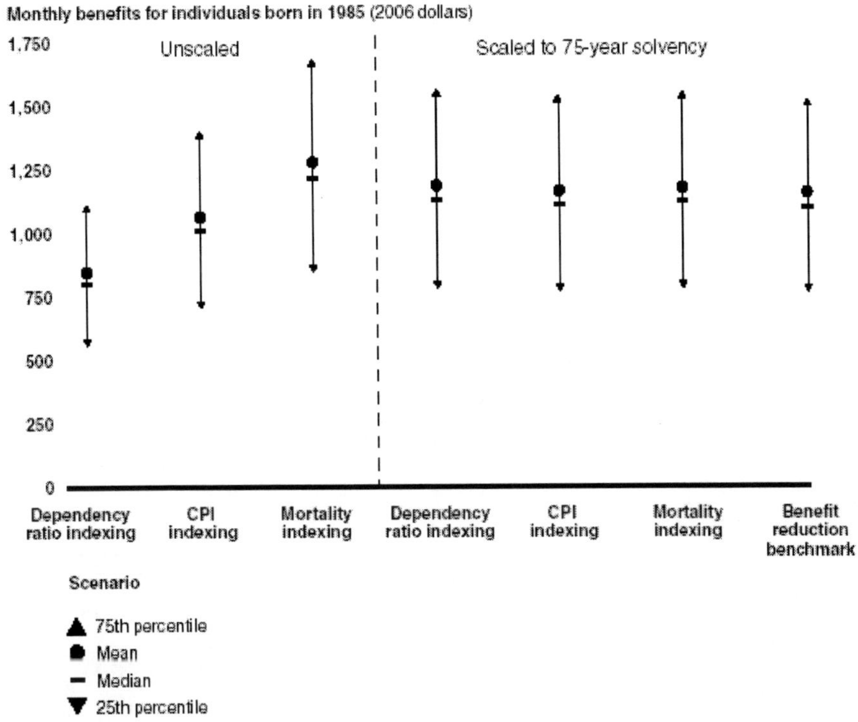

Source: GAO analysis of GEMINI data.

Note: Benefits are for all individuals in the GEMINI 1985 cohort sample in 2052 (the year the cohort reaches age 67). Scenarios are modeled using the intermediate assumptions of the 2005 trustees' report. The dependency ratio index links the growth of initial benefits to changes in the dependency ratio, the ratio of the number of retirees to workers. The dependency ratio index has a 197 percent improvement in 75-year solvency, generating far more programmatic savings than is needed to achieve solvency. The CPI index links the growth of initial benefits to changes in the CPI. The CPI index has a 127 percent improvement in 75-year solvency, generating more programmatic savings than is needed to achieve solvency. The mortality index links the growth of initial benefits to changes in life expectancy to maintain a constant life expectancy at the normal retirement age. The mortality index has a 72 percent improvement in 75-year solvency, which does not generate enough programmatic savings to be solvent. The benefit reduction benchmark is a hypothetical benchmark policy scenario that would achieve 75-year solvency by only reducing benefits. Thus, the benchmark has a 100 percent improvement in 75-year solvency, being exactly solvent at the end of the 75-year period. The scaled scenarios are adjusted to achieve a 75-year actuarial balance of zero. While scaling allows comparisons across distributions over 75 years, the different indexing scenarios are not identical in terms of sustainability. For a more complete description of the indexing scenarios, the benchmark, or the scaling, see appendix I.

Figure 3. Indexing Changes with a Larger Proportional Reduction Have a Greater Impact on the Distribution of Benefits, but Scaling to Achieve 75-Year Solvency Illustrates That the Proportional Effects Have Similar Results

Regardless of the index used to modify initial benefits, most proposals apply the new index in a way that has proportional effects on the distribution of benefits.[39] Thus, benefits at all levels will be affected by the same percentage reduction, for example, 5 percent, regardless of earnings. The left half of figure 3 illustrates this proportionality in terms of monthly benefits. While the level of benefits differs, the distribution of benefits for each scenario has a similar structure. However, the range of each distribution varies by the difference in the size of the proportional reduction. A larger proportional reduction—the dependency ratio index— will result in a distribution with a similar structure, compared to promised benefits. However, each individual's benefits are reduced by a constant percentage; therefore, the range of the distribution, the difference between benefits in the 25th and 75th percentile, would be smaller, compared to promised benefits. This proportional reduction in benefits is also illustrated in figure 4, which compares the currently scheduled or promised benefit formula with our three alternative indexing scenarios. Under each scenario, the line depicting scheduled benefits is lowered, by equal percentages at each AIME amount, by the difference between the growth in covered wages and the new index. Each indexing scenario maintains the shape of the current benefit formula; thus the progressivity of the system is maintained, but the line for each scenario is lower than scheduled benefits, which would affect the adequacy of benefits.

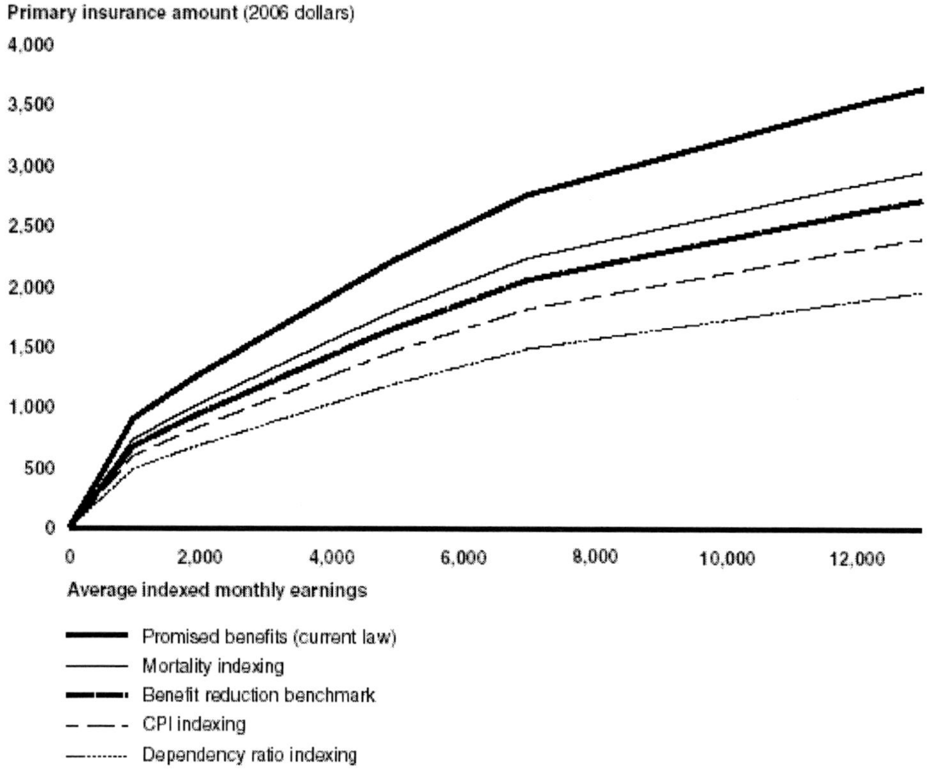

Source: GAO calculations.

Note: The illustrated PIAs are for individuals who become eligible in 2050. The dependency ratio index links the growth of initial benefits to changes in the dependency ratio, the ratio of the number of retirees to workers. The CPI index links the growth of initial benefits to changes in the CPI. The mortality index links the growth of initial benefits to changes in life expectancy to maintain a constant life expectancy at the normal retirement age. For more information on each index see appendix I.

Figure 4. Proportional Indexing Changes Would Maintain the Progressivity of the Current Benefit Formula, but Could Reduce Adequacy (Initial Benefits in 2050)

The proportional effects of indexing are best illustrated by adjusting, or scaling, each index to achieve comparable levels of solvency over 75 years.[40] Thus, for those indexes that do not by themselves achieve solvency, the benefit reductions are increased until solvency is achieved; for those that are more than solvent, the benefit reductions are decreased until solvency is achieved but not exceeded.

The right half of figure 3 shows the distribution of monthly benefits for each of the scaled indexing scenarios and the benchmark scenario. Once the different indexing scenarios are scaled to achieve solvency, the distribution of benefits for each scenario is almost identical in terms of the level of benefits. Differences in the distributions deal with the timing associated with implementing the changes. Scaling the indexing scenarios also reveals that the shape of the distributions is the same. The distributions of monthly benefits for the indexing scenarios are also very similar to the distribution of benefits generated under the benefit reduction benchmark. Therefore, changes to the benefit formula, applied through the replacement factors, will have similar results regardless of whether the change is an indexing change or a straight benefit reduction, because of the proportional effect of the change.

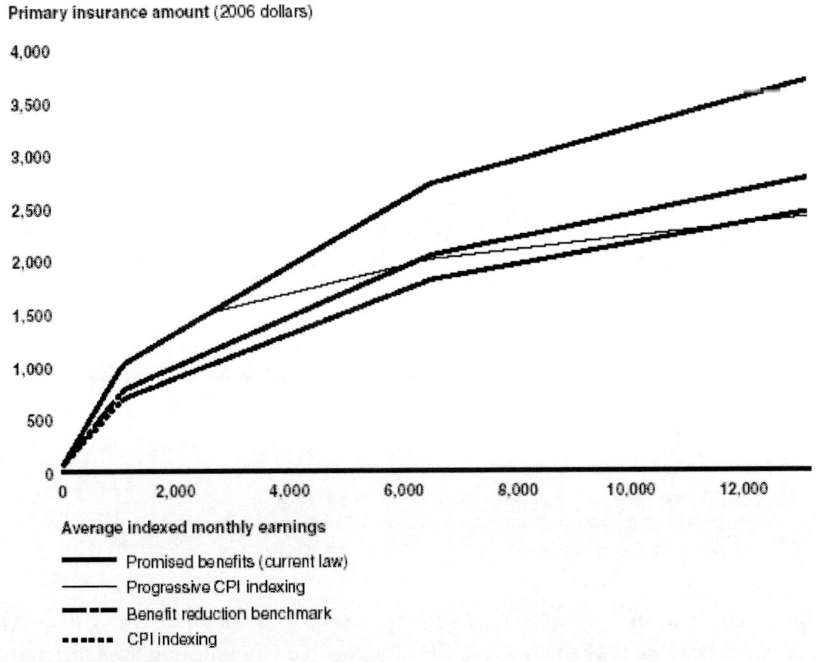

Source: GAO calculations.

Note: The illustrated PIAs are for individuals who become eligible in 2050. The CPI index links the growth of initial benefits to changes in the CPI. Progressive CPI indexing uses different indexes at various earnings levels. Individuals with earnings below a certain point would have their initial benefits adjusted by wage indexing; those individuals with earnings above that level would be subject to a combination of wage and price indexing on a sliding scale, with those individuals with the highest earnings having their benefits adjusted completely by price indexing. However, progressive CPI indexing does not achieve 75-year solvency, it has only a 74 percent improvement in solvency. For more information on the indexes see appendix I.

Figure 5. Lower-Income Individuals Would Fare Comparatively Better under the Progressive Application of the CPI Index than under the CPI Index Alone (Initial Benefits in 2050)

Indexing Approaches Could Also Be Modified to Achieve Nonproportional Effects

Indexing could also be modified to achieve other distributional goals. For example, so-called progressive indexing, or the use of different indexes— such as prices and wages—at various earnings levels, has been proposed as a way of changing the indexing while protecting the benefits of low- income workers. Thus, under progressive price indexing, those individuals with indexed lifetime earnings below a certain point would still have their initial benefits adjusted by wage indexing; those individuals with earnings above that level would be subject to a combination of wage and price indexing on a sliding scale, with those individuals with the highest lifetime earnings having their benefits adjusted completely by price indexing.[41]

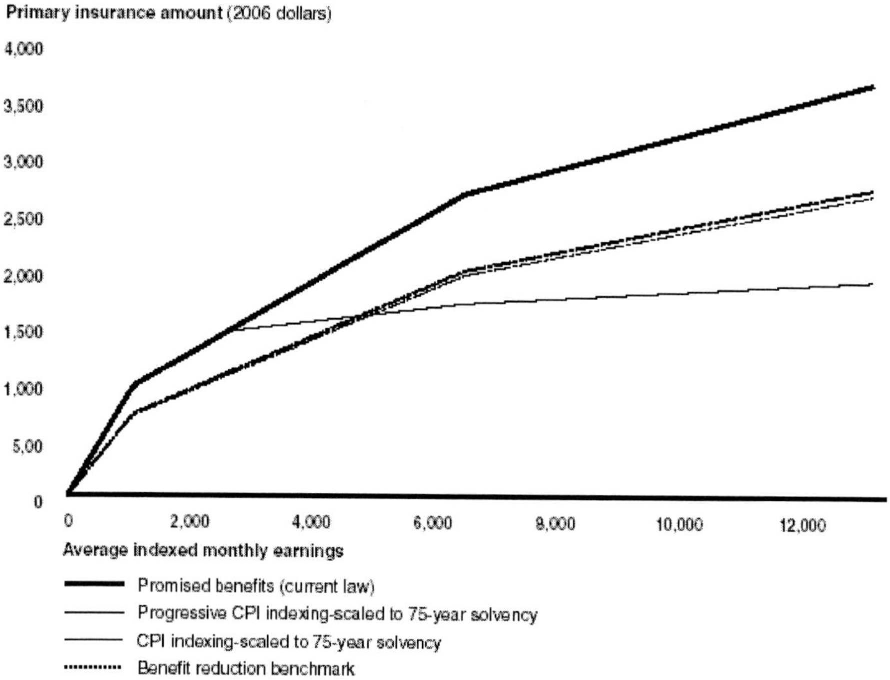

Source: GAO calculations.

Note: The illustrated PIAs are for individuals who become eligible in 2050. The CPI index links the growth of initial benefits to changes in the CPI. Progressive CPI indexing uses different indexes at various earnings levels. Individuals with earnings below a certain point would have their initial benefits adjusted by wage indexing; those individuals with earnings above that level would be subject to a combination of wage and price indexing on a sliding scale, with those individuals with the highest earnings having their benefits adjusted completely by price indexing. While scaling allows comparisons across distributions over 75 years, the different indexing scenarios are not identical in terms of sustainability. For more information on the indexes and the scaling, see appendix I.

Figure 6. Scaling the Progressive Application of the CPI Index to Achieve Equivalent Solvency Demonstrates That Most Individuals above a Certain Point Would Receive About the Same Level of Benefits (Initial Benefits in 2050)

The effect that progressive price indexing would have on the benefit formula can be seen in figure 5, where the CPI indexing scenario is compared to a progressive CPI indexing scenario and to benefits promised under the current program formula.[42] Many lower-income individuals would do better under the progressive application of the CPI index than under the CPI indexing alone. However, a progressive application of CPI indexing does not by itself achieve 75-year solvency, and further changes would be necessary to do so. Figure 6 shows what happens to the benefit formula when each of these indexing scenarios is scaled to achieve comparable levels of solvency over 75 years. Under progressive price indexing, to protect the benefits of low-income workers, the indexing to prices at higher earnings levels begins to flatten out benefits, causing the line in figure 6 to plateau. Thus, under this scenario, most individuals with earnings above a certain level would receive about the same level of benefits regardless of income—in the case of figure 6, a retiree with average indexed monthly earnings of $2,000 would receive a similar benefit level as someone with average indexed monthly earnings of $7,000. Since progressive price indexing would change the shape of the benefit formula, making it more progressive, it would reduce individual equity for higher earners, as they would receive much lower benefits relative to their contributions.

While proposals that have suggested progressive indexing have focused on using prices, any index can be adjusted to achieve the desired level of progressivity, and the results will likely be similar. However, to the extent that wages grow faster than the new index over a long period of time, the benefit formula will eventually flatten out and all individuals above a certain income level would receive the same level of benefits.

Indexing Applied to Taxes Would Have Adequacy and Equity Considerations

Indexing changes could also be applied to program financing. Under the current structure of the system, one way this could be accomplished is by indexing the Social Security payroll tax rate.[43] As with indexing benefits, the payroll tax rate could be indexed to any economic or demographic variable. Under the tax scenarios presented, only the indexing of taxes would change, so promised benefits would be maintained. However, workers would be paying more in payroll taxes, which, like any tax change, could affect work, saving, and investment decisions.

While benefit levels would be higher under tax increase scenarios, as compared to benefit reduction scenarios, the timing of the tax changes matters, just as it did with benefit changes. Since benefits would be unchanged in the tax-increase-only scenarios, we use benefit-to-tax ratios to compare the effects of different tax increase scenarios. Benefit-to-tax ratios compare the present value of Social Security lifetime benefits with the present value of lifetime Social Security taxes.[44] The benefit-to-tax ratio is an equity measure that focuses on whether, over their lifetimes, beneficiaries can expect to receive a fair return on their contributions or get their "money's worth" from the system. With benefits unchanged in the tax increase scenarios, the benefit-to-tax ratios would vary across scenarios because of differences in the timing of tax increases.[45]

To illustrate the effects of the timing of a change in tax rates, figure 7 shows the benefit-to-tax ratios, for four different birth cohorts, for two tax increase scenarios: (1) the dependency ratio tax indexing scenario scaled to achieve 75-year solvency and (2) our tax increase benchmark scenario that increases taxes just enough to achieve program solvency over a 75-year projection period.[46] By raising payroll taxes once and immediately, the tax increase benchmark would spread the tax burden more evenly across generations. This is seen in figure 7, where the benefit-to-tax ratios are fairly stable across cohorts for this scenario.[47] The dependency ratio tax indexing scenario would increase the tax rate annually, in this case with changes in the dependency ratio. Under this scenario, later cohorts would face a higher tax rate and thus bear more of the tax burden, compared to earlier cohorts. This would result in declining benefit-to-tax ratios across cohorts, with later generations receiving relatively less compared to their contributions.

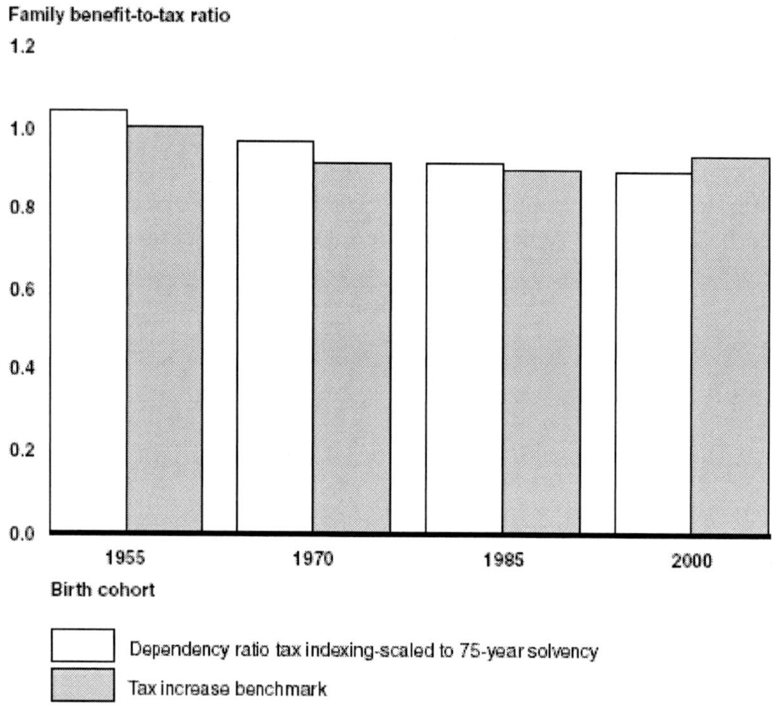

Source: GAO analysis of GEMINI data.

Note: Benefit-to-tax ratios are the sum of the present value of family benefits divided by the present value of family taxes summed for all individuals in the cohort that survive until age 24. Scenarios are modeled using the 2005 trustees' report intermediate assumptions. The dependency ratio tax index links the growth in the payroll tax rate to changes in the dependency ratio, the ratio of the number of retirees to workers. The dependency ratio tax index has been adjusted—or "scaled"—to achieve a 75-year actuarial balance of zero. While scaling allows comparisons across distributions over 75 years, the different indexing scenarios are not identical in terms of sustainability. The tax increase benchmark is a hypothetical benchmark policy scenario that would achieve 75-year solvency by only increasing payroll taxes. For a more complete description of the indexing scenario, the scaling, or the benchmark, see appendix I.

Figure 7. A Onetime Payroll Tax Increase Would Spread the Tax Burden More Evenly across Cohorts than Gradual Increases through an Index

Revising COLA for Existing Beneficiaries Would Have Important Distributional Implications for Multiple Subpopulations

Indexing changes can also be applied to the COLA used to adjust existing benefits. Under the current structure of the program, benefits for existing beneficiaries are adjusted annually in line with changes in the CPI. The COLA helps to maintain the purchasing power of benefits for current retirees. Some proposals, under the premise that the current CPI overstates the rate of price inflation because of methodological issues associated with how the CPI is calculated, would alter the COLA. Figure 8 shows the difference in benefit growth over time under the current COLA and two alternatives: growing at rate of CPI minus 0.22 and growing at of CPI minus 1.[48] Changes to the COLA would also have adequacy implications. After 20 years, benefits growing at the rate of the CPI minus 0.22 would slow the growth of benefits by about 4 percent below the level given by the current COLA and growing at the rate of the CPI minus 1 by about 17 percent. This slower benefit growth would improve the finances of the system, but would also alter the distribution of benefits, particularly for some subpopulations. Since changes to the COLA compound over time, those most affected are those with longer life expectancies, for example, women, as they would have the biggest decrease in lifetime benefits as they tend to receive benefits over more years. In addition, as education is correlated with greater life expectancy, highly educated workers would also experience a significant benefit decrease. There could also be a potentially large adverse effect on the benefits paid to disabled beneficiaries, especially among those who become disabled at younger ages and receive benefits for many years. These beneficiaries could have a large decrease in lifetime benefits.[49]

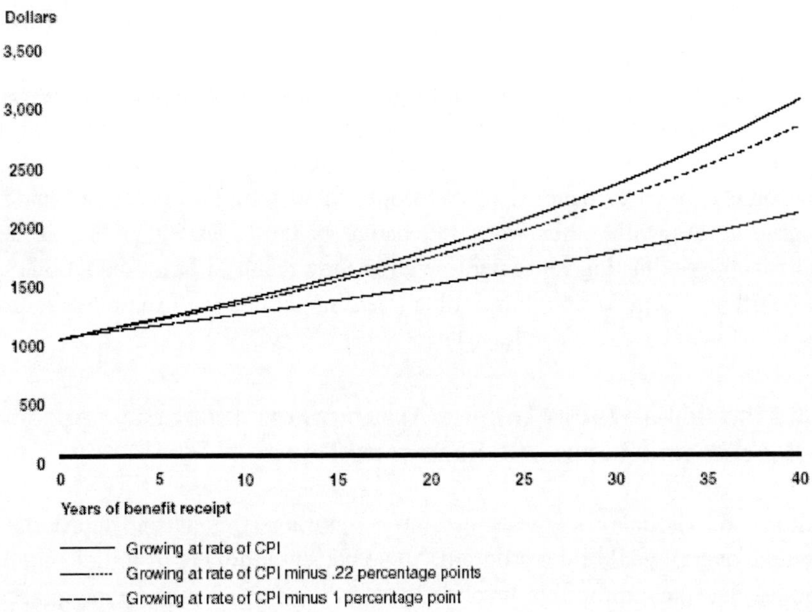

Source: GAO analysis.

Figure 8. The Growth of $1,000 Benefit under the CPI and Two Alternatives Illustrate That Those Beneficiaries Who Receive Benefits Longer Will Be Affected the Most

Reducing the COLA would also have equity implications. Since the COLA is applied to all beneficiaries, reductions in the COLA would lower the return on contributions for all beneficiaries. However, the magnitude of the effect will vary across subpopulations, similar to its effect on adequacy. Those individuals who have the biggest decrease in lifetime benefits will have the biggest decrease in individual equity. While these individuals have a large decrease in equity, they would still receive higher lifetime benefits since they live longer and collect benefits over more years. Individuals with shorter life expectancies will experience a decrease in equity, but they will fare comparably better than other groups that live longer, since their lifetime benefits will decrease much less. Therefore, men, African-Americans, low earners, and less educated individuals would experience a much smaller decrease in equity compared to their counterparts.

KEY CONSIDERATIONS IN CHOOSING AN INDEX

Indexing raises other important considerations about the program's role, the stability of the variables underlying the index, and the treatment of Disability Insurance (DI) beneficiaries. The choice of the index implies certain assumptions about the appropriate level of benefits and taxes for the program. Thus, if the current indexing of initial benefits was changed to price growth, there is an implication that the appropriate level of benefits is one that maintains purchasing power over time rather than the current approach that maintains a relative standard of living across age groups (i.e., replacement rates). The solvency effects of an index are predicated upon the relative stability and historical trends of the underlying economic or demographic relationships implied by the index. For example, the 1970s were a period of much instability, in which actual inflation rates and earnings growth diverged markedly from past experience, with the result that benefits unexpectedly grew much faster than expected. Finally, since the benefit formulas for the Old-Age and Survivors Insurance (OASI) and DI programs are linked, an important consideration of any indexing proposal is its effect on the benefits provided to disabled workers. Disabled worker beneficiaries typically become entitled to benefits much sooner than retired workers and under different eligibility criteria. As with other ways to change benefits, an index that is designed to improve solvency by adjusting retirement benefits may result in large reductions to disabled workers, who often have fewer options to obtain additional income from other sources.

Choice of a Particular Index Implies Assumptions about the Appropriate Level of Benefits and Taxes, Adequacy and Equity

The choice of an index suggests certain assumptions about the appropriate level of benefits and the overall goal of the program.[50] The current indexing of initial benefits to wage growth implies that the appropriate level of benefits is one that maintains replacement rates across birth years. In turn, maintaining replacement rates implies a relative standard of adequacy and an assumption that initial benefits should reflect the prevailing standard of living at the time of retirement. In contrast, changing the current indexing of initial benefits to price growth implies that the appropriate level of benefits is one that maintains purchasing power.[51] In turn, maintaining purchasing power implies an absolute standard of adequacy and an assumption that initial benefits should reflect a fixed notion of adequacy regardless of improvements in the standard of living. Also, any index that does not maintain purchasing power results in workers born in one year receiving higher benefits than workers with similar earnings born 1 year later.[52] This would occur with any benefit change that would reduce currently promised benefits more than price indexing initial benefits would, since price indexing maintains the purchasing power of initial benefits. In the case of longevity indexing, if the growth of initial benefits were indexed to life expectancy, then this implies that the increased costs of benefits that stem from increasing life expectancy should be borne by all future beneficiaries, even if society has become richer. Therefore, the desired outcome, in terms of initial benefit levels at the time of retirement, should drive the choice of an index.

The current indexing of existing benefits with the COLA implies that maintaining the purchasing power of benefits for current retirees is the appropriate level of benefits. Revising the COLA to reflect a more accurate calculation of the CPI retains this assumption. However, adjusting the COLA in a way that does not keep pace with the CPI would change that assumption and imply a view that the costs of reform should be shared by current as well as future retirees.

Similarly, on the revenue side, the program currently uses a constant tax rate, which maintains the same proportion of taxes for all workers earning less than the maximum taxable earnings level. Applying a life expectancy index to payroll tax rates suggests that the appropriate level of taxes is one that prefunds the additional retirement years increased life expectancy will bestow on current workers, but also that the appropriate level of benefits is one that maintains replacement rates, as benefits are unchanged.

Stability of Economic or Demographic Relationships Underlying the Index Is a Consideration

Indexing raises other considerations about the stability of the underlying relationships between the economic and demographic variables captured by the index. The choice of an index includes issues of risk and methodology. Some indexes could be based on economic variables that are volatile, introducing instability because the index generates wide swings in benefits or taxes. In other cases, long-standing economic or demographic relationships premised by the index could change, resulting in unanticipated and unstable benefit or tax levels. While most indexes will also pose methodological issues, these can become problematic to address after the index has already been widely used, and the correction will have implications for benefits or taxes. An example is the current measurement limitations of the CPI. In other instances, the index may be based on estimates about future trends in variables like mortality that could later prove incorrect and erode public confidence in the system.

Some indexes are premised on the past behavior of economic or demographic relationships. If these long-standing relationships diverge for a significant period of time, they may result in unanticipated and unstable benefit or tax levels. For example, the 1972 amendments that introduced indexing into the Social Security program were premised on the belief that over time, wage growth will generally substantially exceed price inflation.

However, for much of the 1970s, actual inflation rates and earnings growth diverged markedly from past experience; price inflation grew much faster than wages, with the result that benefits grew much faster than anticipated. This development introduced major instability into the program, which was unsustainable. Congress addressed this problem when it passed the 1977 amendments.[53] Moreover, even though the 1977 amendments succeeded in substantially stabilizing the replacement rates for initial benefits, a solvency crisis required reforms just 6 years later with the 1983 amendments. High inflation rates resulted in high COLAs for existing benefits just as recession was depressing receipts from the payroll taxes. The indexing of initial benefits under the 1977 amendments did not address the potential for such economic conditions to affect COLAs or payroll tax receipts.

Many indexes have methodological issues associated with their calculation, which can become problems over time. For example, the CPI has long been in use by the Social Security program and other social welfare programs. However, the CPI is not without its methodological problems. Some studies have contended that the CPI overstates inflation for a number of reasons, including that it does not account for how consumers can substitute one good for another because the calculation assumes that consumers do not change their buying patterns in response to price changes.[54] Correcting for this "substitution effect" would likely lower the CPI. Changing the calculation in response to this concern might improve accuracy but is controversial because it would also likely result in lower future benefits and put more judgment into the calculation.

Indexes that are constructed around assumptions about future experience raise other methodological issues. An example is a mortality index, which seeks to measure future changes in population deaths. Such a measure would presumably capture an aspect of increased longevity or well-being in retirement and could be viewed as a relevant determinant of program benefits or taxes. Accuracy in this index would require forecasts of future mortality based on assumptions of the main determinants influencing future population deaths (i.e., medical advances, diet, income changes). Such forecasts would require a clear consensus about these factors and how to measure and forecast them. However, currently there is considerable disagreement among researchers in terms of their beliefs about the magnitude of mortality change in the future.[55] In choosing an index, such methodological issues would need to be carefully considered to maintain public support and confidence.

The Treatment of Disabled and Survivor Beneficiaries Poses Challenges When Modifying the Indexing

Under the current structure of the U.S. Social Security system, the OASI and DI programs share the same benefit formula. Thus, any changes that affect retired workers will also affect survivors and disabled workers. However, the circumstances facing these beneficiaries differ from those facing retired workers. For example, the disabled worker's options for alternative sources of income, especially earnings-related income, to augment any reduction in benefits are likely to be more limited than are those for the retired worker. Further, DI beneficiaries enter the program at younger ages and may receive benefits for many years. As a result, disabled beneficiaries could be subject to benefit changes for many years more than those beneficiaries requiring benefits only in retirement.[56]

These differing circumstances among beneficiaries raise the issue of whether any proposed indexing changes, or any other benefit changes, should be applied to disabled worker and survivor beneficiaries, as well as to retired worker beneficiaries.[57] If disabled worker beneficiaries are not subject to indexing changes applied to retirees, benefit levels for disabled workers could ultimately be higher than those of retired workers. This difference in benefit levels would occur because disabled workers typically become entitled to benefits sooner than retired workers, and thus any reductions in their replacement factors would be smaller. Such a differential could increase the incentive for older workers to apply for disability benefits as they near retirement age.

Excluding the disability program from indexing changes has implications for solvency and raises implementation issues. If the indexing changes are not applied to the disability program, even larger benefit reductions or revenue increases would be needed to achieve fiscal solvency. Since the OASI and DI programs share the same benefit formula, excluding disabled worker beneficiaries from indexing changes might also necessitate the use of two different benefit formulas or require a method to recalculate benefits in order to maintain different indexing in each program. Such changes could lead to confusion among the public about how the programs operate, which may require significant additional public education.

Concluding Observations

Indexing has played an important role in the determination of Social Security's benefits and revenues for over 30 years. As in other countries seeking national pension system reform, recent proposals to modify the role of indexing in Social Security have primarily focused on addressing the program's long-term solvency problems. In theory, one index may be better than another in keeping the program in financial balance on a sustainable basis. However, such a conclusion would be based on assumptions about the future behavior of various demographic and economic variables, and those assumptions will always have considerable uncertainty. Future demographic patterns and economic trends could emerge that affect solvency in ways that have not been anticipated. So, while indexing changes may reduce how often Congress needs to rebalance the program's finances, there is no guarantee that the need will not arise again.

Yet program reform, and the role of indexing in that reform, is about more than solvency. Reforms also reflect implicit visions about the size, scope, and purpose of the Social Security system. Indexing initial benefits, existing benefits, tax rates, the maximum taxable earnings level, or some other parameter or combination will have different consequences for the level and distribution of benefits and taxes, within and across generations and earnings levels. These questions relate to the trade-off between income adequacy and benefit equity.

In the final analysis, indexing, like other individual reforms, comes down to a few critical questions: What is to be accomplished or achieved, who is to be affected, is it affordable and sustainable, and how will the change be phased in over time? Although these issues are complex and controversial, they are not unsolvable; they have been reconciled in the past and can be reconciled now. Indexing can be part of a larger, more comprehensive reform package that would include other elements whose cumulative effect could achieve the desired balance between adequacy and equity while also achieving solvency. The challenge is not whether indexing should be part of any necessary reforms, but that necessary action is taken soon to put Social Security back on a sound financial footing.

AGENCY COMMENTS

We provided a draft of this report to SSA and the Department of the Treasury. SSA provided technical comments, which we have incorporated as appropriate.

Barbara D. Bovbjerg
Director, Education, Workforce,
and Income Security Issues

APPENDIX I: METHODOLOGY

Microsimulation Model

Description

Genuine Microsimulation of Social Security and Accounts (GEMINI) is a microsimulation model developed by the Policy Simulation Group (PSG). GEMINI simulates Social Security benefits and taxes for large representative samples of people born in the same year. GEMINI simulates all types of Social Security benefits, including retired worker, spouse, survivor, and disability benefits. It can be used to model a variety of Social Security reforms including the introduction of individual accounts.

GEMINI uses inputs from two other PSG models, the Social Security and Accounts Simulator (SSASIM), which has been used in numerous GAO reports, and the Pension Simulator (PENSIM), which has been developed for the Department of Labor. GEMINI relies on SSASIM for economic and demographic projections and relies on PENSIM for simulated life histories of large representative samples of people born in the same year and their spouses.[58] Life histories include educational attainment, labor force participation, earnings, job mobility, marriage, disability, childbirth, retirement, and death. Life histories are validated against data from the Survey of Income and Program Participation, the Current Population Survey, Modeling Income in the Near Term (MINT3),[59] and the Panel Study of Income Dynamics. Additionally, any projected statistics (such as life expectancy, employment patterns, and marital status at age 60) are, where possible, consistent with intermediate cost projections from Social Security Administration's Office of the Chief Actuary (OCACT). At their best, such models can provide only very rough estimates of future incomes. However, these estimates may be useful for comparing future incomes across alternative policy scenarios and over time.

GEMINI can be operated as a free-standing model or it can operate as a SSASIM add-on. When operating as an add-on, GEMINI is started automatically by SSASIM for one of two purposes. GEMINI can enable the SSASIM macro model to operate in the Overlapping Cohorts (OLC) mode or it can enable the SSASIM micro model to operate in the Representative Cohort Sample (RCS) mode. The SSASIM OLC mode requests GEMINI to produce samples for each cohort born after 1934 in order to build up aggregate payroll tax revenues and OASDI benefit expenditures for each calendar year, which are used by SSASIM to calculate standard trust fund financial statistics. In either mode, GEMINI operates with the same logic, but typically with smaller cohort sample sizes in OLC mode than in the RCS or stand-alone-model mode.

For this report we used GEMINI to simulate Social Security benefits and taxes primarily for 100,000 individuals born in 1985. Benefits and taxes were simulated under our tax increase (promised benefits) and proportional benefit reduction (funded benefits) benchmarks (described below) and various indexation approaches.

Assumptions and limitations

To facilitate our modeling analysis, we made a variety of assumptions regarding economic and demographic trends. In choosing our assumptions, we focused our analysis to illustrate relevant points about distributional effects and hold equal as much as possible any variables that were either not relevant to or would unduly complicate that focus. As a result of these assumptions, as well as issues inherent in any modeling effort, our analysis has some key limitations, especially relating to risk and changes over time.

2005 social security trustees' assumptions

The simulations are based on economic and demographic assumptions from the 2005 Social Security trustees' report.[60] While the 2006 trustees' report has been released, the assumptions have changed very little from the 2005 assumptions. We used trustees' intermediate assumptions for inflation, real wage growth, mortality decline, immigration, labor force participation, and interest rates.

Distributional effects over time

We simulated benefits for individuals born in 1955, 1970, 1985, and 2000. However, the majority of our figures focus on individuals born in 1985 because all prospective indexing changes would be almost fully phased in for these individuals. However, the distributional effects might change over time. This is because each index phases in over time and reduces the primary insurance amount (PIA) formula factors (or increases the Old-Age and Survivors Insurance (OASI) and Disability Insurance (DI) taxes) at different rates. For example, individuals in the 1955 cohort that survive to age 65 do so in the year 2020, so the benefit reductions (or tax increases), which we specify to begin sometime between 2006 and 2012, depending on the scenario, have only been implemented for about 8 to 14 years. Additionally, members of the cohort that become disabled might becomedisabled prior to the implementation of annual PIA reductions or tax increases. Such issues become less pronounced with the younger cohorts.

Pre-retirement mortality

To capture the distributional impact of pre-retirement mortality, we calculated benefit-to-tax ratios and lifetime benefits for all sample members who survived past age 24. However, our measure of well-being, lifetime earnings, may not be the best way to assess the well-being of those who die before retirement. Some high-wage workers are classified as low lifetime earners simply because they did not live very long, and consequently our analysis overstates the degree to which those who die young are classified as low earners. As a result, our measures underestimate the degree to which Social Security favors lower earners under all of the scenarios we analyze.[61]

Description of alternative policy scenarios

CPI Indexing

To simulate consumer price indexing (CPI) indexing, which essentially links the growth of initial benefits to changes in the CPI, we successively modified the PIA formula replacement factors (90, 32, and 15) beginning in 2012, reducing them successively by real wage growth in the second prior year. This specification mimics provision B6 of the August 10, 2005 memorandum to SSA's Chief Actuary regarding the provision requested by the Social Security Advisory Board (SSAB), which is an update of provision 1 of Model 2 of the President's Commission to Strengthen Social Security (CSSS).[62] As noted in the CSSS solvency memorandum from SSA's Chief Actuary, "[t]his provision would result in increasing benefit levels for individuals with equivalent lifetime earnings across generations (relative to the average wage level) at the rate of price growth (increase in the CPI), rather than at the rate of growth in the average wage level as in current law."

This provision as specified and scored by OCACT in the SSAB memo would increase the size of the long-range OASDI actuarial balance (reduce the actuarial deficit) by an estimated 2.38 percent of taxable payroll. Using the overlapping cohort mode of SSASIM, we estimated this provision as increasing the size of the long-range OASDI actuarial balance by 2.43 percent of taxable payroll, or 5 basis points more than the OCACT scoring.

Mortality indexing

To simulate mortality indexing, which links the growth of initial benefits to changes in life expectancy to maintain a constant life expectancy at the normal retirement age, we successively modified the PIA formula replacement factors (90, 32, 15) beginning in 2009, reducing them annually by multiplying them by 0.995. This specification mimics provision 1 of Model 3 of CSSS.[63] The CSSS solvency memorandum notes that the 0.995 successive reduction "reduces monthly benefit levels by an amount equivalent to increasing the normal retirement age (NRA) for retired workers by enough to maintain a constant life expectancy at NRA, for any fixed age of benefit entitlement."[64]

This provision as specified and scored—using the intermediate assumptions of the 2001 trustees' report—in the CSSS memo by SSA's Office of the Chief Actuary would reduce the size of the long-range OASDI actuarial balance (reduce the actuarial deficit) by an estimated 1.17 percent of taxable payroll. Using the overlapping cohort mode of SSASIM and specifications, which mimic the intermediate assumptions of the 2005 trustees' report, we estimated this provision as increasing the size of the long-range OASDI actuarial balance by 1.39 percent of taxable payroll, or 22 basis points more than the earlier OCACT scoring.

Dependency indexing

Benefits

To simulate so-called dependency indexing of benefits, which links the growth of initial benefits to changes in the dependency ratio, we successively modified the PIA formula replacement factors (90, 32, and 15) beginning in 2010, by reducing them annually by an index that follows the inverse of the increase in the aged dependency ratio from 2 years prior. For example, the reduction for 2010 is given by dividing the 2009 PIA formula factors (90, 32, and 15) by 1.0098, which is rate of increase from 2007 to 2008.[65]

This provision as specified has not been scored by OCACT. Using the overlapping cohort mode of SSASIM and specifications that mimic the intermediate assumptions of the 2005 trustees' report, we estimated this provision as increasing the size of the long-range OASDI actuarial balance by 3.78 percent of taxable payroll.

Taxes

To simulate so-called dependency indexing of payroll taxes, which links the growth of payroll taxes to changes in the dependency ratio, we increased the initial OASI and DI tax rates (both employer and employee combined) in 2009 by a cumulative index that increases annually by the rate of increase in the aged dependency ratio from 2 years prior. For example, the increase for 2010 is given by multiplying the 12.4 percent tax rate (employer and employee combined—10.60 percent for OASI and 1.80 percent for DI) by 1.0098—the rate of increase from 2007 to 2008—to arrive at a rate of 10.70 percent for OASI and 1.82 percent for DI. By 2050 the cumulative index is 1.863, and the tax rates (employer and employee combined) are 19.75 percent for OASI and 3.35 percent for DI.

This provision as specified has not been scored by OCACT. Using the overlapping cohort mode of SSASIM and specifications that mimic the intermediate assumptions of the 2005 trustees' report, we estimated this provision as increasing the size of the long-range OASDI actuarial balance by 6.98 percent of taxable payroll.

Scaling to achieve comparable levels of solvency over 75 years

We modified the aforementioned CPI, mortality, and dependency indexes to "scale" them to achieve comparable levels of solvency over a 75-year period—the same actuarial period used by OCACT in trustees' reports and solvency memorandums.[66] To scale the proposals, we modified the PIAs (or OASI and DI tax rates in the case of the aged dependency ratio tax increase index) by a scaled factor equal to the inverse of the percentage of solvency attained by the original, unscaled version of the proposal. For each year in the 75-year period, the scaling factor is multiplied by the percentage point difference between the unscaled PIA factors and the factors prior to implementation of the proposal (i.e., 90, 32, and 15).[67] The application of the so-called scaling factor to the PIA factors (or OASDI tax rates) conveniently modifies the index in such a way that 75-year actuarial balance is 0.[68]

Table 4. Application of So-called Scaling of PIA Factors for Aged Dependency Ratio Benefit Reduction Index: An Example Using 2050 PIA Formula Factors

Step	Description	PIA formula factor or calculation	PIA formula factor or calculation	PIA formula factor or calculation
1	PIA formula factors in 2009	90.0	32.0	15.0
2	PIA formula factors in 2050	48.3	17.2	8.1
3	Difference between factors in 2050 and initial factors (i.e., the factors in 2009 or prior)	41.7	14.8	6.9
4	Scaling factor[a]	.508	.508	.508
5	Difference multiplied by scaling			
	factor (i.e., step 3 * step 4)	21.2	7.5	3.5
6	New, so-called "scaled" PIA formula factors (i.e., step 1–step 5)	68.8	24.5	11.5

Source: GAO.

[a] The aged dependency benefit reduction index increases the 75-year OASDI actuarial balance by 3.78 percent of taxable payroll. This is 196.9 percent of 1.92 percent of taxable payroll, which is the amount required to produce a 75-year actuarial balance of 0 under the intermediate assumptions of the 2005 trustees' report. The inverse (i.e., 1/x) of 196.9 percent is 50.8 percent.

Data reliability

To assess the reliability of simulated data from GEMINI, we reviewed PSG's published validation checks, examined the data for reasonableness and consistency, preformed sensitivity analysis, and compared our solvency estimates, where applicable, with published results from the actuaries at the Social Security Administration.

PSG has published a number of validation checks of its simulated life histories. For example, simulated life expectancy is compared with projections from the Social Security trustees; simulated benefits at age 62 are compared with administrative data from SSA; and simulated educational attainment, labor force participation rates, and job tenure are compared with values from the Current Population Survey. We found that simulated statistics for the life histories were reasonably close to the validation targets.

For sensitivity analysis, we simulated benefits and taxes for policy scenarios under a number of alternative specifications, including limiting the sample to those who survive to retirement. Our findings were consistent across all specifications.

Benchmark Policy Scenarios

According to current projections of the Social Security trustees for the next 75 years, revenues will not be adequate to pay full benefits as defined by the current benefit formula. Therefore, estimating future Social Security benefits should reflect that actuarial deficit and account for the fact that some combination of benefit reductions and revenue increases will be necessary to restore long-term solvency.

To illustrate a full range of possible outcomes, we developed hypothetical benchmark policy scenarios that would achieve 75-year solvency either by only increasing payroll taxes or by only reducing benefits.[69] In developing these benchmarks, we identified criteria to use to guide their design and selection. Our tax-increase-only benchmark simulates "promised benefits," or those benefits promised by the current benefit formula, while our benefit-reduction-only benchmarks simulate "funded benefits," or those benefits for which currently scheduled revenues are projected to be sufficient. Under the latter policy scenarios, the benefit reductions would be phased in between 2010 and 2040 to strike a balance between the size of the incremental reductions each year and the size of the ultimate reduction.

Table 5. Summary of Benchmark Policy Scenarios

Benchmark policy scenario	Description	Phase-in period	Ultimate new benefit reductions[a] (percent)
Tax increase only (promised benefits)	Increases payroll taxes in 2006 by amount necessary to achieve 75-year solvency (0.98 percent of payroll each for employees and employers)	Immediate	0
Proportional benefit reduction (funded benefits)	Reduces benefit formula factors proportionally across all earnings levels	2010-2040	25

Source: GAO.

[a] These benefit reduction amounts do not reflect the implicit reductions resulting from the gradual increase in the full retirement age that has already been enacted.

SSA actuaries scored our original 2001 benchmark policies and determined the parameters for each that would achieve 75-year solvency.[70] Table 5 summarizes our benchmark policy scenarios. For our benefit reduction scenarios, the actuaries determined these parameters assuming that disabled and survivor benefits would be reduced on the same basis as retired worker and dependent benefits. If disabled and survivor benefits were not reduced at all, reductions in other benefits would be greater than shown in this analysis.

Criteria

According to our analysis, appropriate benchmark policies should ideally be evaluated against the following criteria:

1. *Distributional neutrality*: The benchmark should reflect the current system as closely as possible while still restoring solvency. In particular, it should try to reflect the goals and effects of the current system with respect to redistribution of income. However, there are many possible ways to interpret what this means, such as
   a. producing a distribution of benefit levels with a shape similar to the distribution under the current benefit formula (as measured by coefficients of variation, skewness, kurtosis, and so forth),
   b. maintaining a proportional level of income transfers in dollars,
   c. maintaining proportional replacement rates, and
   d. maintaining proportional rates of return.

2. *Demarcating upper and lower bounds*: These would be the bounds within which the effects of alternative proposals would fall. For example, one benchmark would reflect restoring solvency solely by increasing payroll taxes and therefore maximizing benefit levels, while another would solely reduce benefits and therefore minimize payroll tax rates.

3. *Ability to model*: The benchmark should lend itself to being modeled within the GEMINI model.

4. *Plausibility*: The benchmark should serve as a reasonable alternative within the current debate; otherwise, the benchmark could be perceived as an invalid basis for comparison.

5. *Transparency*: The benchmark should be readily explainable to the reader.

Tax-increase-only, or "Promised Benefits," Benchmark Policies

Our tax-increase-only benchmark would raise payroll taxes once and immediately by the amount of Social Security's actuarial deficit as a percentage of payroll. It results in the smallest ultimate tax rate of those we considered and spreads the tax burden most evenly across generations; this is the primary basis for our selection. The later that taxes are increased, the higher the ultimate tax rate needed to achieve solvency, and in turn the higher the tax burden on later taxpayers and lower on earlier taxpayers. Still, any policy scenario that achieves 75-year solvency only by increasing revenues would have the same effect on the adequacy of future benefits in that promised benefits would not be reduced. Nevertheless, alternative approaches to increasing revenues could have very different effects on individual equity.

Benefit-reduction-only, or "Funded Benefits," Benchmark Policies

We developed alternative benefit reduction benchmarks for our analysis. For ease of modeling, all benefit reduction benchmarks take the form of reductions in the benefit formula factors; they differ in the relative size of those reductions across the three factors, which are 90, 32, and 15 percent under the current formula. Each benchmark has three dimensions of specification: scope, phase-in period, and the factor changes themselves.

Scope

For our analysis, we apply benefit reductions in our benchmarks very generally to all types of benefits, including disability and survivors' benefits as well as old-age benefits. Our objective is to find policies that achieve solvency while reflecting the distributional effects of the current program as closely as possible. Therefore, it would not be appropriate to reduce some benefits and not others. If disabled and survivor benefits were not reduced at all, reductions in other benefits would be deeper than shown in this analysis.

Phase-in Period

We selected a phase-in period that begins with those becoming initially entitled in 2010 and continues for 30 years. We chose this phase-in period to achieve a balance between two competing objectives: (1) minimizing the size of the ultimate benefit reduction and (2) minimizing the size of each year's incremental reduction to avoid "notches," or unduly large incremental reductions. Notches create marked inequities between beneficiaries close in age to each other. Later birth cohorts are generally agreed to experience lower rates of return on their contributions already under the current system. Therefore, minimizing the size of the ultimate benefit reduction would also minimize further reductions in rates of return for later cohorts. The smaller each year's reduction, the longer it will take for benefit reductions to achieve solvency, and in turn the greater the eventual reductions will have to be. However, the smallest possible ultimate reduction would be achieved by reducing benefits immediately for all new retirees by 13 percent; this would create a notch.

In addition, we feel it is appropriate to delay the first year of the benefit reductions for a few years because those within a few years of retirement would not have adequate time to adjust their retirement planning if the reductions applied immediately. The Maintain Tax Rates (MTR) benchmark in the 1994-1996 Advisory Council report also provided for a similar delay.[71]

Finally, the timing of any policy changes in a benchmark scenario should be consistent with the proposals against which the benchmark is compared. The analysis of any proposal assumes that the proposal is enacted, usually within a few years. Consistency requires that any benchmark also assumes enactment of the benchmark policy in the same time frame. Some analysts have suggested using a benchmark scenario in which Congress does not act at all and the trust funds become exhausted.[72] However, such a benchmark assumes that no action is taken while the proposals against which it is compared assume that action is taken, which is inconsistent. It also seems unlikely that a policy enacted over the next few years would wait to reduce benefits until the trust funds are exhausted; such a policy would result in a sudden, large benefit reduction and create substantial inequities across generations.

Defining the PIA Formula Factor Reductions

When workers retire, become disabled, or die, Social Security uses their lifetime earnings records to determine each worker's PIA, on which the initial benefit and auxiliary benefits are based. The PIA is the result of two elements—the Average Indexed Monthly Earnings (AIME) and the benefit formula. The AIME is determined by taking the lifetime earnings record, indexing it, and taking the average of the highest 35 years of indexed wages.[73] To determine the PIA, the AIME is then applied to a step-like formula, shown here for 2006.

$$\begin{aligned} \text{PIA} = \ & 90\% \bullet (\text{AIME}_1 \leq \$656) \\ & + 32\% \bullet (\text{AIME}_2 > \$656 \text{ and} \leq \$3955) \\ & + 15\% \bullet (\text{AIME}_3 > \$3955) \end{aligned}$$

where AIME_i is the applicable portion of AIME.

All of our benefit-reduction benchmarks are variations of changes in PIA formula factors.

Proportional reduction: Each formula factor is reduced annually by subtracting a constant proportion of that factor's value under current law, resulting in a constant percentage reduction of currently promised benefits for everyone. That is,

$$F^i_{t+1} = F^i_t - (F^i_{2006} \bullet x)$$

where

F^i_t represents the three PIA formula factors in year t and

x = constant proportional formula factor reduction.

The value of x is calculated to achieve 75-year solvency, given the chosen phase-in period and scope of reductions.

The formula for this reduction specifies that the proportional reduction is always taken as a proportion of the current law factors rather than the factors for each preceding year. This maintains a constant rate of benefit reduction from year to year. In contrast, taking the reduction as a proportion of each preceding year's factors implies a decelerating of the benefit reduction over time because each preceding year's factors gets smaller with each reduction. To achieve the same level of 75-year solvency, this would require a greater proportional reduction in earlier years because of the smaller reductions in later years.

The proportional reduction hits lower earners harder than higher earners because the constant x percent of the higher formula factors results in a larger percentage reduction over the lower earnings segments of the formula. For example, in a year when the cumulative size of the proportional reduction has reached 10 percent, the 90 percent factor would then have been reduced by 9 percentage points, the 32 percent factor by 3.2 percentage points, and the 15 percent factor by 1.5 percentage points. As a result, earnings in the first segment of the benefit formula would be replaced at 9 percentage points less than the current formula, while earnings in the third segment of the formula would be replaced at only 1.5 percentage points less than the current formula.[74]

Table 6 summarizes the features of our benchmarks.

Table 6. Summary of Benchmark Policy Scenario Parameters

		Annual PIA factor reduction (percentage point)			Ultimate PIA factor (2040) (percent)		
Benchmark policy scenario	**Phase-in period**	**90 percent factor**	**32 percent factor**	**15 percent factor**	**90 percent factor**	**32 percent factor**	**15 percent factor**
Tax increase only (promised benefits)	2006	0	00	0	90.00	32.00	15.00
Proportional benefit reduction (funded benefits)	2010-2040	0.74	0.26	0.12	67.07	23.85	11.18

Source: GAO's analysis as scored by SSA actuaries.

Note: Annual PIA factor reductions rounded to the nearest hundredth of a percent.

APPENDIX II: BACKGROUND ON DEVELOPMENT OF SOCIAL SECURITY'S INDEXING APPROACH

Social Security did not originally use indexing to automatically adjust benefit and tax provisions; only ad hoc changes were made. The 1972 amendments provided for automatic indexing of benefits and taxes for the first time, but the indexing approach for benefits was flawed, introducing potential instability in benefit costs. The 1977 amendments addressed those issues, resulting in the basic framework for indexing benefits still in use today.

Program Did Not Use Indexing until 1970s

Before the 1970s, the Social Security program did not use indexing to adjust benefits or taxes automatically. For both new and existing beneficiaries, benefit rates increased only when Congress voted to raise them. The same was true for the tax rate and the cap on the amount of workers' earnings that were subject to the payroll tax. Under the 1972 amendments to the Social Security Act, benefits and taxes were indexed for the first time, and revisions in the 1977 amendments created the basic framework still in use today.

Table 7. Percentage Increases in OASI Benefits, Prices, and Wages, by Effective Date of OASI Change, 1950-1971

Date of change[a]	Increase in OASI benefit		Increase in consumer price index		Increase in average wages	
	Since prior amendment[b]	Since January 1940	Since prior amendment	Since January 1940	Since prior amendment	Since January 1940
September 1950	81.3[c]	81.3	75.5[c]	75.5	148.8[c]	148.8
September 1952	14.1	106.9	9.3	91.8	12.5	179.9
September 1954	13.3	134.3	0.5	92.8	7.7	201.5
January 1959 (1958)	7.7	152.4	7.9	108.0	19.4	259.9
January 1965	7.7	171.9	7.9	124.5	22.3	340.2
February 1968 (1967)	14.2	210.5	9.3	145.4	18.0	419.4
January 1970 (1969)	15.6	258.9	10.8	171.8	12.2	482.8
January 1971	10.4	296.2	5.2	185.9	5.3	513.7

Source: Martha Derthick, *Policymaking for Social Security,* The Brookings Institution, Washington, D.C., 1979, p. 276. Reprinted with permission of the Brookings Institution Press, and GAO analysis.

[a] Year of enactment, if different from year in which change took effect, is in parentheses.

[b] Average increases for current beneficiaries, that is, people who were on the rolls. At the same time, increases approximately equal to these were promised by statutory formula, to active workers.

[c] Percentage increase since January 1940, when OASI benefits were first paid.

Ad hoc benefit and tax changes had sporadic effects

Until 1950, Congress legislated no changes to the benefit formula of any kind. As a result, average inflation-adjusted benefits for retired workers fell by 32 percent between 1940 and 1949. Under the 1950 amendments to the Social Security Act, these benefits increased 67 percent in 1 year. Afterward, until 1972, periodic amendments made various ad hoc adjustments to benefit levels. Economic prosperity and regular trust fund surpluses facilitated gradual growth of benefit levels through these ad hoc adjustments.[75]

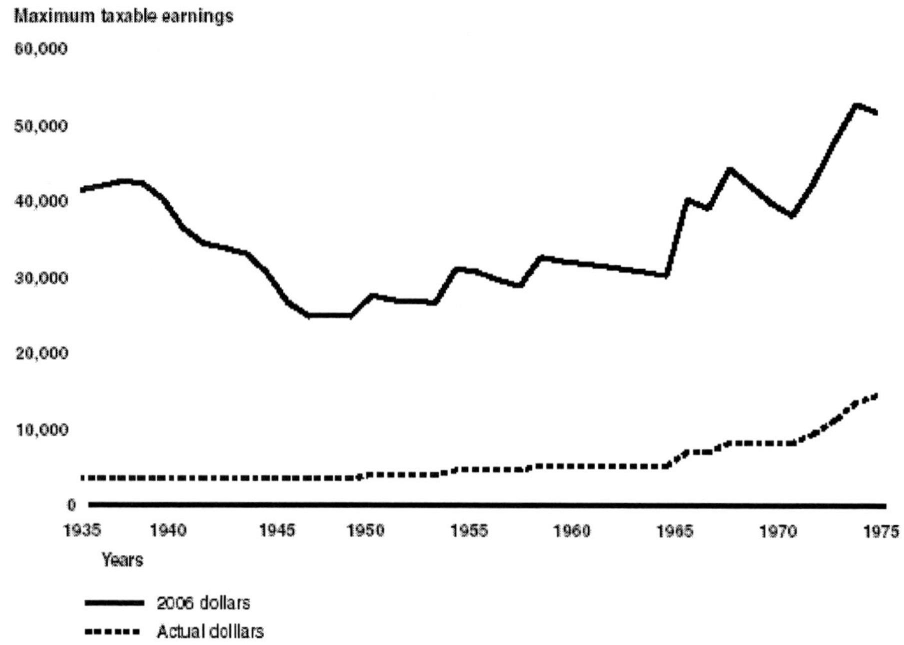

Source: SSA, and GAO analysis.

Note: The maximum taxable earnings level is the level at which earnings are subject to the payroll tax.

Figure 9. Inflation-Adjusted Values of the Maximum Taxable Earnings Level before Automatic Adjustments, 1937-1975

Source: SSA.

Figure 10. Percentage of Total Covered Earnings below Social Security's Maximum Taxable Earnings Level, 1937-2005

In light of the steady growth of benefit levels, the 1972 amendments instituted automatic adjustments to constrain the growth of benefits as well as to ensure that they kept pace with inflation. Table 7 summarizes the history of benefit increases before 1972. It illustrates that between 1940 and 1971, average benefits for all current beneficiaries tripled while prices nearly doubled and wages more than quintupled.[76] Some benefit increases were faster and some were slower than wages increases.

On the revenue side, payroll tax rates have never been indexed. However, Social Security's revenue also depends on the maximum amount of workers' earnings that are subject to the payroll tax. This cap is technically known as the contribution and benefit base because it limits the earnings level used to compute benefits as well as taxes.[77] Just as with benefits, the maximum taxable earnings level did not change until the 1950 amendments even as price and earning levels were increasing. From 1940 to 1950, the inflation-adjusted value of the cap fell by over 40 percent. Also, until the 1972 amendments, adjustments to the maximum taxable earnings level were made on an ad hoc basis. With the enactment of the 1972 amendments, the maximum taxable earnings level increased automatically based on increases in average earnings. Figure 9 shows the inflation-adjusted values for the maximum taxable earnings level before automatic adjustments took effect in 1975.[78] Figure 10 shows that as a result of the fluctuations in the maximum taxable earnings level, the proportion of earnings subject to the payroll tax varied widely before indexing, ranging from 71 to 93 percent.

Indexing in 1972 Amendments Built on Previous Ad Hoc Benefit Increases

The 1972 amendments, in effect, provided for indexing initial benefits twice for new beneficiaries. The indexing changed the benefit formula in the same way that previous ad hoc increases had done.

Approach used for ad hoc benefit increases

Before the 1972 amendments, benefits were computed essentially by applying different replacement factors to different portions of a worker's earnings. For example, under the 1958 amendments, a workers' PIA[79] would equal

58.85 percent of first $110 of average monthly wages plus 21.40 percent of next $290,

where the 58.85 and 21.40 percents are the replacement factors that determine how much of a worker's earnings will be replaced by the Social Security benefit.[80] Subsequent amendments increased benefits by effectively increasing the replacement factors. For example, the 1965 amendments increased benefits by 7 percent for a given average monthly wage by increasing the replacement factors by 7 percent to 62.97 from 58.85 and to 22.9 percent from 21.4.[81] The automatic adjustments under the 1972 amendments increased these same replacement factors according to changes in the CPI. These changes in the benefit computation applied equally to both new and existing beneficiaries.[82]

To illustrate how the benefit formula worked, take, for example, a worker with an average monthly wage of $200 who became entitled in 1959 (when the 1958 amendments first took effect). The PIA for this worker would be

> 58.85 percent of $110 plus
> 21.4 percent of the average monthly wage over $110,
> that is, $200-1 10 = $90, which equals
> $64.74 + $19.26 = 84.00.

When the 1965 amendments took effect, this same beneficiary would have the PIA recalculated using the new formula. Assuming no new wages, the average monthly wage would still be $200, and the new PIA would be

> 62.97 percent of $110 plus
> 22.9 percent of the average monthly wage over $110,
> that is, $200-1 10 = $90, which equals
> $69.27 + $20.61 = 89.88,
> which is 7 percent greater than the previous $84.00.

Now consider the example of a new beneficiary, who became entitled in 1965 (when the 1965 amendments first became effective). For the purposes of this illustration, to reflect wage growth, assume this worker had an average monthly wage of $240.00, or 20 percent more than our previous worker who became entitled in 1959. For this new beneficiary, the PIA in 1965 would be $99.04, which, as a result of the wage growth, is much more than 7 percent higher than the initial benefit for the worker in 1959.

1972 amendments introduced indexing

The 1972 amendments provided for automatic indexing of benefits and taxes for the first time. The indexing approach for benefits was flawed andraised issues that the 1977 amendments addressed; these issues help explain the basic framework for indexing benefits still in use today. In particular, the indexing approach in the 1972 amendments resulted in(1) double-indexing benefits to inflation for new beneficiaries though notfor existing ones and (2) a form of bracket creep that slowed benefit growth as earnings increased over time. Within a few years, the problems raised by the double indexing under the 1972 amendments became apparent, with benefits growing far faster than anticipated.

Under the 1972 amendments, indexing the replacement factors in the benefit formula to inflation had the effect of indexing twice for new beneficiaries. First, the increase in the replacement factors themselves reflected changes in the price level. Second, the benefit calculations were based on earnings levels, which were higher for each new group of beneficiaries, partially as a result of inflation.[83] Thus, benefit levels grew for each new year's group of beneficiaries because both the benefit formula reflected inflation and their higher average wages reflected inflation. For existing beneficiaries who had stopped working, the average earnings used to compute their benefits did not change, so growth in earnings levels did not affect their benefits and double indexing did not occur. Once the double indexing for new beneficiaries was understood, the need became clear to index benefits differently for new and existing beneficiaries, which was referred to as "decoupling" benefits.

The effect of double indexing on replacement rates could be offset by a type of "bracket creep" in the benefit formula, depending on the relative values of wage and price growth over time. Bracket creep resulted from the progressive benefit formula, which provided lower replacement rates for higher earners than for lower earners. As each year passed and average earnings of new beneficiaries grew, more and more earnings would be replaced at the lower rate used for the upper bracket, making replacement rates fall on average, all else being equal.

Indexing Approach Introduced Potential Instability in Benefit Costs

The combination of double indexing and bracket creep implied in the 1972 amendments introduced a potential instability in Social Security benefit costs. Price growth determined the effects of double indexing, and wage growth determined the effects of bracket creep. The extent to which bracket creep offset the effects of double indexing depended on the relative values of price growth and wage growth, which could vary considerably. Had wage and price growth followed the historical pattern at the time, benefits would not have grown faster than expected and replacement rates would not have risen; the inflation effect and the bracket creep effect would have balanced out. However, during the 1970s, actual rates of inflation and earnings growth diverged markedly from past experience (see Figure 11), with the result that benefit costs grew far faster than revenues.

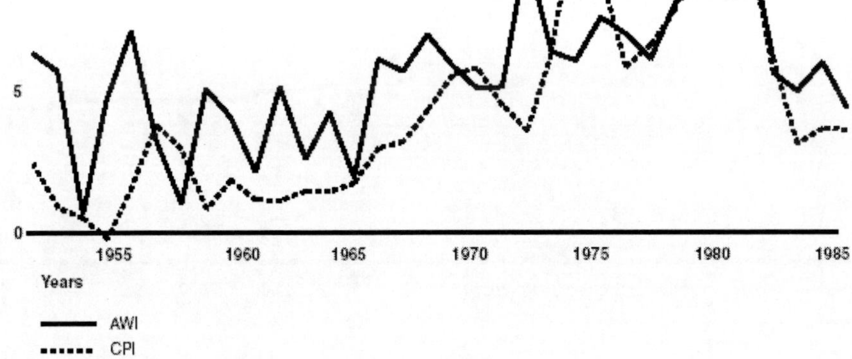

Source: SSA and US Bureau of Labor Statistics.

Figure 11. Changes in Average Wage Index and Consumer Price Index, 1951-1985

In contrast, an indexing approach that stabilized replacement rates would help to stabilize program costs. To illustrate this, annual benefit costs can be expressed as a fraction of the total taxable payroll in a given year, that is, total covered earnings.[84] In turn, this can be shown to relate closely to replacement rates.

$$\frac{\text{Total benefits}}{\text{Total covered earnings}}$$

$$= \frac{\text{Number of beneficiaries} \times \text{Average benefit}}{\text{Number of workers} \times \text{Average taxable earnings}}$$

$$= \frac{\text{Number of beneficiaries}}{\text{Number of workers}} \times \frac{\text{Average benefit}}{\text{Average taxable earnings}}$$

While not precisely a replacement rate, the second term on the last line above—the ratio of the average benefit to average taxable earnings—is closely related to the replacement rates provided under the program. While replacement rates are now relatively stable after the 1977 amendments, it is the first term on the last line above—the ratio of beneficiaries to workers—that has been increasing and placing strains on the system's finances. The inverse of this is the ratio of covered workers to beneficiaries. While 3.3 workers support each Social Security beneficiary today, only 2 workers are expected to be supporting each beneficiary by 2040. (See figure 12.)

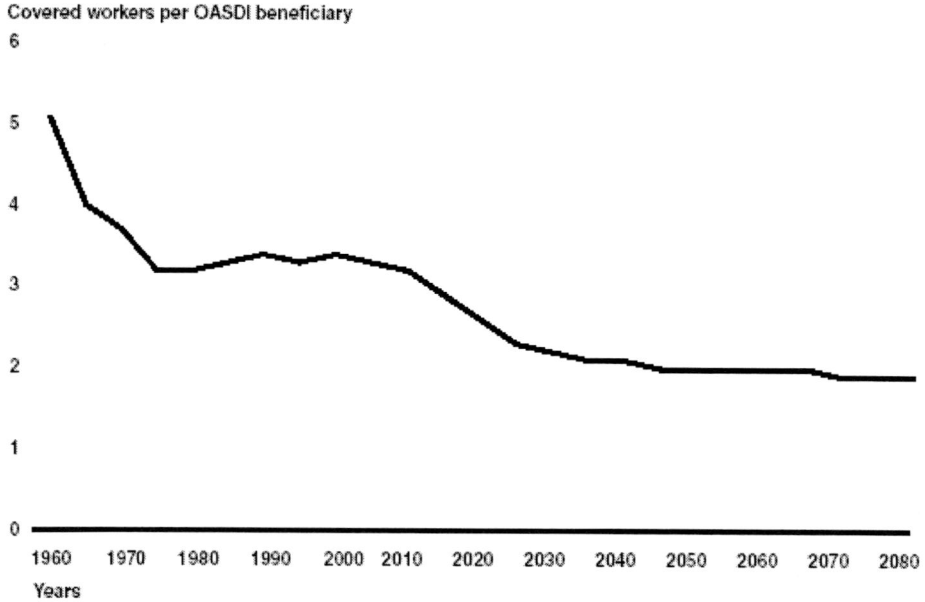

Source: SSA.

Note: This is based on the intermediate assumptions of the 2006 Social Security trustees' report.

Figure 12. Social Security Workers per Beneficiary

Related GAO Products

Social Security Reform: Answers to Key Questions. GAO-05-193SP. Washington, D.C.: May 2005.

Options for Social Security Reform. GAO-05-649R. Washington, D.C.: May 6, 2005.

Social Security Reform: Early Action Would Be Prudent. GAO-05-397T. Washington, D.C.: Mar. 9, 2005.

Social Security: Distribution of Benefits and Taxes Relative to Earnings Level. GAO-04-747. Washington, D.C.: June 15, 2004.

Social Security Reform: Analysis of a Trust Fund Exhaustion Scenario. GAO-03-907. Washington, D.C.: July 29, 2003.

Social Security Reform: Analysis of Reform Models Developed by the President's Commission to Strengthen Social Security. GAO-03-310. Washington, D.C.: Jan. 15, 2003.

Social Security: Program's Role in Helping Ensure Income Adequacy. GAO-02-62. Washington, D.C.: Nov. 30, 2001.

Social Security Reform: Potential Effects on SSA's Disability Programs and Beneficiaries. GAO-01-35. Washington, D.C.: Jan. 24, 2001.

Social Security: Evaluating Reform Proposals. GAO/AIMD/HEHS-00-29. Washington, D.C.: Nov. 4, 1999.

Social Security: Issues in Comparing Rates of Return with Market Investments. GAO/HEHS-99-110. Washington, D.C.: Aug. 5, 1999.

Social Security: Criteria for Evaluating Social Security Reform Proposals. GAO/T-HEHS-99-94. Washington, D.C.: Mar. 25, 1999.

Social Security: Different Approaches for Addressing Program Solvency. GAO/HEHS-98-33. Washington, D.C.: July 22, 1998.

Social Security: Restoring Long-Term Solvency Will Require Difficult Choices. GAO/T-HEHS-98-95. Washington, D.C.: Feb. 10, 1998.

End Notes

[1] We used the GEMINI model under a license from the Policy Simulation Group, a private contractor. GEMINI estimates individual effects of policy scenarios for a representative sample of future beneficiaries. GEMINI can simulate different reform features, including individual accounts with an offset, for their effects on the level and distribution of benefits. See appendix I for more detail on the modeling analysis, including a discussion of our assessment of the data reliability of the model.

[2] These are consumer price index (CPI) indexing, dependency ratio indexing, mortality indexing, and a so-called progressive indexing approach that uses different indexes at various earnings levels. See appendix I for a discussion of these indexes and our scope and methodology, as well as GAO, *Social Security: Program's Role in Helping Ensure Income Adequacy*, GAO-02-62 (Washington, D.C.: Nov. 30, 2001), GAO, *Social Security Reform: Analysis of Reform Models Developed by the President's Commission to Strengthen Social Security*, GAO-03-310 (Washington, D.C.: Jan. 15, 2003), and GAO, *Social Security: Distribution of Benefits and Taxes Relative to Earnings Level*, GAO-04-747 (Washington, D.C.: June 15, 2004).

[3] We focused on workers born in 1985 because all prospective program changes under all alternative policy scenarios would be almost fully phased in for these workers.

[4] See appendix I for a complete description of our benchmark policy scenarios.

[5] Earnings replacement rates measure the extent to which retirement income replaces pre- retirement income for particular individuals and thereby helps them maintain a pre- retirement standard of living.

[6] In 2006, workers receive 1 credit for each $970 of earnings, up to the maximum of 4 credits per year. To be eligible for retirement benefits a worker needs 40 credits.

[7] These estimates are based on the Social Security trustees' 2006 intermediate, or best- estimate, assumptions.

[8] Life expectancy has increased fairly steadily since the 1930s, and further increases are expected. Increases in life expectancy vary by gender, education, and earnings. Women, highly educated individuals, and higher-income individuals generally experience greater life expectancy.

[9] See GAO, *Social Security: Criteria for Evaluating Reform Proposals,* GAO/T-HEHS-99-94 (Washington, D.C.: Mar. 25, 1999), and GAO, *Social Security: Evaluating Reform Proposals,* GAO/AIMD/HEHS-00-29 (Washington, D.C.: Nov. 4, 1999).

[10] For a discussion of individual equity issues, see GAO, *Social Security: Issues in Comparing Rates of Return with Market Investments,*GAO/HEHS-99-110 (Washington, D.C.: Aug. 5, 1999).

[11] GAO-02-62.

[12] One type of indexing took the form of automatic inflation adjustments to the earnings replacement factors in the benefit formula. At the same time, the earnings used in the formula were higher on average for each new group of beneficiaries, partially because of inflation. See appendix II.

[13] Lawrence H. Thompson. "Toward the Rational Adjustment of Social Security Benefit Levels," *Policy Analysis,* Vol. 3, No. 4, Fall 1977.

[14] Wage indexing also applies to other provisions of the program that are not part of the primary benefit computations. Such provisions include earnings test thresholds, maximum family benefits, coverage thresholds, and thresholds relating to disability insurance.

[15] A worker's earnings for a given year are indexed by multiplying them by the ratio of the national average wage for the indexing year to the national average wage in the year the income was earned. The indexing year is the second calendar year before the year in which the worker is first eligible—the year the worker reaches age 62, becomes disabled, or dies. Earnings after the indexing year are counted at their actual value.

[16] In this figure, replacement rates are the annual retired worker benefits at age 65 divided by career-average earnings. Illustrative workers have career-average earnings equal to about 45, 100, and 160 percent of Social Security's Average Wage Index, respectively, for low, medium, and high earners. These three cases have earnings patterns that reflect differences by age in the probability of work and in average earnings levels. Taxable maximum earners have earnings equal to the maximum earnings taxable under OASDI in each year. Using illustrative workers holds other factors equal that might also affect replacement rates. For example, using illustrative workers filters out the effects of changes in the covered population or changes in work and retirement patterns.

[17] See GAO, *Social Security: GAO's Analysis of the Notch Issue,* GAO/T-HEHS-94-236 (Washington, D.C.: Sept. 16, 1994).

[18] Specifically, Social Security's COLAs are based on the consumer price index for urban wage earners and clerical workers (CPI-W), as opposed to the CPI series for all urban consumers (CPI-U).

[19] Andrew G. Biggs, Jeffrey R. Brown, Glenn Springstead, "Alternative Methods of Price Indexing Social Security: Implications for Benefits and System Financing," National Bureau of Economic Research, Working Paper 11406 (2005).

[20] For more information on the CPI and how it overstates the true rate of inflation, see Advisory Commission to Study the Consumer Price Index, "Toward a More Accurate Measure of the Cost of Living," Final Report to the Senate Committee on Finance, Dec. 1996, which is known as the Boskin Commission report. A variety of changes have been made to the CPI since that report, including changes that in turn affect Social Security's COLA. In addition, a new "chained" CPI reflects how consumers substitute one product for another when their relative prices change. This new CPI is not yet used by government agencies, but some reform proposals call for using a variation of it in computing COLAs.

[21] For example, the elderly allot a larger proportion of their expenses to medical care than the general population, which partially depends on Medicare's coverage and premiums.

[22] In earnings-related public pension systems reviewed here, indexation appears in different forms but in all cases affects the way in which pension rights are accrued. For example, in notional defined contribution systems such as in Sweden and Italy, workers earn a notional rate of return on their contributions (based on their earnings), and indexation is implicit in that notional return. In point systems such as in Germany, workers earn pension points (also based on their earnings) that are multiplied by a pension-point value at the time of retirement. There, indexation is implicit in the value of the pension point.

[23] It is important to note that the structure of public pension programs differ across countries, and hence are not strictly comparable. For example, contributions in some cases help finance maternity/paternity and unemployment benefits in addition to old age benefits.

[24] The total employer and employee contributions of 9.9 percent may appear low, but the retirement pension benefits these generate are relatively modest, replacing only 25 percent of average pensionable earnings.

[25] Canada's reserve fund is managed by an Investment Board that operates independently from the government since the late 1990s and invests in both foreign and domestic assets subject to some restrictions.

[26] As in the United States in the 1970s and 1980s, prices at times grow faster than wages; nonetheless, these periods remain exceptional.

[27] A full-career worker is defined as one having earnings between the ages of 20 and 65. The computation reflects the average effect, in OECD countries, for a manufacturing worker with average earnings.

[28] In most OECD countries, the formula used varies by either individual earnings, age or length of service.

[29] Using per capita wage growth, i.e., wage growth divided by the labor force, as an index implies that when the labor force shrinks, per capita wage growth goes up. As a result, benefits increase right when the number of contributors gets smaller, creating an imbalance.

[30] More precisely, the average-wage-growth indexation is reduced whenever the Balance Ratio is less than 1, where Balance Ratio = (Contribution Asset + Buffer Funds)/Pension Liability. The index then automatically becomes average wage growth multiplied by the Balance Ratio, and remains so as long as the Balance Ratio is less than 1. The Buffer Funds are a collection of reserve funds to which part of pension contributions are transferred. These are then invested in domestic and foreign assets with the objective of achieving the highest possible returns. The Buffer Funds play an important role in ensuring the financial stability of the pension program insofar as high rates of return on these funds may partially or fully compensate for any adverse demographic or economic developments.

[31] The longevity factor enters the formula determining initial benefits for a given cohort and does not change for that cohort after the normal retirement age. It ensures that the present value of benefits does not increase with life expectancy across cohorts.

[32] Changes in fertility or longevity are likely to affect the dependency ratio in the long run, but little in the short run.

[33] Benefits at the time of retirement are determined by remaining life expectancy and a growth "norm" of 1.6 percent. Benefits are then adjusted each year for inflation plus or minus deviations from this norm.

[34] Longevity and mortality are differing measures of life expectancy.

[35] See appendix I for more information on these indexes.

[36] We focused on workers born in 1985 because all prospective program changes under all alternative policy scenarios would be almost fully phased in for such workers.

[37] The benefit reduction benchmark is a hypothetical benchmark policy scenario that would achieve 75-year solvency by only reducing benefits. For ease of modeling, the benefit reduction benchmark takes the form of reductions in the benefit formula factors. Each formula factor is reduced annually by subtracting a constant proportion of the factor's value under current law, resulting in a constant percentage reduction of currently promised benefits for everyone. See appendix I for more information about the benefit reduction benchmark. Consistent with the Social Security trustees' report, we use a 75-year projection period in assessing the solvency of different indexing scenarios and our benchmarks. The 75-year projection period has been standard practice for many years, although it does not capture sustainabiity over longer time horizons. We believe it is important to consider sustainabiity, and there are different ways to do so, but this issue is outside the scope of this report.

[38] While the level of solvency differs among these scenarios, the level of benefits under each scenario is lower than promised benefits, and replacement rates have declined in each scenario.

[39] The general application of these indexes is to multiply the PIA formula's replacement factors by a factor that reflects the new index. This is the approach taken by the Social Security actuaries and most proposals. See appendix I.

[40] While scaling allows comparisons across distributions over 75 years, the different indexing scenarios are not identical in terms of sustainability.

[41] For more details on the progressive price indexing proposal, see provision B7 of the August 10, 2005 Office of the Chief Actuary (OCACT) memo at http://www.ssab.gov/documents/advisoryboardmemo--2005tr--08102005.pdf, which was the basis for our analysis.

[42] Progressive price indexing and progressive CPI indexing are two ways of referring to the same proposal.

[43] Under the current system, the maximum taxable earnings level, the level at which earnings are subject to the Social Security payroll tax, is indexed to the growth in wages, but the payroll tax rate itself is not indexed. Some proposals have suggested changing the indexing of the maximum taxable earnings level so that it maintains coverage of 90 percent of all wages. Other proposals have not focused on the 90 percent goal, but rather have suggested raising or completely eliminating the cap. With any of these changes, several issues arise, most importantly whether the benefit formula takes into account these higher earnings. These issues go beyond the scope of our work, and thus we did not analyze changes to the maximum taxable earnings level.

[44] A value less than one, for example, indicates that benefits collected fall short of taxes paid. The present value of benefits or taxes is the equivalent value, at a point in time, of the entire stream of benefits the individual receives or taxes the individual pays in his or her lifetime.

[45] Changing benefits would also affect the benefit-to-tax ratios, which would have adequacy and equity considerations.

[46] The tax increase benchmark is a hypothetical benchmark policy scenario that would achieve 75-year solvency by only increasing payroll taxes. It raises payroll taxes once and immediately by the amount of Social Security's actuarial deficit as a percentage of payroll (1.96 percentage points divided evenly between employers and

employees). It results in the smallest ultimate tax rate that would achieve 75-year solvency and spreads the tax burden evenly across generations. See appendix I for more information about the tax increase benchmark.

[47] Since the 1955 cohort reaches age 62 in 2017, the earliest age of eligibility for retired worker benefits, members of this cohort will spend fewer years contributing to the system at the higher tax rate than the other cohorts. Thus, their benefit-to-tax ratios will be higher than those for the other cohorts. Also, since lifetime benefits grow over time as people live longer, the benefit-to-tax ratios for the tax increase benchmark will begin to increase, as can be seen for the 2000 cohort.

[48] The 0.22 percentage point reduction in the growth of the CPI has been proposed as a modification to the COLA to correct methodological issues associated with how the CPI is calculated. Thus the COLA would be based on a new CPI-W series that would reflect a "superlative" formula, of the type currently used for the new chained CCPI-U. The 1 percentage point reduction in the CPI is another possibility for slowing the growth of benefits that has been analyzed by the Office of the Actuary at SSA.

[49] Since the current benefit formula links the calculation of benefits for all beneficiaries, any proposed changes would affect the benefits of disabled workers as well as retirees. Proposals to reform Social Security often modify the benefit formula without taking into account that the circumstances facing disabled workers differ from those facing retired workers. See the next section of this report for a discussion of this issue, as well as GAO-03-310, and GAO, *Social Security Reform: Potential Effects on SSA's Disability Programs and Beneficiaries*, GAO-01-35 (Washington, D.C.: Jan. 24, 2001).

[50] Most proposals that change the indexing of initial benefits would implement the new index through the benefit formula by multiplying the replacement factors by the difference between the growth in wages and the growth in the new index. In such instances, changing the indexing would not likely pose any serious implementation issues from an agency operational perspective.

[51] Purchasing power reflects the amount of goods and services individuals can afford with a given level of benefits.

[52] This is the so-called notch effect. Such a situation occurred immediately after the 1977 amendments. Notches generate controversy and confusion among beneficiaries because of inequities that result from them. See GAO/T-HEHS-94-236.

[53] For more detail on the 1977 amendments, see appendix II.

[54] For more information on the CPI and how it overstates the true rate of inflation, see Advisory Commission to Study the Consumer Price Index, "Toward a More Accurate Measure of the Cost of Living," Final Report to the Senate Committee on Finance, Dec. 1996; Congressional Budget Office, "Is the Growth of the CPI a Biased Measure of Changes in the Cost of Living?" (Washington, D.C., 1994). In recent years a variety of changes have been made to the CPI, including changes that in turn affect Social Security's COLA. In addition, a new "chained" CPI reflects how consumers substitute one product for another when their relative prices change. This new CPI is not yet used by government agencies, but some reform proposals call for using a variation of it in computing COLAs.

[55] See Ronald D. Lee and Lawrence R. Carter, "Modeling and Forecasting U.S. Mortality," *Journal of the American Statistical Association*, Vol. 87, No. 419, 1992; and Michael Sze, Stephen C. Goss, and Jose Gomez de Leon, "Effect of Aging Population with Declining Mortality on Social Security and NAFTA Countries," *North American Actuarial Journal*, Vol. 2, No. 4, 1998.

[56] For more information on the effects of reform on the DI program and beneficiaries, see GAO-01-35.

[57] Some proposals have suggested reducing the disabled worker benefit only at the time of conversion from DI to retired worker status, but only in proportion to the percentage of their potential working years that occurred in a nondisabled state.

[58] While these models use sample data, our report, like others using these models, does not address the issue of sampling errors. The results of the analysis reflect outcomes for individuals in the simulated populations and do not attempt to estimate outcomes for an actual population.

[59] MINT3 is a detailed microsimulation model developed jointly by the Social Security Administration, the Brookings Institution, RAND, and the Urban Institute to project the distribution of income in retirement for the 1931 to 1960 birth cohorts.

[60] The Board of Trustees, Federal Old-Age and Survivors Insurance and Disability Insurance Trust Funds, *The 2005 Annual Report of the Board of Trustees of the Federal Old-Age and Survivors Insurance and Disability Insurance Trust Funds* (Washington, D.C.: Mar. 23, 2005).

[61] For benefit-to-tax ratios we followed the methodology followed in GAO-04-747; see appendix I of this report for more detail.

[62] See page 3 of http://www.ssab.gov/documents/advisoryboardmemo—2005tr— 08102005.pdf for description of the provision. For the original provision from the President's Commission to Strengthen Social Security, see page 4 of http://www.ssa.gov/OACT/solvency/PresComm_20020131.pdf .

[63] For more information on provision 1 or Model 3, see page 8 of the CSSS proposal at http://www.ssa.gov/OACT/solvency/PresComm_20020131.pdf.

[64] We chose the CSSS specification because it was already scored and readily available. Other constructions or interpretations of a mortality index are certainly possible. For example, life expectancy at birth or some other age could be used. Further, life expectancy could be defined as period or cohort. A period life table represents

the mortality conditions at a specific point in time, whereas a cohort table depicts the mortality conditions of a specific group of individuals born in the same year or series of years.

65 The aged dependency ratio is 0.204 and 0.206 under the intermediate assumptions of the 2005 Trustees' report for 2007 and 2008, respectively.

66 Though we do not present SSASIM or GEMINI results for the progressive CPI index, we also scaled this proposal. For an OCACT scoring of this proposal, which was the basis of our SSASIM OLC estimates for the scaled and unscaled versions presented in the report, see provision B7 of the August 10, 2005 OCACT memo at http://www.ssab.gov/documents/advisoryboardmemo--2005tr--08102005.pdf. To scale this scenario, we consulted with OCACT and only scaled the third and fourth PIA formula factors, as these were the only factors reduced in the original provision. This effectively sped up the rate of indexing so that the benefit reductions were faster than pure price indexing across generations of steady maximum earners. Additionally, we had to slightly raise the scaling value for this scenario because the third and fourth formula factors would need to have been of a negative value beginning in 2065. However, we censored negative values at zero and raised the scaling factor by one percentage point to achieve a 75-year actuarial balance of 0 for the scaled version of progressive CPI index.

67 In the case of the aged dependency ratio tax increase index, the increase from the initial OASI and DI tax rates is multiplied by the scaling factor—again, represented by the inverse of the percentage of solvency attained by the index.

68 Despite a similar 75-year actuarial balance across the indexes studied, each index may have a unique balance in the 75th year because of the unique timing of the benefit reductions (or tax increases) of each index.

69 These benchmarks were first developed for our report GAO-02-62. We have since used them in other studies, including GAO-03-310; GAO, *Social Security Reform: Analysis of a Trust Fund Exhaustion Scenario*, GAO-03-907 (Washington, D.C.: July 29, 2003); GAO, *Social Security and Minorities: Earnings, Disability Incidence, and Mortality Are Key Factors That Influence Taxes Paid and Benefits Received* GAO-03-387 (Washington, D.C.: Apr. 23, 2003); and GAO-04-747.

70 The Social Security actuaries provided these scorings for a previous report and used assumptions from the 2001 trustees' report. The actuaries did not believe it was necessary to provide new scorings using updated assumptions for the purposes of our study, since the assumptions and the estimates of actuarial balance on which they are based have changed little from the 2001 report. In particular, they did not believe that the differences in assumptions would materially affect the shape of the distribution of benefits, which is the focus of our analysis. All estimates related to the indexing scenarios and benchmark policy scenarios were simulated using the SSASIM OLC mode.

71 Advisory Council on Social Security. *Report of the 1994-1996 Advisory Council on Social Security*, Vols. 1 and 2. Washington, D.C.: Jan. 1997.

72 See GAO-03-907, in which we analyzed such a policy scenario under a congressional request.

73 The highest 35 years of salary are used in the calculation of a retired worker benefit. The disabled worker benefit is calculated using the number of years between the age of entitlement and age 21, divided by 5.

74 Other analyses have addressed the concern about the effect of the proportional reduction on low earners by modifying that offset to apply only to the 32 and 15 percent formula factors. The MTR policy in the 1994 to 1996 Advisory Council report used this approach, which in turn was based on the individual account (IA) proposal in that report. However, the MTR policy also reflected other changes in addition to PIA formula changes.

75 Until the 1970s, trust fund projections were routinely exceeded at least in part as a result of actuarial methods that assumed no growth in average earnings.

76 These estimates of average benefit increases include both existing and initial benefits.

77 The contribution and benefit base reflects the program's role of only providing for a floor of protection.

78 In 2006, the maximum taxable earnings cap is set at $94,200.

79 The PIA is the monthly amount payable to a retired worker who begins to receive benefits at normal retirement age or (generally) to a disabled worker. This is also the amount used as a base for computing all types of benefits payable on the basis of one individual's earnings record.

80 The declining replacement factors for higher levels of earnings made the formula progressive.

81 When the maximum taxable earnings level increased, a new replacement factor would be applied to the newly covered portion of earnings. For example, the 1965 amendments increased the maximum taxable earnings from $4,800 to $6,600. Accordingly, the benefit formula added a new component, with a replacement factor of 21.4 percent for the next $150 of average monthly wages.

82 The fact that benefits were changed for both new and current beneficiaries using the same computations came to be known as "coupling" of benefit increases.

83 Part of the growth in wages reflects inflation. Wage growth makes the average monthly earnings for a new year's group of beneficiaries higher on average than for the previous year's group.

84 In a pay-as-you-go system, the payroll tax would equal annual benefit costs as a percentage of payroll.

In: Social Security Reform: Disability, Indexing and Financing ISBN: 978-1-61668-354-2
Editor: Janet U. Burlington

Chapter 8

GREATER TRANSPARENCY NEEDED ABOUT POTENTIAL GENERAL REVENUE FINANCING*

United States Government Accountability Office

WHY GAO DID THIS STUDY

Absent reform, Social Security's financing gap will grow until currently scheduled benefits can no longer be paid in full. Recent reform proposals often include general revenue (GR)—a major change that can have significant implications for the budget as a whole. This report addresses these issues: (1) What information is available about GR in recent proposal scorings by Social Security's Office of the Chief Actuary (OCACT)? (2) What common mechanisms, especially GR mechanisms, are used to increase program revenue? (3) What are the implications of GR for the trust fund and the federal budget? We have prepared this report under the Comptroller General's statutory authority to conduct evaluations on his own initiative as part of a continued effort to assist Congress in addressing the challenges facing Social Security.

WHAT GAO RECOMMENDS

GAO recommends that the Commissioner of SSA direct OCACT to include a summary presentation of its analysis to facilitate comparisons of reform proposals especially with respect to use of GR and federal budget implications. SSA suggested that a table showing how each provision affects the actuarial deficit would be helpful. GAO agrees but remains of the view that a table that can clearly and quickly communicate both trust fund effects and federal budget implications is needed.

* This is an edited, reformatted and augmented version of a U. S. Government Accountability Office publication dated March 2007.

WHAT GAO FOUND

Although focused on the trust fund, OCACT scoring memos are also the primary source of information on how proposals would impact the federal budget. Memos provide information on GR use and its effects, but experts said comparing proposals on this element presents challenges, requiring extensive efforts to understand complex tables shown at the end of the memos.

Fourteen of 17 proposals GAO reviewed provided GR (1) as needed to maintain trust fund solvency or (2) as specified by formula, amount, or source. Nine of the 17 achieved "sustainable solvency" under OCACT's definition using the first approach. This type of unlimited transfer poses the greatest potential risk to the federal budget, especially when combined with benefit guarantees. In proposals reviewed, amounts of GR under both types of approaches ranged up to about twice program shortfall.

In all proposals using GR, the GR was reallocated from the non–Social Security budget. While any additional revenue to the trust fund will help solvency, unified federal budget effects depend on the type of revenue— whether it is new revenue (additional payroll tax revenue or GR that is new to the federal budget) versus reallocated GR. Absent other changes, new revenue would improve the long-term fiscal imbalance while reallocated GR would do nothing to address it. Although raising taxes (payroll or other) or cutting benefits would have tangible consequences for taxpayers and beneficiaries, e.g., less take-home pay or smaller benefit checks, the consequences of transfers from the non–Social Security budget in the form of reallocated GR are less likely to be clearly observable. Reallocated GR, however, is not free. Regardless of how GR is provided to Social Security, it must be paid for at some point. The question is when, and by whom.

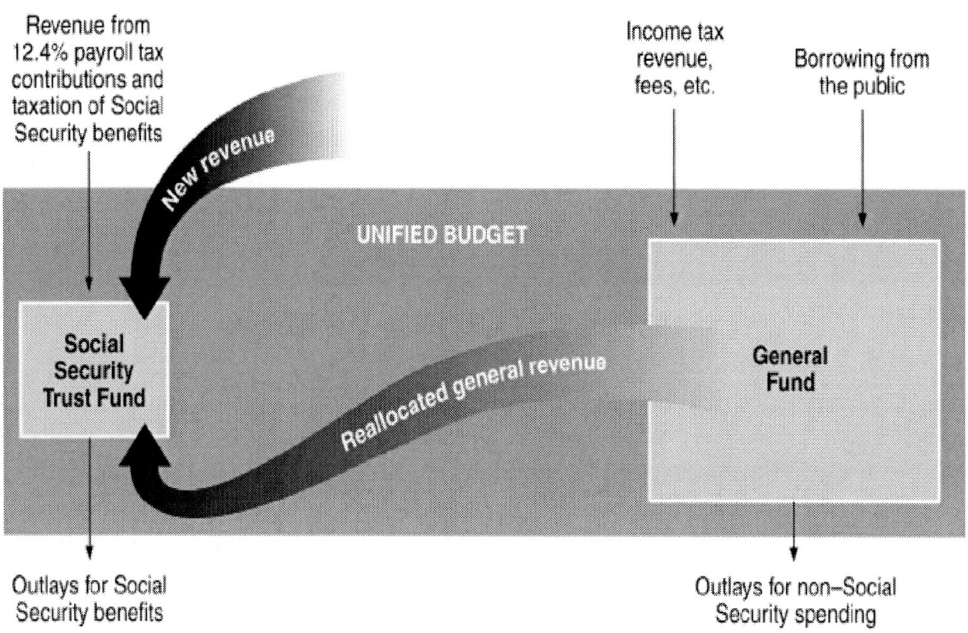

Source: GAO

New Revenue versus Reallocated General Revenue

ABBREVIATIONS

CBO	Congressional Budget Office
CES	Committee on Economic Security
CPI	Consumer Price Index
GR	general revenue
HI	Hospital Insurance
IA	individual account
OASDI	Old-Age, Survivors, and Disability Insurance
OCACT	Office of the Chief Actuary
SSA	Social Security Administration

March 22, 2007
The Honorable Max Baucus Chairman
Committee on Finance
United States Senate

The Honorable Herb Kohl
Chairman
The Honorable Gordon Smith
Ranking Member
Special Committee on Aging
United States Senate

The Honorable Charles B. Rangel
Chairman
The Honorable Jim McCrery
Ranking Member
Committee on Ways and Means
House of Representatives

The Honorable Michael R. McNulty
Chairman
The Honorable Sam Johnson
Ranking Member
Subcommittee on Social Security
Committee on Ways and Means
House of Representatives

Absent substantive reform, the gap between expected Social Security cash revenues and benefits that is expected to begin in 2017 will grow until the Social Security combined Old-Age Survivors and Disability Insurance (OASDI) trust fund[1] is exhausted and benefits at currently scheduled levels can no longer be paid in full. Under the 2006 intermediate Trustees' estimates, Social Security's long-term financial shortfall is estimated at 2.02 percent of total taxable payroll,[2] and its trust fund is projected to reach exhaustion in 2040.[3] Since its inception in 1935, Social Security has been financed primarily by the payroll tax contributions of employers and employees. However, recent reform proposals have often used—and in some cases relied primarily on—general revenue financing[4] to help address the program's financial shortfall. Many of the reform proposals estimated (scored) by the Office of the Chief Actuary (OCACT) at the Social Security Administration (SSA) as achieving "sustainable solvency"[5] for the trust fund would give Social Security significant amounts of general revenue as part of a package of modifications.

Such use of general revenue for Social Security would represent a major shift for this important and popular program. Since enactment in 1935, Social Security payroll taxes have been increased and benefits expanded, but the program's financing framework has remained largely the same. The use of general revenue was proposed both before the actual creation of Social Security and during short-term financing crises in the 1970s and 1980s as an alternative to payroll tax increases, but Congress for the most part has rejected general revenue financing for Social Security. Use of general revenue would change the "self-supporting" nature of the program and has thus been controversial. Some have feared that such a shift would facilitate benefit expansion by undermining the fiscal discipline that requires limiting benefit outlays to trust fund balances; others have feared that use of general revenue would lead ultimately to a change from a universal program to a reduced, means-tested benefit. Since 1983, small amounts of general revenue from taxation of the Social Security benefits of upper-income retirees have been dedicated to the program.[6]

In the coming years, as the baby boom generation retires, the nation will face a daunting and unprecedented long-term fiscal challenge. GAO's longterm budget simulations show that current fiscal policy is unsustainable and, absent changes, will lead to an escalating spiral of federal deficits and debt.[7] Social Security is not the major driver of the long-term fiscal challenge—the cost of government-financed health care is—but Social Security reform has the potential to affect not only the financial condition of the program's trust fund but also the financial condition of the Nation. As the reform debate resumes, it will be important to make transparent the implications of general revenue use not only for the trust fund but also for the federal budget as a whole.

This report seeks to answer the following questions: (1) What information is available about general revenue use in recent Social Security proposal scoring memos by OCACT and how can available information about general revenue use best be presented in order to facilitate comparison of reform proposals? (2) In recent Social Security reform proposals, what common mechanisms, especially general revenue mechanisms, are used to increase revenue to the program? (3) What are the implications of general revenue use for the trust fund and the federal budget?

To answer these questions, we reviewed relevant literature on Social Security and performed an in-depth analysis of 17 OCACT proposal scoring memos done from 2001 through 2006. These included all proposals scored as achieving long-range solvency. Where a proposal was scored in multiple years, we used the most recent scoring. We also interviewed selected federal budget experts representing a range of views on reform approaches and met with officials from OCACT and Congressional Budget Office (CBO) involved in proposal scorings. (See app. I for more details on our scope and methodology.)

We have prepared this report under the Comptroller General's authority to conduct evaluations on his own initiative, and it is intended to assist Congress in its deliberations on

Social Security and retirement issues. The report is addressed to interested congressional committees.

We performed our work between May 2005 and December 2006 in accordance with generally accepted government auditing standards. We requested comments on a draft of this report from the Commissioner of Social Security and incorporated those comments as appropriate. (See "Agency Comments and Our Evaluation" and app. II.)

RESULTS IN BRIEF

Scoring memos prepared by OCACT usually serve as the basis for discussion of the financing changes—including any use of general revenue—contained in reform proposals.[8] These memos focus on the impact of a proposal on the combined OASDI trust fund. Understanding the use of any general revenue in a given proposal, the proposal's impact on the federal budget, and how different proposals compare on these dimensions presents challenges. Although OCACT scorings have evolved in recent years to include estimates of a proposal's use of general revenue and the proposal's year-by-year impact on the federal budget, detailed information on these effects is available primarily in the complex technical tables at the end of the scoring memo.

In OCACT's recent scorings, five different mechanisms were used to provide general revenue to maintain the current Social Security program[9] or to a restructured Social Security system that included individual accounts (IA). These mechanisms can be characterized as providing for either unlimited or limited amounts of general revenue financing. The first mechanism provides for unlimited amounts of general revenue to be transferred to the trust fund as needed to maintain solvency (e.g., a 100 percent trust fund ratio). The other four mechanisms provide limited or defined amounts of general revenue through (1) general revenue transfers to the trust fund specified by formula or amount; (2) refundable tax credits, used to fund IAs; (3) dedication of estate tax revenue to the trust fund; and (4) redirection of Social Security benefit taxation revenue from Medicare's Hospital Insurance trust fund to the Social Security trust fund. Fourteen of the 17 proposals we reviewed used reallocated general revenue, most often to finance program restructuring, and 9 proposals used the mechanism of unlimited transfers as needed to achieve a specified trust fund ratio, which guaranteed "sustainable solvency" for the trust fund under OCACT's definition. (See text box for definition of "reallocated general revenue.") Three proposals did not use general revenue. Of the 17 proposals, 7 increased payroll tax revenues.

NEW VERSUS REALLOCATED GENERAL REVENUE IN SOCIAL SECURITY

In this report, "general revenue" in Social Security is defined as any revenue that does not derive from payroll tax contributions. In this framework, interest on trust fund assets is considered as deriving from payroll tax contributions.[a] All other revenue to Social Security, including revenue from taxation of certain Social Security benefits, is classified as general revenue.[b] This framework accords with the federal budget accounting perspective of our analysis. This conforms to the discussion of general revenue use in Social Security found on SSA's history web site.[c]

Although any additional payroll tax revenue would be new to the federal budget, general revenue may be either new to the federal budget as a whole or reallocated from other federal priorities.

- New general revenue is revenue that derives from a new source, that is, from a new tax or increase to an existing tax. For example, in 1983, the Social Security benefits of upper income retirees were made subject to income taxation, and the revenue from this new tax was dedicated to the Social Security trust funds. From a federal budget perspective, this change represented new general revenue at that time. This change has remained in place and constitutes a permanent form of general revenue in today's Social Security program.
- Reallocated general revenue does not come from a new source. Rather, it is reallocated from existing revenue to the Treasury. Following World War II, reallocated general revenue was used to fund Social Security benefits for military personnel and also a small flat benefit for individuals who were at least age 72 in 1968 but not entitled to Social Security through their work history.

[a] GAO's definition of general revenue assumes that the interest rate used to credit the trust funds reflects the rates for long-term federal marketable government securities, as is the case under current law. The Department of Treasury determines the interest rate earned on trust fund balances for Social Security using a statutory formula that sets the interest rate equal, at the time of issue, to the average market yield on outstanding marketable government securities not due or redeemable for at least 4 years.

[b] From a tax perspective, accounting treatments are more complex. For example, the earned income tax credit, a refundable tax credit available to certain lower income earners, was intended to help offset Social Security payroll taxes for those eligible. See GAO, Tax Administration: Earned Income Credit—Data on Noncompliance and Illegal Alien Recipients, GAO/GGD-95-27 (Washington, D.C.: Oct. 25, 1994).

[c] See http://www.ssa.gov/history/genrev.html.

All proposals we reviewed were scored by OCACT as able to pay benefits as scheduled in that proposal over the 75-year period, but the effects on the federal budget shown in OCACT's technical tables varied widely. For example, the effect on debt held by the public ranged from an improvement of $45 trillion to a worsening of $41 trillion over the 75-year projection period.[10] Unlimited transfers of reallocated general revenue as needed to achieve trust fund solvency—by definition—pose the greatest potential risk to the budget especially when combined with benefit guarantees. In the proposals we reviewed, amounts of general revenue transferred under this mechanism ranged up to about twice total program financial shortfall. Limited transfers, however, were also quite large, in some cases somewhat more than twice program shortfall.

From the trust fund perspective, any type of increased revenue the trust fund receives — new general revenue, reallocated general revenue, or increased payroll tax revenue—will improve the actuarial balance and increase the trust fund's capacity to pay benefits. From the budget perspective, however, new revenue from any source would improve the long-term fiscal imbalance while reallocated general revenue would do nothing to address it, all other things equal. (See Figure 1) New revenue would have tangible consequences for taxpayers, e.g., less take-home pay, while reallocated general revenue is less likely to be clearly observable. Reallocated general revenue, however, is not free. Regardless of how general revenue is provided to Social Security, it must be paid for at some point. The question is when, and by whom.

Regardless of their views on reform, most budget experts we spoke with believed greater transparency was needed concerning the use of general revenue in reform proposals. In view of the long-term fiscal challenge facing the nation, some experts were especially concerned about proposals' use of reallocated general revenue for Social Security. As one of these experts emphasized, the public needs to understand that reallocated general revenue for Social Security is not "free." Reallocated general revenue would need to be paid for now or later through lower spending, higher taxes, and/or more debt.[11] Other budget experts viewed the use of reallocated general revenue as making possible a transition to a restructured Social Security system that would include IAs. These experts viewed the use of reallocated general revenue as a transition cost that would eventually be repaid to the budget as a whole.[12] Most experts we spoke with were concerned about the mechanism of providing for unlimited transfers of reallocated general revenue as needed to assure trust fund solvency. They noted that since this mechanism in effect removes the possibility of trust fund exhaustion, it disables the trust fund's capacity to signal policymakers and the public of a need to take action.

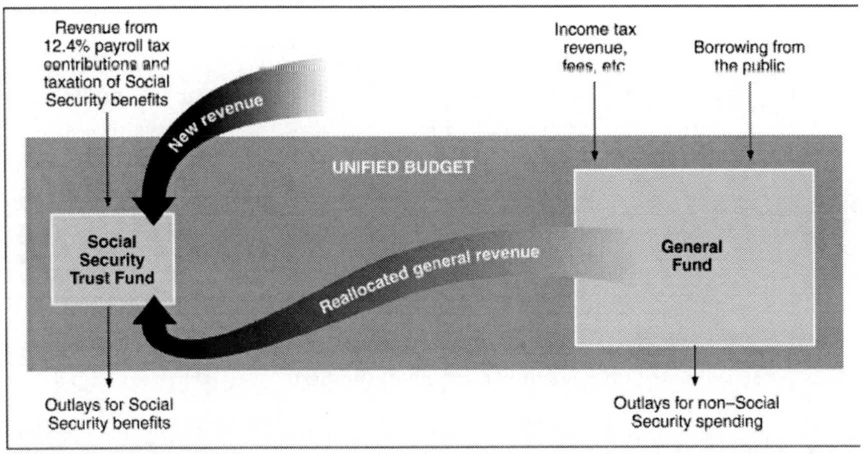

Sourece: GAO

Figure 1. New Revenue versus Reallocated General Revenue in Social Security Reform

In coming decades, our nation will face a serious long-term fiscal challenge that will put America's fiscal future at risk. Substantive reform of Social Security will involve hard choices. OCACT's valuable information and complex analyses could make an even greater contribution to the reform debate if they were more readily accessible to nonexpert users. To improve understanding of proposed changes to Social Security, GAO is recommending that the Commissioner of SSA direct the Office of the Chief Actuary to include a summary presentation of its analysis in future scoring memoranda that will enable policymakers and the general public to quickly and easily compare Social Security reform proposals especially with respect to proposed use of general revenue and implications for the federal budget as a whole. This type of presentational change would not require any additional analysis but could greatly facilitate comparison of proposals to one another.

SSA did not explicitly agree or disagree with our recommendation in its comments. In response to the recommendation, SSA noted that recent OCACT memos had added an additional table ("table d") that, SSA believes, already provides key information on general revenue use in proposals. SSA also expressed the view that a summary table showing the effects on the actuarial deficit of each proposal provision would be helpful. As our report had noted, this table has been included in some memoranda at the request of the proposal's sponsor.

While we agree with SSA that both the technical and summary table it describes add value, we remain of the view that OCACT needs to develop a new table that can clearly and quickly communicate both trust fund effects and federal budget implications of a proposal. Our report acknowledged the value and completeness of OCACT's analyses including those presented in "table d." The message of our report was not that OCACT needs to do additional analytic work. Our message was rather that OCACT's existing analyses need to be summarized and highlighted so that a proposal's implications for both the trust fund and the federal budget as a whole are immediately clear.

BACKGROUND

When Social Security was enacted in 1935, the nation was in the midst of the Great Depression. About half of the elderly depended on others for their livelihood, and roughly one-sixth received public charity. Many had lost their savings. Social Security was created to help ensure that in the future the elderly would have adequate incomes in retirement and would not have to depend on welfare. Instead, the new program would provide benefits based on the payroll tax contributions of workers and their employers. Today Social Security is much more than a retirement program. In 1939 Social Security coverage was extended to the dependents of retired and deceased workers and in 1956 to the disabled. Over one- third of beneficiaries receive benefits for reasons other than old age.[13]

Social Security Is One Part of the Long-Term Fiscal Challenge

Our work on Social Security reform has emphasized the need for change not only because future program revenues are expected to fall short of what is needed to pay currently scheduled benefits in full but because Social Security, Medicare, and Medicaid taken together will consume an increasing share of the budget and the economy. To move into the future with no changes in federal health and retirement programs is to envision a very different role for the federal government. Little room would be left for other federal spending priorities such as national defense, education, and law enforcement. Absent changes in the structure of Social Security and Medicare, some time during the 2040s government would do nothing but pay interest on the debt and mail checks to retirees. Accordingly, substantive reform of Social Security and health programs remains critical to recapturing our future fiscal flexibility.

Overall, the federal budget is facing unsustainable deficits and debt. Our most recent long-term budget simulations provide a compelling illustration of how unsustainable the long-term fiscal outlook is under current policies.

As shown in figure 2, the long-term outlook under plausible assumptions is bleak. A demographic shift will begin to affect the federal budget in 2008 as the first baby boomers become eligible for Social Security benefits. Over time, this shift will cause spending for federal health and retirement programs including Social Security to swell. Long-term commitments for these and other federal programs will drive a massive imbalance between spending and revenues that cannot be eliminated without difficult policy choices and ultimately significant policy changes.

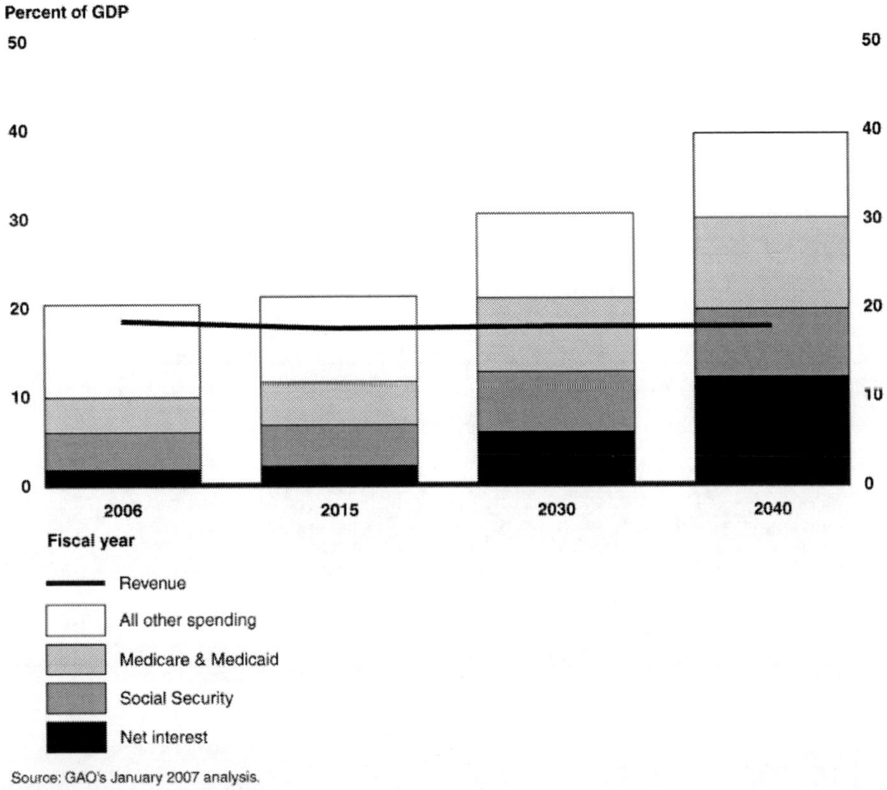

Source GAO's January 2007 analysis.

Figure 2. Composition of Spending as a Share of GDP Assuming Discretionary Spending Grows with the Economy After 2007 and All Expiring Tax Cuts Are Extended

As figure 2 shows, contrary to popular perception, although Social Security grows in size, it is not the major driver of the long-term fiscal challenge. Spending for Medicare and Medicaid is expected to grow much faster. Many specific solutions have been proposed for Social Security, but approaches to reducing health care cost growth remain elusive. Moreover, addressing federal programs such as Medicare and the federal-state Medicaid program will need to involve changes in the health care system of which they are a part. This will be a societal challenge affecting all age groups. While Social Security reform alone cannot eliminate the long-term fiscal challenge, the likely effects of reform on the nation's fiscal future should be clearly understood and taken into account.

Social Security's Trust Fund and the Federal Budget

Social Security's benefit payments and program receipts are tracked in federal budget accounts that are known as trust funds. Trust funds are one type of mechanism created to account for receipts that are dedicated to a specific fund for a specific purpose.[14] Social Security has two trust funds, the Old-Age Survivors Insurance (OASI) Trust Fund and the Disability Insurance (DI) Trust Fund. The combined OASDI trust fund comprises the financial resources of the Social Security system.[15] Social Security has a permanent appropriation that permits the payment of benefits as long as the relevant trust fund account has a sufficient balance.

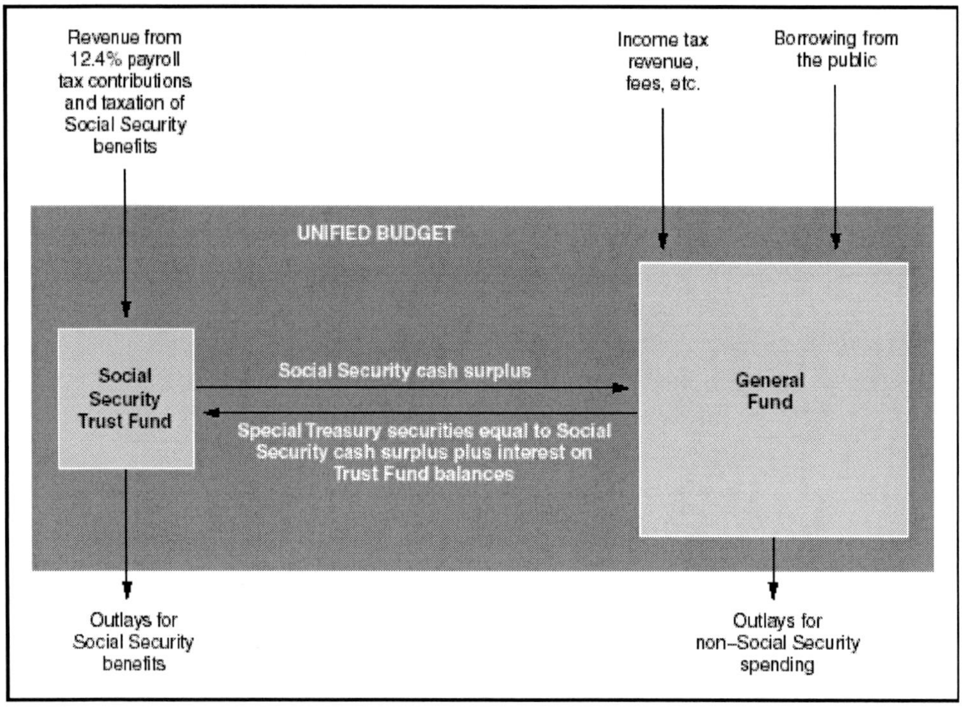

Source: GAO

Figure 3. Social Security Flows Today

Social Security's outlays are limited to trust fund balances, but the program's outlays and revenues are also part of the federal unified budget. Today, Social Security payroll tax revenues exceed benefits. In 2005, the Social Security trust fund paid $530 billion in benefit payments and administrative costs and took in $608 billion in cash revenues, leaving a cash surplus of about $78 billion.[16] By law, the Social Security trust fund must invest any cash surpluses in interest-bearing federal government securities. Throughout its history, Social Security has invested mostly in a special type of nonmarketable securities that, like debt held by the public, are guaranteed by the full faith and credit of the U.S. government. Treasury borrows the cash from Social Security's surplus to pay for other government expenses, and this use of Social Security's excess cash revenues reduces the amount Treasury would otherwise need to borrow from the public to finance other federal programs.[17] (See Figure 3).

These excess cash revenues, however, will begin to diminish in 2009, one year after the oldest members of the baby boom generation first become eligible for Social Security old age benefits. This downturn in the Social Security cash surplus—the difference between payroll taxes and benefits paid—will begin a squeeze on the rest of the budget that will worsen in the coming years, making less cash revenue available for other federal priorities. By 2017 trust fund cash revenues will be inadequate to pay currently scheduled benefits in full, and the Social Security trust fund will need to redeem trust fund assets from the Treasury. To pay the trust fund, Treasury will need to provide cash from general revenues in exchange for those trust fund securities. This can come only through increased revenue, increased borrowing from the public, reduced spending in the rest of the government, or some combination of these. While the trust fund is redeeming its securities, it will continue to pay full benefits, but the redemptions will reduce overall federal budgetary flexibility.

Our Framework for Evaluating Reform Proposals

As we have said previously, Social Security reform proposals will need to be evaluated on a number of criteria. Our work on various aspects of this important program has emphasized that Social Security reform is about more than solvency. To evaluate reform proposals, we have suggested that policy makers should consider three basic criteria:

1. the extent to which the proposal achieves sustainable solvency and how the proposal would affect the economy and the federal budget;
2. the balance struck between the twin goals of individual equity (rates of return on individual contributions) and income adequacy (level and certainty of benefits);[18] and
3. how readily such changes could be implemented, administered, and explained to the public.

Our first criterion of sustainable solvency reflects the need to look at Social Security reform both in terms of its trust fund and in the larger context of the federal budget as a whole. It is different from OCACT's definition, which is focused solely on the trust fund, for which they are responsible.

From a micro perspective, projected trust fund balances can provide a vital though imperfect signaling function for policymakers about underlying fiscal imbalances in covered programs. Tracking the estimated future balances makes it possible in turn to estimate how much more funding is needed to pay for the benefits scheduled in current law. A shortfall between the long-term projected fund balance and projected costs can signal that the fund, either by design or because of changes, is collecting insufficient monies to finance currently scheduled future payments. This signaling device can eventually prompt policymakers to action.

From a macro perspective, however, program solvency measures such as the trust fund exhaustion date and the actuarial balance calculation provide no information about the broader question of program sustainability—that is, the capacity of the future economy and the federal unified budget to pay program benefits over the long run. When a program is not fully self-financed, as is the case with Social Security, projected accumulated trust fund balances do not necessarily reflect the full future cost of existing government commitments. Accordingly, trust fund balances are not an adequate measure of Social Security's sustainability. The critical question is whether the Nation and the government as a whole can afford the benefits in the future and at what cost in terms of other claims on scarce resources. Extending a trust fund's solvency without reforms to make the underlying program more sustainable over the long term can obscure the warning signals that trust fund balances provide, thereby creating a false sense of security and delaying needed program reform.

Evaluating proposals is a complex task involving trade-offs between competing goals. Reform proposals should be evaluated as packages that strike a balance among individual reform elements and important interactive effects between these elements. The overall evaluation of any particular reform proposal depends on the weight individual policy makers place on each criterion.

Social Security Financing Has Evolved, but Payroll Taxes Remain the Principal Financing Mechanism

Since its establishment in 1935 Social Security has been financed primarily by payroll taxes contributed equally by employers and employees. Both tax rates and benefits have changed over time, but Congress has generally rejected proposals for including general revenue in financing Social Security benefits. Payroll tax rates have increased, from a total of 2 percent of taxable payroll in 1937—when payroll taxes were first collected—to 12.4 percent today. Benefits have also been expanded to include workers' families and the disabled.

The question of whether some general revenue should be used to minimize the burden of payroll taxes has been debated since the program's inception. The Committee on Economic Security (CES), tasked by President Roosevelt with designing the program, believed that expected benefit payments would exceed expected payroll tax revenues beginning about 1965 and at that time general revenue should be used to fill the gap. Under this financing arrangement, the general revenue share was ultimately expected to reach about one-third of total revenues. President Roosevelt rejected the idea of using general revenue in program financing. He endorsed payroll tax financing on the grounds that it would ensure the new program would be "self-supporting." A perceived link between benefits and payroll tax contributions would, he believed, serve to preserve the program in the future. Using general revenue would make the program welfare—in President Roosevelt's words, "the dole by another name."

President Roosevelt's financing approach envisioned the buildup of a reserve fund that would serve to fund benefits in the long term, but objections were made to this approach. Some believed that the existence of a large reserve fund would lead to higher benefit levels or other increased government spending; others objected to the underlying concept of prefunding benefits which they believed would lock in specific levels of support for aged beneficiaries in the future. Congressional changes to the program that expanded benefits and postponed scheduled payroll tax increases put the program on a pay-as-you-go basis, that is, revenues from current workers in a given year pay for the benefits of current beneficiaries in that year.

Nevertheless, the issue of whether general revenue should be used to supplement payroll tax financing has recurred throughout Social Security's history. During short-term financing crises in the late 1970s and early 1980s, proposals were made for general revenue use. At that time some opposed this use of general revenue believing that it would obscure the true cost of the program and lead to benefit expansion. Reform legislation passed in 1983 did include permanent use of some general revenue by imposing a new income tax on the Social Security benefits of upper income retirees and dedicating that tax to the trust fund.[19] Although the income thresholds were not indexed to inflation, amounts of revenue to Social Security from this source have been and remain small relative to total program tax revenue.

Since the legislation passed in 1977 and 1983, a temporary build up of trust fund assets has caused Social Security to temporarily deviate somewhat from pay-as-you-go financing. This occurred in part because the large baby boom generation makes the size of the workforce large relative to the beneficiary population. As the baby boom generation retires and is replaced by a workforce that will grow less rapidly than in the past, trust fund assets will be redeemed to pay benefits, but these assets plus payroll tax revenues will eventually be insufficient to pay currently scheduled benefits in full. To deal with this structural imbalance, many proposals have included the use of general revenue to supplement payroll tax financing—often in large amounts relative to total financing and over extended time periods. For example, both proposals made by President Clinton in 1999 and reform models put forward in 2003 by the Commission to Strengthen Social Security established by President George W. Bush included the use of general revenue.

OCACT Scoring Memos Are Primary Source of Information on Reform Proposals, but Detailed Tables Are Difficult to Use for Understanding General Revenue and Federal Budget Effects

OCACT scoring memos are the primary source of information on recent Social Security reform proposals. Since the mid-1990's, OCACT has scored a wide variety of comprehensive reform proposals. Each proposal modifies the OASDI program using one or several of the following provisions that: (1) reduce benefits, e.g. through changes to indexing formulas and/or other methods; (2) increase benefits for special populations; (3) raise revenue through payroll tax increases; (4) use general revenue financing through a range of mechanisms (not always specified as general revenue); (5) invest trust fund assets through government investment in marketable securities; or (6) change the current structure of the program by creating IAs.[20] The format of these scoring memos has evolved over time, partially in response to feedback from users. More recent scoring memos are available on OCACT's web site.[21] In addition, OCACT has begun to post estimates of many of the stand-alone provisions that have been suggested to modify the Social Security program and improve its financial status. Many of these are also included in the various comprehensive proposals.

OCACT's scoring memos typically emphasize two important summary measures: (1) the change to actuarial balance and (2) ability of the trust fund to meet obligations throughout the 75-year period and beyond, an indicator of "sustainable solvency" as defined by OCACT.[22] In recent years, sustainable solvency as defined by OCACT has become the standard by which reform proposals are measured. When OCACT evaluates a reform proposal as meeting the definition of sustainably solvent, the proposal sponsor often highlights this point in press statements and other statements. This measure, however, considers only trust fund effects and not the effect of the proposal on the federal budget.[23]

To discover crucial information on a proposal's general revenue use and federal budget effects, a user of OCACT's scoring memos must consult the detailed tables at the end of the memo. The type and amount of information included in the tables has increased over time. Current tables are generally comprehensive in presenting a proposal's financial effects. Columns display year-to-year changes in the financial operations of the trust fund and the unified budget as well as the cashflow between the trust fund and the general fund of the U.S. Treasury. For those plans that include either government or IA investment in equity markets, OCACT publishes two sets of tables, one reflecting "expected-yield" assumptions on investments and a second set reflecting "low-yield" assumptions. A few of the scoring memos we analyzed included other tables that provide insight into general revenue use. One of these tables shows the impact of each individual provision on the long-range actuarial balance (as a percentage of payroll). This table shows to what extent a single provision, by itself, either improves or worsens the actuarial balance.[24]

Budget experts we spoke with agreed that the tables had evolved and now provide more information but they also said that the tables are difficult to use and take much effort to understand. In particular, they said that the "information is not reader-friendly" and "key estimates of general revenue are not highlighted and it is not always clear if there is a specified source for the general revenue." Our analysis of 17 recent scoring memos generally confirmed this assessment. Policymakers and the public may have a difficult time comparing how different plans get to sustainable solvency and the implications for the rest of the budget, future deficits, and debt held by the public. Similarly, the 1999 and 2003 Technical Panels on Assumptions and Methods, convened by the Social Security Advisory Board, expressed concerns about consistency in presentation of information in scoring memos. One recommendation made by budget experts was for an up-front summary table with crucial information that a reader needs in order to compare plans. Although we found no agreement on precise content for the table, information about benefit cuts, tax increases, and general revenue could somehow be included.

OCACT staff told us that the principal purpose of their scorings was to show the effect of a proposal on trust fund solvency and not on the budget as a whole. They added that they were generally satisfied with the current format for scoring memos, noting that they had not received any negative feedback from users. They did agree that information could be more user- friendly and are considering ways to achieve this goal, for example through the inclusion of visuals. OCACT staff further noted that scoring proposals is resource-intensive. Although some scorings can take up to a year, others must be done under tight timeframes, e.g., when sponsors are planning to introduce legislation. They also told us that they have discussed options for a summary table with selected users but had not found any consensus on what information should be highlighted. OCACT staff emphasized that their scorings are and need to continue to be perceived as objective. In any case, OCACT staff did not think that the use of general revenue should be highlighted above other proposal changes.

More recently, CBO has developed the capacity to do long-term estimates of Social Security reform proposals and has completed five long-term scoring memos to date. OCACT and CBO scoring memos have key substantive and presentational differences. One particularly important difference is the use of different economic assumptions, which results in CBO currently having more optimistic estimates of current-law program finances. Although budget experts we spoke with generally thought that CBO scoring memos have been beneficial analytical tools, they also thought that OCACT scoring memos were likely to continue to be the primary source of information in any debate over reform proposals. Therefore, having OCACT scoring memos provide clear and easily accessible information on any use of general revenue and on the impact of any reform proposal on the broader budget remains important.

Recent Proposals Differ by Revenue Mechanism and Reform Approach Used, but Most Reallocate General Revenue and Aim to Increase Investment Returns

Almost all proposals we reviewed package multiple revenue options and/or benefit changes to achieve sustainable solvency, but they differ[25] in both the broad approach they take for dealing with the long-range solvency problem and the revenue mechanisms they use. Reform approaches can be divided into two broad categories: approaches that maintain the current structure, that is, a pay-as-you-go social insurance program of defined benefits paid for primarily by payroll tax revenue, and approaches that create a new structure that includes IAs.

Provisions that guarantee revenue to the Social Security trust fund can be classified as: reallocated general revenue mechanisms, payroll tax mechanisms, or new general revenue mechanisms (see Text Box). A reallocated general revenue mechanism is any provision that increases revenue to the program by redirecting existing general revenue expected under existing law to the trust fund. Payroll tax mechanisms directly change the amount of payroll taxes contributed and therefore increase payroll taxes flowing into the trust fund. A new general revenue mechanism would establish a new source of income to the general fund and dedicate it to the Social Security trust fund. Examples would be the creation of a national sales tax or increases in income or excise taxes with the revenue from any of these dedicated to the Social Security trust fund. None of the proposals we examined introduced new general revenues. All of them—although described and characterized in various ways—used only mechanisms that would reallocate general revenue and/or increase payroll taxes.

All 17 of the Social Security reform proposals we analyzed include at least one mechanism to increase revenue to Social Security and some use more than one mechanism.[26] Fourteen of the 17 proposals we examined would reallocate general revenue, that is, transfer existing revenue from the general fund; the other 3 proposals did not use general revenue.

The 14 proposals that used reallocated general revenue did so by means of five different mechanisms. These mechanisms can be characterized as providing for either unlimited or limited amounts of general revenue financing. The first mechanism provides for unlimited general revenue; the other four use varying means to provide limited or defined amounts of general revenue financing. Unlike plans with unlimited transfers to assure trust fund solvency, proposals with general revenue transfers limited by specified amounts, source, or formula, could be insolvent at some point in time if the actual financial condition of the program differs from the OCACT estimates.

Unlimited mechanism:

- **Unlimited general revenue transfers to the trust fund of whatever amount is necessary to maintain trust fund solvency (e.g., a 100 percent trust fund ratio).**[27] This mechanism is the most frequently used general revenue option. It is found in 9 of the 17 plans we examined. This provision usually states that general revenue transfers are to be made if, at any time, the combined OASDI trust fund ratio is projected to fall below 100 percent under the provisions of the plan.[28] Transfers of sufficient amount and timing will be made to prevent the trust fund from falling below 100 percent of the annual program cost. In simple terms, funds sufficient to pay projected benefits for the year, that is, to maintain solvency, would be transferred as needed from the general fund to the Social Security trust fund without regard to the amount. This provision alone guarantees program solvency under any circumstance because it provides the trust fund with an unlimited and open-ended draw on the general fund.[29]

Limited mechanisms:

- **General revenue transfers specified by formula or amount.** Six plan sponsors propose using this mechanism, which specifies—in actual dollars, as a percentage of taxable payroll or using a formula—how much general revenue would be transferred to the trust fund in a given year. Transfers would be limited by these specifications. In other words, transfer amounts are made independent of the financial condition of the program as measured by the trust fund ratio).[30]

- **"Refundable tax credits" for individual add-on accounts (or to individuals to offset account contributions).** Alone among the general revenue options discussed, under this mechanism revenue would not be transferred to the OASDI trust fund, but would be outlaid immediately— either to provide funding to individual add-on accounts or to offset the cost of those accounts. The four proposals using this option would either credit the general revenue directly to the workers' add-on accounts (the amount would be determined by the plan's provisions) or include the amount as a credit on the individuals' income taxes to partially offset the payroll tax increase introduced to fund the account. Although in these proposals the add-on accounts would be financed outside of the current program—either entirely or partially funded using reallocated general revenue[31]—they would be considered part of a new Social Security system.

- **Dedication of revenue generated from the estate tax to the trust fund.** This revenue option would dedicate revenue from the estate tax to the Social Security trust fund to help finance the current structure. One proposal would permanently establish a tax of 45 percent on all estates of deceased taxpayers with taxable assets in excess of $3.5 million (as in current law for 2009).[32] The tax revenue would be dedicated to the OASDI trust fund instead of to the general fund.

- **Redirection of those revenues from Social Security benefit taxation that now go to the Medicare Hospital Insurance (HI) trust fund to the OASDI trust fund.** Currently, up to 85 percent of an individual's or couple's OASDI benefits may be subject to federal income taxation if their income exceeds certain thresholds. The income tax revenue attributable to the first 50 percent of OASDI benefits is already dedicated to the Social Security trust fund, but the revenue associated with the amount between 50 and 85 percent of benefits is dedicated to the Medicare HI trust fund. Two proposals would dedicate all of the income from the tax on OASDI benefits to OASDI.

  Reform plans with individual accounts may have indirect effects on income from benefit taxation. Proposal sponsors typically stipulate whether disbursements from individual accounts would be taxed like current Social Security benefits or not taxed at all. If account disbursements are considered OASDI benefits for income tax purposes, income to the trust fund could be greater (or smaller) in cases where the combined traditional benefit and account disbursement yields are greater (or lesser) than under current law. There would be similar implications for the HI trust fund if benefit taxation income is distributed as under current law. Plans that reduce the taxable traditional OASDI benefits and do not tax individual account distributions would lower trust fund revenue from this source.

  Of the 17 proposals, 7 increase payroll tax revenue using one or more of the following four mechanisms:

- **Raise or eliminate the "taxable maximum limit" or "cap" on covered earnings[33] (with or without retaining the cap for benefit calculation).** Incorporated in five proposals, this is the most common mechanism for bringing in new payroll tax revenue. This mechanism would not change the 12.4 percent tax rate but would either increase the level of wages taxed or completely eliminate the cap so that all covered earnings are taxed. This latter option is similar to the Medicare HI payroll tax of 2.9 percent, which applies to all covered earnings. SSA recently estimated that in 2005 about 84 percent of covered earnings were subject to the OASDI tax (i.e., were taxable) and projected decreases in the ratio of taxable wages to covered wages through 2015. After 2015, SSA expects this percentage to be held approximately constant at 82 percent of covered earnings. Four plans propose to increase the percentage of taxable earnings under the "cap" to a level between 87 and 90 percent of covered earnings. A fifth plan would completely eliminate the earnings cap and would tax all earnings at the 12.4 percent rate.

- **Increase the 12.4 percent payroll tax on taxable earnings.** Four plans propose raising payroll tax rates by between 1 and 3 percentage points. None of the plans we reviewed propose an immediate tax rate increase of 2.02 percentage points, the estimated increase needed to achieve 75-year solvency through year 2080.[34]

- **Expand coverage to state and local government employees not currently covered.** Three plans would require those public employers not currently providing Social Security coverage to cover newly hired employees.[35]

- **Tax covered earnings above the "cap" but at a lower tax rate (with or without retaining the "cap" for benefit calculation).** Two proposals apply a rate much lower than 12.4 percent, between 3 and 4 percent, to covered earnings above the established taxable maximum.

Some of the mechanisms to increase payroll tax revenue could also result in increased benefit costs. For example, proposals that raise or eliminate the "cap" on covered earnings or tax earnings above the "cap" may or may not include these wages when calculating benefits. If the wages are included in the benefit formula, benefit costs would increase in the future and the improvement in the actuarial deficit would be smaller than if the wages were not included in the benefit calculation. Expanding coverage to all state and local government workers would bring in additional payroll tax revenue but would also increase the long-term benefit costs as newly covered earnings would entitle affected workers to the associated benefits.

None of the five general revenue mechanisms in the plans we examined would come from new revenue sources and hence would bring no new revenue to the federal budget; the four payroll tax mechanisms would bring new revenue to the budget as a whole. Table 1 categorizes the mechanisms in terms of this framework. The number in parentheses indicates the number of reform proposals that contain this mechanism.

Although there is no analytic link between the inclusion of IAs and the selection of a specific revenue mechanism, in our review we found that most of the time reallocated general revenue mechanisms are used to help structure a new Social Security system with IAs. On the other hand, payroll tax mechanisms are used about half the time to help finance the current program and about half the time in proposals creating a new system including IAs. Table 2 summarizes the reform approach and revenue mechanisms used in reform plans. The numbers in parentheses indicate the number of reform proposals that contain a particular mechanism.

Most proposals—15 of the 17 we reviewed—included provisions aimed at increasing revenue through investment in private markets. Two proposals used direct government investing in marketable securities through the current program structure and 13 created a new Social Security structure including individual accounts.[36] Investing in marketable securities creates the potential for improved returns but increases investment risk for the investing party (the government or individuals). Therefore, unlike reallocated revenue and payroll tax mechanisms, neither investment approach assures additional income.

Proposals for government investment of the trust fund anticipate returns that would increase revenue to the trust fund while in most IA proposals the benefit obtained from any increased returns would be credited to the individuals' accounts and generally included as part of the account distribution. Individual account proposals may redirect revenue from the program or the federal budget but typically compensate for lost revenue through either across-the-board benefit cuts or "benefit offsets"[37] to currently-scheduled benefits. In these proposals, the "total benefit" from the new Social Security system consists of a combination of the traditional Social Security defined benefit (including any modifications/offsets) and the individual account distribution (including any modifications/offsets).

Some plans establishing IAs propose to guarantee benefit levels irrespective of actual returns; they are able to do this by using general revenue transfers. Guarantees would benefit account holders by partially or fully protecting them from risk. However, the increased benefits to account holders would create a corresponding cost for the federal government.

Whenever an account fell short of promised benefits, the government—and, implicitly, taxpayers—would make up the difference.[38]

Table 1. Revenue Mechanisms in Reform Proposals by New and Reallocated Revenue

	New Revenue	Reallocated Revenue
Limited, specified funding source	• *Increase the 12.4 percent payroll tax (4)* • *Raise or eliminate earnings cap for payroll tax (5)* • *Tax earnings above the cap at a lower rate (2)* • *Expand coverage to state/local employees not overed (3)*	• Redirect all revenue from taxation of OASDI benefits to OASDI trust fund (2) • Dedicated estate tax[a] (1)
Limited, no specified funding source		• General revenue transfers specified by amount or formula[b] (6) • Refundable tax credits (4)
Unlimited, no specified funding		• General revenue transfers as needed to maintain trust fund solvency (e.g., a 100% trust fund ratio)[b] (9)

Source: GAO.

Notes: Payroll tax mechanisms are in italics. The number of reform proposals do not sum to 17 since some reform plans contain more than one revenue mechanism.

[a] Sunset provisions in the Economic Growth and Tax Relief Reconciliation Act of 2001 would result in the estate tax being treated in the budget as new revenue in 2010 (the only year that the tax is repealed under current law) and reallocated revenue in all succeeding years.

[b] In some cases, proposal sponsors suggest or assume sources of non-Social Security program savings or increases in revenue to help offset the costs to the general fund. However, the transfers to the trust fund in these proposals would not be contingent on achieving the estimated reductions in federal spending or increases in tax income on which transfer amounts are based.

Table 2. Revenue Mechanisms in Reform Proposals by Reform Approach

	Maintain Current Structure	New Structure with IAs
General revenue mechanisms	• Unlimited general revenue transfers as needed to maintain solvency (e.g., a 100% trust fund ratio) (1) • Dedicated estate tax (1)	• Unlimited general revenue transfers as needed to maintain solvency (e.g., a 100% trust fund ratio) (8) • General revenue transfers specified by amount or formula (6) • Refundable tax credit (4) • Redirect all revenue from taxation of OASDI • benefits to OASDI trust fund (2)
Payroll mechanisms	• *Raise or eliminate earnings cap for payroll tax (3)* • *Increase the 12.4 percent payroll tax (2)* • *Tax earnings above the cap at a lower rate (1)* • *Expand coverage to state/local employees not covered (2)*	• *Raise or eliminate earnings cap for payroll tax (2)* • *Increase the 12.4 percent payroll tax (2)* • *Tax earnings above the cap at a lower rate (1)* • *Expand coverage to state/local employees not covered (1)*

Source: GAO.

Note: Payroll tax mechanisms are in italics. The number of reform proposals do not sum to 17 since some reform plans contain more than one revenue mechanism.

Additional Revenue Improves Trust Fund Solvency but Effects on the Federal Budget May Differ Greatly

The effect of a reform proposal on federal budget balances and debt cannot be determined from its effect on trust fund solvency. The proposals we reviewed illustrate this. All plans included in our review were scored by OCACT as able to pay the plan's benefits in full over the 75-year period. However, plans' impact on the federal budget as a whole varied widely in the scorings. For example, the effect on debt held by the public ranged from an improvement of $45 trillion to a worsening of $41 trillion over the 75-year projection period.[39] The impact of a proposal package on the federal budget is shown in the year-by-year scoring of effects on unified deficits and debt that OCACT provides in its technical tables.

That the impact on the trust fund and the impact on the budget as a whole can differ is not surprising. By definition, any increase in revenue provided to the trust fund—whether new general revenue, reallocated general revenue, or increased payroll tax revenue—will increase the trust fund's capacity to pay benefits. Effects on the federal budget, however, depend on the type and amount of revenue and also on assumptions about payment of currently scheduled benefits.[40]

We compare the impact of new and reallocated revenue on the budget and long-term fiscal outlook under two different assumptions about the payment of currently scheduled benefits beyond projected trust fund exhaustion in 2040.[41] First, assume as OCACT does in its memos and GAO does in its long-range simulations, that currently scheduled benefits would be paid in full throughout the estimating period (i.e., borrowing would increase to fund the benefits). Under these assumptions—and assuming no other changes in spending and/or revenue—either new general revenue or additional payroll tax revenue would replace some of that borrowing and improve the long-term fiscal outlook. Reallocated general revenue equal to (or less than) the Social Security financial shortfall would have no impact on federal budget deficits, debt, or the long-term fiscal outlook. In amounts greater than the shortfall, reallocated general revenue would make the long-term outlook worse, all other things equal.

As an alternative, assume instead that benefit outlays will be limited to trust fund income once the trust fund has reached exhaustion in 2040.[42] Under this alternative, federal budget balances would be the same through 2040 as under the first assumption, then improved over the longer term due to lower annual outlays and less borrowing.

Under this "trust fund exhaustion scenario," new revenue dedicated to Social Security early in the projection period would improve annual budget balances and extend the time period during which currently scheduled benefits could be paid in full. The new revenue would also reduce debt for most of the 75-year period.[43] Any amount of reallocated general revenue on the other hand would increase federal budget deficits, reduce budgetary flexibility, and increase debt held by the public relative to this alternative assumption of trust fund exhaustion. All else equal, the reallocated general revenue would provide additional income to the trust fund and make possible additional benefit outlays, but borrowing from the public would be needed to pay for these outlays.

Use of different time frames can also lead to different conclusions about the federal budget effects of additional revenue including reallocated general revenue. For example, some proposals that restructure the Social Security system to rely more on individual accounts—funded in part through a "carve-out" of current payroll tax revenues—use large amounts of reallocated general revenue at the outset to help make up the gap as benefit reductions from currently scheduled levels are phased in. Those favoring this approach to system restructuring may view the reallocated general revenue as a loan from the rest of the budget that will be paid back. Advocates for these types of changes point out that once the transition to the new system is complete, the cost of the Social Security program will have been reduced compared to paying currently scheduled benefits in full. Some favoring program restructuring have advocated use of an infinite horizon rather than the 75-year time frame traditionally used for actuarial assessment of the trust fund.[44] These analysts view 75 years as an arbitrary cut-off point. They note that the use of this horizon can be misleading where a gap between projected revenues and benefit payments continues to grow after the 75-year window, as is the case with the current program.

Those who oppose using reallocated general revenue to achieve system restructuring include an emphasis on a shorter time frame in their analyses. They point to higher levels of federal spending and debt held by the public over at least the next several decades resulting from this approach to reform. These analysts emphasize that it is in this nearer time frame the baby boom generation will retire and the cost to the government will escalate dramatically, driven by demographics and compounded by federal spending on health. These analysts were concerned that revenue used for Social Security will not be available for Medicare and Medicaid, and absent changes in fiscal policy, spending on the three major entitlements will lead to unsustainable levels of debt long before Social Security restructuring will have reduced federal commitments for that program. These analysts called for a focus on the long-term federal budget problem as a whole and a search for solutions to Social Security's financing problems within that larger context.

In concept, the mechanism of unlimited reallocated general revenue as needed to assure trust fund solvency, used in 9 of the 17 proposals we reviewed, represents the largest potential draw on the federal budget. The amount of reallocated general revenue actually provided to the trust fund in these proposals would vary depending on the financial requirements of the Social Security program, and these would depend on the other proposal provisions. The other four general revenue mechanisms would use specified amounts of reallocated general revenues. That is, the amount of general revenue used would not vary according to the financial requirements of the Social Security program but would be dictated by the parameters of the mechanism, e.g., specified in current dollars or as a share of taxable payroll in specific years.

In terms of size, amounts of reallocated general revenue used by mechanisms in proposals we reviewed varied widely, ranging up to over 200 percent of total program financial shortfall. Estimates for general revenue deriving both from the mechanism of unlimited reallocated general revenue as needed to assure trust fund solvency and from specified general revenue transfer amounts were large in some cases. Table 3 shows amounts of reallocated general revenue by type of mechanism.

Some of the budget experts with whom we spoke suggested an approach we did not find in any of the reform proposals we examined. These experts suggested that plans could establish a new source of general revenue and dedicate the new revenue to the Social Security trust fund. For example, they suggested that instead of payroll tax increases, income taxes could be raised or a value-added tax[45] instituted with all or part of the revenue dedicated to Social Security. Some of the budget experts we spoke with observed that any policy decision to introduce new revenues dedicated to a particular program could have implications for the capacity of the rest of the budget to deal with other fiscal challenges. Enactment of any new taxes for Social Security could affect the public's willingness to bear taxes to fund other important national priorities, such as Medicare. In addition, taxes may have effects on individuals' saving behavior and on labor supply, effects that are beyond the scope of this report.

Table 3. Size of Reallocated General Revenue in Proposals Reviewed by Mechanism Used

		Amount		
	Mechanisms for reallocating general revenue	**As a share of 75-year program financial shortfall**	**As a percent of taxable payroll**	**Number of proposals using mechanism**
Unlimited	General revenue transfers as needed to maintain solvency (e.g., a 100% trust fund ratio)	Up to 184%[a]	Up to 3.5%	9
Limited	General revenue transfers to the trust fund specified by formula or amount	Up to 207%	Up to 4.0 %	6
	Refundable tax credits[b]	Up to 115%	Up to 2.2%	4
	Redirect all revenue from taxation of OASDI benefits to OASDI trust funds	22%-23%	0.4%	2
	Dedicated estate tax	27%	0.5%	1

Source: GAO analysis of OCACT scorings.

Notes:

The numbers shown in this table do not sum to 17 since some reform plans contain more than 1 revenue option.

As shown in this table, "program financial shortfall" is defined as the cost of achieving actuarial balance including the cost of an ending trust fund ratio of 100 percent.

Estimates shown are based on available information in OCACT scoring memos. In some cases, scorings for individual mechanisms were not shown separately.

Where account yields affected the amounts of general revenue a proposal would use, OCACT's expected yield estimate was used.

[a] Based on proposals reviewed as scored by OCACT under their expected yield assumption. Under OCACT's low yield assumption, estimated amounts for this mechanism would range up to 245 percent of program shortfall.

[b] Not transferred to the trust fund; used to fund individual add-on accounts.

Despite their differing views on reform approaches, budget experts generally either believed or advocated that some use of general revenue would be part of reform. Some of them were concerned about the use of reallocated general revenue for Social Security in view of the long-term fiscal challenge facing the nation. One emphasized that the public needs to understand that reallocated general revenue for Social Security is not "free." Reallocated general revenue would need to be paid for now or later through lower spending, higher taxes, and/or more debt.[46] Another expert expressed the view that general revenue would be needed to reduce the political pain involved in reform but cautioned that using general revenue for Social Security could mean an even larger share of federal resources committed to funding programs that serve the elderly in coming decades, further squeezing out other national priorities. Most experts expressed the view that greater transparency about the use of general revenue use in reform plans was needed.

Most budget experts with whom we spoke expressed concern about any provision of reallocated general revenue as needed for Social Security to assure trust fund solvency. These analysts, including some who generally do not find trust fund accounting meaningful, said that the signaling provided by the Trustees' projected trust fund exhaustion date has served a useful purpose by alerting policymakers and the public of the need for program reform. Providing for the use of reallocated unlimited general revenue transfers to achieve sustainable solvency would mean that the trust fund would never be projected to reach exhaustion. As a result, these analysts observed, the true costs of the program would become less transparent while at the same time the public might think that the Social Security financing shortfall had been resolved.

One expert was especially concerned that explicit guarantees that total payouts from accounts plus Social Security would be not less than currently scheduled benefit levels could prove expensive for the federal budget. Such guarantees will likely add to the cost of the Social Security system, because individuals will have protection against downside risks but are allowed by a guarantee to benefit on the upside, this expert said. In earlier work we noted that any proposal that would guarantee benefits and rely on enhanced rates of return on individual accounts to finance longterm solvency may create an additional draw on general revenue that could serve to increase the deficit over the long term.[47] Four of the 17 proposals we reviewed for this report included this type of provision; 3 of the 4 also provided for unlimited transfers of reallocated general revenue to maintain trust fund solvency.

CONCLUSIONS

In coming decades, our nation will face a serious long-term fiscal challenge that will put America's fiscal future at risk. As we have said in our body of work on Social Security, substantive reform of this important program will involve hard choices that will need to modify the program's underlying commitments for the future. To do this—to achieve the goal of saving Social Security and making it sustainable for the future—reform will need to increase program revenues and/or decrease program expenses. These are the only options.

It may well be that some general revenue will be part of reform. If so, this would a major substantive change. Considering both the long-term fiscal situation and the potential implications for Social Security, the use of any general revenue in proposals—reallocated or new—will need to be clearly understood by both policymakers and the general public.

Although OCACT's determination of "sustainable solvency" for a reform plan will remain an important threshold that plans will need to meet, it is not a sufficient benchmark in the context of the long-term fiscal outlook facing the United States. It is also an incomplete metric for comparing and evaluating reform plan financing implications. Given that most recent proposals use reallocated general revenue, a determination of trust fund solvency alone can be especially misleading. By definition a determination of trust fund solvency is not designed to and does not provide any information on how, when, or to what extent a plan is likely to worsen or improve the already daunting future federal fiscal imbalances. Clarity about these broader implications of any proposal will be essential as reform changes are debated.

Although raising taxes (payroll or other) or cutting benefits would have tangible consequences for taxpayers and beneficiaries, e.g., less take-home pay or smaller benefit checks, the consequences of transfers from the non- Social Security budget in the form of reallocated general revenue are less likely to be clearly observable. Reallocated general revenue, however, is not without cost. Regardless of how general revenue is provided to Social Security, it must be paid for at some point. The question is when, and by whom.

OCACT scoring memos have played and will continue to play an indispensable role in the debate by analyzing how proposals would affect the trust fund's finances and in more recent years how proposals would affect the federal budget. OCACT's valuable information and complex analyses could make an even greater contribution if they were more readily accessible to nonexpert users. It would be helpful for OCACT to include near the beginning of each memo a summary of the relative contribution of each provision in a proposal package to trust fund solvency. In addition, OCACT could devise a way to enable policymakers and the public to quickly and accurately grasp how the elements of a proposal, including any general revenue, work together to affect the trust fund and the overall federal budget. This type of presentational change would not require any additional analysis but could greatly facilitate comparison of proposals to one another.

We recognize that developing a summary that would be easily accessible to policymakers and the general public and perceived as fair by all participants in the reform debate will present challenges. The elements of reform proposals are likely to continue to evolve, and new formats and analyses may become necessary. We recognize that a balance will need to be struck between standardizing formats and allowing the information provided to continue to evolve with the debate. Nevertheless, a more standardized summary early on could make clear the relative contributions of benefit cuts and increased revenue from payroll and nonpayroll taxes. In addition, it could illuminate any use of general revenue and how use of such revenue is likely to affect the long-term budget outlook. This summary would be a presentational, not analytical, modification with major potential benefits to greater public understanding of proposed changes to this popular program that is important to virtually all Americans.

Recommendation for Executive Action

To improve public understanding of proposed changes to Social Security, we recommend that the Commissioner of SSA direct the Office of the Chief Actuary at SSA to include a summary presentation of its analysis in future scoring memoranda that will enable policymakers and the general public to quickly and easily compare Social Security reform proposals especially with respect to proposed use of general revenue and federal budget implications.

Agency Comments and Our Evaluation

In written comments (reprinted in app. II) on a draft of this report, SSA suggested that we should direct our recommendation to the Chief Actuary, not to the Commissioner. This change, SSA said, would target the entity that develops the analysis and would also be sensitive to the independence of the Chief Actuary.

As SSA stated in its comments, by legal mandate the Chief Actuary does report directly to the Commissioner. Because our recommendation concerns only the presentation of actuarial estimates—not any change in which estimates are developed nor in the analytical work required to develop them—we believe the recommendation as it stands recognizes and is appropriately sensitive to the independence of the Chief Actuary while at the same time reflecting the organizational structure of the Office of the Chief Actuary within SSA.

SSA did not explicitly agree or disagree with our recommendation in its comments. In response to the recommendation, SSA noted that recent OCACT memos had added an additional table ("table d") that, SSA believes, already provides key information on general revenue use in proposals. SSA also expressed the view that a summary table showing the effects on the actuarial deficit of each proposal provision would be helpful. As our report had noted, this table has been included in some memoranda at the request of the proposal's sponsor.

While we agree with SSA that both the technical and summary table it describes add value, we remain of the view that OCACT needs to develop a new table that can clearly and quickly communicate both trust fund effects and federal budget implications of a proposal. Our report acknowledged the value and completeness of OCACT's analyses including those presented in "table d." The message of our report was not that OCACT needs to do additional analytic work. Our message was rather that OCACT's existing analyses need to be summarized and highlighted so that a proposal's implications for both the trust fund and the federal budget as a whole are immediately clear.

Neither of SSA's two suggestions is fully responsive to this goal. SSA itself noted in its comments that "table d" is "somewhat complicated." With regard to the summary table showing how each provision affects the actuarial deficit, we agree that this table adds considerable value and can help facilitate certain types of comparisons across plans. It does not, however, make clear how each provision or the proposal as a whole would affect the federal budget. It is this kind of information, now available only to experienced users of OCACT memos, that needs to be made more accessible. Given the long-term fiscal challenge facing the Nation, the reform debate needs to take place not simply in the context of trust fund solvency but also in the larger context of the federal budget as a whole.

SSA also provided technical comments, which we incorporated as appropriate.

Susan J. Irving
Director, Federal Budget Analysis,
Strategic Issues

Barbara D. Bovbjerg
Director, Education, Workforce,
and Income Security Issues

APPENDIX I: SCOPE AND METHODOLOGY

To answer the questions in this report, we reviewed relevant historical documents and other literature on Social Security, including GAO reports and testimonies.[48] We undertook a review of the 26 OCACT proposal scoring memos done from 2001 through 2006, ultimately performing an in- depth analysis of 17 of those scoring memos.[49] We eliminated nine of the scoring memos either because they were proposals that were scored in multiple years or because they were not scored by OCACT as able to pay plan benefits in full throughout the 75-year period. Most of the 17 proposals were characterized by OCACT as meeting its definition of "sustainably solvent." We also reviewed proposal scorings done by Congressional Budget Office (CBO) and met with officials from OCACT and CBO who were responsible for proposal scorings. To enhance our understanding of the relationship between Social Security and the federal budget, we interviewed selected federal budget experts from think tanks and other policy organizations who represented a range of views on reform approaches. Some of these experts were former officials of the Social Security Administration and/or Congressional Budget Office.

Our analysis, like the scorings of the Office of the Chief Actuary and recent scorings by CBO, is limited to first order effects of reform changes. Accordingly, second order effects of proposed reforms on the federal budget, such as effects on economic growth, are beyond the scope of this report. This report also does not address the effects of general revenue use on program equity. As discussed in other GAO work, the use of significant amounts of general revenue transfers could change program equity in ways that are difficult to quantify.[50]

APPENDIX II: COMMENTS FROM THE SOCIAL SECURITY ADMINISTRATION

SOCIAL SECURITY
The Commissioner
March 2, 2007

Ms. Barbara Bovbjerg
Director, Education, Workforce and
Income Security Issues
U.S. Government Accountability Office
Washington, D.C. 20548

Dear Ms. Bovbjerg:

Thank you for the opportunity to review and comment on the draft report, "SOCIAL SECURITY REFORM: Greater Transparency Needed about Potential General Revenue Financing" (GAO-07-213).

If you have any questions, please contact Candace Skurnik, Director, Audit Management and Liaison Staff, at (410) 965-4636.

Sincerely,

Michael J. Astrue

Enclosure

SOCIAL SECURITY ADMINISTRATION BALTIMORE MD 21235-0001

COMMENTS ON THE GOVERNMENT ACCOUNTABILITY OFFICE (GAO) DRAFT REPORT, "SOCIAL SECURITY REFORM: GREATER TRANSPARENCY NEEDED ABOUT POTENTIAL GENERAL REVENUE FINANCING"(GAO-07-213)

Thank you for the opportunity to review and comment on the draft report. We appreciate your conducting this audit of the use of general revenue (GR) financing in Social Security reform proposals and the impact of this financing on the unified Federal budget.

Recommendation 1

To improve public understanding of proposed changes to Social Security, GAO recommends that the Commissioner of the Social Security Administration direct SSA's Office of the Chief Actuary (OCACT) to include a summary presentation of its analysis in future scoring memoranda that will enable policymakers and the general public to quickly and easily compare Social Security reform proposals especially with respect to proposed use of GR and federal budget implications.

Comment

We suggest that GAO revise the recommendation from suggesting that the Commissioner of Social Security direct OCACT to develop further analysis to a recommendation directed to the Chief Actuary. This would target the entity that actually develops the analysis in question, and would also be sensitive to the independence of the Chief Actuary. By legal mandate, the Chief Actuary of Social Security does report directly to the Commissioner. However, it is critical to the credibility of the actuarial estimates and analyses produced by OCACT that these be wholly objective and unbiased both in content and presentation. They should not be, nor appear to be, influenced or controlled by any other entity, even the Commissioner.

It should be noted that, for over a year, OCACT has been including an additional table "d" which provides the specific implications for the Old-Age, Survivors and Disability Insurance unfunded obligation of different provisions in the overall proposal. In particular, a separate column in the table has been provided indicating the extent to which GR transfers that do not represent new income to the government affect the unfunded obligation of the program. While somewhat complicated, this table does already provide much of what is called for by GAO. We do agree, however, that general inclusion of a simple table showing the effects on the actuarial deficit of each provision would be helpful.

GLOSSARY OF TERMS

The majority of the definitions provided here are from the Social Security Administration, *The 2006 Annual Report of the Board of Trustees of the Federal Old-Age and Survivors Insurance and Disability Insurance Trust Funds* (Washington, D.C.: May 1, 2006) and GAO, *A Glossary of Terms Used in the Federal Budget Process,* GAO-05-734SP (Washington, D.C.: September 2005).

Actuarial balance The difference between the summarized income rate and the summarized cost rate over a given valuation period.

Actuarial deficit A negative actuarial balance.

Assumptions Values relating to future trends in certain key factors which affect the balance in the trust funds. Three sets of demographic, economic, and program-specific assumptions are presented in the annual Trustees' report.

- Demographic assumptions include fertility, mortality, net immigration, marriage, and divorce.
- Economic assumptions include unemployment rates, average earnings, inflation, interest rates, and productivity.
- Program-specific assumptions include retirement patterns, and disability incidence and termination rates.

The three sets of assumptions are described as follows:

- Alternative II is the intermediate set of assumptions, and represents the Trustees' best estimates of likely future conditions.
- Alternative I is characterized as a low cost set—it assumes relatively rapid economic growth, low inflation, and favorable (from the standpoint of program financing) demographic conditions.
- Alternative III is characterized as a high cost set—it assumes relatively slow economic growth, high inflation, and unfavorable (from the standpoint of program financing) demographic conditions.

In its estimates of reform proposals, OCACT uses the intermediate set of assumptions, which represents the Trustees' best estimates of likely future demographic, economic, and program-specific conditions.

Board of Trustees A Board established by the Social Security Act to oversee the financial operations of the Federal Old-Age and Survivors Insurance Trust Fund and the Federal Disability Insurance Trust Fund. The Board is composed of six members, four of whom serve automatically by virtue of their positions in the federal government: the Secretary of the Treasury, who is the Managing Trustee, the Secretary of Labor, the Secretary of Health and Human Services, and the Commissioner of Social Security. The other two members are appointed by the President to serve as public representatives.

Constant Dollars Amounts adjusted by the consumer price index (CPI) to the value of the dollar in a particular year.

Cost rate The cost rate for a year is the ratio of the cost of the program to the taxable payroll for the year. In this context, the cost is defined to include scheduled benefit payments, special monthly payments to certain uninsured persons who have 3 or more quarters of coverage (and whose payments are therefore not reimbursable from the General Fund of the Treasury), administrative expenses, net transfers from the trust funds to the Railroad Retirement program under the financial-interchange provisions, and payments for vocational rehabilitation services for disabled beneficiaries; it excludes special monthly payments to certain uninsured persons whose payments are reimbursable from the General Fund of the Treasury, and transfers under the interfund borrowing provisions.

Covered earnings Earnings in employment covered by the Old-Age Survivors and Disability Insurance program.

Current dollar "In current dollars" means valued in the prices of the current year. Amounts are expressed in nominal dollars with no adjustment for inflationary changes in the value of the dollar over time. The current dollar value of a good or service is its value in terms of prices current at the time the good or service is acquired or sold.

Debt held by government accounts Federal debt owed by the federal government to itself. Most of this debt is held by trust funds, such as Social Security and Medicare. The Office of Management and Budget (OMB) contrasts it to debt held by the public by noting that it is not a current transaction of the government with the public; it is not financed by private saving and thus does not compete with the private sector for available funds in the credit market; and it does not represent an obligation to make payments to the public.

Debt held by the public That portion of the gross federal debt held outside of the federal government. This includes any federal debt held by individuals, corporations, state or local governments, the Federal Reserve System, and foreign governments and central banks. Debt held by government accounts (intragovernmental debt) is excluded from debt held by the public. Debt held by the public is not the same as public debt or Treasury debt.

Exhaustion Date As reported in the Trustees' Report and for the purposes of this report, the year in which the OASDI trust fund would become unable to pay currently- scheduled benefits when due because the assets of the fund were exhausted.

General fund of the Treasury Funds held by the Treasury of the United States, other than receipts collected for a specific purpose (such as Social Security) and maintained in a separate account for that purpose.

General revenue For a discussion of how it is defined for the purposes of this report, see page 6.

Income rate Ratio of income from tax revenues on a liability basis (payroll tax contributions and income from the taxation of scheduled benefits) to the OASDI taxable payroll for the year.

Inflation An increase in the volume of money and credit relative to available goods, resulting in an increase in the general price level.

Interest A payment in exchange for the use of money during a specified period.

Interest rate For the OASDI trust funds, interest rates on new public-debt obligations issuable to federal trust funds are determined monthly. Such rates are set equal to the average market yield on all outstanding marketable U.S. securities not due or callable until after 4 years from the date the rate is determined. The effective interest rate for a trust fund is the ratio of the interest earned by the fund over a given period of time to the average level of assets held by the fund during the period. The effective rate of interest thus represents a measure of the overall average interest earnings on the fund's portfolio of assets.

Long range The next 75 years. Long-range actuarial estimates are made for this period because it is approximately the maximum remaining lifetime of current Social Security participants.

Maximum taxable limit The limit or "cap" on covered earnings that are subject to the 12.4 percent payroll tax and that can be used in the benefit formula, thereby limiting the size of taxes and benefits. This "cap" is indexed annually for average wage growth and therefore it changes every year. In 2007, the taxable maximum limit is $97,500.

Nominal dollar See under Current dollar.

Outlay The issuance of checks, disbursement of cash, or electronic transfer of funds made to liquidate a federal obligation. Outlays during a fiscal year may be for payment of obligations incurred in prior years (prior-year obligations) or in the same year. Outlays, therefore, flow in part from unexpended balances of prior-year budgetary resources and in part from budgetary resources provided for the year in which the money is spent. Total government outlays include outlays of off-budget federal entities, such as the Social Security trust fund.

Pay-as-you-go financing A financing method where taxes are scheduled to produce just as much income as required to pay current benefits, with trust fund assets built up only to the extent needed to prevent exhaustion of the fund by random economic fluctuations.

Payroll taxes A tax levied on the gross wages of workers.

Present value The equivalent value, at the present time, of a future stream of payments (either income or cost). The present value of a future stream of payments may be thought of as the lump-sum amount that, if invested today, together with interest earnings would be just enough to meet each of the payments as they fell due. Present values are widely used in calculations involving financial transactions over long periods of time to account for the time value of money (interest). For the purpose of present-value calculations for this report, values are discounted by the effective yield on trust fund assets.

Solvency A program is solvent at a point in time if it is able to pay scheduled benefits when due with scheduled financing. For example, the OASDI program is considered solvent over any period for which the trust funds maintain a positive balance throughout the period.

Summarized balance The difference between the summarized cost rate and the summarized income rate, expressed as a percentage of taxable payroll.

Summarized cost rate The ratio of the present value of cost to the present value of the taxable payroll for the years in a given period, expressed as a percentage. This percentage can be used as a measure of the relative level of cost during the period in question. For purposes of evaluating the financial adequacy of the program, the summarized cost rate is adjusted to include the cost of reaching and maintaining a target trust fund level. Because a trust fund level of about 1 year's cost is considered to be an adequate reserve for unforeseen contingencies, the targeted trust fund ratio used in determining summarized cost rates is 100 percent of annual cost. Accordingly, the adjusted summarized cost rate is equal to the ratio of (a) the sum of the present value of the cost during the period plus the present value of the targeted ending trust fund level, to (b) the present value of the taxable payroll during the projection period.

Summarized income rate The ratio of the present value of scheduled tax income to the present value of taxable payroll for the years in a given period, expressed as a percentage. This percentage can be used as a measure of the relative level of income during the period in question. For purposes of evaluating the financial adequacy of the program, the summarized income rate is adjusted to include assets on hand at the beginning of the period. Accordingly, the adjusted summarized income rate equals the ratio of (a) the sum of the trust fund balance at the beginning of the period plus the present value of the total income from taxes during the period, to (b) the present value of the taxable payroll for the years in the period.

Sustainable solvency As defined by OCACT, sustainable solvency for the financing of the program is achieved when the program has positive trust fund ratios throughout the 75-year projection period and these ratios are stable or rising at the end of the period.

Taxable earnings Wages and/or self-employment income, in employment covered by the OASDI and/or Hospital Insurance (HI) programs, that is under the applicable annual maximum taxable limit. For 1994 and later, no maximum taxable limit applies to the HI program.

Taxable payroll A weighted average of taxable wages and taxable self-employment income. When multiplied by the combined employee-employer tax rate, it yields the total amount of taxes incurred by employees, employers, and the self- employed for work during the period.

Taxable wages See under “Taxable earnings.”

Trust fund As discussed in this report, the OASDI trust funds are separate accounts in the United States Treasury in which are deposited the taxes received under the Federal Insurance Contributions Act and the Self-Employment Contributions Act, as well as taxes resulting from coverage of state and local government employees; any sums received under the financial interchange with the railroad retirement account; voluntary hospital and medical insurance premiums; and transfers of Federal general revenues. Funds not withdrawn for current monthly or service benefits, the financial interchange, and administrative expenses are invested in interest-bearing federal securities, as required by law; the interest earned is also deposited in the trust funds.

- Old-Age and Survivors Insurance (OASI). The trust fund used for paying monthly benefits to retired-worker (old-age) beneficiaries and their spouses and children and to survivors of deceased insured workers.

- Disability Insurance (DI). The trust fund used for paying monthly benefits to disabled-worker beneficiaries and their spouses and children and for providing rehabilitation services to the disabled.
- Hospital Insurance (HI). The trust fund used for paying part of the costs of inpatient hospital services and related care for aged and disabled individuals who meet the eligibility requirements. Also known as Medicare Part A.

Trust fund ratio A measure of the adequacy of the trust fund level. Defined as the assets at the beginning of the year expressed as a percentage of the cost during the year. The trust fund ratio represents the proportion of a year's cost which could be paid with the funds available at the beginning of the year.

Unified budget Under budget concepts set forth in the Report of the President's Commission on Budget Concepts, a comprehensive budget in which receipts and outlays from federal and trust funds are consolidated. When these fund groups are consolidated to display budget totals, transactions that are outlays of one fund group for payment to the other fund group (that is, interfund transactions) are deducted to avoid double counting. The unified budget should, as conceived by the President's Commission, take in the full range of federal activities. By law, budget authority, outlays, and receipts of off-budget programs (currently only the Postal Service and Social Security) are excluded from the current budget, but data relating to off-budget programs are displayed in the budget documents. However, the most prominent total in the budget is the unified total, which is the sum of the on- and off-budget totals.

End Notes

[1] In this report, the combined OASDI Trust Funds are referred to as the Social Security trust fund. For more information on federal trust funds and other funds dedicated to specific programs, see GAO's report *Federal Trust and Other Earmarked Funds: Answers to Frequently Asked Questions*, GAO-01-199SP (Washington, D.C.: January 2001).

[2] For explanation of technical terms, see the glossary at the end of this report.

[3] Social Security's financial condition has traditionally been measured separately from that of the rest of the budget by comparing the program's expected revenues with expected costs over a 75-year timeframe. Estimates of the solvency of Social Security's trust funds in this framework have been prepared by the Office of the Chief Actuary (OCACT) at the Social Security Administration (SSA) each year since 1941.

[4] As used in this report, *general revenue* refers to any revenue not derived from payroll tax contributions. (See text box.)

[5] When OCACT describes a proposal as modifying the program so that there is a positive trust fund ratio throughout the 75-year projection period and these ratios are stable or rising at the end of the period, this meets the definition of "sustainable solvency" in the 2006 Trustees' Report.

[6] The Social Security Amendments of 1983 require beneficiaries with income (defined as adjusted gross income plus tax-exempt bond interest plus one-half of Social Security benefits) of more than $25,000 if single, and $32,000 if married filing jointly, to include up to 50 percent of their benefits in their taxable income, beginning in 1984. Revenues from this provision are credited to the OASDI Trust Funds. The Omnibus Budget Reconciliation Act of 1993 required beneficiaries with incomes of more than $34,000 if single, and $44,000 if married filing jointly, to include up to 85 percent of their benefits in their taxable income, beginning in 1994. Revenues attributable to taxation of over 50 percent of Social Security benefits are credited to the Medicare Hospital Insurance (HI) trust fund. These levels are not adjusted for inflation or wage growth, so the percentage of beneficiaries paying tax on Social Security benefits is expected to rise in the future.

[7] GAO's long-term simulations assume that scheduled benefits for Social Security and Medicare's HI Trust Fund are paid through borrowing, that is, by using reallocated general revenue after program trust funds reach

exhaustion. (See textbox, "New Versus Reallocated General Revenue in Social Security.") For more information on GAO's simulations, see http://www.gao.gov/special.pubs/longterm/.

[8] While OCACT has primary responsibility for scoring reform proposals, CBO has more recently begun to publish long-term scorings of some proposals. OCACT and CBO scorings have both substantive and presentational differences including: different assumptions, baselines, and time periods covered. One particularly important difference is the use of different economic assumptions, which results in CBO having more optimistic estimates of current-law program finances.

[9] That is, maintain a modified pay-as-you-go social insurance program of defined benefits paid for primarily by payroll tax revenue.

[10] In constant 2005 dollars under OCACT's expected yield assumption. Estimates are based on OCACT scorings and represent change in debt levels compared to a baseline in which scheduled benefits are paid in full and no other changes are made. Estimates were not available for one of the plans reviewed.

[11] See GAO, *Options for Social Security Reform*, GAO-05-649R (Washington, D.C.: May 6, 2005).

[12] Advocates for these types of changes state that over time, the savings to the government (compared to paying currently scheduled benefits in full) will come to exceed the cost of funding individual accounts.

[13] For more information on the Social Security program, see GAO, *Social Security Reform: Answers to Key Questions*, GAO-05-193SP (May 2005).

[14] In contrast to private trust funds, the federal government does not have a fiduciary responsibility to the trust fund beneficiaries. Congress can raise or lower future trust fund collections and payments by changing existing laws.

[15] In this report, the combined OASDI Trust Funds are referred as the Social Security trust fund. For more information on federal trust funds and other funds dedicated to specific programs, see GAO-01-199SP.

[16] Total receipts to the combined trust funds, including $94 billion in interest income, were $702 billion in calendar year 2005.

[17] If Treasury could not borrow from the Social Security trust fund, it would have to borrow more in the private capital market and pay interest in cash to finance current budget policy. However, Treasury still has to pay the trust fund interest on these securities. For a more detailed discussion of the temporary trust fund buildup and how it interacts with the federal unified budget, see GAO, *Social Security Financing: Implications of Government Stock Investing for the Trust Fund, the Federal Budget, and the Economy*, GAO/AIMD/HEHS-98-74 (Washington, D.C.: Apr. 22, 1998).

[18] See GAO, *Social Security: Program's Role in Helping Ensure Income Adequacy*, GAO-02-62 (Washington, D.C.: Nov. 30, 2001. For a discussion of individual equity issues, see GAO, *Social Security: Issues in Comparing Rates of Return with Market Investments,* GAO/HEHS-99-110 (Washington, D.C.: Aug. 5, 1999).

[19] Since Social Security benefits had previously been untaxed, this was seen by some as a benefit cut.

[20] For a more detailed discussion see GAO-05-649R and GAO, *Social Security Reform: Implications of Different Indexing Choices*, GAO-06-804 (Washington, D.C.: Sept. 14, 2006).

[21] http://www.ssa.gov/OACT/solvency/index.html.

[22] When OCACT describes a proposal as modifying the program so that there is a positive trust fund ratio throughout the 75-year projection period and these ratios are stable or rising at the end of the period, this meets the definition of "sustainable solvency" in the 2006 Trustees' Report.

[23] On the other hand, our criterion for sustainable solvency measures the effect on the trust fund and includes evaluating how a proposal would affect the U.S. economy and the federal budget.

[24] OCACT officials told us that this table was included only when specifically requested by the plan sponsor.

[25] For analysis of benefit and revenue options described in terms of GAO's framework for evaluating Social Security reform plans, see GAO, *Options for Social Security Reform*, GAO-05-649R (Washington, D.C.: May 6, 2005).

[26] Because some proposals were scored in multiple years or were not designed to achieve 75-year solvency, the universe of proposals discussed in this report is comprised of 17 proposals. Scorings can be found at http://www.ssa.gov/OACT/solvency/index.html.

[27] The trust fund ratio is a measure of the adequacy of the trust fund level. It is defined as the assets at the beginning of the year expressed as a percentage of the cost during the year. The trust fund ratio represents the proportion of a year's cost that could be paid with the funds available at the beginning of the year. Having a trust fund ratio of 100 percent or more—that is, assets at the beginning of each year at least equal to projected outgo during the year—is considered a good indication of a trust fund's ability to cover most short-term contingencies.

[28] Most plans specify unlimited transfers to meet a 100 percent trust fund ratio, but one plan specifies transfers to maintain a 90 percent trust fund ratio. This trust fund ratio level still maintains solvency because the program can pay scheduled benefits when due.

[29] In some cases, proposal sponsors suggest sources of non-Social Security program savings to help offset the costs to the general fund. However, the transfers to the trust fund would not be contingent on achieving the reductions in actual federal spending.

[30] Although plan sponsors sometimes propose spending cuts and/or assume revenue increases in non-Social Security programs to offset these general fund transfers; the transfers are not conditional on the savings/revenue increases being achieved and would be made regardless of the success of these changes.

[31] Plans may require individuals to contribute to the add-on account in order to receive credits.

[32] Under current law (as of January 2007), the estate tax would be repealed for 2010 but would be restored with a lower exemption and a higher rate than in effect for 2009. Thus, compared to current law the estate tax in this proposal would be new revenue to the budget only in the year 2010 and reallocated revenue in all succeeding years.

[33] SSA defines covered earnings to mean wages and self-employment earnings that are covered by the OASDI and/or HI programs. Under current law, all covered earnings are taxed at a rate of 2.9 percent for Medicare HI, but for OASDI only covered earnings up to a "taxable maximum limit" or "cap" are taxed at the 12.4 percent rate. This limits taxes as well as the earnings reflected in the benefit formula. The level of "taxable earnings" reflects only the portion of covered earnings that is at or below this cap. This taxable maximum limit is indexed annually for average wage growth and therefore it changes every year. In 2007, the cap is $97,500.

[34] However, significantly larger changes would be required to maintain solvency beyond 75 years.

[35] About one-fourth of public employees do not pay Social Security taxes on the earnings from their government jobs. Extending coverage to include them could result in potentially significant transition costs for some of their state and local government employers. See GAO, *Social Security: Implication of Extending Mandatory Coverage to State and Local Government Employees*, GAO/HEHS-98-196 (Washington, D.C.: Aug. 18, 1998).

[36] For GAO's discussion of the key issues to consider in comparing Social Security and private market rates of return, see GAO/HEHS-99-110.

[37] The purpose of benefit offsets is to compensate the trust funds for foregone taxes and to equitably distinguish between those who do, and those who do not, shift Social Security taxes to voluntary personal accounts. There are different methods for calculating the offset. For a more thorough discussion of offsets, see Virginia P. Reno, Michael J. Graetz, Kenneth S. Apfel, Joni Lavery, and Catherine Hill, eds., *Uncharted Waters: Paying Benefits from Individual Accounts in Federal Retirement Policy, Study Panel Final Report*, National Academy of Social Insurance (Washington, D.C.: January 2005), ch. 9.

[38] For a discussion of issues raised by estimating guarantee costs, see CBO, *Evaluating Benefit Guarantees in Social Security* (Washington, D.C.: March 2006).

[39] In constant 2005 dollars under OCACT's expected yield assumption. Estimates are based on OCACT scorings and represent change in debt levels compared to a baseline in which scheduled benefits are paid in full through borrowing and no other changes are made. Estimates were not available for one of the plans reviewed.

[40] In this section, as elsewhere in the report, our analysis follows that of OCACT in being limited to first order effects.

[41] For GAO analyses of reform proposals using multiple sets of assumptions, see *Social Security: Evaluating Reform Proposals*, GAO/AIMD/HEHS-00-29 (Washington, D.C.: Nov. 4, 1999); *Social Security Reform: Analysis of Reform Models Developed by the President's Commission to Strengthen Social Security*, GAO-03-310 (Washington, D.C.: Jan. 15, 2003); and *Social Security Reform: Analysis of a Trust Fund Exhaustion Scenario*, GAO-03-907 (Washington, D.C.: July 29, 2003).

[42] The Trustees 2006 Report notes that even if a trust fund's assets are exhausted, tax income will continue to flow into the fund. Present tax rates would be sufficient to pay 74 percent of scheduled benefits after trust fund exhaustion in 2040 and 70 percent of scheduled benefits in 2080. For an analysis of an illustrative assumption along these lines, see GAO-03-907. This scenario was developed as an analytic tool, not a legal determination.

[43] The effect on debt by the end of the period would depend on the amount of new revenue raised for Social Security. If this was equal to the 75-year Social Security shortfall in present value terms, debt by the end of the period would be the same as under the alternative assumption. This is because the additional new revenue would have been used to pay for additional benefit outlays of equal size. All else equal, debt at the end of the period would be lower relative to the trust fund exhaustion scenario if the new revenue exceeded program shortfall.

[44] CBO uses a 100-year time frame for analysis.

[45] A value-added tax is a tax levied at each stage of production or distribution on the value added to the product during that stage of production. Value-added taxes are now commonly used in many Western European countries as a source of revenue.

[46] See GAO-05-649R (Washington, D.C.: May 6, 2005).

[47] GAO/AIMD/HEHS-00-29 (Washington, D.C.: Nov. 4, 1999).

[48] In particular this report builds on GAO's analysis of revenue options for reform as discussed in *Options for Social Security Reform*, GAO-05-649R (Washington, D.C.: May 6, 2005).

[49] Scorings can be found at http://www.ssa.gov/OACT/solvency/index.html.

[50] See GAO-05-649R and GAO, *Social Security: Distribution of Benefits and Taxes Relative to Earnings Level*, GAO-04-747 (Washington, D.C.: June 15, 2004).

CHAPTER SOURCES

The following chapters have been previously published:

Chapter 1 – This is an edited, reformatted and augmented version of a Social Security Advisory Board report, Sylvester J. Schieber, Chairman, dated December 16, 2008.

Chapter 2 – This is an edited, reformatted and augmented version of a United States Government Accountability Office publication, Report GAO-07-621R, dated August 10, 2007.

Chapter 3 – This is an edited, reformatted and augmented version of a Congressional Research Service publication, Report Order Code RL34433, dated April 4, 2008.

Chapter 4 – This is an edited, reformatted and augmented version of a Congressional Research Service publication, Report RL33544, dated May 22, 2009.

Chapter 5 – This is an edited, reformatted and augmented version of a Congressional Research Service publication, Report RL32822, dated May 20, 2009.

Chapter 6 – This is an edited, reformatted and augmented version of a United States Government Accountability Office publication, Report GAO-08-26, dated October 2007.

Chapter 7 – This is an edited, reformatted and augmented version of a United States Government Accountability Office publication, Report GAO-06-804, dated September 2006.

Chapter 8 – This is an edited, reformatted and augmented version of a United States Government Accountability Office publication, Report GAO-07-213, dated March 2007.

INDEX

A

B

C

F

G

H

I

J

L

M

R

S

Y